Roy
Buchanan

American Axe

by Phil Carson

Backbeat
Books
San Francisco

Published by Backbeat Books
600 Harrison Street, San Francisco, CA 94107
www.backbeatbooks.com
Email: books@musicplayer.com
An imprint of Music Player Network
United Entertainment Media, Inc.
Publishers of *Guitar Player* magazine and MusicPlayer.com

For copyright credits regarding lyrics, refer to page 276.

Distributed to the book trade in the U.S. and Canada by
Publisher's Group West, 1700 Fourth Street, Berkeley, CA 94710

Distributed to the music trade in the U.S. and Canada by
Hal Leonard Publishing, P.O. Box 13819, Milwaukee, WI 53213

Cover Design: Sonia Chan
Cover Photo: Dean Reynolds
Composition: Greene Design

Library of Congress Cataloging-in-Publication Data

Carson, Phil.
    Roy Buchanan : American axe / by Phil Carson
        p. cm.
    Includes bibliographical references (p.) and index.
    ISBN 0-87930-639-4
    1. Buchanan, Roy. 2. Guitarists—United States—Biography.
Rock musicians—United States—Biography. I. Title

    ML419.B83 C37 2001

                                    2001035451

Printed in the United States of America

08   5 4 3 2

Contents

DEDICATION

For Roy Buchanan.
You made music sweet music
And turned our heads around.

And for Alps, Stein, Beat and Bone, the Nayd, Strauss, Leibs,
Les and Chone —
we caught the big time.

Introduction

Roy Buchanan and his battered 1953 Telecaster got inside your head and grabbed you in the gut. He had eclectic musical tastes, a devotion to craft, and something to say. And he said what he had to say with soul. The foremost impression seared upon my mind more than three decades after first hearing him perform is his sheer emotive power. Roy conveyed feeling, and not just his own. Sometimes it felt as if he knew everyone's feelings. With his '53 Fender Telecaster Buchanan serenaded, inspired, saddened, and hypnotized his audiences, all in the space of a couple hours' performance at the small clubs he preferred. He expressed the known range of human emotions and more, including intuitive matters of the heart and mind that defy adequate description. In Buchanan's hands the Telecaster sang, whispered, and wailed like it never had before, or has since. He could play virtually anything he imagined, and his imagination knew few boundaries. He was that damn good.

To explore Roy's life and times involves a journey to another America, for he lived in a time when places still meant something, before a certain homogeneity crept into everyday life. His birth in rural Arkansas on Sept. 23, 1939, his coming of age in California's austere San Joaquin Valley, his passage through Los Angeles, Shreveport, and Washington, DC, all shaped the man and his music. Places shaped him, and so did the times. Roy jumped into rock 'n' roll virtually at The Creation itself, after Elvis and others brought black rhythm and blues to appreciative white audiences. Over the next 32 years Roy pioneered numerous guitar techniques, developed a unique sound, and touched people as he passed in and out of the limelight. In the end he contributed as much as any individual to the vocabulary of rock 'n' roll, country, and blues.

When you heard Roy Buchanan playing his Telecaster, you knew instantly who it was. In a profession crowded with posers, fakers, and imitators, Buchanan was the real McCoy, a gifted stylist with seemingly unlimited passion for the music he played. He had a way of playing a note, a chord, a whistling harmonic or a steel guitar–like lick at the precise moment when it would have the greatest emotional or intellectual impact on the listener. He touched nerves. This connection with his audience meant that his music, feeding off the crowd's energy, came alive on the stage of a darkened nightclub. He knew how to pace a set and toy with the room's emotional dynamics until late, late at night he might fall into a down-and-dirty 12-bar vamp that would simply ignite the crowd. Yet, in a story full of contradictions, his friends and colleagues all swear that his most beautiful playing often took place in a hotel room after a gig—where, of course, few could hear him.

Buchanan's music was consistently soulful, searing and mysterious, and so was he. Though many great electric guitarists might be said to combine technical virtuosity and emotive power, with Roy Buchanan there was always more, and not all of it good. His seemingly boundless talents were matched by a penchant for forbidden fruits and a confounding predilection for anonymity. Taciturn, deeply shy and sensitive, yet freighted with a journeyman's cynicism, Buchanan carved out a crooked path for himself. He had a talent for dissembling, for mythologizing. He dispensed his own brand of country mojo and, for the most part, people bought it. Country mojo could be a powerful thing. As it turned out, it could not banish demons or bend steel bars.

The story that unfolds here, though it follows just one man's life, illuminates the struggles of this country's working musicians. For every innovator who becomes a star, a handful escape notice. There is a poignancy to the lives of men and women who are somehow compelled night after night to produce joy for the throng, despite the odds that such a pursuit will land them in an early grave. This story bares a gritty world of smoky, alcohol-fueled after-hours dungeons that beckons to many of us, luring us with a sense of escape, and forcing us to face harsh truths that lie at the heart of America and its popular music. It is within these sometimes sordid settings—crucibles of a sort—that American music is forged. Roy Buchanan lived this life, producing sounds of beauty and melancholia, sounds that registered with his audience on a profound level.

That Roy never became a star seems also a quintessentially American story. He never was comfortable as a front man. As one observer has noted, "He was the archetypal sideman. He stepped up, knocked you out, and then stepped back into the shadows." Thus this is not the biography of a star, a celebrity, a well-known face. It is simply an account of an ordinary mortal with extraordinary talents whose work in American vernacular music transformed it into art. There are no limousines in this story, just the endless dotted white lines on the roads that connected town-to-town, gig-to-gig.

Because Roy's life is not well-documented, my own journey in reconstructing it led me to the locations that shaped his life, searching for family, friends, and colleagues who could reach into their past and shed light on a taciturn character and his peregrinations. It is a measure of the humble goodwill Roy created during his life that, with the exception of his wife, Judy, everyone made kind and extraordinary efforts to aid my quest.

Roy had something musical to say—something that came from deep inside him, often beautiful and joyous and too often painful—and it issued forth when he had a guitar, preferably a vintage Telecaster, in his hands. Despite the difficulties and missed opportunities, his soulful honesty lives on.

Phil Carson
Colorado Springs, CO
April 2001

FROM SMITH'S CREEK
TO THE PROMISED LAND

*T*he Arkansas River begins as icy fingers of snowmelt in the high granite of the Rocky Mountains before it drops eastward, parting America's high plains en route to the miasmic Mississippi and the sea. Along the river's lower length, as it carves a path between the Boston Mountains and the Ouachitas in northwest Arkansas, the river slows and meanders, creating fertile bottomlands as it winds to its mouth. Before flood control measures were constructed in the early 1940s, the lower river flooded dangerously each spring, replenishing the soil in the river bottoms. In the 1930s Bill Buchanan and his wife, Minnie Reed Buchanan, farmed those bottoms outside a town called Ozark. The Buchanans lived, as all sensible people did, as their parents had before them, on higher ground, atop the slight hills that rose just beyond the flood plain. For the Buchanans this was the center of a world composed of lush hills and soft, rich soil. In this deeply rural corner of Arkansas life unfolded like a sunflower, slow and easy. War flickered on a distant horizon like heat lightning, terribly near, yet mercifully far.

One summer afternoon in 1944, on the front porch of a rambling, two-room homestead on one of the hills above the river, 16-year-old J.D. Buchanan gathered a couple of friends to fool around with their guitars. J.D.'s youngest sibling, five-year-old Leroy Buchanan, scampered past his brother and his guitar-playing friends. "I heard them playing," Roy would recall many years later, "and I told them, 'You're out of tune.' They got real mad and said, 'Okay, if you're so smart then, tune it up!' So I did. It was just a natural thing." Soon after, Leroy told his father that he liked music. Bill Buchanan was intrigued. He asked his son what kind of music, or which instrument, he liked best. "Guitar," Leroy replied. Bill Buchanan promptly bought Leroy a cheap acoustic guitar.

Thus the story of Roy Buchanan's earliest musical inclinations—according to Roy himself, who later displayed a prodigious talent for forging myth from the most mundane facts. More than 50 years later, J.D. did not recall the tuning incident. But

1

Roy's Aunt Willie Buchanan easily remembered that young Leroy's interest in music surfaced early. Willie got a kick out of watching her young nephew play, or try to play, his first guitar. "Leroy always had a desire, ever since I remember, a desire for music," Willie Buchanan recalled in her Arkansas twang. "He'd get that guitar and pick and pick and pick, and twist around. He *thought* he could play. He'd try. How *funny* he looked, tryin' to play that guitar. I just thought he was showin' off." Leroy learned three chords before his cousin Charles accidentally broke the toy guitar. Years and miles passed before Leroy again picked up an instrument.

THAT LEROY BUCHANAN took such an early interest in the guitar is not particularly surprising, given his surroundings. Music sprang out of the Arkansas hills like the cold clear springs that permeate the Ozarks. J.D.always had guitars around the house and played them just for fun. The boys' uncle made fiddles from scratch as a hobby. Not everyone in rural Arkansas in those days played music, but everyone knew someone who did. Bill Buchanan's cousins, Billy and Amos Gilbreath, were in constant demand for Saturday night dances thanks to their fiddling skills. Perhaps the surprise is that Leroy Buchanan eventually took his music as far as he did, given the humble circumstances of his birth.

Bill Buchanan's clan hailed from Scotland by way of Tennessee and Mississippi, where his father was born just east of the Delta region in the 1870s. John Buchanan made it to the Ozark area sometime in the 1890s after service in the Spanish-American war, long after the Cherokee, Choctaw, and Chickasaw had fled the depradations of white settlement. Some said Bill's grandmother, Mary Casey, might have been Cherokee—a not uncommon matter in Arkansas in those times, though not as frequent as some would have it. This story would be repeated for generations by family members who found a degree of romance in it, and shunned by those who did not. Minnie Reed's people had moved west into Arkansas from Tennessee and Kentucky. In Arkansas a man could raise a family on the productions of a couple dozen acres, if he was willing to part the soft earth with mule-drawn plow. Many a man in those parts pursued such a Jeffersonian ideal, but by the 1930s—with its scorching droughts, foreclosures, and poverty—they were mostly sharecroppers, sustaining themselves and their families off another, more fortunate man's land.

Bill Buchanan and Minnie Bell Reed had grown up around Webb City, Ozark's neighbor on the river's south bank, and married in 1926 when Bill was 23 and Minnie 18. Bill worked a few dozen acres of cotton, sorghum, peanuts, and corn on land owned by his widowed mother, Ada Bell Walden. For unknown reasons—though in the 1930s the cause is easy to suspect—the Buchanans lost their land and later sharecropped on land owned by J. Steven Turner, a prominent local planter. Under the sharecropping arrangement the Buchanans, who owned their mules, kept half the parcel's production each year after they'd paid off Turner for their "draw"—the money for seeds, equipment, perhaps even clothes and food, advanced by the landowner to his tenants. It was a system not unlike the post-slavery plantations worked in Mississippi by black field hands, but it wasn't much like it either. The Buchanans and their neighbors had mobility and choice and were treated fairly by Mr. Turner, in part because he was a trustworthy man and in part because the Buchanans were fortunate in those days in the South to be white.

Ozark took root on both sides of the Arkansas River. The north bank featured the Little Rock & Fort Smith Railroad tracks and therefore it attracted the town's commercial center, while the south bank drew farmers who planted in the river bottoms. Today you can drive over the river on a bridge built courtesy of the Army Corp of Engineers, but in the pre-war era locals depended on a commercial ferry, or they dared cross the ice when the river froze up in winter.

On the south side of a small town split by a river the Buchanans sharecropped by a stream known as Smith's Creek. The creek ran through a tangle of sycamore, red leaf maple, water oak, loblolly pine, and sumac to the Arkansas River less than a mile away. Bill Buchanan was a simple sharecropper, accustomed to only the most basic pleasures. The love of books, or of church, was not among them. Nor did the moonshine that came from the hills tempt him. Buchanan was a hardworking, thrifty, teetotalling man. The Buchanan women attended church on behalf of their men. Bill Buchanan had his own ideas; he did not find church useful. Many years later—after Roy Buchanan had repeatedly told interviewers his father was a preacher—J.D. would say that if Bill Buchanan ever entered a church, "the roof would fall in on his head."

LIFE ON SMITH'S CREEK could be good, and it could be hard. The Buchanans' first child, Clarence Edward, arrived the day after Christmas 1926, either stillborn or unable to thrive. A healthy baby, J.D., came into the world in September 1928. A daughter, Betty, arrived five years later. In 1936 Bill's brother, Johnnie, married Minnie's sister, Willie, and the new couple moved in with Bill and Minnie. The two sisters quarreled, and Minnie took to correcting Johnnie's pronunciation of his own last name. In those days, in that place, many people including Johnnie pronounced the name Buchanan as "Buck-hanon." Some folks in Ozark still do. "Minnie would say, 'You're not pronouncin' that right!'" Willie recalled with a laugh. "She'd say, 'It's Bue-kanon, not Buck-hanon!' Bill and Johnnie's sister, Lena, she'd chime in, 'I've been a Buck-hanon all mah lahf and I'm always gonna *be* a Buck-hanon!" The clan found peace when Willie and Johnnie moved into their own home down the road.

In June 1938 Willie gave birth to her first son, Charles, a baby with dark curly hair. Minnie adored her sister's baby, even coveted him. Bill and Minnie took to bed early on the winter nights preceding Christmas 1938. Minnie grew heavy with child, raising expectations and awakening old fears. By the third week of September 1939 Minnie asked Willie to help with the impending birth of her fourth child. A local physician, Dr. Gibbons, arrived in his Model T early in the evening of September 23. Minnie lay abed in the house's single bedroom, already in labor. Oil lamps lit the room. (The Buchanan home did not have electricity or running water.) After the doctor cut and tied the umbilical cord, Willie washed the baby. "I warshed heem," she said in her Arkansas twang. On the birth certificate recorded exactly one month later, signed by "Bill Buckhanon," the name given for the child is Leroy Buchanan. Leroy would learn to play the guitar.

YOUNG LEROY, like every child, soaked up his immediate surroundings, oblivious to the outside world. His first years in Arkansas and life in the Buchanan household forever imparted a slight Southern drawl to his speech. Arkansas' contributions to Roy's musical education are less fathomable, but the possibilities cannot be ignored. On Saturday nights at some houses, folks moved the furniture out of the main room, rolled up the rug if they owned one (the Buchanans did not), and invited neighbors to a dance. Likewise, neighbors might gather in fall for a "frolic," social gatherings that made harvest chores easier through shared labor. Out came fiddles, guitars, and banjos, often made from the nearby forest, or purchased through the mail from Sears-Roebuck. Traditional folk songs, long ago transplanted from England, Ireland, and Scotland, had been transformed by the isolation and the idiosyncrasies of rural Appalachian and Southern musicians into something new. "Hillbilly," a folksy musical thread in the tapestry that one day would be called "country music," soon emerged. The Buchanans might attend these gatherings to be sociable, but because of a natural reticence and stern upbringings they did not dance. Still, the music played. And Leroy had big ears.

In the 1930s radio transformed rural Arkansas, just like the rest of the country. Johnnie and Willie Buchanan managed, like a million of their fellow Americans in the midst of the Depression, to buy a Model A for $600. The car sported a small radio. "I'll never forget that first radio we had," Willie said. "We'd go down in the cotton fields and people didn't know nothin' 'bout the radios, they's just comin' in. And the people'd just come in like *crazy* to listen to that ol' radio in that car. Everyone in our neighborhood would come to our house and set up 'til midnight listenin' to that ole radio." Radios supplemented local hillbilly music with musical programs from far away—orchestras such as Rudy Vallee and His Connecticut Yankees or Guy Lombardo and His Royal Canadians arrived over the airwaves from unimaginable distances. The songs of "The Singing Brakeman," Jimmy Rodgers, who in the 1930s put a white face on the black country blues, came in loud and clear from Memphis. Though Jimmy Rodgers made the airwaves, his black contemporaries like Robert Johnson and Charlie Patton generally did not. Black purveyors of the country blues could be heard in that part of the South in those days mainly in the juke joints that dotted the backcountry lanes of cotton plantations, unless they'd made it north to Beale Street in Memphis, or south to New Orleans, where blues made it from the plantation to the public house.

Early on Sunday mornings the Buchanan women attended a nearby Pentecostal church while the men made for the river or the woods. By late morning neighboring families had a game of horseshoes under way and, when times were good, a chicken—maybe a catfish—crisping in the frying pan. "Ever-body knowed ever-body," Willie Buchanan recalled of the joys of the sabbath. "Ever-body got to visitin' round. They don't do that anymore."

Despite the Arkansas bottoms' rich soil, time-honored tradition, and Bill and Minnie Buchanan's best efforts, by the 1930s forces outside their control had sent cotton prices into a tailspin. Large-scale farming and mechanized equipment, among other things, depressed prices and displaced hundreds of thousands of field laborers like the Buchanans who knew no other life. A couple hundred miles west, drought and wind parched the earth until the topsoil turned to dust, which swirled into the air, dimming the sky and painting Arkansas sunsets blood red. The Dust Bowl cast a pall over Arkansas and its neighboring states even as the Depression clutched the entire nation in its withering grasp. "If you could save five dollars a year you were in tall cotton," one Ozark resident recalled. In the mid- to late 1930s nearly a half-million people pried themselves loose from this blighted land in the nation's western South and traveled Route 66 to California, the Promised Land. California's soil sustained endless fields of cotton and limitless orchards of fruit, so it was said. Even jobs were ripe for the picking. Hard times made such stories easy to believe. When Minnie Buchanan's older sister, Clara, and her husband, Luther York, made the journey to California and returned to report there really *was* work, Bill and Minnie listened. They had a family to feed.

Sometime after Leroy's second birthday, spurred by hardship, Bill and Minnie Buchanan took their family west by train to Pixley, CA, a small rural farming community just north of Bakersfield in the San Joaquin Valley. Dust Bowl migrants either moved to the city—most often Los Angeles—for factory work in the defense industry, or they remained in farm labor and landed in the San Joaquin. Bill and Minnie chose to stay with what they knew and they worked in the Valley's fields and lived in the labor camps that accommodated other Arkies and Okies who'd sought salvation in the Golden State.

Bill Buchanan found the San Joaquin's vast spaces disconcerting, and its lack of rain daunting. He and his family must have been homesick for some time. In contrast to the comfortable scale of Ozark's lush, wooded hills, the San Joaquin Valley stretched two hundred miles north to south and sprawled nearly a hundred miles wide. Trees were the exception, rather than the rule. From Pixley's modest elevation of 274 feet above the sea, one could look east and just make out the towering, snow-dappled Sierra Nevada through the valley's natural haze. To the west the sensuous, low-lying profile of the coastal ranges appeared like mirages on the horizon. Farming required irrigation. Water cost cash money. Furrowed fields all belonging to someone else ran mesmerizing distances, unlike the well-watered, crazy-quilt, family-tended patches back in Arkansas. Pima cotton ruled, joined by potatoes, grapes, tomatoes, and watermelons. Long summers provided sunshine, and winters often were mild. But winter also brought freezing rains and haunting fog. For farm laborers this meant the dreaded "dead time," when staying alive after the harvests could become a desperate battle.

No one share-cropped here, because leased land had to be paid for in cash rather than crops. Those who toiled at the bottom of the agricultural economy, like Bill Buchanan, found cash hard to come by. Modern farming and the high value of irrigated farm and ranch land in fact promoted an economy dominated by large corporations and conglomerates such as the local Associated Farmers. Bill Buchanan's devotion to farm labor, however, did not make him a devotee of the Valley's fledgling labor unions, violently despised by those who possessed land and water and power. Like many Arkies and Okies Bill had an independent streak that, in one observer's words, made him "immune to the wiles of the organizer." A simple, natural affinity for the San Joaquin's farmers made taking sides a painful step, and the unions' associations with Communism spooked not a few simple men. Bill Buchanan resisted the unions because he wasn't a joiner, not because he wasn't sympathetic to the cause. There seemed to be plenty of back-breaking work to be had picking cotton and harvesting the valley's fruits and vegetables without getting embroiled in politics. The days would be much the same, regardless of one's loyalties. Entire families took to the fields together at daybreak each day, and after a field was picked clean, they followed the procession of harvests from south to north, from cotton to fruit, from day to day, month to month. Toddlers like young Leroy, so he said 30 years later, were corralled into crude playpens woven from cotton stalks at the edge of a field.

THE BUCHANANS STUCK it out for three years, until homesickness outweighed their hopes for a future in California. At the end of World War II, with farm wages depressed by a sudden surfeit of labor, they returned to Ozark. Strawberry prices there had soared and they found their kin in Ozark planting strawberries. The Buchanans joined in to see if this could sustain them too. It did not. But they saved some money, bought a car, and made another journey to Pixley. Leroy and his cousin, Charles, were fooling around the Buchanan home in Ozark when the adults called out that it was time to go. Bill and Minnie were leaving again for California. This time the Buchanans would leave in their own car, a Chevrolet, with neighbor Austin Law driving his pickup truck full of their worldly goods. "We was at Minnie and Bill's, my family and me," Charles said. "Me and Roy was outside playin' when they started callin' for me. It was time to go. We wouldn't tell one another 'bye. We were sad, you know. We'd been playin' in the sand. So we just wrote it in the sand. We wrote 'Goodbye.'"

The family loaded up their Chevy and Law's new three-quarter ton Ford pickup and headed west. In Oklahoma they found Route 66, the two-lane blacktop that John Steinbeck in *The Grapes of Wrath* had dubbed the "mother road, the road of flight," the highway of dreams that linked the Midwest with California. Law was familiar with the entire route. He had developed a lucrative side business ferrying

Class photograph of Leroy Buchanan, young and smiling, circa 1950, Pixley.

neighbors to California and, when they'd had enough, driving them back home again. "We's two nights on the road," Law recalled. High plains, red deserts, soaring mountains all passed by Leroy's window. Two days and nights later—an interminable time for a six-year-old—far from home, the caravan climbed Tehachapi Grade and entered the San Joaquin Valley, the southern end of California's Great Valley. They passed through the "big city"—Bakersfield—and the hamlets of McFarland, Delano, and Earlimart before reaching Pixley. Though he could not know it then, Leroy in years to come would become intimately familiar with Route 66 and America's other cross-country roads. But for the moment the joys and difficulties of childhood unfolded.

Leroy faithfully attended Pixley Union School from July 1945 until his graduation in June 1954, the prime post-war years. His academic records no longer are extant, but his yearbooks for his latter days at Pixley Union reveal interests in sports, shop, and teasing girls. Early on the family lived in a handful of different homes, depending on where Bill Buchanan found work. By 1948 Bill's hard work and dependability had won him a job with Gus Forsblad, a World War I veteran of Swedish extraction. Forsblad found in Bill Buchanan a simple, straightforward, hard-working man he could trust to handle the critical task of irrigating his crops. He put up Bill and his family in a modest two-bedroom, wood-framed house in the middle of several hundred acres of cotton and alfalfa. It would be Leroy's home until he left Pixley for good.

The Buchanans were typical of the town's newer residents. Pixley's population peaked in the 1940s and '50s, fattened by waves of Arkansans and Oklahomans. The town consisted of a modest commercial district that had sprouted where the Southern Pacific Railroad ran north and south and Highway 99 briefly raced alongside. The town, named for the 19th century politician, newspaper editor, and public citizen Frank M. Pixley, supported a fire station, a courthouse, and a post office, a couple of restaurants, a motel, and a lumber yard. As a self-respecting agricultural community it also claimed a cotton gin, a potato packing house, and a hay mill. The *Pixley Enterprise* chronicled local events and brought news of the outside world. The town was not large enough to merit a high school or attract a bank. Churches outnumbered saloons by a nose. A significant number of Pixley-ites frequented one of these establishments or the other. And for those who enjoyed both the excesses of Saturday night could be absolved by a bit of testimony on Sunday morning. Arkies and Okies could be fervent in their religion, and they could be practical. Homes rose along a grid of streets on both sides of the railroad tracks. Sheds stuffed with dirty gray piles of cotton rose at strategic street corners at the edge of town. Beyond, farmhouses dotted the furrowed fields of cotton and grapes that stretched away in every direction.

Bill Buchanan was a good, hardworking man, but it was Minnie who sought betterment for their children. Minnie focused her uplifting energies on her two youngest by getting them music lessons. Music was an integral part of the Pentecostal experience Minnie brought into the Buchanan home from her nearby Assembly of God church. She remembered Leroy's early interest in the guitar and she arranged for Leroy to take lessons from an itinerant music teacher from Bakersfield, a widow named Mrs. Clara Louese Presher. Minnie might have mentioned this to J.D., by then stationed at the U.S. Army's Camp Beale in Northern California. He recalled sending money home to help his folks purchase a red Rickenbacker lap steel guitar for Leroy at White's Music Center in nearby Tulare. Leroy was nine years old. The year was 1948. The guitar purchase and music lessons went hand-in-hand. Mrs. Presher already had numerous pupils in Pixley, Delano, Tulare, Visalia, and Earlimart whom she taught to play piano, guitar, banjo, accordian, and other instruments. Though Leroy expressed interest in playing the standard, "flat top" guitar, his folks favored the lap steel. "There were guitar players all over Pixley, but nobody played steel," Roy explained many years later.

The lap steel guitar derived its name from two things: the steel bar a player held in his left hand, which was used to depress the strings at various frets on the guitar's neck, and the fact that the guitar sat in the player's lap. The fingers of the player's right hand, equipped with finger picks, plucked the strings to form chords and notes. Eventually the instrument would be built with its own stand and foot pedals. Electrified, it would be known as the "pedal steel guitar." By the late 1940s, the lap steel guitar had become an integral part of the country music that the Buchanans could pick up on their home radio set. "I used to try to copy Jerry Byrd, a really smooth player," Roy would recall years later. By the mid-1940s Byrd had become one of Nashville's first session musicians, parlaying his love of lyrical Hawaiian guitar music into a steel guitar sound that would shape modern country music. The steel guitar is not a simple thing to learn, as Byrd once explained to Tom Bradshaw for *Guitar Player*. "To be a good steel guitar player you have to have a good ear. You're really playing by ear, because a steel guitar is the only instrument in the world you play by sight. You got frets there, but if you're a little out of tune the frets have no relevance. Your ear has to hear if you're sharp or flat and make the adjustment. It is an instrument of feel, rather than position."

Pixley may not have had many steel players, but elsewhere they seemed ubiquitous. The instrument had been first captured on "hillbilly" or "country" music recordings in the late 1920s when singers like Jimmie Rodgers and Jimmie Tarlton recorded their own country blues using lap steel guitar accompaniment. By that time black bluesmen and -women had employed the basic technique of applying a steel bar, a knife, or a bottle to standard guitar playing to create another musical style: the bottleneck blues rising out of the Mississippi Delta. Of that development, however, Leroy Buchanan knew nothing.

As influential as his steel guitar sounds were to post-war America, by the late 1940s Jerry Byrd had lots of company. Bob Dunn emerged in Fort Worth, TX, playing guitar and steel for Milton Brown and his Musical Brownies. Leon McAuliffe played steel for Bob Wills and his Texas Playboys, a band that specialized in Western swing. Wills gigged on KVOO in Tulsa from Repeal to the Second World War, helping spread the gospel of country swing and incidentally helping popularize steel guitar sounds. Songwriter Shel Silverstein once said of those sounds: "The steel guitar is the most soulful of all instruments. And if you don't want to get hurt, don't listen to it."

In the little house out in the field at Pixley's edge, an inexpensive radio set brought all this music into the Buchanans' home, as in millions of homes across the West. In the Buchanans' humble household one's appreciation for music was sharpened by the lack of other diversions. Leroy became keen at picking up melodies and the intricacies of steel guitar solos when he wasn't riding his bike, shooting baskets, or doing household chores. He had a knack for instantly memorizing a song's structure and tempo, its guitar solos, even its lyrics. The Grand Ole Opry, broadcast from Nashville and carried over local stations, came on at night in California. Forty years later Roy Buchanan would specifically recall staying up late and hearing "Step It Up and Go," a traditional performed on the Opry that inspired him to become a musician. The Callahan Brothers covered it in the 1930s and Big Jeff and the Radio Playboys in the 1940s, but Leroy probably heard the Maddox Brothers and Rose version in 1947, which featured a young buck on guitar named Roy Nichols.

Used to have a gal, she was little and low
She used to love me but she don't no more
She had to step it up and go

The airwaves were full of country music. Town Hall Party, a live radio show out of Los Angeles that featured the likes of finger-picker Merle Travis, came in over KFI radio out of Compton, CA. Travis played an exciting finger-picking style of lead guitar that opened a world of possibilities to young musicians with big ears like Leroy Buchanan. The airwaves carried a slew of personalities and possibilities: Hank Williams ("I'm So Lonesome I Could Cry"), Jimmy Wakely ("I Wasted a Nickel Last Night"), Lefty Frizzell ("Traveling Blues"), and Tex Williams ("Smoke, Smoke, Smoke That Cigarette") all impressed themselves on Leroy's young mind. Leroy heard Red Foley's 1950 smash "Chattanooga Shoe Shine Boy" and memorized it. (Thirty years later, he surprised his band one night by singing and playing the period piece flawlessly.) He heard Spade Cooley's "Shame on You," Jack Guthrie's "Oklahoma Hills," even Bing Crosby's "Sioux City Sue." Hank Williams grafted country themes and instrumentation atop rhythm and blues, and Ernest Tubb electrified the country blues of Jimmie Rodgers. Country music was in ferment.

The radio brought Leroy music, and with it some notion of a world outside of Pixley. Apart from the family's migration from Ozark, and a weekend or two up in the Sierra each summer, Leroy had no other exposure to the outside world except through school and the family radio. The announcers' thrilling presentation of singers' names and songs might have fired thoughts of stardom in Leroy's young head. But for now, he dutifully took his weekly lessons from Mrs. Presher down at the Assembly of God church. The thrill of the steel guitar sound and his growing ability to play the songs he heard on the radio gave him a task—in fact an identity—he enjoyed.

Down the road, Bakersfield produced its own brand of country music. In the Depression and its aftermath, Arkansas, Oklahoma, and Texas had sent an abundance of musicians to Bakersfield. In the post-war flush of good times the town's honky tonks were jammed with local revelers on Friday and Saturday nights. Live entertainment brought audiences in and, in turn, those audiences supported good music. With the advent of electric, solid-body guitars, steel guitars, and bass guitars created by California companies like Rickenbacker, Fender, and Bigsby, and affordable amplifiers, musicians in Bakersfield had the tools to cut through a club's boisterous revels and be heard above the din. The Arkies and Okies' matter-of-fact ways kept the music honest, raw, and exciting and it coalesced into an infectious strain

Roy acting cool with J.D., far right, and Phil Clemmons, far left, with three unidentified friends, circa 1952.

of country music dubbed the Bakersfield Sound. This funky amalgam of electrified guitars and fiddles, backbeat and vocals, found a home in the smoky honky tonks that produced it, then reached airwaves and jukeboxes. This thrilled the hell out of ambitious locals who built a country music industry in Bakersfield that by the late 1950s earned the town the sobriquet the Western Nashville.

For many locals, having a good old time with loud, loud music late, late at night proved to be a source of great happiness. Naturally, not everyone agreed. The San Joaquin Valley had a strong element of Puritanism, which thrived in the charismatic churches, where direct experience of the Holy Spirit is reflected in fits of ecstasy, speaking in tongues and miraculous healings. Minnie Buchanan belonged to such a church, Pixley's Assembly of God. And the honky tonks existed a world apart from the one occupied by Leroy's lap steel guitar teacher, Mrs. Presher. "She wanted to teach children how to play music," her son, Wallace Presher, said. "That's all she ever wanted to do. She was a Baptist and very religious. She felt that God had given her a gift and that her requirement was to share that gift." She would never step foot inside Bakersfield's notorious honky tonks, Wallace said. "There was a lot of drunkness and violence in those places and she just would not tolerate it. She was dead set against alcohol."

Even in her day Clara Louese Presher was something of an anachronism. Born in 1903 in Spaulding County, GA, south of Atlanta, and raised in Chicago, she attended the Busch Conservatory of Music and earned a bachelor's degree in music from Northwestern University. In Chicago she worked as a union musician, playing organ and piano for traveling big bands. She favored classical music and loved Verdi and Bach. She married a World War I veteran in Chicago and had a child, but lost her husband to his war injuries early in their married life. She eventually moved to Bakersfield with her young son and briefly remarried. By that time she no longer performed in public. In Bakersfield Mrs. Presher taught music through the local Evelyn Scott Studios and, after leaving Evelyn Scott, she honored a noncompete clause in her contract and taught students in outlying towns. Every day but Sunday she loaded her aging Chevrolet with music books and instruments and headed north for the hour's drive to her students' homes. In the case of poor folks like the Buchanans who lived in the country, Mrs. Presher met her students on neutral ground. In Leroy's case, that meant Pixley's Assembly of God church.

Leroy and his younger sister, Linda Joan, did household chores to pay for their lessons. There's no record of how much Mrs. Presher charged, but it couldn't have been much. "She didn't run her business like a business," Wallace Presher said. "She ran it like a love. She gave away a lot of those music lessons. Some of the children she taught up there she didn't charge. She would bring home bags of produce, chickens, and everything else from the farm. These were poor people and these were poor times." As for her teaching philosophy, he added: "She was pretty rigid in her methods. You had to learn the basics. You had to learn to read music, and you had to learn all the fingering techniques long before you got into the actual music."

"[Mrs. Presher] set the foundation for everything I learned on steel guitar," Roy Buchanan would recall years later to Ashley Kahn for *Guitar Player*. "When I went to regular guitar, it was still a steel sound." On another occasion he explained that Mrs. Presher inspired him to express himself honestly. "If I can't feel the music, I can't play. Mrs. Presher was really into that. She would say: 'Roy, if you don't play with feeling, don't play it.'" Mrs. Presher apparently made a valiant effort to teach young Leroy to read music as well. "They used to have a method of teaching that taught by numbers," Roy later recalled. "To count the notes they have all the numbers written out for you. I'd listen to [Mrs. Presher play] and I could memorize it before the next week. It took her two years to realize that I couldn't read music. I was studying her more than I ever studied music. I got a feeling from her." Twenty years later Roy recalled in an interview with Tom Zito the fateful moment when

Mrs. Presher realized her attempt to teach young Leroy to read music had been for naught. "I just played by ear. One day my cousin snitched on me and told Mrs. Presher that I wasn't reading the music. She broke down and started crying." Leroy may have fractured his relationship with Mrs. Presher by learning to play by ear, but after three years of lessons, his ears were his primary teachers.

Freddie Ramirez, a neighbor of Leroy's age, periodically dropped by the Buchanans' house to visit after "roadsiding" hay along Terra Bella, the main road running east of town past the Buchanan place. "I'd go out there and play with him while he was out in his yard, the only one in his family that was around," Ramirez said. "I'd like to hear him play and he was a good friend—easygoing, more or less to himself. A good guy, once you got to know him." Left to his own devices on those long afternoons after school, out in the middle of a sea of cotton and grapes, Leroy got acquainted with solitude and loneliness, and with a deep melancholy that crept into his bones. Maybe it had always been there. Only now he felt its grip. This was not immediately apparent to those around him, perhaps because he was naturally reserved. His younger sister, Linda Joan, noticed.

Though shy, Leroy had a knack for performing. He relished his chances for recitals, despite how nervous they made him feel. His first recitals took place at his mother's church, where he played songs like "Amazing Grace" and "The Old Rugged Cross." School assemblies gave him an even better taste of what it might be like to be one of those performers he heard on the radio. Ramirez remembered Leroy holding school assemblies in thrall. "He was better than the whole band. Everybody listened to him instead of the band. Now, I never did hear him sing, but he played all the Hank Williams songs that were playin' back then just exactly like they were on the record. He would sound *exactly* like the guy playin' guitar. Back then, of course, you didn't hear people play like that unless it was on records or the radio."

LEARNING TO SOAR

··   ····················

L eroy's reputation for playing flawless steel guitar soon reached a couple of local musicians, brothers Marvin and Paul Kirkland. In 1950 Marvin Kirkland was a budding singer and rhythm guitarist. At 21, he was older than Leroy by a decade. "We were looking for *somebody*," Kirkland recalled. "Back in those days steel guitar was pretty big, before the electric guitars got to be so popular. Evidently someone we knew had heard him play. Leroy was a little on the meek side, very quiet around us, maybe because he was the youngest of the group. But he was very serious about playing the steel guitar."

Kirkland's homegrown musical training and his aspirations were not unusual in the San Joaquin Valley. "We just liked guitars, so we'd fool with 'em whether we could hit a tune or not," he said. "We'd sit around campfires at night and make noise. We got to where we thought we were pretty good, thought we'd take the show on the road."

The Kirkland brothers with Leroy Buchanan on steel guitar billed themselves as the Waw Keen Valley Boys. Having a whiz kid on hand helped draw a crowd, and the Kirklands didn't care who got the spotlight as long as they had a paying gig. As Jerry Byrd said many years later in reference to his own youthful beginnings as a player: "A kid can steal a show."

"We played little honkytonks," Marvin said. "We were playing a club up in Tulare and we had to sit Leroy down on the other side of a partition, on the restaurant side, because he was too young to set up there on the bandstand with us. I remember because it was the first time, or one of the first times, he ever played with anybody for money. He had a little red steel guitar, I remember that very well. We didn't make very much. At that time we didn't dream of becoming professionals. Leroy, out of all of us, went on with it."

Leroy kept his day job attending Pixley Union School until June 1954. Though shy, Leroy excelled in his seventh-grade sports programs, earning spots on the school's football and basketball teams in 1952–53. He ran for and won a position on student council. By the following year, however, it seemed his growing interest in the standard "flat top" guitar demanded more of his time, because in eighth grade he was no longer cited for participating in sports. How he obtained his next guitar is not known for certain, but his first standard guitar seems to have been a $14 Harmony f-hole model. Soon he managed to get his hands on a Martin acoustic. He palled around with classmates Darrell Jackson and Darrell Brewer, the first an aspiring singer, the second a guitar player. In June 1954 Roy's yearbook, carefully inscribed, "Leroy Buchanan," was filled with typical graduation messages from his peers. "I hope you and Darrell Jackson have lots of luck in the future," wrote Jerry Hill. Both Judy Brackett and "Bonnie Lou" signed his yearbook, "To a swell guy." "Wanda" wrote: "To a sweet boy. Best wishes in high school." Marcella Bigham wrote: "Best wishes to a mean boy." "To a very good boy, sometimes," added Bonnie Wilson.

Leroy's younger sister, Linda Joan, remembered that at this juncture Leroy enjoyed beating her mercilessly on the basketball court. She recalled another side of Leroy, too. Broadleaf cottonwood trees grew like weeds around the Buchanan house out in the field by the Forsblad's place, but because cottonwoods sapped groundwater and shaded crops, most were taken out. Leroy and Linda Joan nurtured one cottonwood in particular though, one that promised to shade the house and the modest patch of bare ground that passed for a yard. Over the years the two children hauled water from a nearby irrigation ditch to nourish that tree, which indeed spread its branches over the house. As decades passed the tree grew more than 100 feet high and its trunk measured four feet in diameter. In the late 1990s the tree was still there, surrounded by fields of grapes and an empty space between crop rows where a house once stood.

At home Leroy contended with an older sister and a younger one. His elder, Betty, remembered taking Leroy out on her bicycle on the dirt roads that stretched through the fields. On one occasion, when she lost control, she simply jumped free and left her younger brother to his fate among the rows of cotton. Leroy's screams still rang in Betty's ears 50 years later. Linda Joan would recall her older brother's kindness in a similar situation, when she was the youngin' and he had his own bike. "Leroy had a bike and I wanted to ride that bike," Linda Joan said. "But it was too tall for me. It was a boy's bike and I was short. So he would put me on it and I'd go ride. And then I would yell, 'Here! I'm coming!' And he'd catch it for me and slow me down so I could get off."

Unlike Ozark, the outside world sometimes visited Pixley. The *Pixley Enterprise* records that on Sept. 1 and on Sept. 30, 1954, "Cousin Herb" Henson and his "Trading Post" gang appeared at the Pixley Veterans Hall, drawing a crowd of 400. Cousin Herb had earned himself a reputation as a radio and television personality who featured local country music talent out of Bakersfield. The *Enterprise* advertisement does not mention who accompanied Cousin Herb to Pixley, but it is quite possible that Buck Owens or Roy Nichols appeared. Roy Buchanan later recalled having seen both guitarists up close, where he could closely watch their hands and decipher their techniques. Leroy wanted to play guitar like they did, maybe better. Owens and Nichols' Telecaster work, at once refined and raunchy, helped create the Bakersfield Sound that so enthralled Leroy.

By this time country music had developed a split personality. In Nashville Red Foley's protégé, Chet Atkins, pioneered a high-gloss approach that colored every studio session and Grand Ole Opry performance. Nashville eschewed the "western" in "country and western" and largely omitted drums to sweeten and soften the music. Artistically and commercially it was a huge success. As Hank Williams, Ernest Tubb, Kitty Wells, Roy Acuff, and Hank Snow issued record after record, Americans snapped them up by the millions. The radio turned country singers into stars: In the early 1950s the Grand Ole Opry's radio broadcast reached ten million listeners each week.

In Bakersfield the picture was decidedly less glossy. The development of country music in this farming and oil-drilling community depended on lean, mean, and loud. The solid-body Telecaster proved to be a big part of the mix. In the right hands it could sing, sting or cut through a smoky honky tonk like a knife. First made in fall 1950 and dubbed the Broadcaster, this "plank with six strings" departed from the intricate guitar craftsmanship that preceded it. A lawsuit by Gretsch, which made the "Broadcaster" drum set, forced Fender to make a number of units—so-called "Nocasters"—with abbreviated decals that omitted a model name. By spring 1951, however, the rising popularity of television sets inspired the company to dub this model the "Telecaster." The change was a case of shifting identity rather than an evolution in design. Rather than employ ornate finishing touches, Leo Fender purposefully stripped the electric guitar to its barest essentials for his Telecaster model. Fender used an ash body with a cutaway design that allowed the player to reach the higher frets, a maple fret board, a simple volume knob, a tone knob, and a single switch for utilizing either a rhythm or a lead pickup. Advertising copy for the new model boasted "fine fast action," "a wide range of tone effects," and "no feedback." The Telecaster's simple design contributed to its elemental sound, and its clarity and honesty made it instantly popular among the Bakersfield set, whose players knew a good, cheap electric guitar when they saw one. In the hands of Buck Owens or Roy Nichols, the Telecaster became one of the distinguishing characteristics of Bakersfield's new sound—a robust result of attitudes, instruments, and the environs in which they melded. With Telecasters and fiddles interweaving with the steel guitar, and a pounding beat kept by drummer and bassist, the music in Bakersfield's rough honky tonks "had a little more edge to it," said Norm Hamlett, who grew up playing steel guitar in this milieu and went on to spend four decades in Merle Haggard's band, the Strangers. "These guys just played full speed ahead. Partly it was the nature of the honky tonks. You had to have something that would cut, that would get people's attention. A Telecaster, plugged into a Fender amplifier, seemed to get their attention." Leroy was quick to pick up on the jump-right-in-with-both-feet approach favored by local players. The Telecaster had other advantages: If and when the going got rough—a concept young Leroy of course would not grasp for some time yet—a man with a solid-body Telecaster could wield his instrument by its neck, like an axe. "You could play [a Telecaster] and defend yourself at the same time without hurting the guitar," Tele player Fred Carter Jr. once told local writer Bob Price.

The Bakersfield Sound was dance music for Friday and Saturday nights, when truck drivers, oil riggers, field workers, and their blue-collar brethren blew off steam by knocking back a couple of cold beers and taking their honey or a cooperative local maiden out on the floor for a spin. The clubs gave folks looking for good times a place to gather and, together, the venues and audiences nurtured local music. From the Beardsley Ballroom in Oildale, north of town, to the Rainbow Gardens and Rhythm Ranch on South Union Avenue to Cousin Ebb's Pumpkin Center Barn Dance on Bakersfield's south side, live country music provided a backdrop to the euphoria of the post-war boom. New clubs sprouted all the time. In 1950 Joe Limi and Frank Zabaleta took a truck stop at 3601 Chester Avenue, renamed it the Blackboard, and brought in steel player Fuzzy Owen's trio. The Blackboard soon gained notoriety for its music, its fights, and its 40-cent draws. As the 1950s unfolded, the club could count among its regular performers a list of stars nearly as long as the nights they played: Tommy Collins, Lewis Talley, Billy Mize, Buck Owens and his wife, Bonnie, all headlined the Blackboard, as did Wanda Jackson and Red Simpson. George Jones, Bob Wills, Patsy Cline, Tex Ritter, Lefty Frizzell, Tommy Duncan, and Spade Cooley—to name just a few—could be counted among the club's visiting performers. Driving home from the Blackboard one night, singer and lightning-fast guitarist Joe Maphis captured the club's allure and its disappointments—a microcosm of the Bakersfield scene—in his song "Dim Lights, Thick Smoke (and Loud, Loud Music)":

Dim lights, thick smoke, and loud, loud music
Is the only kind of life
You'll ever understand

Dim lights, thick smoke, and loud, loud music
You'll never make a wife
To a home-lovin' man...

A home and little children
Mean nothing to you,
A house filled with love
And a husband that's true,

You'd rather take a drink
With the first guy you meet,
And the only home you know
Is the club down the street

Roy with his father, Bill Buchanan, in starched overalls and fedora, circa 1954.

The Bakersfield Sound rode the airwaves into homes in the San Joaquin Valley and young Leroy Buchanan was paying attention. "I learned from listening to the radio," Roy Buchanan once told an interviewer. "There was a guy in Bakersfield who played a Telecaster. I loved his playing. He became a singer later on. His name is Buck Owens. He's the one who got that whole thing started . . . ."

By this time, though he continued to play the steel guitar, Leroy seems to have reached a new level of skill, confidence, and dedication to the flat-top guitar. "He lost himself in it," sister Linda Joan would recall. "It was hard to get Leroy away from his guitar. He would withdraw into his music." To Linda Joan this stemmed from more than simple dedication. She herself experienced the melancholia, even depression, that cropped up in her family. She is certain today that her beloved older brother felt something similar.

In the fall of 1954 Leroy began to take the bus each day to Delano High School, 14 miles down the highway and, socially, a million miles from Pixley. "I don't think Leroy liked high school," Linda Joan said. "There was a big difference between the 'haves' and the 'have-nots.' I hated high school for the same reason." A hayseed from Pixley had to struggle for acceptance at Delano High School and Leroy's taciturn nature did not aid him in that regard. Music became his solace. He realized it would be his ticket away from Pixley and the loneliness he found there.

The radio set in the Buchanan family's house out in the fields now carried new sounds even more infectious than country music. White singers were adopting black rhythm and blues and garnering prime airplay for their version of "race music," previously broadcast only after midnight. In August 1954 Bill Haley issued "Shake, Rattle, and Roll," a cover of the Joe Turner original released only three months earlier, and *Billboard* magazine ate it up. The trade sheet carried advertisements touting Bill and his Comets as "The Nation's 'Rockingest' Rhythm Group." Truth in advertising might have required the ad to read: "The Nation's Rockingest Rhythm Group (with White Faces)." Black rhythm and blues artists in Memphis, New Orleans, St. Louis, Chicago, New York, Detroit, and other American cities had been rockin' and rollin' since at least the late 1940s. White performers simply brought the music into the mainstream white culture, garnering prime airtime. The music carried the day, infecting white middle-class youths who created a burgeoning market for R&B repackaged as "rock 'n' roll."

In the Aug. 7, 1954, *Billboard*, notice appeared of a new release, "That's All Right, Mama," which Arthur "Big Boy" Crudup had performed in 1947. The new record was backed by "Blue Moon of Kentucky," which had been a hit for Bill Monroe the same year. "[Elvis] Presley is a potent new chanter who can sock over a tune for either the country or the r.&b. markets," the notice read. "On this new disk he comes through with a solid performance on an r.&b.-type tune and then on the flip side does another fine job with a country ditty. A strong new talent." More than 30 years later, Roy Buchanan recalled that another of Presley's efforts in the summer of '55 hit him right between the ears: "Everybody said he did 'That's All Right, Mama,' first, but I heard him do 'Mystery Train' and it really got me excited, so I decided to leave home . . .' " Another time, Roy said: "I was laying in bed one night. I was about fifteen years old. There was a show I listened to every Saturday night. It was called 'Louisiana Hayride.' [Broadcast out of Shreveport, LA.] They said, 'Elvis Presley will be out in a minute.' And all these girls started screamin'. I'd never heard anything like that before. Sure enough they come out and Scotty Moore took off on 'Mystery Train.' [I thought] God, that guy's great! These guys are going to get big." Roy claimed he eventually learned all Moore's solos, note for note. "[He] was so unique and so different. Powerful. Aggressive for those days. Scotty Moore was just bold. It would just grab you."

ATTENDING DELANO HIGH SCHOOL had its moments. Leroy met a new friend, Bobby Jobe, in music class. The two could relate. Both were poor boys from the sticks, both were smitten by country music and rhythm and blues. Jobe lived at H Camp at Shinley's Ranch, just outside Earlimart. "Leroy's folks were from down South and kinda had the blues feeling in their soul," Jobe said 45 years later. "So music come kinda natural for Leroy." As for his new friend's demeanor, Jobe added: "He was pretty shy, man. Yes he was! I don't think he thought about havin' a girlfriend because it would take him away too much from his guitar." The two skipped physical education classes and talked guitars, or got their music teacher to give them a pass to stay in the music room where they could pick all afternoon. "Leroy and me, pickin' guitars is all we wanted to do," Jobe remembered. "So we'd tell Mr. Hayden, 'Mr. Hayden, why don't you get us passes out of sixth period so we can sit here and pick and learn somethin'?' He'd give us our way. During PE class sometimes we'd walk around the track and talk guitars, and what we's goin' to do. Leroy says, 'I ain't goin' do no work, man. I got that guitar and that's all I'm goin' do. I want you to come with me.' Anyways, we'd think about it. He'd say, 'Let's get out of here and go to Las Vegas.' This is 1955. He's sixteen years old!"

Leroy could think big, or at least talk boldly, a talent he might have learned from his older brother, J.D. J.D. had a natural gift for storytelling and fast talk that he had honed as an Army airman at Camp Beale. J.D. excelled at relating momentous events and insinuating himself into the story, whether or not he'd been there—an ancient and honorable prerogative of the storyteller. His prodigious talents in this area, legend among family and friends, may well have helped shape Leroy's sly sense of humor and predilection for myth-making. Quietly watching his brother at work, Leroy learned to tell a tall tale with a straight face.

On leave from Camp Beale, J.D. returned home and took Leroy with him on jaunts to nearby Earlimart, Stockton, and Fresno. J.D. claims to this day that his purpose was to get Leroy work as a musician. His sisters counter that their older brother used Leroy's musical talent to attract women. The effect was the same: Leroy got exposed to music. It was on such a visit to Stockton that, according to J.D., his younger brother heard the blues for the first time. "I had a colored friend, Earl, a guitarist, who was doin' a gig at a black club in Stockton," J.D. said. He suggested that the venue could have been the Lido Club in the Lido Hotel on Laredo Street. "Me and Roy went in there and Roy like to ate that up 'cause he'd never heard the blues before. After that it got to where he'd say, 'I'm gonna learn them nigger blues.' He'd bend them strings on the guitar and say, 'I'm gonna play them nigger blues.' That's exactly what he'd say. And that's the first time, as far as I know, he was ever exposed to it."

The blues had evolved from chants and hollers that enlivened labors in the fields of West Africa music that captive slaves brought to the American South in the seventeenth, eighteenth, and ninteenth centuries. In the South's plantations, work camps, and prison farms, the African pattern of call-and-response was transformed by extreme hardship, grinding poverty, and relentless persecution into several art forms, including gospel music, and a twelve-bar format of three lines known as the blues. The genre was composed of two melodic statements (the call) and a third (the response). The human voice became the blues' primary instrument, but the guitar, banjo, and harmonica provided the earliest, cheapest accompaniment. A man or woman who could sing and play the blues became a valued member of a separate society. Their tales of misery and heartache struck an empathetic note in their audiences. The sharing of a burden made life more endurable. This music took root in the fertile bottomlands of the Mississippi River, particularly between Vicksburg and Memphis. By the 1930s and '40s the lineage of artists that one day would reach Leroy Buchanan's ears had entered history. The names of just a few—Blind Lemon Jefferson, Charley Patton, Son House, Robert Johnson, Lightning Hopkins, Memphis Slim and Memphis Minnie—ring a bell even today. After World War II, others—including McKinley Morganfield (aka Muddy Waters), John Lee Hooker, Chester Burnett (aka Howlin' Wolf), and Elmore James—traveled north to Memphis, St. Louis, and Chicago, where, like their distant brethren in Bakersfield, they used electrified amplification to be heard above the din of the crowd. By the 1950s, when Leroy heard "Earl" in Stockton, the blues were everywhere—practiced both by big bands and singers (and often guitarists) such as B.B. King, Bobby "Blue" Bland, Jimmy Reed, Sonny Boy Williamson, Willie Dixon, Little Milton, and countless others. Along the way from the South to the city, the blues spawned gospel, rhythm and blues, jazz and . . . more.

The blues appealed to Leroy Buchanan. The minor keys resonated inside him as the musical expression of his inner feelings. The pathos inherent in the lyrics meshed with his outlook. Musically, the blues explained so much to a young player. It provided a pedigree for popular music and tied together seemingly disparate musical threads. Now Leroy understood the roots of rhythm and blues, of country music, and of rock 'n' roll. In terms of technique, bending strings on the guitar gave Leroy a new mode of expression and a new level of sophistication. He embraced the blues and he immersed himself in them. And he applied what he'd learned to the emerging, mongrel art of rock 'n' roll.

Leroy soon made another discovery, one that afforded him new, more complex ways of playing in any idiom. His reaction was similar to the first time he heard the blues. "I didn't know what 'jazz' was," he confessed much later in life. "First time I even heard the word was in seventh or eighth grade. I didn't know a modern jazz chord until I was fifteen. The first jazz player I ever heard was Barney Kessel. I got a record called 'To Swing or Not to Swing,' started learning the chords, and found it improved my other playing."

J.D. CLAIMED that before Leroy put down the steel guitar for good, he and Leroy paid to make a recording together at a music store, perhaps in Tulare or Visalia or Stockton. "It was like one of those little machines that you put a quarter in and play. [We got] a little, red record for my mom. I know I was a little disappointed, but Mom was real happy over the thing." (No copies of this record, Roy Buchanan's earliest known recording, have been located.)

By this time Leroy had focused intently on the guitar work of Roy Nichols. Nichols, born in Chandler, AZ, in 1932, was seven years Leroy's senior—impossibly older to a teenager. Nichols had learned country picking from Henry Maddox of the Maddox brothers and as he matured he absorbed Django Reinhardt's swinging jazz style, which lent him a degree of sophistication and fluency that set him apart from most country pickers. Nichols' sound caught Leroy's ear. ("Roy and I always used to say, 'Any damn fool can play country music,'" J.D. once said. "'But it takes a *smart* person to play *good* country music.'") By the mid-'50s, Nichols had played with Lefty Frizzell, a Roy Rogers–style singer with a few hits under his belt, and local crooner Smiley Maxidon. Around this time he sat in on Cousin Herb Henson's "Trading Post" television program, where Leroy might have seen him. Most anyone who lived in that place and time and had an interest in country guitar picking vividly remembers Roy Nichols' distinctive approach. He popularized guttural, staccato runs in an infectious style dubbed "chicken-pickin'." He made a descending run of notes into a sound all his own, a sound Lula Maddox, mother of the Maddox brothers, once characterized as sounding like "a horsey fartin'." His string-bending technique, borrowed from the blues, gave the Bakersfield Sound a whole new twist. Where most of his contemporaries hit a note and bent it up into a sharp, Nichols bent a string, struck it, and released it, lowering the note. His progressive, lyrical style, infused by jazz and blues, transformed country guitar picking into an art. Leroy recognized Nichols' style as a class apart from run-of-the-mill pickers, and he worked on his own technique until he could mimic Nichols' best licks. Leroy studied the way Nichols turned a lick inside out, or played it backwards. Nichols' playing inspired Leroy to conceive of new possibilities. The effect on Leroy's playing impressed the hell out of his buddy, Bobby Jobe.

"*Gawd*, Leroy was the hottest thing that ever *was* on the guitar," Jobe said. "When we were goin' to school he had an acoustic with a pickup in it. A little Martin. He also had a little f-hole Harmony. He was doin' all the Buck Owens stuff. Buck was workin' for Tommy Collins then, and they were doin' 'You Better Not Do That,' and 'Whatcha Goin' Do Now?,' and Leroy had that guitar part just perfect. He could play Merle Travis, Roy Nichols, *anything*."

Leroy and Bobby hooked up at first with other high schoolers, like Leroy's Pixley friend, Darrell Jackson, who sang, and aspiring pianist Bobby Hamilton from Delano. Together they dubbed themselves "The Dusty Valley Boys" and played at school assemblies. Leroy had not quite given up the steel guitar at that point, for Jobe remembers that his friend continued to listen to and emulate steel guitar licks he heard on the radio. "I was over at Leroy's house in Pixley, settin' there, listenin' to the radio, and he played a little steel guitar, a little Rickenbacker, a little red one, set on his knees, okay?" Jobe said. "We're settin' around there and Webb Pierce had just come in with this song, 'Slowly.' Bud Isaac played steel guitar for Webb Pierce." (Isaac was playing a brand-new invention, the pedal steel guitar.) "The kickoff was like 'da da da da' in descending notes: 'Sl-o-o-w-ly I'm fallin' more in love with you . . . .' Leroy said to me, 'You hear that?' I said, 'Yeah.' So he goes out to the barn, picks up a ten-penny nail, a piece of bailing wire, a piece of wood like a little pedal, took it back in the house, and he took that nail and wove it through his strings, behind the bridge, hung the piece of wire to the piece of wood, about an inch from the floor. He'd push that piece of wood down and play his steel and it sounded just like Bud Isaac. Whatever he'd hear comin' down the pike, he'd only have to hear it but one time and he could play it just like any guitar picker: Roy Nichols, 'Sugarfoot' Garland, *anyone*. We'd hear it on the radio. Or we'd get into a cafe or a honky tonk that's got a jukebox in it that had the good songs. So we'd sit there and put our nickels in the jukebox and learn a lot of stuff like that, see? Just play it over and over. Leroy was crazy 'bout blues then. We'd just set around listenin' to B.B. King, Bobby 'Blue' Bland . . . ."

Leroy and Jobe were a couple of teenagers on the make. They hustled the more seasoned talent they met locally, looking for a real paying gig. That talent had to be at least eighteen years of age, of course, look old enough to play in a beer joint, and have a car to get everyone to the gig. Guitarist Custer Bottoms, from Alabama, lived near Jobe outside Earlimart and agreed to give the boys a try. Fiddle player Lewis Lyles, from nearby Corcoran, joined them. The ensemble jelled, and Bottoms and Lyles were delighted to find that the youngsters could hold their own. "We got a job at a little honky tonk up in Tulare called 'The Forty-Niner,'" Jobe said. "Custer, he's the band leader, see? All right. I was playin' rhythm. Back then we didn't have no bass. Leroy played lead guitar on a Gibson hollow-body electric. We played good old country, man. Ray Price, Carl Smith, Hank Williams, stuff like that. *Good* country. Okay. Leroy would do stuff like 'Sugarfoot Rag,' 'Waterbaby Blues,' Roy Nichols' guitar number. 'Course, Lewis on the fiddle would play things like, 'Cabbage Down,' 'Maiden's Prayer.' Whatever people wanted to hear. Custer and I sang vocals. We did Hank Williams, Hank Locklin, Ernest Tubb, you name it. We didn't have no name for the band. We just got up there and picked."

The Forty-Niner was "just a honky tonk," Jobe recalled. "It had a cafe on one side, then the bar on the other side. We'd been there a couple of weeks and gawd, you couldn't even get in. People were lined up as if the Maddox Brothers and Rose were there. So the third or fourth week a state man comes in, flashes the badge, and asks Lewis how old he is. Lewis says, 'Eighteen.' He was *lyin'*! So the state man says, 'Okay, finish tonight and don't come back no more.' He looked at Leroy and said, 'How old might *you* be?' Leroy looked like a kid! Leroy says, 'Sixteen.' The state man says, 'Finish this night and don't you come back!' So he says to Custer— Custer is twenty-six—'What's *your* age?' Custer says, 'Well, I'm twenty-six and I run the band here.' 'You got any ID with you?' Custer got so mad when the fellow checked out his driver's license. Then the state man walked over to me at the other end of the bandstand and says, 'You guys are pickin' good tonight. Too bad you guys gotta quit.' I said, 'I guess so.' He says, 'Well, keep on pickin', son.'"

"We didn't play anyplace in Bakersfield," Jobe added "It was really tight. Union. We couldn't pay the dues. But we played at Delano at the Cellar, the Cuckoo Inn. One of the honky tonks we worked was called the Cowboy Inn. The first time we played we made seven-and-a-half dollars apiece, per night. After three weeks we got a raise to ten dollars a night, apiece. By the time we got busted [at the Forty-Niner in Tulare] we's up to 12-and-a-half dollars a night. We was packin' that place. That's about the most money we ever made. Back in school me and Leroy would have good money in our pockets!"

In addition to country standards Custer Bottoms led his band through Bill Haley's "(We're Gonna) Rock Around the Clock"—a song popularized in 1955 by the first teenage rebellion flick, *The Blackboard Jungle*—and Fats Domino's "Ain't That a Shame," which also hit the charts that summer. Leroy's experiences on stage with Custer Bottoms' band stirred ambitions. "[The audience] was sort of shocked, I think," Roy would recall of these early gigs. "It was something in their eyes when I started playing. It made me feel good. I thought, 'Hey, *this* is what I want to do.'"

LISTENING TO THE RADIO, plugging nickels into jukeboxes, and climbing up on stage gave Leroy and Bobby an education, whether or not they attended classes. By 1955, Leroy and Bobby Jobe were beginning to piece together the music's pedigree. They gradually came to understand that rock 'n' roll and country had roots. They figured out that the country-style acoustic blues from the Delta had something to do with it. And they recognized that the electric Chicago blues practiced by Muddy Waters, Howlin' Wolf, and Elmore James also had a lot to do with propelling rock 'n' roll. Perhaps the two young men even grasped that the Bakersfield Sound and the electric blues grew from similar, if separate, circumstances.

Musicologists and pop culture historians later would argue about the origins of rock 'n' roll, and which artists and songs exemplified its beginnings or propelled it to become a major force in American culture. But to a budding, hick-town guitarist like Leroy Buchanan, these arguments would make little sense. The only thing that mattered was the music he actually heard. That was his education. Where the music came from mattered less than where it could take him. He badly wanted out of Pixley.

Leroy was hardly alone in his affection for rock 'n' roll. One writer later attempted to capture the burgeoning white audience's interest in crossover rhythm and blues: "[The] vocal styles were harsh, the songs explicit, the dominant instruments—saxophone, piano, guitar, drums—were played loudly and with an emphatic dance rhythm, [and] the production of the records was crude. The prevailing emotion was excitement." One senses that this critic meant to convey his reservations about the new sounds, but the elements he described were exactly what fired up America's youth.

It was becoming clear to Leroy that to capitalize on what he'd learned, he would have to leave Pixley. That Leroy had to go, that finishing high school would not be his path, seems to have been a foregone conclusion among his closest friends and family. "It's difficult to talk about Roy because of all my family, I identified with Roy," said Linda Joan. "I can understand his fighting with depression, wanting to get out of Pixley. He wanted to escape. Most of us wanted to get out of there." Jobe remembered that his friend began that process with a quick trip to

Stockton in a naive attempt at landing a gig. "Music was all he cared about, all he dreamed about. He went to Stockton first, worked up there, tryin' to make a livin' playin'. He took off by himself. After he come back from Stockton he came by my house. He said, 'I'm sure glad you didn't go with me, man. I damned near starved to death! I've been so hungry I didn't know what to do. I didn't want to give up so I finally came home.'"

The next departure was effortless, though not deliberate, according to J.D. Buchanan. "I moved to L.A. in early 1955," he said. On a drive to Stockton J.D. and his friends stopped in Pixley and picked up Leroy. "On our way home from Stockton my friend was driving, and when we went through Pixley, Roy and I were both asleep and he forgot to let Roy off at home," J.D. continued. "The next thing I knew, we woke up in Hollywood, where I was living. Roy went home for a while. The next thing I knew, he was back."

Leroy had come to a decision. His brother's presence in Hollywood and his sister's place in Garden Grove, just south of Los Angeles, offered an opportunity. Pixley would never change. A small town spelled doom for anyone with ambitions of becoming a professional musician. One simple snapshot of Pixley's size and resistance to change: In January 1955, Delos O. Howard, the town's lone constable for 46 years, finally retired. The pace of change, if it could be called such, was suffocating. Music was all Leroy dreamed about. His talent could only thrive, let alone flower, in the city. He had to hit the road. Many years later a colleague asked him how he knew he was ready for the proverbial pavement. Roy replied that when he heard a song on the radio and had the licks mastered by morning, he knew. With his future utterly uncertain and his worldly experience minimal, he set forth. But leaving town at age sixteen is never easy. Apparently Leroy felt compelled to mythologize his departure. "He told me, 'I got to go,'" his friend Freddie Ramirez said. "He was sad, like on the verge of tears. It was a sad, sad day. I can remember him leaving. Something about someone dyin'. He had to leave. It was better for him, though at the time we didn't know it. He was gone, gone, gone from Pixley."

HITTING THE ROAD

*I*t is tempting to imagine young Leroy Buchanan on the shoulder of a two-lane blacktop, hitchhiking out of Pixley with guitar in hand, hair blowin' in the wind. Or perhaps aboard a Greyhound bus, staring out the window as the miles fly by, guitar in the seat beside him, en route to L.A. and the glittering big time. In reality, the circumstances of his departure were considerably more mundane. "For some reason Roy didn't want to go to school anymore," recalled his former brother-in-law, Phil Clemmons, who'd married Leroy's older sister, Betty. "I think his mother just didn't know what else to do with him. He was lost up there in Pixley. He came down to L.A. visiting one time and we hit it off real good, because I loved music and liked to play a little. I asked him to come down and stay with us. I brought him down to McNab Street in Garden Grove, where we lived, sometime in early '56."

Clemmons himself wondered what to do with Leroy, who seemed interested only in his guitar. "I worked as a front-end brake mechanic, so I took him to work with me one day. The first thing I had him do was try to pull a wheel off a car. He got grease all over his hands. I looked over and he was just looking at his fingernails. His fingernails were always just perfect for picking. This one was Chet Atkins, that one was somebody else. So he didn't want any part of working in a mechanic's shop." Indeed, Leroy had told his friend Bobby Jobe he "wouldn't do no work," and he meant it. He would play the guitar. That would be his ticket up and out. If that shielded him from dirty, seemingly pointless labor, so much the better. He had a gift and he worked hard at developing it. "It was nothing for me to leave the house at eight in the morning and come home at five and Betty would tell me, 'Roy's been playin' that guitar in his room the whole day!'" Clemmons said.

A photograph from this period shows a teenaged Leroy in a red-striped shirt, his brown hair slicked back, holding a clutch of younger cousins. Leroy's expression is pleasant if somewhat impassive, utterly devoid of guile. It is a clean slate, without the contours of life experience. Yet Leroy knew something inside that the world had yet to discover. For one thing, he had perfect pitch—the ability to discern any note and to tune an instrument by ear. That gift gave him an innate confidence in his talents not immediately reflected in his demeanor. But it was bound to surface sooner or later.

Phil Clemmons did his best to arrange an audition for his young brother-in-law in some sort of show-business venue. "Doye O'Dell had a show on television every week, a country music show, and I managed to get a phone number from a friend of mine," Clemmons said. "We called ahead to let them know we'd be there. I told Roy when we got out of my car, 'You're going to take your guitar with you, aren't you?' He said, 'Well, I don't know.' You wouldn't believe how bashful he was. He said, 'Let's just wait and see what he says.' I said, 'Well I think you ought to take your guitar.' But he didn't want to. We waited in the audience until the show was over, then we went backstage. Doye O'Dell and this other guy come over and introduce themselves and I said, 'This is Leroy Buchanan, the guy I told you about. He'd like to do a little audition for you.' O'Dell says, 'So, you want to play the guitar, huh? Okay, let's hear you.' Leroy said, 'Well, I've got to get my guitar.' O'Dell says, 'I haven't got time for that. You can use mine.' So Leroy takes his guitar and the first thing he does, he starts tuning it. O'Dell grabs it out of his hands and walks away and that was the end of the audition. I said, 'What the hell did you do *that* for?' And Leroy says, 'I wasn't going to play a guitar that far out of tune.'"

The kid had a point. And possibly an attitude. His desire to tune the guitar could have reflected a simple honesty. It might have been a deliberate expression of contempt for a lesser mortal. Quiet, unassuming Leroy Buchanan, despite his outward meekness, had developed a fierce sense of musicianship. And that case of ambition he'd been nursing since his days running with Bobby Jobe had become a quiet fever. "The only thing he ever said about the future was that he wanted to learn to play all different kinds of music," Clemmons said. "Oh, and that someday he wanted to be the world's greatest guitar player."

The first step on the road to greatness would be a doozy. Leroy's personality, as with most teenagers, contained a jumble of contradictions: he was shy and brash, ambitious and naive. Drop such a character in a town full of hustlers, like Hollywood, and things were bound to get interesting. Leroy visited and occasionally stayed with his older brother J.D., who lived in Hollywood. That way Leroy wouldn't overstay his welcome at Phil and Betty's, or get dragged down to the machine shop where he might get his fingernails dirty. In that respect it was out of the frying pan and into the fire—perhaps because Phil talked to J.D. and couldn't help but mention Leroy's aversion to labor. J.D. immediately set Leroy to work helping him build a cinderblock retaining wall at his home. "Roy told me, 'Man, that's the hardest I ever worked in my life,'" J.D. recalled later with a cackle.

Both Phil and J.D. tried to help Leroy land a job as a musician since the kid clearly had his heart set on it. Temperamentally, however, Leroy was not geared toward the sort of self-promotion the business required. "Roy didn't know anyone to call in the entertainment business," Clemmons recalled. "He had no idea how to get it going. So J.D. or someone J.D. knew got him onto Bill Orwig."

Central Casting would be hard-pressed to find a cheesier wheeler-dealer than Bill Orwig. A native of Oklahoma City, OK, he epitomized the proverbial two-bit Tinsel Town hustler—short, stout, and balding, he wore checkered jackets and gabardine slacks. He had no car. His "Jaguar" was forever "in the shop." From the point of view of a couple of kids he soon recruited, though, Orwig "had a pretty good spiel," one observer recalled. A good spiel, perhaps, but not a great one. Dirt stuck to him. He had a reputation. Local 47 of the American Musicians' Union had published a photograph of Orwig in its newsletter with the caption, "DO NOT PLAY WITH THIS MAN." Orwig instantly recognized Leroy's talents and noted the usefulness of the young man's naiveté. He offered Leroy a room at his own apartment and promised to make him a star. Leroy, anxious to get his career moving and to relieve his sister and brother of his care, accepted. His sole possessions, besides a change of clothes, were a hollow-body Gibson electric guitar and his Martin acoustic.

Orwig soon snared 18-year-old drummer Spencer Dryden in his web as well. Spencer, a year older than Leroy, had grown up in Southern California's coastal towns and, after getting the hot rod scene out of his system, had gotten a few years of jazz and rock drumming under his belt. Hanging around Hollywood drum shops and Local 47's union hall helped him make connections. One led to Bill Orwig. Dryden ignored the union's warnings and soon Orwig had two members of a group that he envisioned would fill 1956's sudden market for rock 'n' roll bands. Preferably clean-cut, white bands. Dryden was a good deal more worldly than his new friend Leroy. "He knew how to play guitar," Spencer would recall. "But he didn't really understand what was going on around him—he was absolutely naive. When we played together he was still Leroy, a kid with a soft-spoken drawl who played the shit out of that guitar. He and I had a similar love of rhythm and blues and down-home rock 'n' roll, so we hit it off real well."

Orwig soon recruited Tommy Oliver on piano, Jim Gordon on sax, Frank Isari on trombone, and Lyle Ritz on bass. He outfitted his band in hideous striped jackets in repugnant colors, with matching shirts and pants. "This is at the beginning of everything," Dryden said. "Nineteen fifty-six. Elvis is king. James Dean is still alive. It's bobby sox and rock 'n' roll. And everybody is looking for an 'in.' None of us knew what we were doing. But Bill Orwig had a scheme." The hustler named his band the "Heartbeats." Because none of them could sing convincingly, he cast the Heartbeats as backup for "The Pharoahs," a three-man, black doo-wop group. Later Orwig convinced singer "Little Julian" Herrera to front the band. "All of a sudden we're making money," Spencer said, still surprised after 40 years. "It was a phony Hollywood trip, like the Monkees or the Spice Girls. Bill Orwig was a little race-town hustler, without his Jaguar, saying, 'I can put this together.' He had some kind of inside track to Jack Gilardi, who at that time was a big-time agent in Beverly Hills. I remember going into Gilardi's office in Beverly Hills, right on Rodeo

Drive, with my drums and Leroy and the guys have their little guitars and tiny amps. We audition for this guy." Gilardi was looking for a band to appear in Jayne Mansfield's movie, "The Girl Can't Help It." The Heartbeats didn't get the part.

Orwig did manage to hustle a few gigs. Because he owned a big, four-door, '49 Ford, Spencer Dryden was elected to drive everyone around. One of the band's first shows was an engagement at the Tulare Auditorium in distant Tulare, just north of Leroy's home town of Pixley. Half the band piled into Dryden's car for the drive north. J.D. Buchanan and his wife, Shirley, were freshly married and they drove J.D.'s '56 convertible Pontiac Starchief in the caravan as well. When the water pump blew on Dryden's Ford, the group had to stop on "the ridge"—tiny 4,183-foot Tejon Pass, the link between the Los Angeles basin and the San Joaquin Valley—to repair it. Frank Isari took the mouthpiece from his trombone and sat and played. That tickled Shirley Buchanan. While a mechanic replaced the water pump on Dryden's car the Buchanans ducked inside a cafe for a cup of coffee. Each table had its own jukebox, the kind with page after page of hits. In August 1956 those pages held a lot of history-in-the-making: Elvis Presley now topped the charts with "Don't Be Cruel" backed with "Hound Dog." "Heartbreak Hotel" and "Love Me Tender" were not far behind. Carl Perkins, Roy Orbison, and Johnny Cash crowded Elvis for the public's attention.

Back on the road, an hour and a half later, Dryden recalled, Leroy pointed out the back window. "He says, 'That's Pixley. That's where I grew up.' I'm looking out at absolute flatness. One or two citrus trees. A lot of dust." The flatness, the citrus trees, and the dust may have helped explain Leroy's naiveté. But the rural terrain spooked Dryden. He was as much a city boy as Leroy was country.

Tulare's Veterans Memorial Building is a functional, four-story building painted pink. It opened on Memorial Day 1956, just months before the Heartbeats arrived. It still stands, and it is still pink. A proposal in the 1970s to paint the building a different color met with round condemnation from the community. The first floor features an enormous auditorium and stage. Fats Domino played the hall two weeks before the Heartbeats. Police Chief Ed Houck had threatened to cancel Fats' show due to "numerous derogatory reports on the effects of this band" from a prior gig in San Jose. At San Jose, "dance enthusiasts" who couldn't gain admission to Fats' sold-out show grew restive, "a beer bottle was thrown and mass fighting ensued." Fats' show in Tulare produced seven arrests for isolated fighting, raising concerns about subsequent rock 'n' roll performances. But an item in the *Tulare Advance Register* dated Aug. 4, 1956, hinted that the Heartbeats' upcoming show would be tamer. "Amvets Plan Dance," read the headline announcing Leroy Buchanan's first "major" professional gig. "Tulare Amvets are winding up last minute preparations for a rock and roll dance to be held in the Memorial auditorium tonight from 9 o'clock to 1 a.m. Featured at the dance will be the Rock and Heartbeats, a Hollywood orchestra." (No doubt the band's name was intended to read "Rockin' Heartbeats.")

As the band unloaded its gear at the Tulare Veterans' Memorial Building, Shirley Buchanan had a chance to take in the scene. Tommy Oliver, who had traveled separately, seemed rather struck with himself. He was not the only one. His girlfriend appeared in bobby socks and saddle shoes and a pink poodle skirt, her pony-tailed hair dyed cotton-candy pink. She had brought her poodle. The dog's coat also had been dyed pink. "We were living on a shoestring at the time and it just seemed to me that people should have better things to do with their money than to match themselves up with their dog and his fur," Shirley said. The music, she remembered, was "loud and fast."

Musically the Heartbeats were not breaking any new ground. According to Dryden, "Most of it was just blues changes, almost all instrumentals. Basically we had about eight tunes, and we played them over and over and over again. When I was writing for the Heartbeats, I would include these blues changes that I heard on the late night R&B stations. It was basically one, four, five. The simplest of changes. Leroy knew exactly what to do. We put our hearts into it, but I don't think it ever gelled." Despite Dryden's sober assessment of the band's abilities, a positive review of the show appeared in the *Tulare Advance Register* on Monday, Aug. 6. On page 2, under a headline, "Rock 'n' Roll Dance Proves Success Here," a reporter wrote: "Tulare rock and rollers danced to the music of the Rock and Heartbeats [sic] from Hollywood Saturday night and their actions received an unofficial okay from the city council, the memorial district board and the police . . . ." The dance drew 450 and transpired "without a hitch." In fact, the Amvets declared they had "no intentions of stopping the youngsters from rock and roll dancing and believe under the correct supervision and management such dancing should be allowed." The story dutifully concluded, "Police Chief Ed Houck said he appreciated the efforts of the youngsters and believed that dancing is something the city can use." Such was the cautionary language employed in public discourse in a day when parents and police feared everything and anything that might provoke unfathomable and uncontrollable behavior in teenagers. Rock 'n' roll certainly fit the bill. But the Heartbeats weren't raising anyone's pulse. The band's brand of rock 'n' roll was relatively harmless, certainly not the rollicking menace created by Fats, Elvis, or, say, Jerry Lee Lewis, another devil-boy about to make the scene.

IRONICALLY, THE HEARTBEATS soon played a bit role in a movie that seemed to mirror, even mock their own real life circumstances—if taking direction from Bill Orwig could be likened to "real life." The mid-1950s spawned numerous teenage rock 'n' roll movies and a deluge of adolescent science fiction, so it was only a matter of time until the Tinsel Town hustler got his boys on the silver screen. The '50s teens and rock genre played on a pretty consistent theme. The first film to feature rock 'n' roll on its soundtrack—Bill Haley and His Comets supplied it—was 1955's *Blackboard Jungle*, which cast Sidney Poitier as a troubled youth. Films began to feature rock 'n' rollers onscreen as well, either as rebellious teens, or aiding and abetting them. *Shake,*

Heartbeats publicity shot, circa 1956. Note that the original photograph was retouched to give Leroy sideburns and disguise his boyish looks. The hideous, regulation Heartbeats jacket is recognizable in the period teen film Rock, Pretty Baby.

Rattle and Rock! with Fats Domino and Joe Turner, released in 1956, followed the travails of teens whose parents saw rock 'n' roll as a source of mayhem. That theme held for another period flick, *Rock, Pretty Baby*, a wonderfully cheesy, maudlin, teen romance-and-angst flick. John Saxon is cast as the confused but deep-thinking young man who nears high school graduation, contemptuous of the medical school he faces (his father is a doctor) and with zeal only for a $300 electric guitar. The guitar's purchase will enable his band to play important gigs prior to graduation, thus keeping alive the hope of "making it." Onscreen, his father, played by Edward Platt (the Chief on the 1960s sitcom *Get Smart*), refuses to let John tap his medical education money for the guitar. "One band in a thousand makes the grade!" Dad storms. "I can't let you throw your life away." Toward the end of the film, during a high school music contest, the main competitors to John's band—the Heartbeats—take the stage. The scene is shot from some distance away, but Leroy and his band mates are easily recognizable because they are wearing Orwig's famously unattractive striped jackets. The band hops around for several minutes in an exaggerated attempt at playing along to overdubbed music, before John takes the stage and delivers a heart-stopping performance. In a clumsy plot twist, the MC, Johnny Grant, announces that the Heartbeats—"our musical acrobats"—have won the contest. The cameras, of course, follow John and his buddies, including Sal Mineo, through their final lines and the Heartbeats' half-minute of fame is over.

Years later, Roy Buchanan still turned red at the thought. "We worked with a choreographer [and] we'd jump all around," he laughed in early 1988 in an interview with Ty Ford for *Maryland Musician Magazine*. Dryden also cringed at the memory. "Yeah, we danced as if we were playing the music. I thought it was stupid at the time. Every one of the movies I made in the '50s had to do with the alienation between the younger generation and the older generation. We were supposed to be juvenile delinquents making jungle music. That was the basic thrust of every script—young James Deans playing the booga-booga music."

WHILE THE HEARTBEATS tangoed with Hollywood greatness, Orwig scared up more big ideas. His next epiphany involved a girl singer named Alys Leslie. Alys' shtick? She emulated Janis Martin, "The Female Elvis Presley." Orwig's interest was understandable. Martin had just scored a hit with her original, debut song, "Drugstore Rock 'n' Roll," which sold three-quarters of a million records in 1956 and won her spots on television variety shows and *Billboard*'s vote for "Most Promising Female Vocalist." "They took us into a studio on Vine Street in Hollywood in the Capitol Records building, a big round building that looks like a stack of 45s," Spencer said. "This was a building where great records had been made. Frank Sinatra recorded there, Stan Kenton—idols of mine. Alys is wearing 'petal-pushers,' a pony-tail and little bows and a little sweater or blouse, with strange little shoes. She had maybe two tunes she could sing. We laid down the two tunes and I have no idea whatever happened to them." This bizarre episode would be wholly unimportant, other than it represents Buchanan's first studio experience.

Orwig hustled the band onto musical bills anywhere he could. One gig sent the band by plane with Mamie Van Doren and the Andrews Sisters to a package show at the Fresno fairgrounds. Another engagement had them backing the Pharoahs on a giant R&B show at the Shrine Auditorium in Los Angeles, headlined by Gene Vincent, with Big Jay McNeely, the Platters, the Penguins, and others. Vincent had recently broken his leg and he performed that night in a full leg cast, Dryden recalled. "We did our three tunes and got off. It *was* a big rush! That was the first time I'd done anything like that." But, he added: "This band, very honestly, despite how good the players were, just wasn't that good. I think this was *it* for Roy though, because he was so young."

The original Heartbeats maintained a sporadic pulse for perhaps six months before succumbing to full cardiac arrest. In time, former Heartbeat Lyle Ritz would hook up with Phil Spector as a session musician in Los Angeles. Tommy Oliver played piano on television's *Name That Tune*. Dryden eventually played drums for the Jefferson Airplane and, later, the New Riders of the Purple Sage. Leroy? His road remained under construction at this point. First he moved back in with his brother and sister-in-law on Lennox Avenue in Hollywood. On Christmas day 1956 the three were out for a walk and a large tumbleweed bounced past. "What if Christmas trees were tumbleweeds?" Leroy asked aloud. Shirley never forgot the remark, which seemed so strange at the time.

J.D. played his younger brother records by Hank "Sugarfoot" Garland and Grady Martin and took him to a few clubs around town to see Johnny Otis and Tal Farlow. "That's where he kicked off on that jazz thing," J.D. would recall. "He really went wild because of Tal Farlow and Barney Kessel. He got to watchin' 'em and he said, 'I'm goin' to *steal* it!' He combined all this together and got in on that blues thing." Now Leroy added jazz chords, phrasings, and a sense of swing to his growing repertoire of techniques. He would recall seeing Johnny Otis in this period and being impressed by Otis' guitarist, Jimmy Nolen. Born Johnny Veliotes in Vallejo, north of San Francisco, in 1921 to Greek parents, Otis' love for black culture and music led him to take the last two syllables of his last name as a stage moniker. In the 1940s he came up playing black clubs like the Barrelhouse Club in Watts, discovering singer Little Esther Phillips and guitarist Pete Lewis along the way. His recordings for Newark, NJ–based Savoy Records brought him a string of R&B hits in 1949–1952. His eye for talent plucked Jackie Wilson, Hank Ballard, and Etta James from obscurity in the 1950s. He did the same for Jimmy Nolen, in time for Otis' 1958 Capitol hit, "Willie and the Hand Jive."

Otis himself credited Nolen with founding the funk school of guitar. Born in 1934 in Oklahoma City, OK, Nolen jumped on his first national tour in 1955 with Jimmy Wilson, a blues singer whose hit "Tin Pan Alley" (later covered by Stevie Ray Vaughan) sent him cross-country that year. Nolen drew on records of the day for his own style, and later said his influences included T-Bone Walker, Muddy Waters, and Wayne Bennett, who recorded with Bobby "Blue" Bland. In Los Angeles in 1955 and '56 Nolen recorded a number of solo efforts for the Federal label, including a version of the Erskine Hawkins Orchestra's 1940 number, "After Hours." The following year he joined Johnny Otis' band, replacing Pete Lewis. Nolen played the catchy rhythm guitar part on "Willie and the Hand Jive," and later credited Bo Diddley for his inspiration. Nolen's funky, sixteenth-note rhythms foreshadowed Curtis Mayfield and others who ultimately garnered fame in the funk guitar genre.

Nolen's approach caught Buchanan's attention. "I loved the way the guy stood, the way he looked," Roy would recall of Nolen in a 1985 interview with Ashley Kahn for *Guitar Player*. "He was working a little club in L.A. with the Johnny Otis show, and they had different guests in front of the band all the time. I think it was T-Bone Walker in front that night, but it was Jimmy's playing that floored me. I noticed that he knew how to back people really well. I tried to become like that—not just taking the lead solos all the time, but complementing the singing or whatever was happening. Jimmy wasn't a very loud player . . . . I guess I got that from him, too. Jimmy was constantly switching his volume and tone all around. Back then he used one of those big, fat Gibsons. I owe Jimmy a lot. He was my first real influence in the blues. It gave me an advantage over other white players 'cause I used to think Johnny Otis' R&B show *was* rock and roll. Then, when I worked in white bands, I tried to play like Jimmy Nolen, bending strings and all that. Everybody would say, 'Wow! How'd you learn to do that?!' "

THAT LEROY LISTENED attentively to the popular music broadcast on radio is abundantly evident in a series of home recordings he made in this period. Leroy was once again staying with his sister Betty and brother-in-law Phil Clemmons in Garden Grove. Phil bought a Voice of Music Model 710 reel-to-reel tape recorder especially for Leroy. "We'd just have a ball with that tape recorder running," Phil recalled. A tape that survives, Roy's earliest known recordings, contains 21 songs, many of them covers of hits freshly released in 1957. Leroy plugged his pickup-equipped Martin guitar directly into the tape recorder and sang into a microphone. The tape opens with "Fallen Star," a simple, brief rendition of a James Joiner song popularized by Nick Noble that year. A score of vocal numbers and several instrumentals follow. Roy sings or duets with Clemmons on Little Richard's "Miss Ann," Ricky Nelson's "A Teenager's Romance," Buck Owens' "Down on the Corner of Love," Fats Domino's "I'm Walkin'" and "Blueberry Hill," Johnny Cash's "Folsom Prison Blues," and Jim Reeves' "Four Walls." On these songs and a few others Leroy carefully recites the lyrics in a youthful but surprisingly resonant voice with a slight Southern accent. "At that time I was the only one he'd sing in front of," Clemmons said. "If we had neighbors over, or took him to a friend's house, he'd never sing. He was too bashful."

Leroy's seemingly effortless recitation of lyrics on more than a dozen songs, many of them new releases at the time, underscored a telltale aspect of his burgeoning talent. "We'd hear a song on the radio," Clemmons said. "Maybe I'd try to sing it, but couldn't remember the words. Why, *he* knew the words. He had an excellent memory. He could hear a record once or twice and he knew the thing by heart. He was just as good on the words as he was on the melody."

The instrumental tracks on this seminal tape also open a window onto Roy's progress as a guitar stylist. Though some are merely practice exercises—one features soft noodling on the guitar, then a few amazing jazz runs and chords—there are

*Roy, center, with a later incarnation of the Heartbeats: (from left) Chuck Hix, "Paul,"
"Allen," and "Dan," circa 1957.*

complete tracks, including an uptempo country melody on one track, a blues on
another, a sweet, slow, whimsical melody on yet another. The tape closes with a
low-key but deft country blues piece that displays sophisticated rhythms, dexterous lead work, and feeling and nuance reminiscent of the acoustic blues master
Robert Johnson—then not 20 years in his grave—or even Lonnie Johnson, one of
the progenitors of the electric blues guitar. With a few exceptions, both the vocal
numbers and the instrumentals are relatively complete and reasonably well-polished.
While singing "Give My Love to Rose" though, Leroy began to laugh and he
abruptly shut off the tape recorder.

In another effort to help his young brother-in-law, Phil Clemmons took Roy
to get a close look at rock 'n' roll the way it ought to be played—loud and raunchy,
with a big back beat. The Louisiana blues-rocker, Dale Hawkins, famous for his
supremely gritty hit, "Susie Q," was in town. This was something more gutsy than
the kind of antiseptic music the Heartbeats played, and Leroy was hooked.

LEROY WAS STAYING with his brother J.D. when Orwig phoned to ask the young guitarist to tour the Southwest and Midwest to promote *Rock, Pretty Baby*. Orwig assured
him he had a new band to back him. Probably Orwig was just making good on
flimsy promises he'd made to the film's producers about promoting the film with a
rock 'n' roll band. Leroy's face betrayed uncertainty. J.D. and Shirley could see that.

Leroy with Mickey Rooney, circa 1956.

But at the time it seemed like Orwig was the only game in town. J.D. and Shirley urged Leroy to consider an easier way to make a living. He wouldn't hear of it, Shirley recalled. "We told him, 'This is a rough world to get into, a lot of guys fall by the wayside. Why don't you find some other line of work?' And he said, 'You know, the Everly Brothers were down to their last guitar pick when they hit it big.' You just couldn't talk him out of doing what he had to do."

Orwig's tour sent the band, including its new frontman, Chuck Hix, a 16-year-old guitarist and singer, across the West by bus in summer 1957. They stopped in small towns in tandem with local screenings of *Rock, Pretty Baby*. Margaret Lewis was growing up in Levelland, TX, thirty miles west of Lubbock, on the Lone Star state's Llano Estacado, or "Staked Plains," near the New Mexico border. She had just begun playing music with her band Margaret Lewis and the Thunderbolts when the Heartbeats appeared at her high school one afternoon. That evening they would play one of the town's three movie theaters before a screening of *Rock, Pretty Baby*. (Three theaters allowed the town to accommodate white, Hispanic, and black theater-goers.) "The girls all went crazy over them," Lewis recalled. "They were just so nice. Roy, I remember him being very shy, real quiet." Lewis made sure she got a signed photograph of the group before they departed.

THE BAND MOVED ON to a series of performances throughout the Midwest. By October, however, everyone in the band—but one—had dropped out and returned home. Orwig probably had stopped paying them. Somehow, for some reason, Leroy soldiered on. He did not yet understand that sticking with the guitar did not equate to sticking with Orwig. That fall, Kansas' Wichita *Eagle* ran a picture of him standing alone, with his dark hair combed straight back over his head, strumming his big Gibson f-hole. "CHORDS TUMBLE OUT" read the caption line. "Rock 'n' roll chords tumbled out of Roy Buchanan's guitar Thursday afternoon at the McClellan Hotel. The 18-year-old singer and musician arrived in Wichita Saturday to welcome the opening of his [*sic*] new picture, 'Rock, Pretty Baby,' at the Civic Theater Monday." Somewhere along the way that summer Leroy had become "Roy."

Relations between the guitarist and his manager must have been shaky at best. At a star-studded musical jamboree in Oklahoma City, Orwig arranged from distant Hollywood to have Roy photographed with Mickey Rooney, Johnnie Ray, and Patti Page, all major stars of the day. Rooney, a precocious film star, had made more than 70 movies since his youth in the 1930s. Johnnie Ray's "Just Walking in the Rain" had just hit No. 2 on *Billboard*'s pop charts, as had Patti Page's "Allegheny Moon." Orwig probably traded on his contacts in the movie world to pull off the photo session, and one can easily imagine him proffering the photos to Roy in lieu of the latter's long-promised pay. ("Roy, these photographs are going to *make* your career! Do you *understand* that?!") One shot shows a playful, casually dressed Mickey Rooney with his arms around Roy, faking on the guitar, while Roy—dressed in white tails, a plaid bow tie, and cummerbund—bashfully hangs his head. One publicity shot captured Roy in a straw hat, holding his Gibson, perched on the back of a wagon drawn by the Budweiser Clydesdales. (In the background a stadium sign reads: "Johnnie Ray . . . Lou Walter's Latin Quarter Revue.") Ultimately, however, Orwig double-crossed the impressionable young guitarist, leaving him stranded in Oklahoma City. As Spencer Dryden recalled: "I remember Roy calling me from Oklahoma City. I had moved back in with my parents. Roy said, 'Listen, man, Bill put us on the road, but he didn't give us any money. We're stranded. I'm in Oklahoma City. Can you help get me back home?' At that time I really didn't know what to do for him. I didn't have any money. But Roy made it back." "Back" in this case turned out to be the short hop from Oklahoma City to Ozark, his point of origin 18 years earlier. His Aunt Willie agreed to take him in for the time being. It was a Buchanan's pleasure to have kin staying over.

If Roy considered the apparently circular nature of his travels, it might have spooked him a little. He'd worked too hard to become a charity case in his ancestral home. Apparently he had decided he'd seen the last of Bill Orwig. He'd come that far by his 18th birthday. Forty years later, an Orwig cousin in Oklahoma couldn't provide much information on his illustrious relative. In the Orwig family, mentioning Bill's name had always been taboo. It's easy to see why. Before he died in the late 1980s in Norman, OK, he was cited for illegally keeping an African lion in his backyard.

Roy arrived in Ozark by bus and stayed several months, bunking with his Aunt Willie and cousin Charles and hanging around with a gaggle of cousins he hadn't seen for years. Charles and Roy hunted and played some guitar together. "He taught me my first chords," Charles recalled. "I'd ask him what he's playin', and he'd say, 'Oh, that's one of them modern chords.'" In Roy's parlance that meant jazz chords. Charles' black '49 Ford got them around. Charles did not hot rod on the road. His impetuous brother, Bobby, had died the year before in a car wreck at Hurricane Creek, on the road between town and the Buchanan place, barely a year after James Dean perished in his own car wreck in Hollywood. Roy and Charles just wanted to take it easy. Sometimes they would sneak off and "drink a little wine," for which Charles had acquired a taste. "Roy was worried for me," Charles said, laughing at the memory. "He said, 'You're gonna have to leave it alone, or you'll get to be an old wino.'" The two cousins attended street dances or drive-in movies with Charles' two sisters, Johnie Pearl "Doodle" Buchanan and Phillis Buchanan. Roy even dated one of their friends, Edna Patterson. That fall the Buchanan cousins might have seen their choice of cheap teenage rebellion flicks like *Hot Rod Rumble*, vintage science fiction thrillers like Boris Karloff's *Voodoo Island, The Incredible Shrinking Man,* or numerous rock 'n' roll pictures like Elvis's *Love Me Tender*. Johnie Pearl remembered that the gang watched *Rock, Pretty Baby* at the local drive-in and all were duly impressed that Roy had been in a real Hollywood movie. She knew, too, that Roy was in Ozark because he was broke. "When you run out of money in Arkansas, you do the best you can," she said. "Roy went off to the cotton fields in the river bottoms around Paris. He said, 'I'd sure hate for somebody important to see me doin' this to get money.' He was worried about every car that come down the road. What's he goin' to do if they see him out there in the fields with the rest of the hands? Anyway, we used to sit around and they'd play their guitars. One night Roy kept tryin' to make him a song. He said, 'If I could just make me a song I'd have it made.'"

Phillis Buchanan, two years younger than Roy, got a kick out of her older cousin. "He played his guitar all the time and said he was going to make something of himself." Roy made an equally good impression on Edna Patterson. Forty years later she still spoke thoughtfully of the young guitarist she dated in the summer of

1957. "I really looked up to Roy," she said. "He was a nice fella. I didn't know him all that long. He told me he'd been in the movies. Everybody said he was shy, but he didn't act that way around me. When he left it was no big deal. He said, 'We'll be seeing each other.' But that was it." "Later," Phillis said, still giggling at the thought, "Edna would say she'd dated a *movie star*."

The circumstances of Roy's departure from Ozark in fall 1957 are not known. Somehow he managed to reach Tulsa, OK, that winter, or the following spring. Tulsa, 120 miles west of Ozark, would have been an easy hitchhike or a cheap bus ride. He subsequently managed to get work as a staff musician on Tulsa's *Oklahoma Bandstand*, the High Plains' answer to Dick Clark's rock 'n' roll juggernaut, *American Bandstand*, broadcast out of Philadelphia. Over the years Roy would give several versions of how he landed on Oklahoma television, backing itinerant rock 'n' roll singers. Perhaps Roy remained under Bill Orwig's spell and an incarnation of the Heartbeats appeared on *Oklahoma Bandstand*, as the guitarist once suggested in an interview. Another time, however, Roy said he stayed with a single mom and her daughter in Tulsa after they found him at the bus station and helped him get the television gig. In any case, the job put Roy on a collision course with the "Shreveport Tornado," Dale Hawkins. Hawkins spun across the country that year, propelled by his hit, "Susie Q." "They [the show's producers] asked me if we'd back [Hawkins] 'cause he didn't have a band," Roy once recalled. "When we got through, Dale said, 'Do you wanna go to Louisiana?' I said, 'Sure.'" As with many stories Roy would tell, this account sounds plausible enough. According to Hawkins, however, Roy approached *him*. "He said, 'Can I play some with you?' I said, 'Come on.' He said, 'Where you goin'?' I said, 'Home.' He said, 'Can I come with?' I said, 'Come *on*!' The reason he came with me is that he dug what I was doin' and wanted to be in on it." And then Roy was gone to Louisiana.

FARTHER ON UP THE ROAD

....

Music flowed out of the wiry, wavy-haired Dale Hawkins like a mountain spring. Raised on a plantation called Goldmine, outside Monroe, LA, where he'd been born in 1938, Hawkins came from country soil. Dale's mother taught school and his dad played in local hillbilly bands. His parents divorced when Dale was three, and not long after his father perished in a fire. His teen years, spent shuttling between relatives, brought self-reliance. His grandfather, Marshall Taylor, contributed to his musical education by taking him to a local black nightspot called Tom Ram's Club. There he made a discovery: "Black people in Louisiana loved Hank Williams as well as the blues," Hawkins said. Fortunately, he added, he was "raised on both sides of the tracks. I got to hear Lonnie Johnson, some of the early Lightnin' Hopkins, *and* Hank Williams." Diverse sounds surrounded him: the stone gospel of the black Baptist churches, the deep Delta blues, swamp boogie emanating from nearby clubs, the rhythm and blues that poured out of New Orleans, and pop music on the radio. Hawkins grabbed his chances. He became a valued salesman at Stan's Record Shop in Shreveport because he could sing new, popular songs to help the largely black clientele decide which records to buy. The store's owner, Stan Lewis, who numbered among his friends Leonard and Phil Chess of Chess Records in Chicago, loved that. After hours, Dale parked cars at the famous Louisiana Hayride, the country and rockabilly showcase that rivaled Nashville's Grand Ole Opry, cadging quarters until the cops ran him off. When his progress in becoming a professional singer slowed, he lied about his age to get into the U.S. Navy. Upon his return to civilian life a year later at age 18 he ducked a chance at college to cut his musical teeth in Bossier City's freewheeling avenue of clubs. The "Bossier Strip" began on the east side of Shreveport's Red River, which snaked across Louisiana to the Mississippi. "At that time there were a lot of clubs on the strip—the Hi-Lo, the Sho-Bar, the Boom Boom Room, the Diamond Head," Hawkins recalled. "When we started out, none of us were old enough to get in through the front door. We didn't have cars. Shit! We'd ride *bicycles* to the gigs."

Hawkins attracted a number of talented, like-minded musicians in their teens like moths to flame. Together they explored the Big Beat and where it could take them. The gang included guitar ace James Burton, who developed the signature lick on "Susie Q" when they recorded the tune in Shreveport in 1956. "Dale had this little blues band thing, singin' the blues, playin' different blues clubs," Burton said. "I was under age, so I had to get a permit to play the blues clubs. The clubs were lined up on 'The Strip,' where Texas Avenue turns into Highway 80. It looked like a mini–Las Vegas. Not wild, just rockin'. Rednecks, they *love* that music. The place I first played with Dale was called the 'It'll Do Club.' That's where we were playin' when we did 'Susie Q.'" Local DJ, producer, and songwriter Merle Kilgore encountered Dale Hawkins at this juncture and believes the abundantly talented singer also managed to be in the right place at the right time. "Dale was the hottest thing in Shreveport," Kilgore said. "He was a black man in a white body. That's what everybody wanted to hear, like Elvis. He was all over that stage." When he heard Dale and his boys performing "Susie Q," Kilgore hustled them into the studio—one of the rooms at Shreveport's radio station KENT—and nailed down a demo. Later, Stan Lewis got a composing credit on the record for assisting on another, cleaner studio take that he forwarded to the Chess brothers in Chicago. The Chesses put out the hit on their R&B subsidiary, Checker Records.

It tickled Hawkins that women of color called Stan's Record Shop asking about the black boy who cut "Susie Q," but complaining that his diction needed improvement for the sake of their race. The implied compliment (for a white musician) extended to Burton's guitar work. "When we recorded 'Susie Q,' we used to get letters at Stan's shop, letters from all kinds of listeners on the radio, sayin' 'Who's that little black boy playin' guitar?'" Burton said. "Stan thought that was funny. I was just doin' my thing."

Dale Hawkins rode "Susie Q" to national fame. After its release in April 1957 it rose to number 27 on the *Billboard* Hot 100 by July 1957, later cracking the Top Twenty. It reached No. 7 on *Billboard*'s Rhythm and Blues charts, proof of its crossover power, and a reflection of Hawkins' diverse influences and broad appeal. The song's raw elements—from Burton's primal guitar lick, mixed up front for effect, to A.J. Tuminello's insistent cowbell hammering out the song's primordial beat—helped the song gel in that magically infectious, rock 'n' roll way.

The song belonged to a new wave of rock 'n' roll hits that shoved the lead guitar into the spotlight, rivaling the traditional importance of the piano or the saxophone. And the song's earthy beat made it danceable. The Susie Q in the song's title referred to a popular dance by the same name that swept black clubs in the late 1930s. "Doin' the Susie-Q" evolved from the Lindy Hop, with a nod to the Jitterbug. The name of the popular dance then was bandied about in song for fully two decades before Hawkins sent his own song up the charts. By 1956 Johnny Otis had issued his hit, "Willy and the Hand Jive," which featured a line about then-popular dances: "She can 'Walk' and 'Stroll' and 'Susie Q,' and do that crazy 'Hand Jive' too . . . ." How Dale Hawkins conceived his hit even he is no longer certain, though he has provided varying accounts. In one he recalled hearing the Clovers' "I've Got My Eyes On You," which provided the feeling that inspired his own hit. (Hawkins and Burton still spar over the songwriting credit. Hawkins believes it his own creation, while Burton holds that his trademark riff created the hit.) Years later, Roy said that Hawkins told him he'd seen Howlin' Wolf in Shreveport in 1955, crawling across a stage moaning, "Sooozeee Q!" and that that inspired Hawkins' hit. Hawkins, in his frank parlance, said that particular account is "horseshit." But the Shreveport Tornado, as Hawkins became known, never hesitated to credit the song with launching his career. " 'Susie Q' opened all the doors," he said. "Though bein' a white artist on a black label, I was ridin' the line. A lot of time you couldn't get airplay because it was on a 'black' label. So we had to break it city by city. That's when I started learnin' about the record business. See, rock 'n' roll was coming in and they couldn't stop it."

Hawkins' hit led to further recording sessions, first in Chicago in late 1957, then in Shreveport in June 1958, where Hawkins recorded his second Top 40 hit, "La-Do-Dada," with Joe Osborn on guitar, at radio station KWKH. "La-Do-Dada" would climb to No. 32 on *Billboard*'s new Top 40 chart that fall. Later that month Hawkins traveled north on a tour that included a gig on *Oklahoma Bandstand*, where he met Roy. So when the two young rockers returned to Bossier City, where Hawkins' brother, Jerry, had an apartment over the Skyway Club, the Shreveport Tornado had already carved quite a path for himself.

Barksdale Air Force Base sprawled to the south of the Skyway Club. The flight paths seemed to pass directly overhead. "We'd be asleep some nights and it seemed like those planes were about to crash into the building," Jerry recalled. Bossier City lay just east of Shreveport, home to the Louisiana Hayride, which ten years earlier had brought its country and rockabilly showcase to Pixley. Now Roy had a chance to attend in person, though whether he ever played on the show, as he later claimed, is not known. His professional gig required backing the Hawkins brothers in the clubs along the Bossier Strip. Barksdale Air Force Base's personnel supplied a good portion of the audiences that packed the clubs on the Strip where these young rock 'n' rollers cut their teeth. When the older Hawkins took off to tour alone, Jerry fronted the band. "We played the Skyway Club four or five nights a week, then we'd do a matinee on Saturday afternoon," Jerry said. With Dale Hawkins out of town Jerry's band was dubbed the Jayhawks, and it included Roy and Joe Osborn on guitars. "We were really R&B, rock 'n' roll," Jerry said. "If Chuck Berry came out with a song, we'd buy the record and learn it. Little Richard? We'd learn to do it. We learned songs by the Platters, the Coasters, Chuck Willis. We'd do a bit of Elvis, Bobby Darin, Paul Anka, Buddy Knox, Buddy Holly—you name it." Between Dale's local appearances and Jerry's gig at the Skyway Club, Roy had full-time work playing rock 'n' roll, rhythm and blues, and flat-out bad-ass blues with guys he liked. For Roy, age nineteen, that had to be the cat's meow.

"Roy was extremely shy," Jerry said. "I don't ever remember Roy having a serious girlfriend. But he was one hell of a picker. I don't even think Roy knew how good a guitar player he was." Jerry noticed something else that would sometimes confound those who saw Roy play the most emotionally wrenching blues. "He seemed strangely *unconcerned* when he was playin'." Except that he unconsciously ground his jaw from side to side as he worked out his solos.

Dale Hawkins sure could pick 'em. Having already employed ace local guitarists such as Sonny Jones, James Burton, the amazing Carl Adams, and Kenny Paulsen, Hawkins now added Roy Buchanan to a remarkable string of journeymen who filled his lead guitar spot. Roy would be followed, briefly, by Scotty Moore, who'd helped put Elvis in the spotlight, and, later, by Fred Carter Jr. and Hank Garland. How likely was it that a half dozen of the best guitarists in rock 'n' roll would be in Shreveport in the late 1950s, all working for Dale Hawkins?

"Roy had good rhythm," Hawkins recalled. "To me, if a guitar player can hold a good rhythm and play some lead, he's got potential. Roy could do it. When we got home from the *Oklahoma Bandstand*, he was down there in Bossier City with some really good musicians, some great guitar players. James Burton. Kenny Paulsen. Carl Adams. Carl Adams was probably one of the greatest guitar players who ever lived. He had these two fingers blown off by a shotgun when he was a kid. Instead of pushing strings, Carl would pull them. It gave him a style as unique as hell."

"Plus," Hawkins added in reference to Roy's education, "we played *so* many nights. *God!* Did we ever play." When Roy joined the fold, Hawkins' band already consisted of Joe Osborn on guitar, A.J. Tuminello on drums, and the Mathis brothers, Marc and Dean, on bass and piano. The Mathis brothers—Louis Aldine "Dean" Mathis and his brother Marcus Felton Mathis—had been around town playing music for some time. Originally from Georgia, they would have a hit as "Dean and Marc" with "Tell Him No" in 1959. As the "Newbeats" the brothers would hit No. 2 in 1964 with "Bread and Butter." Roy taught Marc to play guitar. The Lewis sisters—including the same Margaret Lewis who had met Leroy Buchanan back in Levelland, TX, and her sister, Rose—sang backup. In Levelland, Margaret had won a talent contest and a spot on the Louisiana Hayride. Her success on the Hayride and her love of song kept her and Rose, both only 15 years old, in Shreveport, where they met Hawkins. According to Margaret, Roy hadn't changed much. "He seemed like the same shy guy, a little more mature. Both my sister and I liked him as a friend. He was the kind of guy you trusted. We'd go to Harry's Barbecue to hang out after the shows, or the Kickapoo, and have hamburgers, or barbecue sandwiches. Roy was always there. He was real fun to be with after you got to know him because he had a good sense of humor, a dry sense of humor, and never was unruly. He was always telling us, 'Watch out for these musicians.' Joe Osborn was like that too. He was not a fast talker. Dale? Now, *Dale* was another story."

Hawkins' club performances with Roy Buchanan on guitar helped fuel the mad beast of early rock 'n' roll. Alas, those performances were not documented on tape, a loss to history. Indeed, field recordings—let alone professional soundboard recordings—from the late 1950s are rare. Yet it seems clear that, based solely on the ability to rock an audience, Dale Hawkins' hard-driving club work would have distinguished his band from most American groups working in rock 'n' roll in 1958. Like so many working bands of that era, one hit record got Hawkins the gigs where he could really work on an audience and attract a following. In contrast, there were plenty of groups out there with more hits, but which nonetheless lacked the musicianship, the soul, and the style to thrill a live audience. Roy would say, many years later: "Dale's best things were never recorded. He always had dreams of Top Ten stuff, he strived for it, and I played what he wanted . . . . I liked the shows—not the big shows where we'd do 'Susie Q' and two others—but the stuff we did in the clubs. Then we'd do blues, spur of the moment things. Dale would make 'em up as we went along." Hawkins later returned the compliment. "It's like what Roy said about me. The best of Roy was never touched."

By the time Roy appeared in Bossier City with Hawkins, James Burton had left the band and hooked up with country and rockabilly singer Bob Luman. Before Burton left Bossier City, however, he and Roy became friends. Burton, born in Shreveport a month earlier than Roy in Ozark, a few hundred miles to the north, played the Louisiana Hayride with Bob Luman while Roy played elsewhere behind Jerry Hawkins. "We sat in, jammed a little bit in the clubs around Bossier City," Burton recalled. "We went out some nights after they got off work. Roy and I used to go sit in with Kenny Lovelace's band at a place called the Stork Club over in Bossier City. Roy seemed to lean toward the blues feel quite a bit. When we went out and sat in, we played blues. Roy was quite laid back. He would kinda sit back in the corner until he had a few drinks, then he was ready to talk to anybody."

According to Burton, *he* pioneered the use of banjo strings on the Telecaster to make it easier to bend strings when playing blues, an innovation Roy later claimed credit for. "When you listen to those old blues records, you know damn well they're not playin' bottleneck on every song," Burton said. "I figured there's got to be some way to do that. So I experimented. Roy might have picked up on that later, but that was my thing." As if in afterthought, Burton added: "We never had any competitiveness."

Burton left town with Bob Luman, but the two returned periodically to play the Hayride. On one such visit Roy and the Mathis brothers hatched a plot to tease James. "Me and Roy and James Burton were real good friends back then," Marc Mathis would recall. "In fact, me and Roy pulled a little trick on ol' James one time. We did it because James was kind of a show-off. He'd play the guitar behind his head. Roy told me, 'We're goin' to *git* him! We're goin' to *git* him!' They had a friendly rivalry goin' and I was caught in the middle of it. Well, James came into town. And he didn't know Roy was in town. So I'm out on stage with my guitar. Roy got backstage, behind the curtains. He was actually playin' and I was fakin' like it was me. I told James to sit in with us. James could put his guitar behind his head and play—he'd do that all the time on stage. He was great! So when he did it this time I unbuckled the guitar strap and swung the guitar out in front of me with one hand on the neck. Meanwhile, Roy's playin' the hell out of his guitar backstage. The guitar'd come back and I'd grab it and pretend to be playin' like crazy. I'd look over at James and he's lookin' back at me, *astonished!* Then I'd swing the guitar out again and do the same thing. He couldn't *believe* I could play like that. Finally, James just took off his guitar and left. I had to run out to the parking lot to tell him it was just a trick, and we all went back in and had a beer together."

Soon after his arrival in Bossier City, Roy got his chance to back Hawkins in the studio—his first real shot at recording rock 'n' roll. At a June 1958 session at the KWKH radio station where he'd recorded "Susie Q," Hawkins, Roy, Dean and Marc Mathis on piano and bass, and D.J. Fontana on drums recorded the instrumental "Crossties," a laid-back set of blues changes with a stone groove. Sheldon Vizell blew a cool tenor sax solo before Roy stepped out with a well-crafted rock 'n' roll solo. "We started doin' that just as a kind of fill-in, to take a break at shows," Hawkins said of this number. The same lineup recorded another Hawkins-style pop tune, "Superman," in the same session. On his approach to recording at this stage, Hawkins said, "You find or create your song. You learn it by performing it. Know what you want when you're puttin' it down in the studio, so you don't waste precious time. To be perfectly honest, I don't know how to do it any other way. Most everything we did in the studio was cut live." "La-Do-Dada," recorded at a different session without Roy, backed with "Crossties," reached No. 32 on *Billboard*'s Top 40 chart that October.

BY THAT TIME HAWKINS, Roy, and the Mathis brothers had piled into Hawkins' brand-new 1958 station wagon, pointed it north, and burned up the better part of 1,000 miles to play the upper Midwest. After dates in Nebraska or Minnesota, accounts differ, the band headed for recording dates at Leonard and Phil Chess' studio at 2120 South Michigan Avenue in Chicago. Chi-town had spawned its own brand of electric blues a decade earlier, when blues musicians from the Mississippi Delta moved north and plugged in, and the Chess brothers made their fortune recording the best. The Chesses were hard-working, Polish immigrants who had parlayed the success of their first nightclub, the Macombo Lounge, into a stake in the jazz-oriented Aristocrat Records in 1947. By 1950 the brothers had bought out their partner and renamed their label Chess—their Polish surname had been Czyz. Chess' alter ego, Checker Records, released much of their R&B and rock 'n' roll catalogue. In time the pair attracted the best blues writers and performers of the day, a long list that included Howlin' Wolf, Sonny Boy Williamson, Little Walter Jacob,

DJ Freeman Hoover with (left to right) Dale Hawkins, Melvin Rogers, Roy Buchanan, Marc Mathis, and Dean Mathis in 1958.

Willie Dixon, Bo Diddley, Muddy Waters, Elmore James, John Lee Hooker, Jimmy Reed, J.B. Lenoir, Otis Rush, Memphis Slim, Memphis Minnie, and Etta James. The Chess brothers captured the best of the electrified blues and sought part of the expanding rock 'n' roll market by taking a chance on an artist like Dale Hawkins, one of the first white singers recorded at Chess.

"We cut 'My Babe' at Chess studios," Hawkins said. "In fact, we rehearsed the damn song as we were driving in, just singin' that old blues song. Willie Dixon took that from Sister Rosetta Tharpe. She'd sing, 'This train, this train is a clean train, this train . . .' Willie slapped some new lyrics on that thing and he and Little Walter had a hit!" Little Walter Jacob's vocal and harmonica stylings added greatly to Chess Records' success in the 1950s, as did his harmonica work on Muddy Water's recordings. His original version of "My Babe," recorded in January 1955, had a slower beat and mellower tone than Hawkins' cover. The track featured Little Walter's harmonica where, three years later, Roy's guitar would deliver a solo. Little Walter's original went to the top of the R&B charts in 1955, one of his last best-sellers.

Roy played his f-hole Gibson on "My Babe." "It was a hollow body," Hawkins recalled. "If you listen to the sound on our version of 'My Babe,' you'll hear it. I just said, 'Roy, grab me an 'E' and hold it.'" Roy took off at an edgy pace, Hawkins started snappin' his fingers to the beat, the band fell in with Dean Mathis pounding the piano keys, and a staple of the Chicago blues got recast as rock 'n' roll. Roy achieved his bold, rhythmic guitar line by deadening his low E string with the heel of his right hand, a technique known as "dead thumb," employed by every self-respecting guitarist of the day. "Dead thumb" is especially well-suited to generating rhythm, and in early rock 'n' roll, every player, regardless of which instrument they played, had to contribute rhythm to propel a song. Roy's solo on "My Babe" is economical and deft. On this track, in fact, Hawkins, Roy, and the Mathis brothers demonstrated that the hottest act in the country—Elvis backed by Scotty Moore on guitar, Bill Black on bass, and D.J. Fontana on drums—had nothing on Hawkins' band, nothing at all. Nothing but a little fame and fortune, anyway.

During the same session, the group recorded a number of other tracks, but none, apparently, with Roy on lead guitar. But there were other aspects to Chicago that surely opened Roy's eyes. "We fuckin' kicked ass," Hawkins said in his inimitable fashion. "We went down to the Southside with Muddy, the Wolf, and Little Walter. Willie Dixon was cool, and Little Walter became a good friend. He was the first guy I ever saw smoke a joint! Leonard kept those guys in new suits and cars. Me? Leonard Chess kept me runnin' all over the world."

HAWKINS DESIGNED his performances for maximum effect. Open with a rocker, slow things down with a ballad, stir it up or get down and dirty with a blues number. Dale Hawkins worked the stage, driving his band until it was squeaky tight, and inflaming his audience to dance all night. He had written more than a dozen of his own songs by then and he made sure his band knew the blues and rhythm and blues songbooks. The William Morris Agency booked Hawkins' tours and had the band zigzagging across the nation to capitalize on "Susie Q," "La-Do-Dada," and "My Babe." The fact that, beyond those songs, Hawkins never again cracked the Top 40 made no difference to his audiences. This was live rock 'n' roll and Hawkins delivered all the energy, swagger, and menace—even innocence—the genre promised. "We had a lot of fun in the clubs," he said. "There were times we'd play a set and never stop playing until the set was over. Just go right from one song into another. Or we'd kick off some blues and just play the shit out of it. We'd have a set laid out, but it would be like . . . " Hawkins paused, then in a conspiratorial whisper, slyly added, "we could take detours! I'd lean over and say, 'Hey boys, we got a one, four, three, in D minor. Let's *go!*'"

Rock 'n' roll generated thrills—a prime attraction, then as now. Musically it was not complicated, but it required a lot of sweat and blood to make it good. "I was one of the hardest task masters in the world," Hawkins said with pride. "After each set we'd have a meeting and I would go over whatever went wrong. And go over it and over it. I was one of the few people that could handle Roy. Not physically, but spiritually. I could make him play what I wanted." Hawkins wanted a band that knew how to back him, but which could break loose on cue. "I was adequate, but Dale would really make you work," Roy later recalled. "He wouldn't leave you alone for a second and I was all for that." Under Hawkins' tutelage Roy's technical abilities and musical sensibilities sharpened and matured. He learned to back the singer, or burst forth to take a solo. He learned what sort of solo would be appropriate to a particular song. As to the solo's content, he let his imagination roam. He listened to sax players and borrowed their phrasings. He learned to mimic the percussive feel of the drummer, or the pianist. He developed the chops to play what he imagined—a rare ability indeed—and Hawkins gave him room to move. For all his discipline and focus, Hawkins also gave Roy a chance to experiment with sounds. The guitarist had discovered that an amplifier's speakers, naturally busted—or purposefully slit—produced a sinister fuzz tone. So did pouring water on the tubes until, overheated, they turned purple. The effect added grit and an edge to the sound, an effect that a decade later could be accomplished via an electronic pedal. Roy could coax bell-like pedal steel guitar tones out of his instrument employing a technique known to guitarists as "contrary bends," or "oblique doublestops," where two strings are played while one is bent. And he discovered the joys of controlled feedback, another component of the rock 'n' roll sound that derived from the electric blues. "I got the idea of using feedback strictly through an accident," Roy told Todd Everett in 1981 for *Record Review*. "I was using a Gibson acoustic, with a DeArmond pickup on it—you couldn't *stop* that thing from feeding back. When I used it with Hawkins, it blew everybody's mind. I blew a speaker out one night, and that was it. [I got] the whole sound: feedback and fuzz tone. I couldn't eliminate it with that Gibson and I couldn't afford to buy any other kind of guitar."

Roy learned a few other tricks of the trade. Certain white pills could help you through your 30th performance in as many days, or just one interminable night. Cold beer made those pills go down easy. This aspect of his education began innocently enough. He did what everyone else was doing, just to get through the barbaric, endless tours with one change of clothes and a guitar. As someone once said, however, "The chains of habit are too light to be felt until they are too heavy to be broken." At this point Roy remained blissfully ignorant of any weight upon his shoulders.

In September 1958 Roy turned 19 on the road in one of the era's hottest performing rock 'n' roll bands. Aspiring singer Fred Mastroni caught one of Hawkins' shows that fall at the Tower Theater in West Philly and later recalled that between Roy's dead-thumb rhythms and Merle Travis–style finger-picking the guitarist simulated an entire band. "I was just a kid, seventeen, and I went with my girlfriend," Mastroni recalled. "Buchanan came out on stage with a drummer, and blew the place away. No bass, nothing but a drummer and Roy, and Dale up front. It was nuts!"

HAWKINS' FRENETIC ROAD TRIPS in this period, with Roy Buchanan in tow, cannot be reconstructed. If a tour schedule started simply, it might be amended on the

Unidentified marquee during Dale Hawkins' touring heyday, circa 1958.

spur of the moment by a phone call from the William Morris Agency, creating a geographical nightmare. Just a phone call and a scribbled note on a napkin could send Hawkins' station wagon and trailer full of musicians and instruments careening to another point on the compass hundreds of miles away. "Chess called me one day," Hawkins said. "*Fuck!* We had to drive my station wagon and a U-Haul trailer all the way from Duluth, Minnesota, to New York, record 'A House, a Car, and a Wedding Ring,' turn right around that night when we got done with the recording and go all the way back and play the next night. It was *tough*." ("A House, a Car, and a Wedding Ring" was released late in 1958 with "My Babe" on the flip side, and the record reached No. 88 on *Billboard*'s Hot 100—Hawkins' last song to chart.) There'd be excitement of every stripe at each gig: rock 'n' rollers, then as now, were Gypsies. As they pulled carefully into town they looked a bit ragged, perhaps exotic, possibly dangerous to local women and their virtue, or to local men and their egos. While most people worked nine-to-five, Monday through Friday, rock 'n' roll Gypsies rolled from town to town, keeping odd hours, living a life never even hinted at in the antiseptic rock 'n' roll movies of the day. They might be simultaneously welcomed and shunned, while making the music for people's lives.

Life on the road had its downsides. Hawkins and Roy might be on stage doing what they loved, but fatigue often made it seem like torture. Some nights they were so pepped up on amphetamines they grinned like sweating zombies. Men got jealous when their dates stared too long at the boys in the band and if the musicians smiled back that sometimes made exiting the stage a dicey proposition. Macho locals might taunt musicians, or anyone else, for that matter, who looked different and therefore posed a threat to their fragile sense of normalcy.

"We were in Claxton, Georgia, and after the show we got invited over to this little club," Hawkins recalled. "It was a paratrooper's club. So this guy at the bar calls me a 'faggot.' He never should have done that, 'cuz I popped his ass. Talk about some country boys whupping some ass. We whupped the piss out of 'em, man. Roy took his jacket off, threw it over a guy's head and hit 'em with something and we cleared out of there. Afterwards we stopped in this gas station. I go to pay and one of the paratroopers is standin' in the front door with a baseball bat. I said, 'Go ahead, motherfucker.' And he comes down like, *wup*! Another comes 'round the corner with a .22 rifle. Roy reaches into the back of the station wagon, grabs our .30-.30, and cocks it. I said, 'Anybody want to call the game?' Those suckers hauled ass out of there! Poor Melvin, the drummer, it took us hours to find him! He took off."

"We lived on the road," Hawkins said with a rueful smile. "We carried one change of clothes. To play some clubs we had to wear ties and jackets. We were always trying our best just to look decent. I'll tell you something about Roy. We were playin' the Roundtable in New York. That Roy, he was always doing somethin'. He came downstairs to play that night and he's got what years later you would call a Beatles haircut. I said, 'Get your motherfuckin' ass back upstairs or I'm going to fine you.' I think he made about nine dollars that week. It tickled the shit out of me. But I couldn't let it go or the rest of the guys would be pullin' something."

"People have to *know* Roy," Hawkins insisted. "He was searchin' for something all the time. He'd say, 'I just don't know what to believe.' I'd say, 'Leave it alone. Don't confuse yourself.' I was probably one of the few people that could ever pull it out of him. I heard so many stories from Roy. He was a good storyteller, a good bullshitter. That cat had a way of getting into your head. The best thing to do with Roy—what I always did—was say, 'Look, we gotta go *this* way *now*. You comin'?' But he would tell me all kinds of tales, man. One thing he told me I'll never forget. He wanted to make it with a nun. I think he was serious, but I never did ask."

The road demanded that weary musicians burn up hundreds of miles after one gig to reach another. Roy learned to sleep sitting up in a vehicle traveling 60 miles per hour. For some reason—probably laziness, bad eyesight, a general lack of interest—he did not, or would not, take the wheel. "We had to put Roy in the backseat with his guitar," Hawkins said with a knowing laugh. "He just didn't give a shit. I don't think he even had a driver's license."

By 1959 Roy had been on the road for three years. He'd racked up thousands of miles with Dale Hawkins and made a couple of near-hit records. He had learned to drink, to fight, to take pills, to avoid driving. On a run to Chicago with Jerry Hawkins and Joe Osborn he might have learned even more, though some of his compadres doubted it. "We played in Calumet City at the Club Southern, owned by Al Capone's nephew," Jerry recalled. "It was a gangster place. There must have been 15 strip joints and we were booked into the only place that had country music. We started at eight o'clock at night and worked 'til four in the morning. Eight sets a night, seven days a week. We'd seen the nightlife before, but when you have 20 strippers trying to hit on you every night, it makes you grow up kinda quick."

FLYING WITH
THE HAWKS

5

*I*n early 1959 Hawkins sped up and down the East Coast, sharing marquees with Fats Domino, Jackie Wilson, and Bobby Darin. Buddy Holly was gone by then, killed in January in a plane crash. Though Hawkins often traveled solo on such tours, relying on the tour's own house band to back him, he wanted to make a splash this time. He brought Roy along to provide the rhythms, menace, and flash that stirred a crowd to frenzy. It was worth the extra cost to bring a sideman who could kick ass. Hawkins could save money or have some serious fun. He chose fun. Apparently, audiences appreciated his choice. Fred Mastroni, for one, caught Hawkins' performance in Philadelphia on this tour and 40 years later he remembered only Roy. The guitarist could simulate an entire band, Mastroni exclaimed, using a dead thumb bass line and dexterous finger-picking that danced over the top. With a slow, steady increase in tempo, Buchanan would turn up the heat until an audience boiled over.

After a whirlwind tour up and down the coast, however, Hawkins and Roy parted company, seemingly for good. Economics intruded. Few artists could afford to tour with their own band, and Hawkins' momentum had crested. His records no longer climbed or even reached the fickle charts. Probably few bands in America could rock as well as Hawkins' unit with Roy Buchanan. But hit records proved to be the damnedest things to conjure up. Without them the singer's cachet with promoters started to slide and demand for his services slackened. Hawkins could still make the rounds alone, relying on pickup bands to back him, but no longer could he take a guitarist along. After more than a year of nearly constant travel, it was time for a break, anyway. Roy—as with every sideman before him and since—chafed under his frontman's authority and pay scale. Ennui played a role. "We *lived* on the road," Hawkins recalled. "After about a year of workin' with Roy, well, I don't know how to do things any other way except my way. Most guitar players ended up hating me, but they were very successful when they left."

Dale's brother, Jerry, still had steady gigs locally in Shreveport and Bossier City and he had a recording contract with Ebb Records. So Roy made a beeline for Louisiana. He figured he could make a living playing for Jerry, at least for a while. He'd figure out something later.

Being based in the Shreveport area brought him innumerable invitations to record at KWKH for a parade of singers, among them Jerry Hawkins, Al Jones, Bobby Jay, and Merle Kilgore. Kilgore, who later went on to direct operations for Hank Williams Jr., recalled: "Roy wouldn't take a dime from me for doin' sessions. I'd say, 'Here's five dollars.' He'd say, 'Nah, I don't want any of that, man.' He'd do demos for me, but he wouldn't take any money at all, and he was just barely hangin' on."

None of the records Roy made in Shreveport in this period hit the contemporary charts, though Al Jones' "Loretta" and Bobby Jay's "So Lonely" still sound great today. The first track was a playful, upbeat rockabilly number that featured Roy's cascading pull-offs and country-style picking. On the second track Bobby Jay is clearly emulating Elvis Presley's cool swagger, and Roy plays a tasty, laid-back solo. By this time Roy must have understood the vagaries of the music business in America: Great music does not necessarily sell. Many, many great records would be made in rock 'n' roll's early days—including in Shreveport in 1959—but there could only be so many hits. Besides, on a hit, a sideman had no claim anyway; he received a modest, one-time fee for his session work in the studio. Record sales generated modest royalties for the artist—that is, the front man, the singer, the presumed star. The lion's share of royalties, however, accrued to whomever owned the publishing rights to the hit. It might be the songwriter, but it could just as likely be the producer, a record company official, or even a disc jockey who agreed to play the song frequently enough to ignite record sales. Record companies often paid DJs in cash, but sometimes particularly cozy relationships were rewarded with publishing rights, a piece of the proverbial action. That is, until the payola scandal rocked the recording industry that very year, after Congress had already investigated rigged television game shows. Yes, you could make money in the recording industry, but only if you were a business-savvy songwriter, a producer, a DJ, or a singer with a hit on your hands.

Roy was none of these. He simply had a gift for playing guitar. He was a sideman, and in the eyes of promoters and record companies, sidemen were expendable commodities, even when their level of musicianship helped make songs into hit records. This attitude explained why Elvis Presley unceremoniously dumped guitarist Scotty Moore and bassist Bill Black in September 1957. The pair had played an integral role, along with drummer D.J. Fontana, in launching Elvis. Their performances and recordings with the singing star had supplied some of the excitement that made him The King. After the singer and his band had achieved a degree of success, the sidemen had the temerity to point out to Presley and his predatory manager, "Colonel" Parker, that the singer's original agreement with them called for sharing record royalties and increased performance fees. In order to get

Elvis' attention, Scotty Moore and Bill Black threatened to quit, and they were dismissed. Ironically, many observers believe that, despite Elvis' continued commercial success as a singer, his records and performances never again possessed the magic conjured by Moore and Black for Sam Phillips' Sun Records in 1954–57. Closer to home, James Burton had naively assumed that his inventive guitar hook on Dale Hawkins' "Susie Q" had garnered him a songwriting credit and, therefore, a share of royalties. He found out the hard way that his assumption was wrong. That was the sideman's lot, at least in those days. Though Burton himself went on to craft a successful career as the ultimate sideman—he played in L.A. studios behind the likes of Frank Sinatra, and from 1969 to 1977 he too served as Elvis' guitarist—he was a rare bird, an artist with a sense for business. For most sidemen, the prospects were dimmer.

In pop music especially, the itinerant sideman, the journeyman, was a working stiff who drew just enough salary to maintain a set of stage clothes, keep an instrument in working order and perhaps develop, if not slake, a thirst for forbidden fruits. In rock 'n' roll, as in jazz or blues, sidemen were anonymous, and meant to be. In rhythm and blues they were often expected to smile, perhaps perform choreographed dance steps behind the singer and, not incidentally, play their asses off all night long, night after night, all on a pittance, until they had nothing left to give. They had options, of course. They could always return to utter obscurity in, say, their hometowns and sell insurance. But the allure of rocking and rolling often kept musicians on the road years longer than sense dictated. The disregard for common sense and the cultivation of a certain feeling of desperation, of recklessness, fueled genuine rock 'n' roll. Roy Buchanan instinctively chose the Gypsy life and tried hard not to look back. But if the going got rough he could always glance into a rearview mirror and see Pixley and its implicit offer of isolation, loneliness, and boredom. That image probably made any other road look pretty darn good and, for a moment, he could forget that the road he had chosen had its own hazards.

IN THE SUMMER OF 1959 Jerry Hawkins, guitarist Joe Osborn, drummer Chris Bourcier, and Roy were living this life, holed up at the Skyway Club with only a handful of local gigs and the embers of ambition smoldering inside them. They wanted fame and they needed to eat. As summer dragged on, the four young men decided to take a road trip to the entertainment world's Promised Land—Los Angeles. They loaded Hawkins' '58 Ford station wagon and headed west to L.A., home to Ebb Records, Jerry's label. "We didn't have a gig or anything, we just went out lookin'," Jerry recalled. They took Route 66 all the way. The road's stupendous scenery triggered Roy's memory of a similar trip he'd made as a child: red dirt hills, sagebrush-covered high plains, pine-clad mountains, and barren desert all slipped past their whirring wheels. Upon arrival in Los Angeles, Hawkins decided he didn't like the scene, turned around, and scooted right back to Bossier City. "Los Angeles was just too rough for me," he said ruefully, 40 years later. "The whole lifestyle! I just didn't want to be there so I went back."

Osborn and Roy were more desperate. They loved the thrill of performing live rock 'n' roll and nothing else they knew—and they didn't know much else—could compare. The two musicians were fast friends and mutual admirers. "Roy was way ahead of his time," Osborn observed. "He was playin' a big, hollow-body Gibson and playin' things that nobody had even thought about. His string-bending was more than anyone else was doing. One time we were playin' a club and the bartender couldn't see him and he asked us, 'What kind of an instrument is that guy playin'?' He didn't even recognize it as a guitar. Roy could play a whole song without playin' one straight-on note. Down in Vegas we starved to death for a while. I knew this country singer, Bob Luman, needed a band. James Burton told me about the gig, 'cause he'd moved on to play for Ricky Nelson." Luman had his first hit late in 1957 with an instant cover of Billy Lee Riley's "Red Hot," a rockabilly number released in September. By fall 1959 he was on a roll.

"Roy and I camped out on the doorstep of Luman's hotel until he showed up," Osborn continued. "He was about to go to Las Vegas. That whole Town Hall Party show was going to Las Vegas to open the Showboat. We told Bob we'd like to go with him. At that time, we wanted to do *anything*. We had long hair down to our asses before long hair came in. We had clothes at the laundry that we couldn't afford to get out. Bob rehearsed us and, of course, we were great, so he got us haircuts and our laundry back and took us to Vegas. Roy and I were both playin' guitar in this band. After we went to Vegas, somehow we lost a guitar and wound up with one guitar between us. I don't recall what happened to Roy's Gibson; somehow he traded that one in on a Telecaster. We had a guitar between us and we borrowed a bass, a Kay bass. Bob liked the way I played his country shit, so Roy was playing that Kay bass while I played guitar. About that time Bob added a girl singer who did a lot of old standards. I didn't know any of those things and Roy knew 'em all, so we switched. I went down to the music store and bought a Precision bass and Roy took the Telecaster. The next night I was the bass player."

Joe Osborn's conversion to bass changed his life. He spent the 1960s and '70s as one of the most sought-after session bass players in Los Angeles—another ultimate sideman. As a member of "the Wrecking Crew," with drummer Hal Blaine and guitarist Larry Knechtel, Osborn played on hundreds of hits by a Who's Who in Los Angeles' pop music recording scene. Later, after opting out of the fast-lane, he performed similar musical services in Nashville.

Roy's encounter with the Fender Telecaster also proved to be a rare match of musician and instrument. Roy had always loved the Telecaster's sound, ever since watching Buck Owens and Roy Nichols in Pixley. It is unclear whether he actually owned and played one professionally prior to this stint with Joe Osborn. But from that point on, the Telecaster would be his guitar of choice. He liked its lightness and simplicity, to be sure. But it was more than that. The Telecaster's plaintive cry, its trebly insistence, its cutting demand to be heard, meant something to him. Unleashing its searing power answered a need.

Suddenly Roy was busy on the road with Bob Luman. Luman took Roy, Osborn, and Jerry Hawkins' former drummer, Melvin Rogers, on the road. They played Los Angeles' *Town Hall Party* on KTTV television on Oct. 2, 1959, and several tracks were recorded. Luman featured his rendition of Ray Charles' No. 1 R&B hit from 1955, "I Got A Woman." Luman actually fashioned himself after Elvis' version, which became a hit after Ray Charles released it—another example of the potent crossover market for rhythm and blues delivered by a white singer. As Luman affected his heartthrob vocals, Roy, Osborn, and Rogers backed him with a hopping Scotty Moore–Bill Black–D.J. Fontana–style rockabilly sound. Roy's manic pull-offs created an edgy cascade of notes that pushed the songs along. Roy, now 20, also stepped into the spotlight to play a raucous uptempo instrumental number dubbed "Roy's Guitar Boogie"—a speeded-up 1950s rock 'n' roll party anthem, a rollicking guitar workout. While it didn't do justice to Roy's talent and technique at that time, it nonetheless revealed that Roy knew how to play loud and fast, a standard operating procedure in rock 'n' roll.

Luman entered the studio that fall to record a few pop songs, with Roy on guitar. The singer's "The Class of '59" and "Dreamy Doll," both minor hits, didn't really require Roy's singular talents. But another Luman track titled "Buttercup" was very much built around Roy's moody dead-thumb intro and his trebly, Scotty Moore–style solo, which pushes past the singer on its rush to the spotlight, imbuing the piece with tension.

That fall in Los Angeles Roy and Osborn met up with their old buddy James Burton. "We went down to a little club called the Sea Witch and sat in and played and hung out," Burton recalled. "Roy spent a couple days at my hotel room. After that, I never really saw him again." In December Luman traveled to Tokyo, Japan, to capitalize on his overseas popularity. Like Hawkins, Luman knew that if he wanted to duplicate the sound on his records in performance, he had to take Roy. The two were greeted at Tokyo's airport by a throng of teenage Japanese girls, members of the famed Shochiku Girls' Revue, armed with bouquets of flowers. A photographer caught the two American rock 'n' rollers suspended in a sea of smiling, female teens, and though Bob shows off a bouquet with a smile, Roy looks a bit grim. The two made a four-week tour of Asia, which took them, among other places, to military bases on Okinawa and Formosa, now Taiwan. Upon his return to the States, Luman headed to Texas to visit his ill mother. Suddenly the band was "at liberty"—in other words, Roy, Joe, and Melvin were out of work.

ROY VISITED HIS BROTHER, J.D., in Hollywood, probably out of necessity, since he had no place else to land. Together the brothers drove north to Pixley. It would be the first time Roy had seen his folks in nearly three years. He could not have called them. The Buchanans didn't own a telephone until the mid-1960s.

Roy (in striped jacket) with Bob Luman, in Tokyo in December 1959.

And he wasn't a letter-writer. Probably J.D. had kept the folks abreast of Roy's adventures.

Nothing about Pixley or its people had changed. That was comforting in a way, though Roy saw through new eyes his good fortune in escaping. Feelings tugged at him. Roy and J.D. had a good visit with their folks and they clowned around in the yard, teasing J.D. about losing his hair, posing with each other as the others took turns snapping a handful of black and white photographs. Roy told his folks about the strange and wondrous places he'd been with Dale Hawkins and Bob Luman: Shreveport, Chicago, New York, Las Vegas, even Japan. His luxurious pompadour and his performing outfits provided tangible proof that he had achieved the first part of his dream: making a living as a professional musician. As for becoming "the greatest guitarist in the world"—an adolescent conception, to be sure, though a noble ambition—well, he already had some of the hottest chops in rock 'n' roll. Yet it was some comfort to his folks to see that his bashful manner hadn't really changed.

While visiting his folks, Roy stayed with his old friend, Bobby Jobe, rather than bunk at the cramped house out in Gus Forsblad's field. The peripatetic guitarist quickly grew restless. "He stayed with me for a couple of weeks in Delano," Jobe recalled. "After they got back from Japan, Luman had to go to Texas, said he'd call Leroy in a week. We hung around, pickin' some, go by his folks' house, drink a little beer. One morning Roy said, 'I wonder why Bobby hasn't called me?' He was getting antsy, see, wantin' to get on that stage. I said, 'Maybe somethin' happened. He'll be callin' ya.' Roy said, 'Well, I don't know.' He went on all day like this. He said, 'Well, let's go to momma's house, she's got my uniforms and things.' His mom had ironed and starched every stage uniform he had. She did it so beautiful. She said, 'What are you going to do?' Roy said, 'Momma, I'm going to Las Vegas.' She said, 'You're supposed to wait for Bobby to call you.' 'No, Momma, I've got to get down there and go to work.' So he took the uniforms and hugged his momma and dad and we went back to Delano to my house. He called the Showboat. He said, 'This is Roy Buchanan. Do I have a job up there?' He told me to listen close. I could hear the gal on the other end. Someone said, *'Get over here, you've got a job right now!'* That night I put him on the bus to Las Vegas and that was the last time I saw him."

Whether Roy saw Luman again isn't known, but the relationship was doomed. The singer soon entered the US Army for basic training, an echo of Elvis' exile. Whether Roy's eyesight or some other infirmity kept him from service, or whether he was simply movin' too fast for the armed services to catch up with him, remains unknown. Roy stayed in Vegas at the Showboat, where he reunited with Joe Osborn, and the two hustled a living. They played behind now-long-forgotten entertainers such as "Carrot Top" Anderson ("an old hillbilly with a funny suit" Osborn recalled) and Sterling Bly. For a couple of young men from down Arkansas and Louisiana-way, living in Las Vegas at the peak of its notoriety, backing singers who entertained mobsters, Hollywood types, and gamblers of every stripe, provided a certain allure. "When you're stuck in Bossier City you never saw anybody," Osborn said. "So it was the first time I'd ever been that close to anybody who was somebody." Though Las Vegas held the young men's attention for a time, they still dreamed. All young rock 'n' rollers harbored a vision that ultimately featured their names on the country's most prestigious marquees and their records blaring from every radio. Unfortunately, this dream contrasted sharply with Osborn and Roy's immediate circumstances: they were backing celebrity hillbillies in Las Vegas! Then a tornado swept through town.

"We were at the Showboat about two months when Dale Hawkins drug us out of there and sent us out to New Jersey," Osborn recalled, still astonished after 40 years. "This might have been early 1960. It was cold, I know that. Dale rescued us! He kept showing up in our lives. It's really strange. He sent us to New Jersey to back his brother Jerry again, in a lounge show." After Jerry Hawkins' gig in New Jersey ended, the band instinctively headed back to Bossier City once again, to regroup. Roy and Osborn had been gone about a year, with Roy getting as far as Japan. But this time Bossier City wouldn't be more than a stopover. "That's where we got split up somehow," Osborn said. "James Burton came by. He'd never seen me play bass and he said Ricky Nelson was putting together a band and they needed me. I didn't see Roy again after that."

ROY'S LIFE ON THE ROAD IN 1960–61 can be glimpsed only through a ragged pastiche of recollections and recordings. These sources fit together only roughly, like pieces of a puzzle that have warped and no longer neatly interlock. Sometime in 1960 Hawkins swung through Bossier City, grabbed Roy, and headed back out onto the road. In New York City they recorded Hawkins' latest songs in sessions produced by the celebrated duo of Jerry Leiber and Mike Stoller. Leiber and Stoller—two young, white, suburban kids from California—had struck pay dirt in the rhythm and blues field in 1953 with "Hound Dog," recorded by Big Mama Thornton. When Elvis covered "Hound Dog" in 1956 the song and, with it, Leiber and Stoller, got launched into the pop stratosphere. Now, in New York, with Leiber and Stoller directing the session, Hawkins waxed three tracks with Roy on hand. But the producers' magic did not propel the singer back onto the charts. They did notice the guitarist's talent, though, and told him to stay in touch.

At some point, Hawkins landed a Saturday morning television program in Philadelphia devoted to rock 'n' roll. That's where Ed Montini, a jazz saxophone player from Mantua, NJ, entered the picture. As Montini recalled: "We auditioned one day for Dale. Roy was already with him. Here comes this hillbilly with his Telecaster and an old Magnatone amplifier. I said, 'My God, what's *this*?'" Then Roy plugged in. "I say to myself, 'Where are these chords coming from? Wait a minute, this hillbilly can *play* that damn thing!' He was playing rock 'n' roll using progressive, modern jazz chords! Jazz had been my life up to that time and let me tell you, that man could play *anything*."

Hawkins took his band to the usual hot spots on the Jersey coast—Wildwood, Somer's Point, Atlantic City—and to the Philadelphia axis that included Camden and Allentown, all the way to the clubs on 14th Street in downtown Washington, DC. The group either played clubs or joined a bill with other pop stars such as Bill Haley, Bobby Day, Brian Hyland (remember "Itsy Bitsy Teenie Weenie Polka Dot Bikini"?), the Righteous Brothers, Dion and the Belmonts, Chubby Checker, and Freddie "Boom Boom" Cannon. Hawkins and Roy apparently went their own way, while the other sidemen split off.

Ed Montini and a drummer named Stan Weinberg hooked up with a couple of singing brothers named the Perry Mates and headed to Rodell Studios, one of only two professional recording facilities in DC. As Montini recalled: "We had something we thought was really good, something commercial, called 'The Kick Step.' So we went into the studio. I wanted to get that Buchanan sound on there also, so we hired him to play on that track and, I think, a couple of others. He just happened to be in DC and we asked him to join us. He said, 'Yeah, if I can record 'After Hours.' That, plus get paid.'"

Leveraging his invitation to a session into a recording opportunity of his own was a gambit Roy would invoke again and again over the years. If someone wanted the benefit of his distinctive guitar on their record, which everyone knew elevated the mundane to the sublime, then they could give Roy a chance to record his own tracks.

Though he had developed a sense of commerciality, first by listening to the radio, then by playing with Hawkins, Roy wanted to see what he could do if he played something he just *felt* like playing. The guitarist had heard and admired Jimmy Nolen's 1956 Federal Records version of "After Hours," the song long known as the "black national anthem," popularized by the Erskine Hawkins Orchestra in 1940. "It was one of the best blues I knew at the time," Roy once said. "Instead of makin' up blues of my own, I wanted to pick something that was more or less a standard."

Roy would later claim to have recorded "After Hours" in 1959, but those who lived the early days of rock 'n' roll have a habit of turning back the clock a year or two in their minds, still vying for recognition of their seminal work. For many reasons, 1960 is more likely. Given Roy's masterful command of the blues idiom evident on the tape that survives, however, the precise date is moot. The guitarist displays a magical finesse, an almost heartbreaking fluency of lasting value, whether the track was recorded in 1959, 1960, or 2020. Roy's maturing way with a solo is fully evident, particularly at the languid, swinging pace he employed on this track. He finds an almost lazy groove, yet he tosses off amazingly fluid runs with an easy touch that takes one's breath away.

Roy had learned to articulate a melody, and think through a solo. He began by stating the melody as simply as possible, perhaps adding a melodic afterthought to be sure he had everyone's attention. Then he'd start playing with the rhythm of the melody line, bending notes for feeling. With the band sailing away behind him, Roy would depart on his own, reworking the melody from the ground floor up, adding inflections, spinning a web, always having something to say. A pregnant pause might precede an eerie wail. If he played quickly, it was to express an emotion, not for flash. Techniques that became Roy's trademarks are in glorious evidence on "After Hours": the guitarist's dexterous manipulation of the Telecaster's volume control that swelled a note until it cried out like a human voice, the oblique doublestop bends that mimicked the sound of a pedal steel guitar, the flawless, hypnotic staccato runs all are in place. While his technique is astonishing, it's his almost quirky phrasing that adds an enervating element, a sheer vitality, to his sound. His ideas matter. By this time Roy could articulate his feelings as guitar phrases, punctuating his musical statements, confessions, and supplications with periods, commas, and exclamation marks. Roy's skill transformed the guitar into a vehicle for expressing his thoughts, his desires, his melancholy soul. He was tapping a deep tradition. As musicologist Alan Lomax wrote in *The Land Where the Blues Began*, "In Southern folk tradition the admired player is the one who can make his instrument speak, and this tendency is ultimately African . . . Each of the exactly milled and tuned strings of the guitar offers a range of notes that, with the subtle manipulations of finger work and slide, can be made to emit the nuance of speech and really talk the blues in every register, as well as define wordless feelings with the utmost delicacy. Most heartbreaking of all are the sounds that come out of the treble strings, choked high up on the neck, which are made to cry out in ineffable agony, as well as ecstasy, as the mood turns from sorrow to orgasm."

The eloquence and depth of emotion Roy coaxed from his guitar seem to come from a person somehow far older than his 21 years. Where this deep kinship with the blues came from nobody really knew—except perhaps for Roy, and he didn't talk about that stuff.

The fate of this sterling track? Later Roy would say he managed to get the "After Hours" tape into the hands of Philadelphia DJ Harvey Moore, who landed him a deal with Bomarc, a subsidiary of Dick Clark's Swan Records. When Moore finally spun the record on his show, the phones purportedly lit up. Roy also claimed that to foster wider distribution he also reached Leiber and Stoller in New York with a copy of "After Hours." "They wasn't interested in it," the guitarist said with asperity, 20 years later. "They said it was great, great blues, but blues don't sell." In fact, without a patron saint behind it, the record died at birth.

THE PROMOTIONAL GENIUS associated with early rock 'n' roll knew no bounds, judging by Stan Weinberg's account of what transpired next. The players knew a DJ, who suddenly seized upon a plan to promote the band. "Basically, he concocted an idea that Roy had been found somewhere in Europe by Gypsies, surrounded by wolves," Weinberg recalled. "The story would be that he'd become friendly with the wolves. He could talk to them. The Gypsies had taught him to play the guitar. It was *unbelievable!* This DJ says, 'Meet me at the so-and-so hotel,' a big hotel in Philadelphia. So we went down there, checked into the hotel—Eddie, Roy, myself. Here comes the disc jockey with this other guy, a very dapper-looking man. Right away we knew this guy was a hood. This was the guy who would do the publicity. He had connections with certain magazines that would publish this story. The scenario was, 'Roy will come out in his beard with these two wolves in chains, billed as 'The Wolf Boy.' He'd been found in the woods in, like, Hungary. Lots of publicity before the first appearance. People would be clamoring, 'Who *is* this guy?!' "

"Anyway," Weinberg lamented, both disappointed and relieved, "nothing ever happened. That was the end of that. They never even got into how they would handle getting the wolves."

Somehow Montini and Weinberg reunited with Dale Hawkins and Roy, and the band took off for Canada. No doubt they hit the usual destinations: Toronto, Hamilton, Windsor, perhaps Ottawa. The road meant many things, and getting wacky was prominent among them. Hawkins and Roy had never lost their appetite for amphetamines, and that meant the guitarist could behave strangely. According to Ed Montini, they *all* were getting a little wacky. "We used to sit around the pool until four or five in the morning, just plain high. I don't know how else to say it. Me and Roy had two separate rooms, with an adjoining door, which we left open. So one night we went to bed. I fell asleep. All of a sudden there's moonlight coming in the window and I look over and there's Roy on his haunches on his bed goin' 'Ahhhoooooooo!' He was howlin' at the moon like he was a wolf! He was *into* it! I have no idea where he got this," Montini confessed, still astonished after nearly 40 years. "We never saw movies. That was *him!*" The sax man added, as if in explanation: "We were pretty hip cats in those days."

When it came to good, clean fun for hip cats in those days, Roy was just like any other young man from the sticks: he enjoyed fast cars, amphetamines, and guns, and he got bored on long-distance drives. As Weinberg recalled, the drive home from Canada held the usual attractions. "Roy had a .45 he carried in the back of his amp in case somebody gave him a hard time he couldn't handle. On our way back to the States, around two or three o'clock in the morning, they were firing that .45 at all these highway signs—and hittin' 'em."

This cast of characters next appeared in Washington, DC, when Dale Hawkins and his band, with Roy on lead guitar, played an extended engagement at the Rocket Room from Tuesday, Oct. 18, to Sunday, Oct, 30, 1960. "The Rocket Room was right across from the Greyhound bus station, owned by a couple of brothers named Baumstein," Weinberg recalled. "Nothing fancy. Naugahyde chairs, plastic tables. No food, strictly alcohol. This is prime time in Washington for live music." According to Montini, Charlie Daniels and the Jaguars had opened the room and Dale Hawkins and his band were the first out-of-towners to headline. "The whole scene was different then," Montini said. "We'd usually play Tuesday through Saturday, from 9 at night until 2 in the morning. Five hours was standard."

Local sax master and bandleader Joe Stanley may have played on this engagement. He was definitely at the club when a young female acquaintance of his stopped in on a whim and forever altered Roy's picaresque lifestyle. Judy Owens visited the club that night with a couple of friends. She had grown up in Mount Rainier, MD, the youngest of five children in a middle-class Catholic family. She attended Immaculate Conception Academy, where Joe Stanley once accompanied her to a school dance. "She was a typical teenager, just like everyone else," Stanley remembered. Judy Owens had grown up by the time Joe saw her again at the Rocket Room in late October 1960. She had long dark hair, a vivacious smile, and a lithe figure. She was taking classes and working at Catholic University. One of her school friends was seriously ill, and Owens and others took their ailing pal out for a night on the town. "We wanted to do things she'd never done before," Owens said. "I had heard Dale Hawkins was at the Rocket Room, but I didn't go to clubs. But I loved 'Susie Q' so we decided to go down there. When we went in there was no band on. We were the only three females. I thought, 'Oh my God, what did we get ourselves into?' The first thing I heard was a guitar. I looked up and the guitar player had his back to us. Then he turned around. He had a beard and he was really unusual-looking for those days. Picture it now, this is 1960. Nobody back then wore a beard. Nobody had long hair. His hair was long for those days, with bangs, so he was a weird-looking character. I noticed him right off. Then when the band got back up and we were dancing I noticed his eyes even more, and he noticed me. He impressed me so much with his playing, I watched him all night long. I noticed that at every break he would go over to the bar and get some drinks and go downstairs. So when the lights came on at closing, my friend Mary said, 'Where are you going?' I said 'I'll be back in a minute. I'm going to meet this guy.' She said, 'Judy, you're *crazy!*' I said, 'Not only that, I'm going to marry him.' I actually introduced myself to him. He was the strangest and yet the most handsome and beautiful person I had ever met." Judy saw Roy a few more times that fall, locating him at various clubs in DC and being sure he noticed her. Then he was gone to Canada again with Dale Hawkins. Bands could play Hamilton, Windsor, and Toronto in rapid succession, often staying for a week-long engagement at each club. In Toronto, a several-mile-long strip known as Yonge Street hosted the clubs where rock 'n' roll was welcome.

"That whole time was a blur," Ed Montini cackled, many years after this particular stint in Canada. "We used to have some pretty wild parties. Miss Toronto was in on it. I couldn't begin to tell you half the things that went on, first because you wouldn't believe it and, second, because we couldn't have it getting around." Montini recalled that "waves" of guitarists came to see Roy rule the stage. "All these local guitar players would come to see him and he'd just turn his back," Weinberg added. "I'd say, 'Roy, what are you doing that for?' And he'd say, 'I don't want them to steal my licks.'" According to Montini, Roy's striking good looks and charisma as a "guitar man" did not always set well with the men in the audience. "We were playing at Le Coq D'Or" on Yonge Street in Toronto, Montini said. "The band had to move at 12 o'clock every night into the restaurant. This guy's wife kept making eyes at Roy. The guy is getting madder and madder. He'd had a snootful. While we're moving our instruments, he starts after Roy. I can attest that Roy didn't want anything to do with this woman. The husband goes after him and is going to punch him out. Roy takes his Telecaster by the neck, like an axe, and hits the guy over the head with it. Down he went, man, like a ton of bricks, and the cops hauled him away."

IT SO HAPPENED that Dale Hawkins' cousin, Ronnie Hawkins—a wild, raunchy performer who hailed from Fayetteville, AR—was also in Toronto at this time with his band, the Hawks. The Hawks contained a couple of musicians who would go on to form one of the greatest rock 'n' roll groups, the Band. One of the players was Levon Helm, who hailed from Helena, AR, and whose experience driving a tractor down on the farm apparently gave him the requisite skills to pilot Ronnie Hawkins' Cadillac, in addition to his duties singing and drumming in the band. Stan Szelest, lured from Buffalo, NY, played rock 'n' roll keyboards with a vengeance that he backed with his fists. Another Hawk came in the form of a teenage guitarist named Robbie Robertson, a native of Toronto. Born in 1943 to a Mohawk mother and Jewish father, Robertson spent his early summers on the Six Nations Indian Reservation, where folks listened to Hank Williams and Lefty Frizzell. He'd learned the rudiments of guitar and hovered eagerly around the Hawks when Fred Carter Jr., the band's guitarist, quit and Hawkins gave him a chance. When he first joined the Hawks he traveled to the South and learned what made Southern rock 'n' roll musicians tick. "You could hear music comin' out of the night," Robertson later told Tony Scherman for *Musician*. Everything gets flatter and flatter, and wetter, and swampier, and you smell the dirt . . . People walked in rhythm and talked this sing-song talk . . . Everything sounded like music." Robbie threw himself with "blind, violent amibition" into succeeding as a Hawk.

Ronnie Hawkins could see that Robertson's guitar work needed improvement. The young Hawk needed to learn finesse, how to back a singer, and perhaps acquire a few of the professional chops that could wow an audience. Chops like Roy had in abundance in *his* arsenal. With Dale Hawkins and his band set to disappear soon, Ronnie Hawkins lured Roy away "to try to advance Robbie." To Dale Hawkins that was stealing. "Everybody that I had, Ronnie at one time or another tried to get!" Dale would recall, still pissed off after 40 years. "I'd love to skin Ronnie's ass!" For Roy, however, this assignment was just temporary.

As Roy later recalled, Ronnie Hawkins told him, "'I know a guy who's got potential on guitar. His name is Robbie Robertson. Would you mind staying long enough to teach him how to play a little bit?' I told him I couldn't stay with him for long. So I stayed with 'em maybe a month . . . and showed [Robbie] how to complement the singer—not just be a guitar player and take the show and not know anything else." As Roy explained in 1981 to Mike Joyce for *Unicorn Times*, "Ronnie was very strict about how he was backed and Robertson would either overplay or underplay. He'd be playing lead when Ronnie was singing and it just wouldn't work out. So I showed him how to do it, because that's what I was really into, backing up people and making them sound good."

Apparently the process began with intimidation. "Roy came around," Robertson recalled in a 1985 film interview. "The second time I had ever met him, this guy was like a gun slinger coming to town, right? He got up, plugged in, looks at me, like, so I thought, 'Okay. You wanna *dance? Let's dance!'* And I was just at the stage where I was starting to get pretty good. I was still very young, maybe 17 years old. And he did this thing like—we started to play, and we were going to, like, swap solos—he was tuning the guitar while playing, 'Bowarrrring . . . .' And it was like Bruce Lee swinging around one of these things before he fights you. By then you're already horrified by what this man has just done before your eyes. So he did all these tricks, weird sounds, and bending things . . . and playing with volume control. It was a very, very frightening experience."

Roy *had* been around and he looked the part. He'd been on the road virtually nonstop for more than five years, without a real home. He'd covered tens of thousands of miles, poppin' pills, drinking beer, and unleashing at every stop the calculated mayhem that was rock 'n' roll. He had his chops together and he knew it. And he let Robertson know it. His unsettling gaze broadened the gulf between his 22 years and Robbie's 17. "He was a bohemian of the period," Robertson told Tony

Scherman for *Musician*. "I thought he was really . . . the most remarkable guitar player I'd ever seen. I remember asking him how he'd developed his style, and he said with a straight face that he was half-wolf." Spookiness aside, Robertson could see his mentor was dead serious about his craft. "Roy had really high goals," Robertson added. "He wanted to be a completely remarkable musician."

Roy had an equally unsettling effect on the rest of the Hawks. "Roy had strange eyes, didn't talk to anyone, and looked real fierce," Levon Helm recalled in his book, *This Wheel's on Fire*. "He just stood there and played the shit out of that guitar." Just standing there and playing the shit out of anything was news to the fledgling Hawks, who were trained by the Hawk himself to put on a *real* show. "Ronnie was always teaching us that when you play you're having a great time," Robertson told Barney Hoskyns, author of *Across the Great Divide: The Band and America*. "It was 'Now you move up here, now you move over there.' Show business! Then Roy came along and said, 'Enough of this up-and-over bullshit, you can be just as effective just by pulling energy out of the music.' And that shit started to embarrass me, all the leg kicks and stuff. I hated it." By the end of this brief sojourn, Roy had imparted to Robertson only as much as he cared to. Robertson stole as much as he could.

Roy's stipulation that he wouldn't stay long worked for Ronnie Hawkins. He wasn't about to put up with Roy's weirdness. "Roy was kind of laid-back," Hawkins said. "You didn't know if he was super-intelligent or just out of this world. When he came to me he had long hair and a beard. At that time Roy was playing games quite a bit. He tells me he's a werewolf who's going to marry a nun. '*Jesus*, son,' I tell him. 'If you are, we've hit the big time. We're getting out of the goddamn bars, baby. I mean, once a month, when the moon's full, we can do the *Ed Sullivan Show*." Roy demurred, indicating that conditions had to be *just* right. "So it's about the right time of month, and we went out on the beach waiting for the moon," Ronnie Hawkins recalled for Peter Goddard's biography, *Ronnie Hawkins: Last of the Good Old Boys*. "[Roy] wasn't stoned. He wasn't on drugs. He said, 'Ronnie, I know you're going to think I'm crazy.' And then I started thinking about how foolish I was, standing out on the beach, waiting for Roy Buchanan to turn into a wolf." There were other reasons Roy would not make a good, devoted Hawk. The manager of the club where they were playing complained about Roy's bohemian appearance. Word got back to Roy. That night he appeared for the Hawks' usual gig with his head completely shaved, including his eyebrows. "He looked like a friggin' Martian!" Ronnie Hawkins exclaimed later. But there'd be no Martians in the Hawks. "He could play anything I wanted him to play, and play it better than anyone else. Robbie was super good for his age, but Roy had been out there longer. He was the master. But Roy had many things to do and it just wasn't going to work out. What he needed was discipline. Playing day and night with a goal to go to. He was too much of a free spirit for the times. I've always been the boss."

Roy soon departed Toronto, leaving in his wake a rock 'n' roll unit soon to acquire three new members and an attitude that could no longer endure the up-and-over routine. Once Rick Danko joined the Hawks as a singer and bass guitarist, and Garth Hudson and Richard Manuel came in on vocals and keyboards, the Hawks would shed their role as Ronnie Hawkins' crack backup band and venture into America seeking fame and fortune on their own. In time they would find both, first as Levon and the Hawks, later as the Band, the counterculture's favorite ragtime band. Bill Avis, road manager for Ronnie Hawkins in 1961, once described the Hawks at this juncture. His picturesque image might have been fixed in Roy's own rear-view mirror as the guitarist departed Canada. "The first thing you noticed was how good-lookin' this band was," Avis told Barney Hoskyns. "Clean-cut, tall young men immaculately dressed in hip suits, cuff links, good haircuts. They just looked *sharp*."

WITH DALE HAWKINS disappearing once again over the horizon on a solo jaunt, Ed Montini convinced Roy to return to DC to put together a band. They hooked up with drummer Stan Weinberg and a one-time hairdresser and bass player named Vince Brando. The four musicians were soon persuaded by sax man and bandleader Joe Stanley to become the latest incarnation of his long-running group, the Sax-tons. Throughout the spring of 1961 the Saxtons played Guy's and the Roundup in DC's Southeast quadrant, plus the Rocket Room at 14th and I, and the 4400 Club in the northern suburb of Mount Rainier, MD. Roy roomed with Joe and his wife in Seat Pleasant, MD. This incarnation of the Saxtons soon fizzled, however. "We fired Joe," Weinberg recalled with a bitter laugh. The foursome—Weinberg on drums, Brando on bass, Montini on sax, and Roy on guitar—quickly regrouped as The Bad Boys. All four shared an apartment on Georgia Avenue Northwest. The Bad Boys earned a spot as house band at Woody's on Kennedy Street from May to July and scratched up one-nighters at familiar clubs like the Rocket Room, Benny's Rebel Room, and Rand's. Brando and Weinberg shared vocal chores on the group's reper-toire, which included songs by Ray Charles, Louis Prima, and the requisite Top Ten covers. Weinberg wrangled a summer engagement for The Bad Boys at the Tropi-cana Ballroom in Virginia Beach, VA, at the mouth of Chesapeake Bay, 200 miles south of DC. When the Tropicana, a popular club on Atlantic Avenue, the town's high-gloss resort strip, didn't immediately renew the band's contract, Weinberg struck a deal with the Top Hat, down the street. The band was that good and every hot spot featured live entertainment in those days. Weinberg convinced Roy to sing on stage for the first time in his life. "I said, 'You can sing.' He says, 'Nah, I can't.' I say, '*Bullshit! You can! You* can do this!' Roy would say, 'Well, I guess I'll try it.' Every night he sang two songs."

As far as anyone knew, Roy had never had a lasting girlfriend. When he returned from Canada, he did not see Judy Owens for months. The two had seen each other only a few times after their initial meeting at the Rocket Room in October 1960. She liked to talk. He would listen, enjoying her attention. When Roy disappeared to Canada, Judy's initial determination to snag the bohemian guitarist definitely wavered, but her interest remained. "When he got back into town he didn't call me," Judy told Mark Opsasnick, author of *Capitol Rock*. "A girlfriend of mine called me and told me he was in town and I said, 'Well, who cares? He didn't call me. I'm not going back down [to the club where Roy was playing].' And she coaxed me into going down. She said, 'You *have* to, it's the last time they're going to be in town. So I went down and he had a full beard and didn't even look like the same human being. He was playing at Guy's, a little dumpy dive in a bad section of Southeast Washington, with The Bad Boys. When I saw Roy down there he was all enthusiastic about the band."

Roy and Judy must have seen each other with some degree of frequency after that, before The Bad Boys left town for their Virginia Beach gig, because she soon appeared there. Stan Weinberg had mixed feelings about the woman pursuing his guitarist. "She liked him a lot," he recalled. "I don't think he wanted to be around any women. He didn't look like he was interested in her at all. She used to cry all the time and this-and-that."

During the Tropicana gig, Roy suddenly needed money. "Roy wanted to borrow $200 from me and I didn't have any money," Weinberg said. "I said, 'Let me see what I can do.' So I went to the club owner, whose name was Moose. He said, 'What can I do for you?' I said, 'Roy here needs $200 and I don't have that kind of money.' Moose said, 'Stanley, I'll tell you what I'm going to do. I don't know Roy. I know you. I'm going to give you $200. What you do with it is your business. But I'm holding you responsible.' So he gives me $200. I said, 'Now Roy, don't let this man down. Pay him back.' He says, 'I will, I will.'"

The $200 had to cover a ring, a marriage license, the gas money to get Roy and Judy to the closest justice of the peace—in Elizabeth City, seat of Pasquotank County, NC—and back, and perhaps a bottle or two of Champagne. Exactly when Roy proposed marriage isn't clear. He liked Judy's manner, and her good looks sweetened the deal. It was long past time to have a woman in his life, yet little in his experience had prepared him for a serious relationship with a woman, let alone marriage. Roy took the plunge anyway. "He got down on his knees and asked me to marry him," Judy recalled. "The whole bit shocked me to death." Somehow Judy survived the shock long enough for the mad dash to Elizabeth City in Stan Weinberg's car on July 20, 1961. The werewolf married the nun—though the two roles could be reversed, or so close friends sometimes said, confidentially. The ups and downs of marriage seemed to find a poster couple in Roy and Judy. "They drove each other crazy," said one close family friend.

The Top Hat gig didn't last, though not because the band wasn't attracting a crowd. En route to a gig one day Ed Montini made a sudden U-turn and another car ploughed into his, breaking his collarbone and sending him and Roy and Judy to the hospital. "I couldn't play," Montini said, "and my '53 Chevy BelAir was demolished." Roy and Judy sustained only minor injuries, but that was it for the band, and everyone went their separate ways. Weinberg never saw his buddy Roy again. "Roy was not comfortable in the spotlight. He didn't like it, didn't want it, wasn't interested in it. He was always kind of a quiet guy. I never saw him get upset. So to me he was a very peaceful, quiet guy. He let his guitar do the talking." As for ambition, it smoldered in everyone's chest. But Roy had once told Weinberg, "Hey, I'd rather just get paid $20 a night and play my own stuff."

"I don't really know exactly what Roy wanted because he never really said," Weinberg offered. "He was a very private guy. He was a country boy and that's the way he wanted to stay. I was always amazed. I thought, 'Look at the talent this guy's got. He could write his own ticket.'"

Roy and Judy returned to Mount Rainier, where they stayed with Judy's mother and sister at Judy's family home. Judy loved being home, but for Roy it was difficult to go from hanging out with The Bad Boys to hanging out with his mother-in-law in suburban Maryland. The situation stirred him to action. He jumped on the phone. Ronnie Hawkins had a session coming up in New York City and he needed help. Robbie Robertson had the lead guitar role nailed down, but Hawkins needed a bass player. Where some might balk at taking second fiddle to a former student, Roy leapt at the chance. In the second week of September Roy and Judy traveled to New York, where Roy met up with Hawkins, Robertson, Levon Helm, possibly Richard Manuel, and sax man King Curtis. Over several days the group recorded a number of covers, including "Susie Q" and "Matchbox." Without Hawkins, Helm sang "Farther On Up the Road" and "Nineteen Years Old." These recordings establish that Robbie's guitar fills had become admirably menacing and his solos had achieved "that stinger thing," all backed by the solid rhythms of Helm on drums and Roy on bass. After the sessions were over, the couple got stuck with a hotel bill. Roy called a DJ in New Jersey who sent just enough money to get them to the Philadelphia area for a job with a local group of rockers known as Bobby Moore and the Temptations. (After the emergence of the Motown group by the same name, Moore's group became the Temps.)

The group was based outside Camden, NJ, just across the Delaware River from Philadelphia. The Buchanans got an apartment in Bellmawr, south of Camden, across the street from Dick Lee's Musical Club, where the Temps worked as the house band. The Temps were a talented, hard-working band composed of three Moore brothers: Bob, the frontman; John, his twin; and their younger brother Butch. In performance, with Roy on lead guitar, they could effectively rock a joint and they won a devoted following in the Philly area. They also recorded numerous tracks that, released on the Swan, ABC-Paramount, and Daisy labels, achieved a degree of local success. The Moore brothers befriended their quirky guitarist, helped him with a paycheck, and gave him the occasional spotlight. Still, he was only a hired gun, and that suited Roy just fine. Whereas Robbie Robertson, for instance, had joined a band that would define his career—and provide the camaraderie and inspiration of equals for support and direction—Roy's taciturn, even diffident nature seemed to forever cast him as a mercenary. His gigs lasted only as long as they suited him, or as long as he could hold things together. Between his long experience on the road, his quirky personality, and the amphetamines he was taking, he'd become a little erratic.

The Temps gig lasted more than a year, from the fall of 1961 until the spring of 1963. Roy needed a steady gig and the Temps provided it. Together they played straight-ahead rock 'n' roll, blues, originals, and popular covers. The band performed consistently at Dick Lee's—a rectangular box made of cinderblocks with a faux stonework facade—where they attracted a faithful crowd. People went to see the Temps, but they returned to hear Roy. The band traveled to other venues as close as Philadelphia or as distant as Allentown, 50 miles away. No doubt many people who heard the band never knew Roy Buchanan's name. That was the promise of American roadhouses in those days: They might be inhabited by local, anonymous virtuosos who could pick more dexterously, or blow more eloquently, than any star. No one ever caught the sidemen's names, then the night would swallow them, leaving nothing more than a trail of astonishment.

Along the way, Roy made a few friends among local musicians. In Allentown to play the Cameo, he'd always see Charlie Whaland, who played bass in local bands under the stage name Danny Charles. "The Cameo was one of the greatest places in the world!" Whaland recalled. "It was a dark, dingy nightclub down in the bad section of town. They had an incredible amount of people in there. There were always a lot of women. If you were looking for sex, you could get it. There was no doubt about it. I remember one woman there known as 'Juicy Lucy'. . . .Anyway, you played in the center of the bar, which was oval, close to the door. The band had their feet at bar height. In the back were tables and a dance floor." After the show Roy and Charlie would head out to have a few beers and play their guitars. Roy's first inclination, apparently, was not to score at the Cameo. "Roy got plenty of attention from women, but he was shy!" Whaland said. "He didn't talk well with women. He couldn't talk about anything but music and weird shit . . . ." As for where the "weird shit" came from, Roy had a hobby. "We'd stay up all night playin' guitar," Charlie recalled. "Roy would say, 'We'd better get some sleep.' And he'd give me some pills. The next morning, I remember somethin' irritatin' me and I opened my eyes and here's Roy stickin' a pill in my mouth to wake me up!"

BOB MOORE TOOK ROY into a Philadelphia studio sometime in the fall of 1961 to cut the first of a handful of tracks the guitarist would record with the Temps on Dick Clark's Philly-based Swan Records. The past four years working for Dale Hawkins paid off. Buchanan had mastered the art of providing well-crafted rhythms, fills, and fiery solos on demand. In the first session, Roy played on three tunes. Two of them were maudlin love songs that drip with melodrama, despite Roy's exquisite guitar fills in the background. The third, "Ruby Baby," was a rocker

"Potato Peeler," the record that captured Roy's trademark whistling harmonic for the first time.

featuring Roy's piercing lead work and a fuzz-drenched solo that screamed out as the song faded. (One of the prevailing theories on the use of fade-outs held that if the recording faded as the band began to cook, fans would want more, either in performance, or by buying the next record.) Roy still harbored ambitions, for he cut his usual deal to lead the band on two tracks of his own choice. "Mule Train Stomp" featured his Roy Nichols–style chicken pickin' and an overdriven amp on a tune that could be described as "Rawhide" on amphetamines, with key changes and background yells courtesy of the Temps. Though monotonous, the song does give Roy a showcase for his instrumental skills. "Pretty Please," Roy's other choice, was a cool, 12-bar blues in the vein of "Crossties" and "Whiskers," featuring Roy's gorgeous steel guitar–sounding country chords that set him apart from his contemporaries. Underneath his stoic demeanor, Roy was still trying to "make it." His face could be deadpan, while the music that flowed from his fingers raged. Because he lacked a strong voice he consistently chose to record instrumentals. Unfortunately, pop instrumentals were not yet well-accepted—the Ventures' signature instrumental, "Walk, Don't Run," issued only a year earlier, in 1960, was considered ground-breaking in that genre. Roy's two tracks got released on Swan under his own name, though the market's reaction is lost to history. Apparently a couple other tracks, clearly Roy's work, were released under the pseudonym of "The Secrets," including "Twin Exhaust," an early adventure in distortion (and released on *The Early Years*). The Secrets' tracks fared no better than the Temps' records; they did not catch fire.

The recording sessions with the Temps garnered Roy a steady role with Swan Records, and he ended up laying down guitar tracks for a procession of artists. Freddie "Boom Boom" Cannon, whose "Way Down Yonder in New Orleans" hit the Top 40 in 1960, used Roy on a session. Danny & the Juniors, who'd had the No. 1 hit of 1958 with "At the Hop," employed Roy for their "Peppermint Twist" sessions in January 1962. Of this session work, however, Roy later told DJ Ashley Kahn: "It didn't move me. I felt like a robot."

Drummer Bobby Gregg collaborated on a couple of Swan sessions that produced minor guitar history when Roy hit a "pinched harmonic"—a high squealing overtone created by plucking a string between pick and thumb—on a song titled "Potato Peeler." "It was a mistake," Roy once told Ashley Kahn. "When the record came out, the guitar players said, 'How'd you do that?' Somewhere in the back of my mind I was tryin' to hit those high notes that the rhythm and blues sax players hit. Like Junior Walker . . . I think I was subconsciously tryin' to get that sound. People said that I'd done it before in person and I just wasn't aware of it." In any case, Roy is credited with a technique now considered standard for rock guitarists' repertoires, used by Robbie Robertson and ZZ Top's Billy Gibbons, among others.

This flurry of side work should have earned Roy a moment in the sun, but instead it brought bitter disappointment. Gregg had found Roy in the studio developing a riff that Gregg promptly convinced him to record as a guitar showcase titled, "The Jam." With Roy leading the band on guitar, the song hit *Billboard's* Rhythm and Blues charts in 1962. An entire generation of guitarists judged themselves by their ability to play "The Jam," in addition to mimicking hits like "Mashed Potatoes," "Green Onions," "Walk, Don't Run," "Louie, Louie," and others. Gregg surreptitiously claimed the songwriting credit on "The Jam," and thus the bulk of royalties, a move that instilled in Roy a deep, long-lasting mistrust of front men and the music business. Forever afterward, Roy would tell how Gregg's maneuver had cost the guitarist money, opportunity, and recognition. Roy also liked to recount how he paid back Gregg in kind. The drummer had an important upcoming gig that would feature "his" hit, "The Jam," and he offered Roy—the only guitarist available who could play the song—a pittance to play for him. Roy agreed. And never showed up.

Aspiring R&B singer Fred Mastroni ran into the guitarist at the Sound Plus studio in Philly in October 1961. Mastroni had seen Roy playing with Dale Hawkins at the Tower Theater in West Philly in 1958 and been blown away. Now the two became friends, and at Mastroni's behest they recorded a half-dozen tracks at Sound Plus. A number of the tracks were simply '50s style pop, including a still-appealing rave up, "Daddy, Daddy," which featured Mastroni on vocals and Roy on a six-string bass guitar tuned one octave lower than standard guitar and played with a bone-crunching fuzz tone. Once again Roy insisted on recording a couple of his own tracks. One such effort yielded an untitled, unreleased instrumental that features an uptempo, country-style blues with guitar and saxophone trading licks and then echoing each other, careening into the fade-out. Roy's soulful picking on this tape predates by nearly a decade similar efforts by later luminaries such as Duane Allman, and it still sounds fresh and exciting. "There was only one take of everything we did," Mastroni would recall. "I told Roy what we were going to do and brrrmmp, there he was. We didn't rehearse anything. I'd hum a couple of bars, and *bang!* it was done."

Roy returned to the studio to help record the Temps' "The Shuffle" and "Mary Lou," which were released on ABC-Paramount Records to little fanfare, despite their solid groove. In time the group also recorded "Trophy Run" and "Braggin'," the former an instrumental built around Roy's guitar work and featuring a screeching Telecaster intro, the latter a rough-and-tumble blues featuring Butch Moore's excellent harmonica work that would be echoed more than a year later by the Yardbirds. The London band, featuring a young Eric Clapton on lead guitar, hit the scene in 1963 and a year later recorded with blues harmonica great Sonny Boy Williamson, who, while in England, met several British bands, including the Rolling Stones. Back in the States Williamson related his trip to Levon and the Hawks. The English bands, Williamson said, were "awful." "They want to play the blues so bad, and they play it so *bad.* They buy me everything, they treat me like God, but they can't play worth a shit."

Butch Moore's recollections of Roy's tenure with the Temps appears to be tainted by a long-standing belief that he and his brothers not only rescued Roy from evil, but taught the guitarist virtually everything he knew. "He had nothin' and nobody," Moore said. "He was a pretty good guitar player, but he became great with us." As for the Temps' performances at Dick Lee's, Moore conceded that Roy often drew the crowds. Unfortunately, he added, Roy seemed to have a monkey or two on his back. "His wife was on him all the time," Moore said. "We were all good-lookin'. Roy had bangs and a beard, the beatnik look. The girls loved him as much as they loved us, and Judy didn't like that. She was very jealous and came around to the shows as much as she could. He'd try to keep her away." By now Judy was pregnant with their first child, Laurie, who would be born in March 1962. Under the circumstances Judy could be forgiven for keeping close tabs on her husband and his increasingly freaky behavior. As with many relationships, that which attracted could also repel. Roy's bohemian approach looked good from a distance, but up close it could be vexatious in the extreme. His lifestyle increasingly seemed to revolve around amphetamines to perform, marijuana to cool out, and beer to come down. He was known to go missing in action after a gig. In sharp contrast, Judy wanted a large family and she would have one. Three months after the birth of their first child, Judy got pregnant a second time. Roy worked consistently to provide, but his wife let him know she didn't care for the trappings of his business. Though it was a life she chose, one can hardly blame her for misgivings. "Roy was messed up," Butch Moore stated flatly. "He was on a lot of stuff. We tried to get him off of it. He was a very strange guy. I taught him how to play harp. We'd be waiting to go play and we'd have to look for him. He'd be down by the river, sittin' in a rockin' chair, playin' harp." Or he might be shooting a bow and arrow, another hobby he'd taken up.

The Temps' performances, with Roy as resident virtuoso, created a reputation for the group, one that spread from Philadelphia to the resorts along the Jersey shore. Troy Page was a beatnik bass player in 1961–62 when he got in the habit of stopping at Dick Lee's to watch Bob Moore and the Temps and, more to the point, Roy Buchanan. Troy, like Roy, had a goatee and longish hair. According to Page, the public in the early 1960s had yet to recognize the value of different lifestyles. Someone with long hair and a beard could walk through a store and, Page recalled, "People would say, 'Oh! He's a hippy.' Or, 'No! He's a religious nut.'"

Dick Lee's was a rectangular room with a bandstand at one end, booths around the walls and tables to one side of the dance floor. It held fewer than 100 people. "On Saturday nights it was wall-to-wall people," Page said. "You couldn't move! You had to struggle to get through the crowd. The Temptations put on a good show. Bobby would do 'The Glide' in his patent leather shoes. Today they call that the 'Moon Walk,' but not even Michael Jackson could do it better than Bob Moore. Roy, he just stood back there. His chin had a funny movement, grinding side-to-side. I guess that was the way he felt his music." The band might do a ballad like "In the Still of the Night," or the Temps' own, "Am I the One?" and the next minute tear down the house on "Green Onions," a hit in 1962 for the all-instrumental group Booker T and the MGs, with the Memphis guitar slinger Steve Cropper on lead. At a certain point, a signal would be given, the lights would dim, and a spotlight would shine on Roy. "'Malagueña' was the big one," Page recalled. Malagueña had been penned by Ernesto Lecuona in 1948 for his suite, "Andalusia." (The song became popular in Anglo circles as "At the Crossroads.") "The whole place just sorta shut down when Roy started playing 'Malagueña,'" Page said. "He had some kind of crazy touch or feeling. I can't describe what it was. Maybe it didn't happen to everybody, but I'd be standing there with my mouth hanging open, the hair standing up on my arms. He had long fingernails on his right hand and all of a sudden he'd get this thing goin', he'd move the tempo up, like an express train, he'd be goin' 90 mile an hour. I'm wonderin', 'When you get goin' that fast, how do you get out of it?' He'd put the pick in his mouth and rap the strings with his long nails and get some crazy sound, then all of a sudden he'd be back in a standard tempo."

"A lot of the stuff he played, he played for musicians," Page said. "To this day every guitar man in South Jersey crucifies the E chord in imitation of Roy. He had guitar players sittin' all around that bar, tryin' to figure out what he was doing. I remember one particular time Les Paul and his son came in. They had a little tape recorder with them. But they got in a hassle at the door because they weren't dressed right, or something. Roy told me they'd been in before. He was very low-key. He could have had a big head. I mean, how many times does Les Paul come in to record you?"

By that time Les Paul had long since achieved celebrity as a performer with his wife, Mary Ford. His fame as a master guitarist and electronic inventor had been recognized in 1952 when Gibson issued its first Les Paul signature model guitar. Not only had he revolutionized the form and function of the modern electric guitar, he was an intrepid musicologist who made it his personal and professional business to encounter—to track down, if necessary—the great players of his time, famous or unsung. Paul once explained to DC music enthusiast Kevin Loftus how he learned about Roy. He found himself traveling to and from gigs in New Jersey and Pennsylvania on Route 46, where he checked the nightspots for players. A like-minded soul, possibly rocker Bill Haley, told him, "Hey, there's a guy down here who really plays the hell out of the guitar, and he's different. He's cruisin' down his own lane. His name is Roy Buchanan."

"We'd never heard anything quite like what Roy was doing. He interested the hell out of me. He's not playing an arpeggio the way you learn an arpeggio. If you had studied the instrument you played it right straight on, the chromatic scale you're taught in school. This guy was anything but conventional—he was just out there. He was unrestricted, as far as what he played. If he felt like getting from here to there, it didn't matter how he got there. If he didn't pick it, he plucked it with his other fingers. There were no rules with Roy."

Paul advised a colleague, guitarist "Thumbs" Carlisle, to go see Roy. "I told him, 'I don't think he plays like anybody. He's a mixture of everything. He's half blues, half country. He's not jazz.' It's like trying to describe what a banana tastes like. What attracted me to Roy was that there were no barriers at all. Whatever he felt like doing he did. He went off the fingerboard completely. He would just go up off where there were no frets. He also developed a thing that you can only do on a Tele-caster guitar—that is, you could hit a note and you could bring [the volume knob] up with your little finger and you could do your wah-wahs with it. It became part of his style. I did approach him to make recordings for Epic/Columbia with The Moore Brothers, but he wasn't interested. And he went *that* away."

Before Roy vanished again into the American night, Seymour Duncan, today a guitar pickup wizard in California and a talented player in his own right, was taken by his uncle to see Roy perform. "I wanted to go see every band that I could, to see what the guitar players were doing," Duncan recalled. "Everybody talked about this guy Roy Buchanan. He was bending strings. He played harmonics, which nobody had ever heard anyone do before. In between songs he'd be doing all these hand stretches. He showed me how to stretch all your fingers, so that when you begin to play you're already nice and loose. Guitar players never did that. He's the only guy I *ever* saw do that. That was real important to him, how limber he was. I remember going to Dick Lee's after I got off work. It would be 2 a.m. in the morning, there'd be eight people in the bar, and Roy would be playing his ass off. You have to respect that."

In this period, amazingly enough, an aspiring young guitarist named John Wynne, all of 13 years old, stood outside a Philadelphia club during a Temps gig and convinced a patron to take his portable tape recorder inside. The result has survived: a sonically crude, though musically revealing tape of Roy burning it up with The Temps in 1962. The band delivers competent versions of Bobby "Blue" Bland's 1957 hit, "Farther On Up the Road," Bill Doggett's "Honky Tonk" from 1956, a comic vocal number, James Brown's 1962 hit, "Night Train" (written and originally performed by Jimmy Forrest in 1952), "Malagueña," and what can only be described as a guitar freak-out based on the theme to Rimsky-Korsakov's "Flight of the Bumble Bee." The whole affair sounds pretty casual, with Roy toying with his solos on the first two tracks. On "Night Train" he plays the saxophone part on his Telecaster using the oblique bends that mimic the steel guitar. One senses from the sparse applause that this may have been a poorly attended matinee performance—until "Malagueña." A drum roll sets a dramatic mood (one can imagine the lights dimming), then in true flamenco fashion, Roy establishes the song's rhythm by thumb-picking on the lower strings while overlaying dramatic, finger-picking leads. The result is difficult to describe, but with changing dynamics, quiet passages, and a crescendo, the guitarist's finale draws a small explosion of applause. The guitar cadenza that follows "The Flight of the Bumble Bee" theme—is a free-form run of notes and chords, with screeching feedback—perhaps an outlet for a sideman getting terminally bored with his gig and beginning to slip.

In fact, one denizen of Dick Lee's later described a night when word spread up and down the street that Roy had gone absolutely haywire. At 2 a.m., the typically reserved guitarist had been seen running up and down the bar with his guitar plugged in, creating musical mayhem and stirring an after-hours audience to hysteria. This particular performance signaled the beginning of the end of his gig with the Temps.

Precisely what prompted the Buchanans' return to Judy's mother's house in Mount Rainier in spring 1963 is not clear. One suspects, from the foregoing incident, that Roy and the Moore brothers may have reached a mutual parting of the ways. The birth of the Buchanans' second child probably contributed. Donald, later known as Roy Junior or Little Roy, was born in March 1963. Many of the first wave of rock 'n' rollers had pregnant wives by this time and, therefore, strong incentives to adopt the acquired habits of a domestic lifestyle. In Roy's eyes the Temps gig had undoubtedly grown old after a year and a half. Roy's professionalism apparently wavered as his interest waned in playing the same gig day in, day out. The precipitating factor in Roy's departure, of course, might have been something else entirely. More than one observer has insisted that the Temps gig came to an end when Roy shot someone with his bow and simply had to leave town in a hurry.

*T*hirty-first Street in Mount Rainier, MD, ran through a leafy, turn-of-the-century neighborhood of brick bungalows where most residents owned their homes and greeted each other with the assurance of familiarity. Mrs. Owens had lived at 4215 31st for decades; it was Judy's childhood home. Not much had changed in the neighborhood since Judy and Roy left almost two years earlier. Ruth and Vivian Weinstein, longtime neighborhood fixtures, still ran Harry's Market a few blocks from the Owens home. For these two, one new blade of grass stood out in stark relief. In June 1963 when a strange-looking young man appeared at Harry's Market to buy milk and diapers the sisters paid close attention. Why, it was that Roy Buchanan, Judy's husband! The couple was roosting again at Mrs. Owens' house. With his long brown hair, his beard, and unsettling eyes Roy cut quite a figure. He hardly ever said much, though he responded politely in a soft Southern drawl when caught in conversation. Perhaps he was just shy, but one simply couldn't tell *what* he was thinking. The Weinstein sisters suspected the worst and watched him like hawks. There was something a little strange about this one, all right.

The Weinstein sisters' perspective spoke to the prevailing culture of Prince George County. Bohemian characters were not in demand. Suburban, predominantly white, blue-collar Mount Rainier lay well south of the Mason-Dixon line. Tolerance for diversity in race, ethnicity, or lifestyle was not a local trait. "Respectable" folks often belonged to the Ku Klux Klan. Confederate flags flew from front porches. In the vernacular of one latter-day observer, Mount Rainier in the early '60s was "a wild-ass, Southern white enclave." The arrival of a long-haired musician was unlikely to be viewed as a positive development.

For Roy the move to Mrs. Owens' house resembled a recurring nightmare. His happy-go-lucky lifestyle of arising at noon, poppin' pills, and playin' past midnight had come to an abrupt end. Suddenly he was back in his mother-in-law's home, surrounded by squalling babies and a relentlessly pedestrian existence. The first time he landed in Mount Rainier, circumstances beyond his control had brought him. He had escaped, Houdini-like, by conjuring up a session with Ronnie Hawkins and a gig with the Moore brothers that ran for more than a year. This time his own reckless ways had made smoking ashes of his job with the Moores. This time—with two already in the brood and Judy soon pregnant again—Roy could not slip his manacles. Judy, in contrast, enjoyed being back in her mother's house and pregnant once again.

Roy, all of twenty-three years old, would have to carve out a living locally using the only tools at hand—his Tele and amplifier. Fortunately, the time and place were ripe for working musicians. As with many American cities in the early '60s, Washington, DC, offered a relatively vibrant nightlife. Clubs clustered in several downtown areas and diverse audiences ate up the gamut of popular music on offer. That meant an abundance of work for a journeyman with Roy's talent.

Washington had a split musical personality, a reflection of the South's cultural duality. In the 1930s and '40s DC had swelled with white immigrants and blacks, as President Roosevelt's New Deal and the World War II years produced a surfeit of government jobs. White southerners brought hillbilly music and bluegrass, idioms that by the 1950s were known as country music. Black immigrants brought rhythm and blues and soul and gospel. Music crosses a lot of boundaries, but at least on the surface, in Washington, the races mixed less than, say, in Shreveport, LA. During the 1940s, '50s, and '60s, each audience enjoyed its favorite music via separate radio stations and nightclubs. Radio served as the cross-pollinating medium. Whites who loved "race music"—that is, the blues and R&B—simply had to stay awake late at night when black stations broadcast their fare.

Black audiences frequented clubs around 14th and U streets in the city's northwest quadrant, an area of 14th variously dubbed the Boulevard, or the black Broadway. In the '40s the Casino Royal hosted black pop singers such as Nat King Cole, the Mills Brothers, Cab Calloway, Ella Fitzgerald, and others. The Blue Mirror catered to jazz. By the '50s the Howard Theater provided an even larger venue for black entertainers and audiences. Even the suburbs of Prince George County, east of the city, had black-only nightspots such as the Evans Grill in Forestville, southeast of the capital. The Evans Grill was a mainstay of the South's so-called chitlin circuit, which provided a post-war venue for beloved performers such as Duke Ellington, B.B. King, Ray Charles, James Brown, Bill Doggett, Sam Cooke, and the Drifters.

Whites had their venues in DC and the Maryland suburbs, too, where taverns catered to Southern tastes in crooners and "gittar twangers." By the '50s promoter Connie B. Gay capitalized on the local devotion to live music by bringing in artists such as Hank Williams, Patsy Cline, Lefty Frizzell, Ernest Tubb, Hank Thompson, Ray Price, Jimmy Dean, Hank Snow, and Bob Wills, to name a few. This was an era when people poured from their homes in the evening to mingle, socialize, dance, and participate in the world—a world far removed from the insular, home-bound video and television culture of more recent times. The new element in Washington's musical mix, of course, was rock 'n' roll, which promised—or threatened, depending on your view—to bring the two races together. Bill Haley had gigged in DC as early as '53, and Elvis Presley hit town on his first national tour in '56. Long before Dale Hawkins and Roy appeared in 1958—the year Bo Diddley himself moved to Washington from New Orleans—the town had spawned rock 'n' roll nightclubs and developed a bit of a scene. Down on 14th Street a clutch of clubs, like Benny's Rebel Room, catered to revelers. Other venues included the Rocket Room at 1200 New York Avenue NW, Rand's at 1416 Eye Street NW, the Hayloft at 1411 H Street NW, and the Alpine Room at 312 Kennedy Street NW. Several of the city's main roads snaked outwards to the northern suburbs and another burgeoning nightclub scene. Rhode Island Avenue ran northeast, where Bass' and the 4400 Club at 4400 Rhode Island Avenue offered devotees of the new music a chance to mingle. Bladensburg Road boasted the Dixie Pig and the Crossroads, a former striptease club at 4103 Baltimore Avenue. Television also capitalized on the craze for rock 'n' roll. Beginning in 1956 DJ Milt Grant hosted a Saturday television show that showcased rock 'n' roll acts from around the country, including appearances by Dale Hawkins and his amazing guitarist. Hawkins played Milt Grant's show several times in 1958–60, planting the seed of Roy's eventual status as local legend.

To be sure, Roy had company on the DC scene—other ace guitarists operated at that time, including, among white players, power chord meister Link Wray, Jimmy Carter, Demetri Callas, and a young player named Jorma Kaukonen, who would migrate west and join the Jefferson Airplane. Among DC's "colored" players, blues man Bobby Parker had a long run of popularity beginning in the '60s. The DC area also included jazz giant Charlie Byrd, country picker Roy Clark, and a well-known classical guitar teacher, Sophocles Pappas. You had to be good to cut it on the DC scene, and the competition kept everyone on their toes.

AT HIS MOTHER-IN-LAW'S HOUSE, Roy set about hustling gigs. He probably called Joe Stanley first. The sax man had known the Owens family for years and his band, the Saxtons, had steady gigs. He obliged by putting Roy in the lineup whenever he could. The Saxtons gigged often at the Dixie Pig, the 4400 Club, and at Bass'. The guitarist also met and gigged with Cole "Sammy" Ghoens, aka Danny Denver, a local lounge crooner with enough talent and showmanship to garner consistent bookings and feed a few musicians. Roy joined the band known as Danny Denver and the Soundtracks, later the Soundmasters, for local gigs at the Crosstown Lounge and Strick's. Singer Fred Mastroni showed up in DC occasionally to visit and play.

Familiar faces were welcome; the bohemian guitarist felt like a fish out of water. He found Washington, DC, much different from Shreveport, even Philadelphia and the hip spots on the Jersey shore. "He hated Washington when he first came down here," Judy recalled many years later. "He said it was filled with a bunch of snots and it was hard to please them."

Working with Joe Stanley and Danny Denver was just a gig. Roy needed a real break and that took time. In the summer of 1964, however, he met a kindred soul, someone else with an eye on the big time and enough talent to have a shot at it. Singer and rhythm guitarist Bobby Howard had played with power chord king Link Wray for years. (Wray had achieved local notoriety with his overheated guitar work, his band the Raymen, and 1958's hit "Rumble," featured in the 1994 film *Pulp Fiction*.) And more importantly, Howard had gigs with his band, the Hi-Boys. In September 1964 Roy joined Bobby Howard and the Hi-Boys for a few months of steady gigs at Rand's downtown and at the Alpine Room on Kennedy Street NW ("For Young Adults, 18 to 80"). The singer later recalled, in a rare interview, that when he met Roy the guitarist was selling encyclopedias.

Howard and Roy found themselves in the midst of a trans-Atlantic musical phenomenon known since as the British Invasion. Essentially, British wannabe rockers had avidly absorbed American rock 'n' roll and blues and R&B throughout the 1950s and now they were exporting it back to its land of origin, with a fetching accent. The Beatles led the charge with their historic appearance on the *Ed Sullivan Show* in February 1964, followed by a raucous appearance at the Washington Coliseum, the first concert of their first American tour. The sensation produced by the Beatles' DC appearance impressed local rockers, and it irked them, too. From that moment on, British groups ruled or rivaled American bands on the American pop charts. As many DC players later testified, young white musicians in town were drawn more to R&B and soul than to the British copy cats then clogging the airwaves. Then there was the issue of authenticity. In the crudest terms, Roy Buchanan was the real McCoy that the Beatles' three guitarists wanted to be. Michael Bane, in his book, *White Boy Singin' the Blues*, called the Brits' efforts "a carnival funhouse mirror reflection of the American musical scene." For their part, the Beatles were effusive in their praise for the American rhythm and blues groups they emulated. The Rolling Stones, who would arrive on America's shores for the first time in July 1964, also had no illusions about their work. They knew where it came from, and they advanced its cause. To their credit, the British bands typically were quite humble. Asked on the snowy February day of their Washington, DC, appearance whether they or the snow would last longer, the Beatles said: "The snow."

They were wrong, of course. For years the Beatles, the Animals, Peter and Gordon, the Rolling Stones, and Herman's Hermits battled Americans like Roy Orbison, the Supremes, the Beach Boys, Jan & Dean, James Brown, and Bob Dylan for the top of the US pop charts. The British Invasion's effect on American bands, however, was powerful. Bobby Howard and Roy Buchanan may have been the real McCoy, but they saw the graffiti on the wall. In November 1964 they renamed their band the British Walkers. Former Hi-Boys Mike Kennedy on drums and Junior Gill on bass formed the group's rhythm section. Mitch Corday, a local hustler, managed the group. He had a talent, according to one observer, for "naming bands after something you thought you'd heard of." Alan White worked for Corday at that time and recalled: "Bobby Howard was a very clever fellow who in concert could only manage, 'Eh, luv, luv,' in a quasi-British accent, but everyone thought they were British." To aid the illusion Roy shaved his beard and joined his band mates in getting a "Beatles haircut" and wearing matching suits with English collars, with shiny, narrow-toed mod boots. The band recorded a regionally successful single, "I Found You," at Columbia Recording Studios in New York City, which featured distinctly Beatlesesque vocals and melodic hooks. On Dec. 4, 1964, *Cashbox* declared that the British Walkers possessed "a fine style and a smooth delivery that serves them well on this Liverpool-sounding rock ballad."

ROY HADN'T LOST his distaste for hokey get-ups and stupid dance steps. He was desperate! (The challenge presented by the British Invasion for American musicians was widespread; even the late king of Texas underground rock, Doug Sahm, formed a band at that time dubbed the Sir Douglas Quintet.) With "I Found You" garnering strong regional airplay, the British Walkers commanded sell-out appearances in the DC area, including stints at the Roundtable in Georgetown, from November 1964 to March 1965. When Howard hit the road, however, he had to leave his ace lead guitarist behind. Judy, expecting the couple's third child, put the kibosh on Roy's yearning to travel. Bobby Howard replaced Roy with local guitarist Jimmy Carter around January 1965, leaving Roy searching for another gig, perhaps one within easy driving distance of home. The guitarist's world began to shrink.

Still, Roy's name got around. Singers like Big Al Downing and Phil Flowers and, once again, Danny Denver, employed Roy to lend his sound to their bands. Sonny Pekerol noticed that during a stint at the Hayloft with one singer or another, Roy got in the habit of bringing his bow and arrow along to the gig. One afternoon a soused heckler got under Roy's skin. According to one purported eyewitness, the guitarist calmly reached behind his amplifier, drew forth his medieval tools, and fired. Some say the heckler received a flesh wound, while others say he was merely pinned to the wall through his clothing. In either case, Roy's response clearly departed from standard operating procedure for an entertainer.

In March 1965 Roy and Judy moved into their own apartment on Queenstown Drive in Mount Rainier. Sensing Roy's need to make more money, big band drummer Walter Salb invited the guitarist to teach at his shop. "Roy was a legend here in town," Salb recounted 35 years later. "I'd been to see him play with some country band. He was a little down on his luck, and I said, 'Come over and teach.' I never thought it would last, but I needed him. Every kid wanted to do a Beatles thing. The guitar had become the most popular instrument in the world. Kids wanted to learn three chords and become a star. Roy wasn't naturally a great teacher but he had such awesome talent and he had a great rapport with people in a quiet, Southern way." Salb saw in Roy not the ambitious talent Ed Montini had known, but, perhaps daunted by disappointments, someone resigned to his

Publicity photograph of the British Walkers, circa 1964. Note the mod haircuts and the shiny, narrow-toed boots, both favored by British pop musicians.

THE BRITISH WALKERS

Exclusively
CRUSADER RECORDS

Direction
PARAMOUNT ARTISTS CORP.
1745 K Street. N.W.
Washington, D.C.
Phone 296-6280

fate. "Roy never really had any ideas of fame and fortune," Salb said. "All he wanted to do was play the damned guitar and make some money. He had none of the rock 'n' roll bullshit illusions about fame. He had that real loose, Southern thing. He just wanted to play."

Between giving lessons the two would jam on bossa novas and other forms new to the guitarist. "I'd show him the structure and where it was going," Salb recalled. "I remember showing him 'The Girl from Ipanema.' It wasn't 30 seconds before he could play rhythm patterns, play lead all over it, and follow every goddamn change. It was almost instant. He was fascinated, a true player. He didn't care about the idiom. Bebop and jazz fascinated him because of the structure. It was more complicated, challenging, than the blues." The guitarist, in turn, showed the drummer a few things about the richness of the blues. "He had such an impeccable sense of timing. He was really a soul player," Salb said. He paused for thought. "Even when Roy was smokin' on the guitar, though, there was always a great melancholy. I sensed that underneath it all."

Roy stuck with teaching all of three months. "One Saturday he didn't show up and it was a loaded schedule," Salb said. "Finally, he called and said he couldn't stand it any longer. We had gotten along because I didn't put any pressure on him. The pressure Roy put on himself. Teaching just was not what he wanted to do."

Playing on stage, in fact, was what Roy wanted to do. Fortunately, Sonny Pekerol had just put together a band known as the Outcasts, with Pekerol on bass guitar and vocals, Steve Sneed on drums, and Vince Gedeon on keyboards and sax. They needed a lead guitarist. "We called ourselves Sonny Gordon and the Outcasts because Roy felt I needed a stage name," Pekerol would recall. "Roy had an answer for everything and, of course, I listened, because he was 'the man.'"

The Outcasts became popular at Rand's, at 1416 Eye Street NW, and at the Starlite, nearby at 1419 Irving Street NW. South Carolina singer Chuck Tilley occasionally lent his talents. Mike "Pokey" Walls, then a local teenage singer/drummer, caught the Outcasts at Rand's. "Every place had two bands, for nonstop music," he said. "That was a DC tradition. When it was break time for the performers, they went into Bill Doggett's 'Hold It,' because everyone knew it. You couldn't screw it up. One by one, the players in the second band would get up on stage and take over on their instruments, while the guys in the first band stepped down, keeping 'Hold It' going. We had an hour break, so I walked up the street to Rand's to see what was going on. The Outcasts were playing the Beatles' 'I'm Down,' and Chuck Tilley was singing his ass off. The DC bands didn't like the Beatles back then, we liked soul music. But I said to myself, 'Gawd! These guys are fucking awesome!' I noticed Buchanan right away, in dark clothes, with his beard, long hair, and bangs. I also noticed that his fingers were extraordinarily long. The pinky on his left hand was as long as the finger next to it."

Pekerol lured the guitarist into his band and made the most of it. In a three-inch ad for an Oct. 14, 1965, gig at the Starlite, the copy proclaimed in large letters: "NOW! 'MR. GUITAR HIMSELF,' ROY BUCHANAN with the Outcasts." Though Judy delivered Roy to his gigs, Pekerol drove him home—after the two had spent the wee hours of the morning parked down by the Potomac River, strumming their Martin acoustics, waiting for sunrise and for the amphetamines to wear off. If not happiness itself, this at least represented a familiar lifestyle, and it gave Roy a little breathing room from his sometimes fractious domestic situation.

Certain esoteric satisfactions accrued, upon occasion. The Starlite sat on Irving Street, around the corner from the Birdland, a black club. Pekerol knew the local headliner, Bobby Parker. "He was kind of like King Farouk, bein' the big guitar player around town," Pekerol explained. "One night he invited me over to Birdland to jam. He'd never heard of Roy Buchanan. So we went over together. We were the only white people in the place. Roy got up and played 'After Hours' and brought the house down. Bobby picked up his guitar, left the stage and, as he passes me, he says, 'What're you tryin' to do to me, man? Make me look bad?' He was furious!" Roy had always taken the road less traveled, in contrast to some of his more successful contemporaries. Around the time he played Bobby Parker's pants off in an obscure DC club—on Oct. 1, 1965, to be precise—Bob Dylan played his first electric set at New York City's Carnegie Hall, backed by none other than the Hawks, with Robbie Robertson on guitar. It is said Dylan had originally wanted to hire James Burton and Joe Osborn to back him, but Burton characteristically had a prior, lucrative commitment—he played in the house band on the *Shindig!* television program. No one could knock Burton for taking a predictable path, least of all Roy, who could bring home only a fistful of dollars on any given night, and those nights being few and far between. The Buchanans and their three small children suddenly moved to a new apartment, clear to Silver Spring, MD, after failing to pay the rent at their place on Queenstown Drive.

Meanwhile, Bobby Poe had taken up management for the Kalin Twins, a duo of singing brothers who'd hit it big in 1958 with their single "When." The Kalins had managed to leverage their one hit into three years on the road before they settled in their hometown to perform in local nightclubs. By 1965 the Kalins needed a backup band, and Bobby Poe and Mitch Corday arranged for Roy and his former British Walker mates, Junior Gill and Mike Kennedy, to fill the role. The band's saxophone slot got filled by various musicians. "Just before Roy we had two guitarists," Hal Kalin said, "but when Roy joined we realized he could magically play rhythm and lead at the same time. It saved us one guy's salary." To get his two-fer-one to the gig, Kalin was willing to drive to suburban Silver Spring, pick up Roy, drive downtown to the show, and return his guitarist home in the wee hours of the morning. Hal stopped in at the Buchanans' apartment on Christmas, 1965, and presented the couple's two toddlers with wristwatches. "They were thrilled," the singer recalled. The Kalins had regular gigs at Benny's Rebel Room at 829 14th St. NW, run by the bald and beloved Benny Mendelssohn, and the Rocket Room at 1200 New York Avenue NW, which Roy had played years before with Dale Hawkins. The rooms were typical of the blue-collar nightclubs of the era. They weren't dives, but they weren't high-class either. Benny's didn't charge a cover to get in, but the long, narrow room had "the smallest tables I'd ever seen in a nightclub" Herb Kalin would recall, so Benny could jam in as many servicemen and their dates as possible. The bandstand extended along one of the long walls. If patrons didn't order a beer swiftly enough, they would be asked to leave. At 2 a.m., the room closed, and Benny charged everyone two dollars to get back in, when no alcohol could be served, but coffee and hamburger plates were available to meet liquor law restrictions. The Kalins, like many bands in that day, booked into a room for six nights per week, two or three weeks running. The two singers dressed in tuxedos, while the band wore business suits with long, thin ties—"more like a funeral than a band," Herb acknowledged. Roy, Kennedy, and Gill played dance music to warm up the room, with Junior Gill acting as MC, occasionally hamming it up with a joke or an Elvis impersonation. Then the house lights dimmed and two spotlights caught the Twins as they strode out on stage to sing the hits of the day. The spotlights focused on the stars, making the band practically invisible to the audience, which worked well for the musicians. Roy had a habit of wedging a burning cigarette into the headstock of his guitar—though the Kalins noticed that sometimes he slyly substituted a joint of marijuana.

Today the brothers concede that their arrangements and choice of repertoire could be "square," but Roy helped them out. "He would show us a new lick, or a new beat—old songs, but with a blues feel," recalled Herb. "He actually helped us get off the pop kick we were on." "They were all strictly head arrangements," Hal added. "No charts." Roy introduced the Kalins to the music of Jimmy Reed and they adopted Reed's "Ain't That Lovin' You Baby," among other songs Roy suggested.

Still, Herb Kalin had the same impression Walter Salb had about their mysterious virtuoso. "Roy was not ambitious. He needed somebody behind him to push him. He just wasn't commercially oriented. He didn't care that much about success." Yet he cared about his craft. The Kalins recognized his talent by sharing the spotlight. "In the middle of the show we would call him down from the bandstand and he would stand in the middle of the room, surrounded by dancers, who stopped to listen. He'd play 'Malagueña' or take a solo." The guitarist enjoyed his time in the spotlight, yet he never allowed himself to confuse one thing with another, as Alan White, earlier associated with the British Walkers, discovered.

"'Malagueña' always blew everyone away," White said. "Well, we're all downstairs in the dressing room at the Rocket Room one night and I walked up to Roy and I said, 'Man, that was fantastic. You are the best, baby!' He started laughing. I said, 'What are you laughing about?' He said, 'Well, if you're going to be a big time booking agent, you've got a lot to learn.' I said, 'What do you mean?' So he picks up an acoustic guitar, puts one foot up on a chair, and plays 'Malagueña' with both hands. Everybody stops what they're doing. The Baumstein brothers come out of their office. The place is dead silent as he plays the song all the way through. At the end all the musicians broke into genuine applause. He turned to me and said, 'What I did upstairs was flashy.' He set down the guitar. 'What I just did was artistry.' He was just being matter-of-fact, and he was right. He wasn't showing off. He was just showing me the difference."

The Kalins and their sartorially challenged sidemen would head out after a gig for a bite to eat at the California Steak House on 14th Street, next door to Benny's Rebel Room, or they'd attend a party, where their quiet guitarist, with a few drinks under his belt, might become more sociable than usual. "I used to go to parties with Roy after jobs," Herb said. "I always got along with him. He did allude to someday he would do something to get attention and we didn't know exactly what he was referring to." Looking back over that period, Hal added: "He was definitely an introvert. It's amazing how many musicians never get up and dance, never do anything. They can play the music, but they don't want to participate in it. They're up there playing and most of 'em don't even know how to dance. All they do is play the music."

From Roy's perspective the gig couldn't last. By August 1966, during an extended engagement at Bass' in Mount Rainier, Roy couldn't make himself go through the motions any more. "One night when I went up there to pick him up," Hal recalled, "Judy came to the door and said, 'By the way, Roy's not coming to work today. He's quitting show business.' I said, 'Where *is* he? I've got a job tonight.' He came out of hiding in a closet and said, 'Yeah, I can't take it anymore. I'm quitting.' I argued with him. 'We've got a *job* tonight!' But he refused to leave the apartment. An hour before we were to go on, he suddenly decided he couldn't take the pressure of show business anymore! I can't remember how we got by that particular night. We did eventually hire another guitar player. We were irritated as hell at the time, but we also realized that he was kind of screwed up so we didn't hold it against him. We were friendly after that. He was a good enough musician that he could've gone with any group he chose. He got along with everybody and everybody liked him. I don't know what the problem was. I guess he needed a change."

THE MAN WAS NOT "quitting show business," of course, but he did need a change. Roy's mercurial spirit and his innovative genius were coupled with an inability to accept the mundane grind of a job that repeated more or less the same show again and again. Six sets per night six days a week crimped his soul. Yet he had to have a gig. As fall 1966 rolled around, Fred Mastroni, Roy's old friend from Philly days, tipped him off to a gig at the New Jersey shore. Roy somehow convinced Judy that the gig would be worth packing up the three children and moving to Somers Point, where he'd played so often in the early days with Dale Hawkins, The Bad Boys, and the Temps. Eventually she acquiesced, glad to have her husband in a regular job and close enough to keep an eye on. Roy may not have mentioned right away that the band he would join was named the Monkey Men.

The Buchanans got an apartment in Somers Point while Roy played guitar for his simian cohorts in the small circuit of clubs—Tony Martz's, the Dunes, the Bayshores—long familiar to touring musicians. In contrast to their last tour of duty on the Jersey shore, the scene had definitely changed in just a few years. Real craziness was loose in the country by this time and rock musicians were heading in progressive directions. Theatrics were in vogue, as were psychedelic drugs. The Monkey Men excelled at theatrics and, possibly, more.

When Mike "Pokey" Walls came to town with the Chartbusters and played Tony Martz's, true to habit, he checked out the local bands, including the Monkey Men, at the Bayshores, a club built out over the water. "The Monkey Men were like a biker-hippy band," he would recall. "They were like the Yardbirds, who had a 'rave up.' The Monkey Men had a thing they called a 'happening.' They'd tell Roy, 'Just freak out, man!' And Roy would do this wild stuff on guitar." They really got crazy, Mastroni said, with a smoke machine and lights flashing. One singer dressed as a preacher stood behind a pulpit spewing biblical passages, while another, dressed as a Nazi, cut the heads off dolls filled with meat. Even the Monkey Men's shenanigans did not ruffle Roy's stoicism. "No matter how wild the Monkey Men got, Roy just laid back and played his guitar," Mastroni said. The band's stated ambition was to make an appearance on the *Ed Sullivan Show* and commit suicide. "That was their ultimate goal," Roy later recalled. "Well, as soon as I found out about the suicide bit, I said, it's time to move on again!"

Mastroni himself played in town with a band called the In-Sex. "We were one of the first bands to have strobe lights, fog, fireworks, you name it," he said. "We'd ride offstage on motorcycles with chickens tied around our necks. We used to hang people in effigy. In fact, Alice Cooper played opposite us in 1967 and went to the West Coast with it."

Seymour Duncan, who'd been just a young teenager when he encountered Roy at Dick Lee's in Bellmawr a few years back, came through town with his band, the Sidekicks. Roy trusted Seymour as few others, so the latter got further insights into the master's techniques. "At that time the Monkey Men played 'Suspicious,' and Roy would mute his strings to make the guitar sound like a trumpet," Duncan said. "No one else could do that. Instead of playing straight notes, he would bend into them. You could feel the control he had over his playing style." How did Duncan get the famously reticent Telecaster master to open up? "I never came across as this guy who wanted to get everything I could from him. I was asking more technical things. Roy knew I liked *how* the guitar worked, along with the guitar playing. What made the guitar sound as it does? Why do different guitars sound different? He was learning, too. He already knew how to take a simple instrument and get the most complex sounds out of it, sounds that were scary. At times, in fact, there would be a certain psychological tension in the clubs when Roy played. I don't know how to describe it. You're watching the band and you know Roy's going to do something. He's going to come out and kick ass. It depended on his mood, and on who was in the audience, but when he felt feisty, he'd come out and blow you away."

As the autumn crowds thinned, the Monkey Men disbanded and Roy and Judy returned to Mount Rainier, inevitably staying at Mrs. Owens' house on 31st Street once again. Not long after their return, Roy and Judy left the kids with their grandmother and drove out to the Maryland shore. They had a wonderful day on the beach and a romantic evening. By the time they checked out of their motel the next day, Judy was pregnant with the couple's fourth child. The carefree weekend was an island in a stormy sea.

IN 1967 IT WAS THE SUMMER OF LOVE and new sounds were penetrating the music scene revolving around DC's Georgetown University. The proliferation of bands in the Georgetown bars offered Roy employment and, by all appearances, a minimum of pressure. Prominent among the clubs was an establishment known as the Silver Dollar. On April 6, 1967, the "New" Silver Dollar advertised "Go-Go Girls Nightly, Continuous Entertainment, Dancing, and The Fourmost, Featuring Roy Buchanan." Photographer John Gossage, then manager of the Discophile, a nearby hip record shop, frequented the Silver Dollar. The street-level club had two round windows—thus its name--and, inside, the long, thin room ran to a bandstand in back. Gossage and his classmates found Roy there and had a revelation. The guitarist was world-class, virtually unknown, and all theirs. "Roy met all the mythic givens that a bunch of wealthy kids around Georgetown could want," Gossage explained. "They wanted something authentic and Roy's certainly from another world. He plays the music they want to hear, requests, in what essentially was a covers band. He could easily imitate Cream." Seeking advice on his own fledgling guitar efforts, Gossage approached Roy backstage and found him low-key and approachable. "We talked about mystical things," Gossage would recall. "His sense seemed to be that the music just comes through you. You don't think about it." One detail in the unknown virtuoso stood out. "The eyes!" Gossage exclaimed. "He had those Rasputin eyes, like two beacons. I remember the intensity of them. He was slightly scary. He wasn't that much older than I was but he seemed a lot older. He was from that other world, that redneck world. He was slightly alien and he had this gift."

Guitarist Tom Guernsey, recently of the Hangmen, recalled his first encounter with Roy. "We thought we were hot shit," he recalled good-naturedly. "We were ridin' high, and I'm the lead guitar player. There were a lot of bands around at that time and we were coming out of the suburbs. We weren't a sham, but we weren't as good as some of the bands that were working every night down in Georgetown. We got 'in' the easy way by making a demo record that took off. We were downtown one night, gloating in our glory, going bar to bar, and there's this little bar called the Silver Dollar. I remembered that I'd heard of this guy, Roy Buchanan, and said, 'Let's go check him out.' We went in and sat down. The place was a dive. There were, maybe, 15, 20 people in there. I want to think the band was playing 'Groovin'' and Buchanan looked totally bored. He had his Telecaster pickup set to the bassy end. He looked like he was asleep. He was playing just the basic bar chords to the song. It's probably been built up in my mind, but the way I remember it . . . He's playing chords, no fills, kind of on autopilot. Then he came to a solo and I remember he flipped his pickup switch over to the treble side and—I don't remember what he played--but I was completely stunned. It was unhealthy. I suddenly realized that I was not on the same planet as this guy. I left befuddled, a little depressed. At first I said to myself, 'I'm going to practice like shit. I'm going to the woodshed and practice and come back and blow him away.' It didn't take me long to figure out that I just didn't have those kind of chops and never would. But I became a big fan. I had never seen anyone who could dig into notes the way he could." The juxtaposition of Roy's talent and his circumstances, gigging in a covers band, puzzled Guernsey. "I'm not a psychiatrist, but part of his thing seemed to be, if he was out of the limelight, playing with a mediocre band in a club where half the people weren't listening, he was free to be himself." That may have worked for Roy, but his lifestyle grated on Judy. Guernsey was at the Silver

Dollar one night when Judy arrived unannounced and launched into a huge row with Roy. "The bartender said to me, 'Get up there and play!' to cover the noise. I think I played 'Louie Louie' for 20 minutes."

WHEN JIMI HENDRIX arrived in Washington, DC, to headline five nights at the city's Ambassador Theatre, he sold out every show. Bassist Stan Doucette once claimed, though he later backed away from his story, that Hendrix came to the Silver Dollar one night during his Ambassador run, and jammed with Buchanan for hours. At that time Roy was gigging six nights a week at the Silver Dollar and other Georgetown bars with a litany of bands named, variously, the Devil's Sons, the Outsiders, the Four Skins, and other imaginative tags. With Stan Doucette on bass, Bobby Jones on drums, and Dennis Carl "Stoney" Lucci on keyboards and vocals, a band dubbed the Fourmost, sometimes the Uncalled Four, appeared in spring and summer 1967 at the Silver Dollar, among other venues. The Uncalled Four moniker had come easily, Bobby Jones said. "My dad would yell at us, 'That loud-ass music is uncalled for!'" It was all a far cry from the Monterey Pop Festival and the new generation of artists whose flamboyance and talent had made national news that June.

By fall a band called the Poor Boys, featuring Roy, contacted Norman Joyce at Philadelphia's Jolly Joyce Agency. Mr. Joyce told the boys there was plenty of work for a rock band in the Philly–South Jersey area. The band and their families moved to one of Roy's old haunts in Bellmawr, NJ, home to Dick Lee's Musical Bar, across the river from Philly. The agency arranged to have the band photographed goofing around in a junkyard for their publicity photo and sent them, when not booked solid into Dick Lee's, to Allentown and Bethlehem, PA, and to the Jersey shore, to venues in Wildwood and to Joe Pop's Shore Bar on Long Beach Island. The winter of 1967–68 provided constant gigs to nourish these bohemian souls.

Sometime in that period a bit of karma caught up with Roy. Back in 1961 he had borrowed $200 from Stan Weinberg to get married. Stan, in turn, had borrowed the money from Moose, the manager at the Top Hat in Virginia Beach. A year later, in 1962, Weinberg and his old sidekick, Ed Montini, were playing in Ocean View, NJ. "In walks Moose," Weinberg said. "He sits down at ringside. You couldn't miss him. He wore black horn-rimmed glasses. I said, 'Christ! I *know* why he's here.' Anyway, he says, 'Where's my money? That man never sent me a dime.' So I went to the club owner and got an advance on my pay and gave it to Moose. We sat down and had a drink together. Well, several years later, Roy was back in business, playing all over with The Poor Boys. I told a friend of mine, a pretty big guy, that Roy Buchanan owed me $200 and that he's playing locally," probably at the Jersey shore. "I said to this friend, 'There's a hundred bucks in it for you.' He goes down there. He sees Roy. He tells Roy, 'You owe Stan Weinberg $200. Get the money or I'll break every finger on your hands.' Roy got the money!"

A snapshot of Roy Buchanan and the Poor Boys, appropriately, in a junkyard, from July 1967. Roy is kneeling in the foreground, with bassist and singer Stan Doucette and Stoney Lucci on the right. Bobby Jones is on the left.

No, Roy was not exactly in step with the times: while the stars of psychedelia made a statement for their generation at Monterey, Roy was getting dunned by a goon in a darkened club.

STILL, THE CLUB SCENE had its moments. Stan Doucette remembered one night at the Aztec Club in Bethlehem, PA. "The club catered to a mostly Mexican audience, so towards the end of the night they asked for something Spanish, and Roy played 'Malagueña.' They shined a single spotlight on Roy, and we got off the stage. The whole place got very quiet. He sat there with a beer in one hand, tapping the strings of his guitar in a minor chord. He got louder, then stopped suddenly, placed his beer on the floor and stood up. With the spotlight on his hands he started picking the melody to the song, faster and faster, and the crowd began to yell like at a bull-fight. His hands were moving so fast they were a blur. Everyone was screaming and throwing coins and dollar bills! One man ran up with a tray of shots of tequila, and Roy drank one. Then he dropped his right arm to his side and went silent. The place became quiet again, and Roy began picking the melody to 'Lonely Bull,' and the crowd went berserk! When he finished I rushed up to him. He said, 'Look.' The fingertips of his left hand were bleeding. He said, 'I gave them what they wanted.' I said, 'You sure did, now let's go home.' Normally, Roy didn't like to be touched, but people were slapping him on the back and, that night, he didn't mind."

In the end the Jolly Joyce Agency could not offer enough gigs to feed a band and their dependents, and the situation got on everyone's nerves. "The band broke up in Wildwood when Roy went off on Stan," Jones says. "One night Roy had been out all night with the guys from another band, called the Temptations. It was a big holiday weekend and they were kinda blasted. We were up on the bandstand when Roy came in, sorta in a trance. He circled around through the crowd, got up on stage, plugged in an extra-long cord, and grabbed a mike. He yells, 'All right you motherfuckers! Now we're really going to *do* it!' Which was totally out of character for Roy, who was normally sorta quiet. He jumped off the bandstand, ran over to the bar, jumped up on it and ran up and down playin' 'The Jam,' the rocker he'd done with Bobby Gregg. It paralyzed the place! People spread the word, 'Buchanan's freakin' out!' and bands left the other bars to see it. People left their cars in the streets and rushed in." The scene fascinated everyone but the bar manager. "We got fired that night," Jones recalls, matter-of-factly. "The manager said, 'I knew it! I knew somethin' was going to happen! We've never heard music like this. If you guys don't get outta here I'm going to have a heart attack!' Later, Roy took out after Stan. Roy always carried this little hammer in his pocket for self-defense and he chased Stan into a closet and beat on that door until it looked like a hundred slug holes in it. He just freaked out." The debacle snowballed and band members and their families had to flee their apartments in Bellmawr, grabbing what belongings they could before getting locked out for failure to pay rent. Roy lost his prized red Rickenbacker steel guitar, the one he'd used in his lessons with Mrs. Presher nearly 20 years earlier. "That was his one and only possession, something he'd carried around all his adult life," Jones added. Thirty years later, the Buchanans' eldest, Donald, could still vividly recall the family's flight, providing a glimpse at the ordinary human cost of an itinerant musician's life. Roy and Judy gathered their clothes and three children and fled to Mrs. Owens' house on 31st Street in Mount Rainier.

THE YEAR 1968 turned life in America into a virtual kaleidoscope of disparate events— the good, the bad, and the unfathomable. In Roy's cloistered world, the spring brought intriguing news: Hendrix was returning to town. Jimi had just released his second album, *Axis: Bold As Love*, and was scheduled to play two shows at a ballroom inside the Washington Hilton on March 10. This time John Gossage made sure Roy had a ticket to see Hendrix perform. Gossage and his friend Paul Dowell would cover the event and interview Hendrix for a local underground paper known as *The Quicksilver Times*. The photographer wanted to build his rock 'n' roll portfolio for a book proposal and he indeed emerged from the day's work with an enduring photographic record of Hendrix in action in '68. Gossage had caught a couple of Hendrix's shows at the Ambassador Theatre the previous August and was determined that Roy experience Jimi, too. So when Roy stopped in at the Discophile record shop where Gossage worked, the photographer gave him a ticket to the earlier of the two shows at the Hilton. It seemed to Gossage like a rare opportunity to expose Roy to the hottest performer on the concert scene, but his secret mission really was to turn Hendrix on to Roy, if chance allowed. Roy definitely expressed interest in seeing Hendrix, Gossage recalls, though his wife was due with their fourth child any day. "When the 'Are You Experienced' album came out the previous August, Roy had been quite blown away by it," Gossage says. "It mattered to him. People were always handing him stuff, 'Oh, you've got to listen to Jeff Beck.' He didn't pay much attention to any of it. But Hendrix mattered." As it turned out, Judy had the couple's fourth child, Patty, on March 9. The next afternoon, while Mrs. Owens looked after her daughter and new granddaughter, Roy took a few hours off and headed for the Hilton. Judy had come through well. There was no good reason to miss *Hendrix*.

No doubt Roy hung at the margins of the young crowd to witness Hendrix's take-no-prisoners approach. The Voodoo Child opened with his riveting rendition of Howlin' Wolf's "Killing Floor," a soft reading of his magical paean to love titled, "The Wind Cries Mary," a down-and-dirty blues workout, "Red House," and delivered the psychedelia of "I Don't Live Today" in addition to a few of his radio hits, such as "Foxy Lady," "Fire," and "Purple Haze." After the first set, Gossage and Dowell followed Hendrix up to his room to take photographs and ask questions, while the rock star flirted with a young woman. "Hendrix was very nice, soft-spoken," Gossage reports. "We tried to convince him after the last show to go to the Silver Dollar and see Roy Buchanan. I remember talking to Jimi about Roy, and saying, 'This is someone you should see. He's the most phenomenal guitar player, outside of you. He came to your show.' Hendrix gave no sign that he knew who Roy was. It was real clear he had more interest in the young lady than he had in hearing any more rock 'n' roll."

GOSSAGE MADE IT to the Silver Dollar that night hoping Hendrix had decided to have a look for himself. Undoubtedly Jimi heard the same line—"there's a local guitarist you *must* see"—at every stop on his tours. In any case, Hendrix did not show up at the Silver Dollar that night. Later, at Roy's nightly set at the Silver Dollar, Gossage asked Roy if he'd gone to the concert earlier. "Yeah, I saw him," came the typically laconic reply. "He went on to play several Hendrix songs that night, you know, with one hand, while drinking a beer—all of Roy's bar tricks," the photographer says. "But from that point on, he had nothing but good things to say about Hendrix."

The contrasts between the two guitarists couldn't have been greater. Hendrix, all of 25, was a Seattle, WA, native, and he flashed flamboyant as the psychedelic warrior in his concert appearances. Dressed in outlandish outfits that combined bellbottoms, silk shirts, embroidered vests, scarves, and a black bowler adorned with gold chain, he moved to the music in erotic ways, and took to new heights the guitarist's shtick of matching his facial expressions to his screaming guitar. He was

Jimi Hendrix at the Washington Hilton, March 10, 1968.

black, a lefty, and played louder than anyone ever had previously—a pretty exotic picture that attracted groupies like moths to flame. Hendrix employed the high-end Stratocaster and the most expensive and powerful amplifiers and embraced the evolving technology of effects pedals.

Roy, then 28, had been in the business more than twice as long as Hendrix. The sartorially challenged hillbilly from Ozark and Pixley, in contrast, stood stock still while playing. He rarely displayed emotion, preferring instead to dwell solely on his craft. Roy was long married and the father of four. He stuck with his tried-and-true Telecaster and his modest Vibrolux amp, and took justifiable pride in producing sound effects with his hands alone. Where Hendrix sought the spotlight, Roy preferred the shadows.

Seeing Jimi seemed to produce a few revelations in Roy, one deeply disturbing. Technology had eliminated one of his competitive advantages: Electronic gadgetry, in the form of sound effect pedals, now allowed any player to produce the wah-wah effects that Roy had painstakingly pioneered on the Telecaster using only his hands and the volume and tone control knobs. The fuzz tone Roy had achieved using ripped speakers and overheated amplifier tubes had become readily available at the flick of a switch. The deep, gritty sound Roy had forged through a decade-long journey across America was now available in a box—and *that* was being hailed as revolutionary. Few could appreciate the irony of this as Roy could. Of course, a player had to have something to say, otherwise effects proved useless. Beyond the music itself, Roy grasped that Hendrix's stage act changed the way the game would be played. As an entertainer, Roy understood the power of theatrics. He possessed a keen commercial sense, and he was willing and able to explore virtually any commercially viable form of music. He simply wasn't capable of jumping around. Roy, being a shy, country boy, believed deeply in the intrinsic power of the music itself, without any visual spectacle. Ironically, so did Jimi, and he eventually regretted his theatrical approach. As he and his music progressed he felt less like jumping around and more like just playing his music, while his audiences seemed to demand the same old shtick. In that sense, although no one understood it at the time, Roy's down-home approach could not be surpassed merely by Hendrix's wild stage presentation. Still, Hendrix had won the spotlight.

Roy concluded that he would have to focus on his strengths, and continue to hone the remarkable control he had developed over his sound. That meant sticking with the elemental tone of a highly amplified Telecaster, and drawing on a songbook composed of the basic threads of American popular music, including country, blues, jazz, and roadhouse rock—no loud shirts, no leaping around, no stage act. Still, he absorbed from Hendrix the techniques he admired.

"Hendrix had made a leap in the kind of guitar playing that Roy also was investigating," Gossage said. "He'd found things that Roy had not found. I think Roy envied Hendrix's ability to write songs. The one comment I remember from Roy was that 'Hendrix had the fat tone, distortion-thing down.' This was the competition. Roy had once said to me, 'Clapton is a good guitar player.' And he left it at that. That Roy was on par with these guys, at this time, was not in question. It was a matter of fact. But I think he'd really *seen* the Hendrix show: the Marshall amps, the moves, the singing, the songs. He thought, 'I can't compete with that.' That brought him back to his roots, in a way. He might have been drawn to make his sound more contemporary. But seeing Hendrix made him realize, 'I'm *this* guy, and he's *that* guy.' After seeing Jimi he went back to the pure Telecaster sound as his claim to fame. And it was wondrous. It wasn't in the amps. It was in his hands."

In interviews in later years, Roy often paid tribute to Hendrix, waxing eloquent over the guitarist's style and delivery, though with a few justifiable caveats. Roy once told an interviewer, "To me Jimi meant the end to a lot of the trash that was happening. He opened the way for guitarists to really experiment and he advanced the guitar." Yet the two men's approaches to music and the guitar separated them, philosophically. "Whenever you play on a smaller amp, you're more in control," Roy observed in 1980 to John Swenson for *The Complete Music Magazine*. "I've always said that Jimi Hendrix's amps and guitars played *him*, he didn't play them. In other words, at that volume you have to work off of what's happening because you never know exactly what's gonna feed back and what isn't. When you're playing through a smaller amp, when you hit a note, you've gotta hit it. It's gotta be there." On the other hand, Roy recognized that the Voodoo Child had tapped into something. "I thought that the way Jimi Hendrix's playing was so abstract was really neat," he told Todd Everett for *Record Review* in 1981. "He was an electronic genius, the Les Paul of the '60s."

Les Paul had the unique perspective of having seen both Roy and Hendrix early on in their respective careers. In 1962 or '63, when Roy had been on the road for five years, Paul caught him at Dick Lee's in Belmawr, NJ. Les ran into Hendrix in 1965, before the latter had achieved any notoriety, also in a New Jersey club. "Roy Buchanan and Jimi Hendrix had some things quite in common," Paul said in an interview with journalist Kevin Loftus and John Adams of New York City's public television station WNET. "It seemed as though I was hearing them come first from Roy Buchanan, whom I'd heard prior to Jimi Hendrix. I was hearing a lot of effects. For instance, those high harmonics that'd come in and they'd just squeal at you. They were not related, necessarily, to what was goin' on at that time, but they sounded great. Mostly they would give you one helluva lift. I liked that. Roy would play runs that no one is going to write and make any sense out of 'em. But they sure fit. And that interested us an awful lot. Roy Buchanan probably was one of the creators in the pioneering of unusual sounds. It seems as though he, like a lot of us guys, were out there looking, chasing sound, and trying new things. I was doing my thing, Roy was doing his thing and, later, Jimi Hendrix did his thing. These things attracted us to one another. We included it in our style, we tried to absorb as much of it as we could. As for others, in many cases, if you don't understand it, don't try to play it. It became a natural thing for Roy Buchanan to play what he played. He just belonged there. But it didn't belong with anybody else. The same thing applied to Jimi Hendrix."

As it turned out, there *was* a significant connection, a chain of events that led from Roy to Hendrix, though no one knew it at the time. Roy's protégé, Robbie Robertson, had played guitar on blues singer John Hammond's second album, *So Many Roads*, recorded in 1964 and released in early 1965. The record reflected some of Robertson's search for, and mastery of, "that stinger thing" that he had sought to absorb from Hubert Sumlin's style. Robertson's performance on Hammond's album also reflected the the wild, squealing Telecaster picking style imparted to him by the wolf-man, Roy Buchanan. When in the summer of 1966 Hendrix met Hammond in Greenwich Village and the two formed a band, Jimi told his new friend that he'd been heavily influenced by the guitar stylings on *So Many Roads*.

IN THE "OLD-SCHOOL" VIEW—in the eyes of professional rock 'n' rollers like Roy who'd been at their craft since the '50s—the psychedelic movement meant two things: a lot of incompetent players were flooding the market, and the audience for live music had expanded. The sometimes amorphous nature of the new music tended to be forgiving if technical prowess was lacking. It certainly didn't require the razor-sharp ability to rock on command, as in the movement's early days. Still, a younger generation wanted to hear live music and that meant that a local musician like Roy could pick up a gig virtually any time.

Having grown up on the music of the 1940s and '50s, Roy could offer a broader perspective than most local musicians. In the Georgetown clubs that catered to the local college students he performed languid versions of his old standbys, "Susie Q," "Malagueña," and "After Hours," as well as a few standards, like Bill Justis'"Raunchy," from 1957, or Jimmy Reed's "Baby, What You Want Me to Do?" from 1960. He could throw in a few Hendrix covers such as "Purple Haze" and "Foxy Lady," from Hendrix's 1967 debut album. Done to a slightly slower tempo, the Hendrix songs served as vehicles for whimsical explorations. On "Purple Haze" in particular the guitarist used his patented busted-speaker and overblown amplifier tubes–fuzz tone and toyed with the melody, sometimes picking it out with ringing harmonics that mimicked an Oriental theme. The guitarist effortlessly delivered Cream's "Sunshine of Your Love," which had hit the airwaves that spring. While lesser guitar players were inspired to attempt Eric Clapton's leads in the song, Roy easily mastered the lead guitar part and pushed it to the limits. He tossed off an instrumental version of Bobby Gentry's "Ode to Billy Joe," a hit from the previous year that he liked to work out on. He'd knock off down and dirty shuffles and uptown blues as well. His amusement at the sudden cachet of "psychedelic" sounds—not to mention his personal brand of cynicism—is reflected in comments he made to writer Bill Holland years later: "How did I play that psychedelic shit? I'd already done it years before, if you want to know the truth. It was just feedback and busted speakers–type stuff. You just give a little volume to it . . . ."

On a good night Roy and his pals delivered robust sets—five or six of them, in fact—every hour on the hour. They might play a five- or six-night engagement. They could play pretty much whatever they wanted, as long as it pleased the crowd, a condition any journeyman could appreciate. Inevitably, however, as in the past, the grind blunted Roy's enthusiasm. He had continued his liberal, even reckless use of amphetamines and in this period his playing sometimes possessed a jaded quality. In a rare tape from May 1968 his performance ranges from razor-sharp to oddly distracted. The music exudes a certain ennui, a mesmerizing, hypnotic quality. The overall effect is part genius, part garage band. Still, when it was fresh, the music blew away the aficionados in the audience who grasped the stature of Buchanan's playing.

While obscurity provided a level of artistic freedom, a simple contrast between Roy and his old friend, James Burton, at this juncture highlights the guitarists' respective paths. As Roy toiled in anonymity in Georgetown, Burton led the band that would back Elvis Presley in the singer's 1968 comeback performance in Las Vegas. That was typical of the difference in approach between the two players. Buchanan, the lone wolf, would not have wanted the job backing Presley. But any professional musician would have to admire Burton for landing a lucrative, prestigious gig.

One night a local young hotshot named Danny Gatton, five years Roy's junior, visited the Silver Dollar and fell under the Telecaster master's spell. Forever afterward, Gatton's guitar style—more an eclectic repertoire of techniques collected from other people's styles than an original sound—often mimicked Roy's. Some mistook Gatton's amazing dexterity for originality, and spoke of a rivalry between the two. Indeed, a virulent lore has sprung up in DC circles that the two would don disguises, even false beards, to catch each other's act. Or that a confederate would call one of the guitarists on the pay phone from a bar where the other was performing, and leave it off the hook, so one could listen in on the other. Over the years, however, it became clear that Gatton had speed, great musical sense, stunning chops, and a sensibility that allowed him to play virtually any style. In contrast, Roy had a trademark sound, a wholly original approach, a depth of soul, and the ability to express it in unique phrasing that made him one of the premiere stylists in American popular music. Take your pick.

For Alan Scheflin the choice was easy. When he heard Buchanan, a world opened. All of age 24, Scheflin already taught law at Georgetown Law School and philosophy at Georgetown University. He remembered a trip to the Discophile, where John Gossage was working. "John said, 'Do you like Eric Clapton?' I said, 'Yeah.' He said, 'Well, then listen to Albert King.' And he put Albert King on, and it was clear Clapton had taken that stuff note for note. I thought, 'Jeez, that's really amazing.' So for a while John educated me as to what was going on, and introduced me to people who really knew the music. He said, 'Listen, you like guitar music. Go across the street to the Silver Dollar, you'll hear the best guitar player in the world.' So I went."

"There aren't words to describe what it was like hearing Roy Buchanan for the first time around 1967," Scheflin said, his voice still tinged by wonder. "Nobody was playing that kind of music. It was riveting, so intense it captured your complete attention. Yet it was musical. The guitar had a sinewy, infectious quality, like a snake that penetrated your soul. Roy's awe-inspiring command of the music always impressed me. There's no tentativeness. Some players will sound tentative because they don't want to take chances. Roy would just as soon jump off a cliff. James Burton, for instance, could make something sound melodic and commercial, but Roy was more interested in sound. His raw guitar sound just grabbed you. I'll never forget his fingers. They were wonderful to behold—like spiders that danced across the strings. Sometimes one hand would freeze and the other would dance, sometimes they both danced. There was a poetry, a ballet, in the way his hands moved."

Mike Botto also attended Georgetown University then. He too was smitten with the "magical world" of the electric guitar. "The audiences at the Silver Dollar loved Roy, and he responded in kind," Botto said. "It was cool if you were a fan, because you could literally sit five feet from Roy Buchanan with nobody between you and him. Oh, it was awesome. You could buy one beer and sit there for four hours." Eventually, admirers like Botto met Roy and got friendly. The student asked the guitarist if he could tape a set and Roy assented, with the provision that the result not be circulated. Botto subsequently made a 90-minute stereo tape that opened a window onto Roy's music at this time. "He really liked the psychedelic, bluesy music popular in that time," Botto said. "After all, he'd been experimenting with feedback since the late '50s. He didn't have to work to come up with these sounds, they just came out of him. Guitarists would come to see him. He was very consistent, from night to night, in his ability to go off into that other level where he's just playing his heart out, especially if he had a good audience. When he got into a song and went off on it, it was an experience you don't often get. There's a couple songs on that tape that really capture that. There's some melodic stuff there where he follows a thread . . . He told me one time that when he's playing like that, he's not even thinking about it. He's thinking about the next song, or what he's going to do tomorrow, and the stuff just comes out of him. He'd take Top 40 stuff and push it over the edge. When he was playing from the depths, it sounded like he was crying, or screaming, or it would get incredibly beautiful. There was so much there. I think playing was the only way he could get it out, and I don't know if it served him well."

Though the cultural chasm between performer and audience might appear great—a poor boy from down Arkansas-way, consorting with upper-middle-class college students nearly ten years his junior—Botto didn't detect any distance on Roy's part. "I think he appreciated the fact that we were there to hear the music." Yet Roy did have a natural reticence and, occasionally, a chemically induced mood that could prevent one from getting to know him. Botto simply brushed that off and invited the guitarist over to his house to relax. This proved deeply beneficial for Roy. "We took him over to my house after his set, smoked pot, and listened to music," Botto said. "He liked it. He literally stopped doing speed in any significant way. When I first met him he was doing a lot of speed. I mean, hundreds of pills. He was right on the edge. One day he told me that he'd been doin' so much speed and had been up for so long, his fingernails hurt, and his teeth hurt. He was just a wreck. The pot helped him get over what he was into with the speed. Wherever I bumped into him after that, all over the country, through the years, he'd introduce me to people as 'the guy who saved his life.' It meant something to him." As Roy later recalled: "One night these total strangers, these college kids, saw the kind of shape I was in on stage and dragged me off to their place for a couple of days. They really managed to talk me off drugs."

The "cure" seems to have coincided with a growing awareness in Roy that his personal path and the road to success in the music business had long since diverged. Perhaps his impending 29th birthday weighed on him. He had a family of five to feed and gigging at clubs did not pay enough for him to cover the rent, buy groceries, and meet other mundane living expenses that many take for granted but that too often become issues in a professional musician's life. Roy's spirit was exhausted, his soul drained. Perhaps he decided, or agreed with Judy, not to pursue further work in the Georgetown clubs. The lifestyle had been ruinous. Just as the transition from little money to no money threatened his and his family's existence, however, Sammy Ghoens, aka Danny Denver, called and offered Roy a decently paying gig as lead guitarist in his country/pop band, the Soundmasters. Roy ruefully accepted. The irony must have been supreme even for him. He couldn't go on playing his own music because of the unbearable grind of relentless club performances, the psychic drain of toiling in obscurity and the temptation of getting high. Suddenly, desperate for money, he hired on with a star-struck lounge act who, nonetheless, had a great voice, a popular stage show, and steady gigs playing for the DC and Maryland bouffant-and-pompadour country crowd. Roy donned a suit and delivered appropriately twangy country guitar for smiling Danny Denver. It sounds jarring, but Roy also had the resignation of the journeyman: Playing the mercenary simply meant drawing on different aspects of his musical heritage to bring home some cash.

The Soundmasters sometimes included Roy's old friend Stan Doucette on bass guitar, and they played every country room in the DC area that would have them. One regular gig took them to the Stardust in Waldorf, MD, a redneck enclave south of DC, where they recorded a lasting testament to Danny Denver's stage act titled *Live! at the Stardust*—lots of straight country, loopy medleys and impersonations, plus maudlin pop. Denver could veer from Merle Haggard to James Brown in one breath and the results were as bizarre as could be expected. So, apparently, was the milieu: at the Waldorf Club in southern Maryland, Doucette recalled, caged go-go girls danced above the stage while Denver, "a gifted bullshitter," worked the crowd.

Though Judy Buchanan forever sang Danny Denver's praises for the number of times he pulled Roy's chestnuts out of the fire, others were less impressed. The Kalin Twins had occasion to cross paths with Danny and they were disturbed at what they found. As Herb Kalin recalls, "He came to see us working one night, and I went to see him working one night. I was interested in him because we'd do impersonations and I'd heard that he did them too. I found him to be absolutely out of his mind, almost impossible to talk to—I'm talking serious mental illness, not just weird. As an entertainer he was very good. His impersonations were funny. After the show, he brought me backstage and he said, 'Now, I want to tell you something. I don't tell many people. One of these days I'm going to be the biggest name in show business. I'm going to be far bigger than Elvis Presley. In fact, I've already had offers . . . I could go on the [Johnny] Carson show tomorrow.' He went into this ridiculous thing about how great he was, how he would astound the world . . . There was something wrong there."

That never bothered Roy, at least at first. But inevitably the familiar grind of six sets a night, six nights a week doing the same damn set again took its toll. After several months with the Soundmasters a certain weariness crept into Roy's soul. He wanted out of the gig, out of "the lifestyle" he had resumed. Judy was increasingly concerned about her husband's erratic behavior and she called their old friend, Marc Mathis, in Nashville, for help. Mathis, who'd played with Roy in Dale Hawkins' band, brought him down to the country music capital, got him a room on Franklin Road across from the Acuff-Rose music publishing offices, and landed him a gig and a session. With Roy in Nashville, no money, and few prospects, Judy and the children moved back into Judy's mother's house in Mount Rainier. "At that time," Judy recalled, "he was living in the fast lane. I was concerned about him, and overwhelmed. We weren't making any money, we were surviving."

First Mathis took Roy into the studio to record five pop vocal tracks Marc had written with Larry Henley. (They never saw release.) That much went smoothly. Roy's gig as lead guitarist in the house band at Boots Randolph's Carousel Club, however, "went to hell" in a couple weeks, according to Mathis. "He was a mess," Marc recalled. "I tried to set him up with a session, then I went on the road. When I got back someone called me and said, 'I thought you said he could play.' I said, 'He *can* play. He's probably the best guitar player I've ever heard in my life!' Well, they told me that he had gone to the session, sat down, laid the guitar face down in his lap, and didn't speak to anybody. I called him, and he was higher than a kite. I went over to the motel and I said, 'Roy, I got some bad news for you.' He said, 'They didn't like me.' I said, 'You never played nothin'!' He said, 'When I walked in, I could tell they didn't like me.' I said, 'Roy, man, I don't know what else to do!' He apologized: 'I'll straighten up.' I told him I'd pick him up for another session and go there with him. I was desperately tryin' to help him. So for about two weeks he was doin' great. I had to leave town again, go out on the road. I came back and went to his room and he was gone." Unfortunately Roy *was* gone. He had fled problems in DC by running to Nashville, only to reverse the process a few weeks later.

With his 30th birthday still ahead of him, with Judy pregnant yet again, desperately needing normalcy in his life, Roy laid down his axe and picked up a pair of scissors. He enrolled in the Bladensburg Barber School on Annapolis Road through the auspices of the Maryland Department of Employment Security's Manpower Development and Training Act. The course lasted 30 weeks. Just as Jimi Hendrix embarked on a brief tour of European capitals in early January 1969, Roy met Gilles J. Maisonneuve, owner and instructor of the barber school. "Mr. Gil," as he still is known to his students, supervised Roy as the guitarist learned the fundamentals of his trade. As long as Roy showed up each morning for hair-cutting lessons and a little practice on unsuspecting locals, the state paid him $42 per week, plus $25 each week for food for his five dependents. On his character reference form, he gave Mrs. Owens' address in Mount Rainier where he and Judy were living, once again. He allowed that he was a self-employed musician of ten years' duration who'd been born in Ozark, AR, 29 years earlier. His education, he scrawled, had ended in the 10th grade.

His apprenticeship lasted until the first week of August. He collected a few dozen dollars each week from the state of Maryland and rarely picked up a guitar.

There was a degree of comfort in total obscurity. Roy experienced some relief that he'd laid down a burden. His immediate world was quite familiar and, for the moment, that was enough. In June, Judy had given birth to the couple's fifth child, David. Judy had the throng she'd always wanted, and Roy did his best to feed them, clipping strangers' locks.

CONSIDER A SNAPSHOT of the world that lay outside Roy's vision. It was in August 1969 that the Band, aka the Hawks, issued its first record, *Music from Big Pink*. Critical reaction was universally ecstatic, from the Beatles to Cream to Al Kooper, who wrote in *Rolling Stone* that "I have chosen my album for 1968. *Music from Big Pink* is an event . . . It's that good old, intangible, can't-put-your-finger-on-it 'White Soul' . . . like church music." Kooper lauded Robbie Robertson's songwriting skills—and those of Richard Manuel—though he did not cite the guitarist's skills with a Telecaster. Instead, he captured the essence of the Band's success when he said it was "a fortunate blending of the right people in the right place, etc. . . . " Indeed, the Band succeeded as an ensemble, the whole proving stronger than its parts. Each member had chosen community over the lonely path of the journeyman. That summer, Eric Clapton hitchhiked to the Catskills to pay homage and to taste the American roots he would never have. Ronnie Hawkins heard *Big Pink* and wasn't quite sure what to make of it. He later told Barney Hoskyns that he was "shocked," having anticipated that the group's first record might approximate "Howlin' Wolf on Benzedrine." "I mean," Hawkins sputtered, when *he* knew them "they didn't even *like* country music." But, the Hawk allowed, "When Robbie brought me the tape I said, 'Goddamn, that's country as hell. But it's funky country, and I like it.' "

On a more distant horizon, perhaps beyond Roy's awareness—certainly beyond his concern—the Beatles were rumored to be disbanding. The Jimi Hendrix Experience *had* exploded, as had Cream. In July word spread that the Rolling Stones' charismatic Brian Jones had been found lifeless in the pool at his estate, Cotchford Farm, south of London.

Meanwhile, Roy attempted to master the various applications of scissors and comb. His graduation from barber school came just two weeks shy of the three-day Woodstock Music and Arts Fair in Bethel, NY, an event that may well have escaped his notice. Many pop concert-goers that summer demanded that the music be "free" for "the people," a sentiment that, had it ever reached Roy, would surely have drawn bemusement. Peace and love were okay with Roy, but as a journeyman he would not take a shine to playing for free.

With a good word from "Mr. Gil," Roy went to work in August 1969 in a barbershop in Clinton, MD. An unconfirmed anecdote has him clipping a patron's ear and abruptly taking his craft elsewhere. Later, Roy cut hair at a shop in the Montgomery Mall in Prince George County. There is no evidence to suggest that Roy ever cut hair effectively. But, if he is to be believed—and that is a gamble—fate found him at his job one day that fall.

"I was doin' a guy's hair the day I first saw it," Roy later recalled. "A guy comes walkin' down the street and I recognized my guitar. I'd never seen it before. I'd never seen this particular guitar. But I knew that guitar was mine. I walked out, right in the middle of a haircut, and I said, 'Where'd you get the guitar?' He said, 'Some guy in Virginia sold it to me.' I just told him, 'I want it.' Usually you'd start trouble like that. He might think I was trying to take it from him or somethin'. But I said, 'What kind of guitars do you like?' He said, 'I like real beautiful guitars.' I said, 'I'll get you the most beautiful guitar you've ever seen and I'll trade you straight across.' I left work that day, and I knew a friend of mine who had connections. [I told him]: 'I want a purple Telecaster.' And he had it before the sun went down and brought that guitar out to me and I went by where the guy was playin'. I said, 'Here's your guitar. Where's mine?' He said, 'Here it is.' We swapped, man. That was it. It was like he knew it was my guitar too for some reason. It just belonged to me. I don't know why or how to explain it. It was *mine*."

It's a great story, one that is disputed by Roy's good friend and hanging buddy from this period, Elwood Brown. Brown told writer Bob Berman that Roy was playing with a Les Paul in this period. Other guitarists would bring Roy their guitar "finds" to see what he thought. According to Elwood, Roy swapped the Les Paul for Charley Jones' latest discovery, a 1953 Telecaster. Roy liked the sound so much the two never swapped back.

In any case, Roy's excitement at finding his instrument—a chipped and weathered 1953 Telecaster, serial number 2324, with its honey-finished, cutaway ash slab, maple neck, and black pick guard—meant his love for playing music had not died. He found kinship with a guitar whose tone ran as pure and clear as the bells of heaven. Many years later *Guitar World* magazine wrote, more tersely, that the 1953 Telecaster "featured long sustain and an ability to perform at louder volumes . . . [it] combined economy and durability." Economy, durability, solid sustain, and the ability to perform at loud volumes? This guitar became the instrument through which Roy would express his joys and sorrows, his thoughts and dreams, for many years to come.

THE CRUCIBLE

*B*arbering didn't last. Roy gave it his best effort but, as autumn chilled the air, it brought the realization that cutting hair wouldn't support his family and, of course, it couldn't compare to the thrill of rock 'n' roll. The only benefit, and a not inconsiderable one, was that it allowed him to escape the steep-sided trench he'd dug for himself in the course of more than a dozen years in the entertainment business. The years toiling in the Georgetown clubs, indulging in amphetamines and beer and dabbling in everything else, including psychedelics like LSD, had dulled the edge of his secret ambition to be the greatest guitarist in the world. He might well be, but he worked in obscurity, unrecognized for his pioneering techniques and emotive powers. His growing family filled his world with joy, even as it narrowed his options. A certain resignation crept into his bones. He was all of 30 years old and, for a rock 'n' roll guitarist, heading over the hill. He wasn't hustling for a record contract, or a gig. Still, though the thought of "making it" had long since become a bitter joke, laying down his axe entirely proved impossible. He dusted off the '53 Telecaster and considered his options.

He may have hooked up with Danny Denver and the Soundmasters by this time. It is certain, however, that at this juncture Charlie Daniels called. Charlie, a guitarist and fiddler, had opened the Rocket Room in DC way back in 1959 with his band the Jaguars—at the same time that Dale Hawkins and Roy Buchanan blew through town, leaving the place in tatters. Yes, Roy and Charlie went way back. Being Southerners—and, therefore, the truest of the true early American rockers— there had been a rapport from the beginning. "I went down to the Rocket Room on an off night and saw them," Daniels says. "Roy was like this wild guitar player. Nobody in DC was playing that way. They were doin' that Southern blues-rock kind of thing. "Susie Q". . . Three-chord, straight down the middle, rock 'n' roll type stuff." A decade later, in September 1969, Charlie Daniels had already entered the producing business in Nashville, thanks to a connection with producer Bob Johnston, who had successfully recorded Bob Dylan, among others. Daniels moved on to a relationship with Polydor, where someone listened when Daniels described his old friend, Roy Buchanan. "Everybody in the music business knew who he was," Daniels would recall. "Roy was hard to hide. He was just brilliant. There was some interest by Polydor. Things fell into place and we did an album." The sessions began in October at Woodland Studios in Nashville. Woodland, a former movie theater, at that time featured one large room for recording. Daniels gathered his longtime crony, singer Taz DiGregorio, keyboardist Bob Wilson, bassist Tim Drummond, and Karl Himmel together at Woodland, with local sound engineer Ernie Winfrey handling the console. "I had grown up in Nashville listening to WLAC—to rhythm and blues—so this was right up my alley," Winfrey recalled. "Charlie told me what to expect before Roy even got to town. I was gleefully rubbing my hands together in anticipation of doing this album."

Just to get Roy into the studio had been a chore for Daniels. At first the guitarist disavowed any interest in recording. His new, more cynical attitude towards the music business translated into an almost shamanistic reticence to have his sounds captured on tape—in contrast to his attitude just a few years earlier. A modest advance from Polydor may have turned the trick, in tandem with Daniels' good ol' boy charm. The sessions began in October but only lasted a few days at a time because of Roy's reluctance to stay away from home. The band reconvened the following January, then again in July 1970, completing a baker's dozen tracks that ran the gamut from a gut-wrenching blues—on which DiGregorio sang the lyrics to T-Bone Walker's "Stormy Monday"—to Leonard Cohen's haunting "Story of Isaac," to some classic Charlie Daniels–style country rock and a bit of melodramatic early '70s schlock. For the most part, Daniels wrote the songs and directed the sessions. Roy insisted on playing a blues and the "Stormy Monday" jam scratched that itch. But, for the most part, he played the role of sideman rather than featured artist. On "Story of Isaac" Roy developed a signature lick that would later became his personal anthem, "The Messiah Will Come Again." In contrast to earlier days, when Roy played on other people's sessions in exchange for a chance to record his latest showcase, the guitarist did not arrive at Woodland bursting with ideas and eager to explore them. By this time Roy had been through his own private hell and he did not seize the day. At this stage he knew better what he didn't like than what he really wanted. Roy arrived at Woodland with an open mind, but no material. Daniels had to build *something* around Roy's talent and deliver it to Polydor. Daniels' instinct told him to make a record his own way, and coax the mercurial virtuoso into adding the spice. Roy was easy, at first.

For the most part the results were pedestrian. Daniels' songs are classic '60s and '70s rock: a bit melodramatic, occasionally trite. There's country picking, ballads, and rock 'n' roll. Predictable, and yet . . . There's a glimpse of the band's potential at the tail end of a typically unremarkable song, "Billy Joe Young," when the band meanders off for a couple of minutes of playful, tasty jazz riffing. But it was not to be.

By November 1970 plans were still on for the release of an album culled from the Woodland sessions, but a month later Roy told an interviewer: "I'm just not playing well on it, and I don't get the chance to really let loose." By the new year the deal was off. Later, Roy would claim *he* had canned the LP because it misrepresented him. Daniels recalls that Polydor itself did the canning. "It just didn't work out. Nobody knew quite what to do with Roy, including myself."

During the sessions at Woodland, Roy BS'd with his band mates, swapping stories and telling whoppers. With Roy it was hard to tell one from the other. He let it be known that he'd been approached to play for the Rolling Stones, but declined. "I remember that story being discussed at that time," Winfrey would recall without prompting 30 years later. "I didn't know anything about it, except that, basically, the Rolling Stones had asked Buchanan to play with them and he turned them down. But I don't know where that story came from." Daniels too is mystified about the purported offer. "I never heard that story before," he said with a chuckle in 1997. "I don't know where that one got started. I did two shows with the Rolling Stones in 1975, but I have never even been within ten feet of them. Roy would have been a heckuva addition to that band. He might have changed their whole thing, you can never tell. But I cannot figure where that story came from."

In fact, no one does, though the odds point to Roy. Nonetheless, it became a cornerstone of the Roy Buchanan Legend. The story grabs the imagination and provokes consternation. *Turned down the Stones?!* The premise itself is highly unlikely: One of the most renowned rock groups of all time somehow learns of and contacts a world-class though anonymous journeyman who lived with only the tattered remnants of a local following around Washington, DC. Yet the jaded maestro remains aloof, preferring poverty and anonymity to selling out. The magnitude of the artist's sacrifice—apparently for principle alone—is supreme.

The story has holes. Brian Jones left the Rolling Stones in mid-June, 1969, and, two weeks later, he died. The Stones hired Mick Taylor in time for their July 5 concert appearance in London's Hyde Park, which suggests little if any time for the sort of contact Roy alleged. From January until the fall of 1969 the guitarist had put down his Telecaster and taken up a pair of scissors. Perhaps the Rolling Stones did call, and Roy really was nuts enough to turn them down. What else did the guitarist have on his plate that could produce the sort of confidence in the future required to dis the Stones? Well, during the Daniels sessions, Roy slipped into the studio with his old crony, Danny Denver, and recorded several tracks of some serious trash. Denver's saccharine melodies and maudlin lyrics produced titles like "A Girl I Used to Know," "Wedding Bells," "Another's Arms," "If You Get Tired of Hurting Me," and "Oh Lonesome Me." On "Okie from Southern Maryland," Denver's tribute to Merle Haggard (and a complete theft of Haggard's "Okie from Muskogee"), Denver sang, "We don't smoke marijuana down in southern Maryland . . . " "We don't let our hair grow long and shaggy, like the hippies down in Georgetown way . . . " Another unfortunate inspiration led Denver to lay down a version of Muddy Waters' "Got My Mojo Workin'," complete with Little Richard–style cries, and mind-bogglingly cheesy results. Roy of course was too principled to play for the Rolling Stones, but he could back a lounge singer who'd declined steadily since the early 1960s when Roy first met him.

In fact, after the studio work with Daniels and Denver, Roy returned to the stage as lead guitarist in Denver's Soundmasters, which had become the house band at the Crossroads Restaurant and Supper Club at 4103 Baltimore Avenue in Bladensburg, MD, a redneck club within spitting distance of the Bladensburg Barber School. Ten years earlier, "Uncle George" Saslaw had converted a former roadhouse known far and wide as the Del Rio into a country music emporium. In the late '30s and '40s the Del Rio had hosted traveling big bands and attractions that included stripper Belle Starr. Local legend had it that the building stood atop a graveyard for slaves. To devotees of blues mythology, the Crossroads' name triggers a reference to bluesman Robert Johnson, who, according to lore, met the Devil himself at a crossroads in the Mississippi Delta and traded his soul for otherworldly musical skills. But in the harsh reality that was suburban Bladensburg, the allusion simply meant that the club stood at the intersection of Bladensburg Road and Baltimore Road, or Route 1. In an island among the crisscrossing roads rises a monument known as the Peace Cross, a memorial to World War I participants built in 1925.

Radio spots broadcast on WBOM's *Country Fun Time* evoked the flavor of the place. "Hello friends! It's the old 'Tom Cat' down at the Crossroads of country music, Maryland's oldest and largest entertainment hot spot. The Crossroads Restaurant and Supper Club, 4103 Baltimore Avenue, Bladensburg, Maryland, at Peace Cross. Presenting the best in country and rockabilly music for your dancing and listening pleasure. You'll be entertained by the fantastic Danny Denver and his Soundmasters. See and hear Danny Denver sing songs like ["Knock Three Times," a No. 1 hit for Tony Orlando and Dawn in 1971, plays for a few bars] . . . ."That's the great sound of Danny Denver. We'll be back with more music from Danny in just a moment. You know, friends, Maryland's finest and largest dance floor is available to you with plenty of free parking at the Crossroads. You'll hear Danny Denver and his Soundmasters featuring Roy Buchanan, the World's Greatest Guitar Player. There's more, too! Every Sunday night there's a go-go contest with a $50 prize. Be sure and go to the Crossroads Restaurant and Supper Club [open] . . . every night, Tuesday through Sunday, from 9 p.m. until 2 a.m. Enjoy the best in country and rockabilly music, plus your favorite beverages till 2 a.m. every night. Seven nights a week. Come on out tonight and tell Big John, Uncle George, and all the staff to seat you to see Danny Denver and the Soundmasters."

So in the fall of 1970, as the radio announced that Jimi Hendrix had met an untimely end in London, Judy drove Roy in their black Chevy station wagon from their place at the Whitfield Towne Apartments in Lanham, MD, to the Crossroads, where the guitarist would emerge carrying his battered '53 Tele in his hands—he had no case for it. Six nights each week, five 45-minute sets each night. Inside, according to those who made the pilgrimage, the situation was down-home for everyone who belonged in that milieu, and decidedly hostile to those who did not. The layout was simple: once inside the door, a long bar stretched away on one's left, tables lined the perimeter of the room and filled the back of the room, while the area in front of the stage—*Maryland's finest and largest dance floor!*—allowed plenty of room to swing your honey through the paces set by Danny Denver and the Soundmasters.

The room was dimly lit, the waitresses aggressive, the women's beehive hairdos reached for the ceiling, and men might wear polyester shirts, jeans, and cowboy boots or work-a-day shirts with their first names stenciled above the breast pocket. When the younger, long-haired Georgetown crowd found out their discovery from the Silver Dollar had resurfaced at the Crossroads, and began to invade this redneck haven, tensions were palpable. Early 1971 forced the war in Vietnam into everyone's face and divided American society. Hamlets on Bladensburg's order of sophistication were polarized. They didn't smoke marijuana down in Bladensburg, either. And long hair meant one thing: You weren't livin' right, you were hippy scum, and if you didn't toe the imaginary line of expected behavior you were going to get the shit kicked out of you. The Crossroads' cloistered world—and Danny Denver's audience—had been breached by outsiders. Usually the outsiders came on week nights when the crowds were smaller and there'd be less opportunity for getting hassled. "It's a scary place," chuckled John Gossage, who made the journey out of the city to this distant and strange suburb. "This is redneck heaven. There's a war going on over in Vietnam and here there's a lot of tension. We're like Roy's friends, come to hear him, so we'd sit next to the bandstand and go backstage between sets, thinking Roy will protect us. The waitresses are utterly aggressive about drinks. You took your last sip—we'd nurse a beer for an hour—and before you even put the glass down, it was gone. 'Want another?' We had very little money and wanted to spend the evening listening to Roy, but the waitresses would say, 'You're taking too long with that beer!'"

In fact, the star of the show wasn't that happy either. On weeknights many in the audience had come to see the sideman, not the front man. They found the scenario far from the glory days of the Silver Dollar. "It was bittersweet," recalled Alan Scheflin. "The club had good fidelity, so you could really hear the guitar player, but Danny Denver would, for a variety of reasons, keep Roy under tight rein. People were there to see Roy and that bothered Danny's ego."

Still, Roy's voice came through the music. A nineteen-year-old guitarist named Nils Lofgren would make the journey to the Crossroads to see Roy, his mentor. "I felt uncomfortable with my long hair," Lofgren said. "But it was clear I was a friend of Roy's, so I never ran into any confrontations. I minded my own business." And he continued to learn, not only about playing the guitar, but about Roy Buchanan. "It's all like a haze to me," Lofgren continued. "I remember seeing Roy at the Crossroads with Danny Denver. At this point I knew Roy and he knew my love for his playing was genuine. I would go backstage between sets and visit. He'd show me things on the guitar. He seemed really friendly and accessible. The rap is that we're all tortured souls, Roy more than most. But my personal experiences, which are my only frame of reference, were all positive, from A to Z. He was never anything but warm and friendly toward me. People said that he turned his back to the audience to 'protect his licks,' but if you had some precious technique to guard, you wouldn't go to some dumpy bar in Bladensburg with Danny Denver and play for four hours."

Yet players did begin to show up at the Crossroads, and Roy could tell from the way they stared when he played just what they were after. One night Lofgren showed up and it became clear musical sparks would fly that evening. "During the break I went backstage and Roy had this weird look in his eye. He explained that there were four steel guitar players up from Nashville that were really there to look down their nose at Roy. They'd heard about him and how he made a regular guitar sound like a pedal steel and they were out there in the audience getting drunk, getting ready to put him down, put him in his place—like you're supposed to be hot, but you're really not. Roy felt a bad vibe from these guys, an attitude. In a good-natured way, with a kind of a smirk, he let me know he was going to . . . Well, he had a mischievous look in his eye and he went out and for the next two sets he stood right in front of these guys and played the most searing, scary, pedal steel–Roy Buchanan blues I'd ever heard in my life. He left no doubt with anybody—even these guys—that he was the master. Roy took great pride in that. He went out of his way to be spectacular. I got the impression that Roy and them then had a mutual understanding that no one ever was going to play what Roy played. Roy at his best was not just technique. Ninety percent of it is one's soul and expressing it. You have to learn enough to express what you're feeling, but your feelings can't be learned. So it was the quality of his soul that always came through. He advanced the guitar by playing lines that were so classically melodic, yet so searingly soulful, that they took on a new importance that the guitar hadn't had until that point." As for the mechanical aspects of his craft, Roy had a few other things to impart to Lofgren. "Roy encouraged me to use higher action on my guitar strings to get more of a singing sound out of it, more sustain. There was a warmth and presence to his playing that I tried to emulate, without copying. But he also taught me an emotional aspect of playing, something that made me want to get out everything I felt or heard. You got the impression that whatever Roy heard in his head he could play. Hendrix did that too. To this day, I've got to watch myself, because I can't play everything I hear."

It wasn't long before journalists found the Crossroads as well. Bill Holland of the *Washington Star* heard from Gerry Mulé, guitarist for the local band Rents Due, about the virtuoso at Bladensburg's finest country and rockabilly emporium and had a look for himself that fall. Holland had grown up in DC listening to jazz, blues, and early rock 'n' roll. He'd seen Elvis Presley in 1955 on a boat ride down the Potomac River. At home he heard Chopin and Muddy Waters. He too puzzled over his country's fascination with the British Invasion. He'd been away in the Peace Corps from 1963 to 1965. "When I came back it was a whole new world—the counter-culture, Dylan, all that stuff," he remembered. "I went away having heard Sam Cooke, Muddy Waters, the real shit on AM radio. I thought, 'What are these skinny Brits trying to do? This is *terrible*. Why does my sister dig it?' That's why when I finally bumped into Roy, this guy was a working-class musician with a lot of . . . I could hear that *he* heard what the black artists were trying to do. And took that and added his own."

"You didn't have to have working-class roots to dig Roy," Holland said. "And I felt confident that my opinion of what Roy was doing was informed." Holland could see that the Crossroads was a world apart from Georgetown and that Roy, the journeyman, could play in either. Roy could play whatever form of music was necessary to land a paying gig. "They just played other people's tunes," Holland said of journeymen in general. "They weren't going to write a rock opera or talk about the Vietnam War. Their whole background was providing loud entertainment for people who did not come to hear them."

The scene at the Crossroads wasn't pretty, according to Holland. "Danny Denver is doing a show set, but way grades down from Vegas. He would wear orange Banlon short-sleeve shirts that fit him when he was young and skinny, but since had shrunk, and black slacks. He would come on stage with his hairy belly showing—as ugly as three dogs in a meat locker. He had a pretty good voice—unsophisticated, but he could do it. They'd give Roy a solo spot and he'd do 'Malagueña' or a plain old blues. He had a little Fender amp. He turned it backwards. I heard he did that so other guitarists couldn't cop his settings. But it mellowed out the sound, it refracted the sound so it wasn't a laser beam of guitar at your ear. He seemed to have defined his palette early on—what he wanted that Telecaster to sound like. And he got it. He was trying to get the human cry. He put a Telecaster note through a Fender amp until it blurched—instead of one thin tone, it would be the sonic equivalent of a Steinway piano, which is known for having a fantastically fat series of overtones—so that the sound was fat and even through the bass and treble qualities. So it wouldn't just be a C, but a C with all its overtones. It almost becomes physical, something you could chew. It wasn't a pure tone. 'Purity' doesn't lend itself to being mongrel. The basis of Roy's tone was, get as much out of that amp and overdriving the tubes to make them turn purple. He wanted that impure tone. Why does it grab you? It's psycho-acoustics. Maybe it's impenetrable. Many times I listened to Roy and realized he was mesmerizing a room. I asked myself why. Why him? Why that guitar tone? I never found an answer. Except that *he* knew. He intuitively knew he'd been given that talent."

Holland also thought he saw through the mystique that Roy did nothing to dispel. In other words, he was hip to Roy's jive. "Roy was uneducated and often he didn't use the right word," the writer recalled. "He would use country mojo on people to bolster himself. Roy would talk about graveyard spirits and all that shit and

I'd just roll my eyes. Basically it was for effect. He might have even believed in it. Jimmy Swaggart, Jerry Lee Lewis, those guys really believe in the Devil. Maybe Roy did too. But I think he often was simply hoodwinking people. He would try that shit out on people who were susceptible. He was quite a con artist."

Nonetheless, Holland became well enough acquainted with Roy to visit the musician at his apartment in Lanham. He is unsparing in his recollections. Apparently Roy was back to his old habits. "Roy was strung out, always trying to get high on pot, speed, alcohol. He always seemed very brooding, nervous, far-away. He wasn't always there. He'd give you the soulful eyes, but you got the impression the wheels weren't turning inside. Judy was trying to keep him away from that stuff all the time. It must have been horrible. I called Roy at his apartment in Lanham and was invited to come out. Judy and Roy were very nice to us—I went out with my wife. Judy would look everyone over. I liked Judy, but she was really high-strung, a little screechy. You could just see him getting headaches." By this time Tom Zito from the *Washington Post* had been to the Crossroads as well. Zito had been part of the Georgetown set in the late 1960s and by late 1970 had talked his way onto the *Post* to write about rock 'n' roll. In a front page article in the *Post*'s feature section on Dec. 9, 1970, Zito described a visit to the Crossroads in all its glory. "The Crossroads really isn't the kind of place that ought to be remarkable. It's a suburban tavern . . . [and] inside it's dark and musty and the waitresses constantly pick up your beer bottle to ask if you want another. The atmosphere is the greasy 1950s all grown up: women in tight pants and high bouffant hairdos, men with their locks neatly slicked back . . . ."

"What makes the Crossroads remarkable," Zito wrote, "is the presence of one man, Roy Buchanan, who provides what may well be the best rock guitar picking in the world."

With those words, the guitarist's so-called career got a life-sustaining jolt. Zito added a few of the stories *he'd* heard, and perpetuated others, including the one about the Stones' alleged invitation.

"Buchanan reacts to all this with a great amount of disinterest—a disinterest that generates its own mystique," Zito wrote. " 'I'm only a guitar player,' he says, scoffing at the praise others heap upon him." "Once you get in the spotlight, the pressure starts building and it can really bring you down," the guitarist told the writer. "I've already spent too much time on the road. I could have worked with a lot of name bands, but I've got five big responsibilities and a sixth one on the way."

Two months later the *Post* article got reprinted in *Rolling Stone* and the guitarist's quest for anonymity reached the pages of the country's premier pop music magazine. By that time either Roy or Polydor had killed the LP from the Charlie Daniels sessions and Zito interceded with the label, garnering an opportunity to lure Roy back into the studio. In late March Zito produced and attempted to play drums on a session with Roy on guitar and vocals, Joe Bayliss on keyboards, and Don Monahan on bass, with Cory Pearson engineering. The band recorded Cream's "SWABLR" and "Lawdy Mama"; "Hey Joe," the Billy Roberts song made famous by Hendrix; Roy's old standbys, "Malagueña" and "Susie Q"; a new one dubbed "Roy's Blues"; and Chuck Berry's standard, "Johnny B. Goode." Two weeks later the same personnel gathered, but with Bing McCoy on keyboards, and recorded a medley of "After Hours" that segued into the piercing riff Roy had used on "Story of Isaac" with Charlie Daniels, a version of Junior Walker's "Shotgun," and, as always, more blues. At best, the sessions produced some interesting music, but nothing one could build an album around. Considering the electricity and emotion he could generate in a dingy nightclub, it became clear that capturing the guitarist in the relatively antiseptic atmosphere of the recording studio would be akin to bottling lightning.

To catch that lightning at the peak of the storm, however, Zito says he personally escorted Peter Green—then the ace guitarist for Fleetwood Mac—Rory Gallagher, Eric Clapton, and Paul McCartney's brother, Mike McGear, to the Crossroads to see Roy. Zito even claimed years later to have set up a recording session at Capricorn Studios in Macon, GA, with the Allman Brothers in spring 1971. Word was that Duane Allman had heard of Roy and was conducive to recording with him. When the time came Roy refused to go, according to Zito. To some, this sort of behavior was inexplicable. To Zito, the matter seemed simple and apparent. "My theory, for what it's worth, is that the dynamics of his marriage had a profound effect on what he did. There was a part of Judy fascinated by the trappings of the rock 'n' roll world, and she was petrified that if he became successful, he would leave her. I think in many ways that defines what happened to his career. I seem to recall some connection with the Jehovah's Witness group. When Roy told me he couldn't go to Macon for that recording session he said, 'It's the Devil's music.' I don't know whether he or Judy actually believed that, or whether that was the easiest way to control what Roy did." In any case, Roy didn't really have to go anywhere. Many of the most important rock guitarists of the day made a journey to the Crossroads, including—apparently—Jerry Garcia of the Grateful Dead, probably in late August 1971 when his band played the University of Maryland. After that Garcia's picking style evolved with an echo of Roy's own Telecaster technique woven in. On the other hand, stories have exaggerated the number of luminaries who appeared at the Crossroads. According to one of Roy's Crossroads cronies, Elwood Brown, "If half the people who they say came in, came in, Roy would've had to play the Crossroads for ten years!"

With Zito's *Post* article reprinted in *Rolling Stone* in February 1971, people took notice. "Guitar freaks started coming out, hippie kids, just to see Roy," recalled Holland. "For a while Danny took it gracefully, and even made comments—'And now here's a solo by somebody everyone came to see'—as he gave Roy a solo. He wanted to be gracious, but he realized what was going down. Suddenly, Roy had his own nights." Before that transition took place, two people in particular made the pilgrimage to the Crossroads and both had an effect on Roy's emancipation from his long seclusion.

New Yorker Bob Berman had heard of Roy in the 1960s from his friend, guitarist Link Chamberland, and when he saw the *Rolling Stone* article he simply headed down to Bladensburg from Rye, NY—a six-hour drive one-way—on a work night. Berman played a little guitar himself, so when he finally reached the Crossroads, expectations had been established. "It was Danny Denver and Roy . . . Roy is playing rhythm, fills, some shuffle, and Danny is singing! I said to myself, 'No! It *can't* be!' You expected a *lot* more. But before I could take a seat, Roy let loose with a solo that absolutely floored me. Then I realized we were at the right place. It really was one of the greatest moments of my life hearing him play for the first time."

When the band took a break, Bob headed to the dressing room, on the left side of the stage. He waited, mentioned Link Chamberland's name, and gained admission to the large closet that served as a dressing room. "It was a great introduction and we started talking," Berman recalls. "Roy was a nice guy, very accommodating. We had a terrific conversation. I asked him if he would do an interview for *Guitar Player* magazine and he said 'Sure.'" Berman had done a bit of writing, but nothing major. When he called the magazine with news of his "discovery," the editors gave him a green light. Berman drove back to Rye that night, worked all day, and returned the next night. "I didn't drink or do drugs or even drink coffee," he laughs today. "I was so high from this music that I was up for almost two days straight." Berman made it his mission to publicize Roy's existence and with his interview pending, he mimeographed a sheet of paper for anyone who would read it extolling the guitarist's virtues. "The band will not knock you out," he wrote in reference to the Soundmasters. However, Roy "is the most original and versatile guitarist I have ever heard . . . pure taste." Berman went on to describe Roy's various techniques, pedal-steel effects created by "just his hands," tremolo work nonpareil, chicken pickin' that would make Chet Atkins take notice, classical to "shock" Segovia, slurs, sustains, harmonics "like church bells ringing"— all the while noting that "his humility is amazing." To sum up, Berman concluded, "Listening to Roy play is like getting laid out by an express train because the effect is the same—you end up in a state of shock not knowing what has happened." Berman helpfully included the Crossroads address, directions from New York City (250 miles, four hours), and the Soundmasters' schedule: Tuesday through Sunday, 9:30 p.m. to 2:00 a.m.

When the time came for the interview Berman visited Roy with Elwood Brown, and they taped a conversation that would be published in March 1972—essentially the first in-depth interview of Roy's career. Roy readily discussed his early family life, his interest in music, and his choice of instrument. Why the guitar? Berman asked. "It sounded like a versatile instrument, and I've always liked different types of music," Roy replied. He went on to name his influences, a list that included Roy Nichols, Chet Atkins, Hank Garland, Grady Martin, Barney Kessel, and B.B. King. And he included his early bosses, including Dale Hawkins and Ronnie Hawkins. Was he bitter, "working so hard for so little money," in the early days? "No, I mark

Bob Berman captured Roy fooling with Berman's Stratocaster during interviews in late 1971 for a Guitar Player *magazine piece published in March 1972.*

everything up as experience," the well-traveled 31-year-old said. "You learn not to do things that way again." And what had kept him going over the years? "I always wanted to play what I felt, but working with other people it had to be kind of commercial. Even when they let me do what I wanted, they held me back to a certain point. I couldn't go all the way, because they were interested . . . in making a Top Ten record. But anymore it seems like anything sells. You have more freedom. You can play jazz and the kids are buying it. Blues—whatever you want to play. But I'm still commercial." Is it true he turned down the Stones? "Yeah . . . The main reason I decided not to go with them, beside the fact that I don't want to travel, was that I didn't know the material, and I didn't figure I could do the job right. To sit down and learn all those songs, that would have taken a lot of work. I guess I'm lazy."

BERMAN FORGED AHEAD, asking about Roy's guitar, his strings, techniques, and patented sounds. How often did the guitarist change his strings? "When they break." Don't they lose their sound before that? "Probably." In terms of craft, did he prefer a one-piece maple neck on his Telecaster, or a rosewood job? "It was the grain in the wood that I think I liked," came the response. "The feel of it makes it better. It's harder for me to bend a note on a rosewood neck. Maple is easier to work

Another Bob Berman photograph of Roy, this time with his trademark 1953 Telecaster, seems to capture the guitarist in a pensive mood.

with. And I like the action high. It keeps your technique built up, for one thing. You won't get lazy if you have to work a little harder. I have a tendency to get slouchy with the strings too low." Roy allowed that he kept the thumb of his left hand around the guitar's neck for strength and balance while making chords and notes, that he bent strings by pushing them up, and that his multi-finger-picking technique derived from learning on steel guitar. Though he currently used his fingernails, he admitted using fingerpicks on his Tele as well. If he had to flat pick, he figured, "the smaller the pick, the better I can get around." When Berman pressed him to explain how he achieved the pedal steel sound, Roy did his best, then laughed. "Now that I've figured out what it was, I'll never be able to do it again! Most of the things I'm doing I'm not even aware of what I'm playing. I know how to get the sounds, but I can't explain it to someone else. If you asked Jimi Hendrix how he did all those things, I'll bet you a dollar to a nickel he couldn't have told you." The guitarist expressed his preference for vintage guitars and amplifiers. As for whether he could read music, or listened to the radio, he added: "Well, I don't read, and I don't listen to the radio. If I decide I want a new lick, I just lay in bed and think of it . . . When I try them out on the guitar, I know whether to keep them or not." Advice for young musicians? "If I had it to do over again, I'd probably learn to read. And I'd spend more time practicing, and learning harmony and theory. The more you know about it, the better off you are."

LOOKING BACK, Berman has only fine things to say about the guitarist. "Roy was an unassuming person. I never found him to have any ego. There was no competitiveness with him regarding the music, as I found with other talented players—or especially less talented players. He just played for the enjoyment of playing. He had a great appreciation for whatever anyone else was able to do." Berman sighs. "Roy was always dealing with the demons. At that point in his life he was fairly straight. He was smoking his Viceroys and drinking his Schlitz." And the music came through. "Nobody could touch Roy for a combination of feeling and tone. When he came on the scene with national recognition, there was just nobody out there who had such an impact on listeners as Roy Buchanan. He was phenomenal. His approach to soloing was so damn original."

John Adams came to think so as well. He'd been at the New York public television station WNET for ten years as a music supervisor, and he knew a good story when he saw one. Perhaps his Canadian heritage gave him a keen sense for the American-ness of his subjects. Born on Prince Edward Island in 1932, he moved to Nova Scotia, ended up in Cambridge, MA, then he did his US Army basic training at Fort Carson in Colorado Springs, CO, in 1956–58 before shipping out for Germany. "As Elvis went in, I had just left," he recalled. Finally, he moved to New York in 1961 to work for National Educational Television, the predecessor to PBS. His beat was "music operations," from ballet to rock 'n' roll.

Adams' colleague Eliot Tozer had been a science producer with a taste for country music; he'd put together a documentary on Merle Haggard in 1968. In February 1971 Tozer gave Adams a copy of the *Rolling Stone* article on Buchanan published that month. "Eliot asked me, 'What do you think?' I said, 'Ah, I don't know.' Prior to that I hadn't had much experience with rock. I'd been involved in jazz and classical circles over the years. That hadn't been my only exposure. Earlier, in 1967, at the Monterey Jazz Festival, WNET filmed a blues afternoon with B.B. King, Janis Joplin and Big Brother . . . I'm watchin what's goin' on on stage. She was terrific. Later, in 1970, we did two rock programs out in San Francisco, one with Santana, the Jefferson Airplane, and the Grateful Dead. That turned my head around. It opened my mind further to the electric guitar and what players were doing. Everybody said, 'Don't drink the Kool-Aid.' I didn't go near it. I was particularly taken by Santana. Not Santana so much as that damn drummer Mike Shrieve and his conga player. Shrieve was unbelievable.

"Ultimately, what got me was the expansion in the use of guitars that I'd never heard before. I was essentially a jazz person. San Francisco opened my mind further to the electric guitar."

Regardless of their skepticism regarding the *Rolling Stone* article touting "the world's greatest unknown guitarist," Adams and Tozer got the go-ahead from Curtis Davis, director of cultural programming, to visit the Crossroads and assess for themselves whether they had a worthy subject for a documentary television program. "We went down and Tom Zito took us to the Crossroads and, of course, Roy was with this country guy [Danny Denver], a whiskey baritone, who wouldn't let him play," Adams recalled. "Well, Roy finally soloed and I couldn't believe this guy. Tozer and I were flabbergasted. I thought, 'Maybe there's something wrong with me. If this guy's so good, how come he's not a star?!' He played in tune, he made sense. He had a *sound*." It was all there: the mournful themes of country music, the innate grasp of the blues, a generous dollop of jazz sensibility and technique, the fierce railing of rock 'n' roll—all delivered without hesitation, without error, in that seductive Telecaster tone, which could be muted and mood-setting, or trebly and biting.

"We needed something to take back," Adams recalls. "We had nothing to show for what Roy sounded like. So he loaned me an acetate of a demo he'd done—told me it was recorded for Leiber and Stoller—called 'After Hours.' People back in New York heard it and they were flippin' out. When I get going and want to do something, I will go nuts. I played that acetate for anybody who wanted to listen to it, to watch the 'Wow!' That's all we had."

Earlier, Adams told his acquaintance, the jazz guitar master Mundell Lowe, that he'd discovered someone—*something*. Lowe's understandable reaction? "How come he ain't rich?" Nonetheless, Lowe agreed to attend the Crossroads with Tozer and Adams. "We're talking about *Mundell Lowe*, one of the ace technical guitar players in the world," Adams explained. "Intrigued, Mundell went with us to the Crossroads. And Danny Denver wouldn't let Roy play. This might have been a Friday night in March 1971. Finally Roy solos and does one of his rushes. I'd seen it before, so I was watching Mundell. He rose in his chair with the music and when Roy hit his climax, Mundell said, '*Wow!*' to himself. Later, to me, Mundell confided, 'This guy's a real guitar player.' Well, that did it for me."

Still, Adams and Tozer would have to convince their boss, Curtis Davis, who was a classical composer, a graduate in music composition from Columbia University. So they took him to a performance that Tom Zito had arranged for Roy at Gaston Hall on the Georgetown University campus. It would be the first in many years to feature Roy's name as the main attraction. "It was exciting for the community, like a coming-out party, because it rewarded Roy for his sacrifices and the audience for having supported him for so long," recalled Alan Scheflin. "Roy's family was there, people from Polydor. There was a real sense that this was something special." Despite a mediocre job on drums by Zito, Roy nonetheless rose to the occasion and, John Adams noted, Curtis Davis was amazed as well.

With the decision taken to make a documentary on Roy's life and times, Adams and Tozer spent some time in DC getting to know the artist. "Roy took to me," Adams said. "Later he always said: 'I knew you were the one that was going to make this work.' He sensed that there was a connection between the two of us. But he was smart. He knew he was using me. The other comment I remember from that time had to do with music. Roy's line was, 'I like anything that's good.' After talking about jazz players, his comment was, 'They all sound like each other. I wanted to find my own sound.' He meant the tone of the guitar—plus the remarkable chops and improvisational creativity he ultimately developed, that no one else to this day could perform."

Tozer and Adams moved swiftly, designing a biographical documentary that would open up with a trip back to California for Roy and his family to see Bill and Minnie Buchanan in Pixley. Roy had not been home to see his folks in nearly ten years. Communication must have been sporadic at best; Roy was not a letter writer and the Buchanans in Pixley did not own their own telephone until 1969. But when Adams returned to DC to gather his subject and head to the Golden State he found the situation complicated by personalities. Tozer and Adams eventually got the Buchanans and a WNET crew airborne to Bakersfield in July. The crew traveled ahead to Pixley to set up their cameras and capture the homecoming as it unfolded. Turned out Minnie had her arm in a cast. When Bill told her that Roy was coming out to see them, she'd been up on a ladder. She got so rattled she fell and broke her arm. Bill was his usual, quiet self. Roy's sister, Linda Joan, however, bristled with hostility at the television crew. "She thought we were there to rip-off Roy," Adams recalled. "She called us 'users.' She really was hostile to us."

But the homecoming went smoothly. There in the front yard of 380 South Park, where Roy's folks had moved a few years back, everyone had a heartfelt reunion. Roy introduced Judy and their children and everyone seemed oblivious to the cameras capturing it all on film. In the kitchen, Roy talked while his mother worked on feeding the contingent. "I was about 15 when I left home," Roy reminisced. "My father said, 'If you ever need a place to stay you know where you can come.' I came back a couple times, a few years later. He's the kind of person that believed I could do anything I wanted to do. I wanted to play music. He figured that'd be all right. I'd take care of myself." Interjected Minnie, "Then when you start to do anything, do the best you can. That's all. [The best that] anybody can expect of us as the Lord expects the best of us when we've done the best for him," she added.

"My mother, my father both worked," Roy continued, for the camera. "My mother, she worked like a man. She could work harder than many a man. She was always strict, but not in the kind of way that ties you down that much. We could do pretty much what we wanted to, as long as we didn't break any laws or hurt anybody. We went to the movies on Saturday and Sunday, always church on Sunday." Quietly, almost under his breath, he added: "My daddy, he was a preacher back then. My mom, she taught Sunday school." Perhaps Roy felt compelled to perpetuate the myths he'd told Tom Zito in his first major write-up the previous November. Making a fib like that for the cameras while the folks were right there! That required a degree of brazenness. When it came to reciting his life story, he gave a somewhat mythical account to the camera. "Well, I left home, 'bout 1955 I think it was. Matter of fact this little town right here is where I left from. First place I went to, I went to L.A. I played around there, when I could, in different clubs. Of course, I was kind of young, it was hard for me to play, so I'd just bum most of the time. Finally, got me a group together. We took off. First place we went to was Texas. We played mostly nightclubs. Like I say, I was still a little young, but we managed to hit a lot of small towns, playin' blues. Mostly for colored people back then. They's about the only ones diggin' it. We toured through Oklahoma, Texas, and, finally, we went to . . . Canada. I wound up in Philadelphia. When I traveled I usually scraped up enough money to catch a bus. I can remember sleeping in fields, I can remember sleeping in bars. I was lucky if I could sleep in a bar, you know? Talk the owner into it. I'd usually make enough money to eat. There was a few times I couldn't do that. I remember one time in Chicago I got stranded and I worked myself all the way back here. Tried to start again. By just playin', three or four dollars a night. I can remember some lonesome times, all right? I think the lonely thing is kind of born inside of a person. That's what makes him play. Your soul seems to be completely someplace else from other people, lonesome people. My dad used to call it 'the blues.' I think he was right."

Out in the yard Roy sat in a chair and played his Telecaster, plugged in but with the volume low as a whisper, circle picking some ethereal magic music that seemed to capture the mixed feelings, the melancholia, and some of the joy of being back among kin. "I always liked any kind of music," he told the camera. "I wanted to play it all. I never considered myself really good at any of it. But people liked to hear me play. 'Course if they liked to hear me play I liked to play it. I liked to play a little jazz, a little country, a little blues. Anything I could hear I'd try a little. And I tried to work it all into one thing. I think that's one reason people noticed my playing." Later, the crew took Roy next door to Minnie's Assembly of God Church, where Roy joined a rousing chorus on a foot-stompin' hymnal, keeping a straight face, barely. He'd been away from the church a long time. Oh, yes he had. But he had sober words when asked where the church fit in, growing up in Pixley. "I found something in church I don't believe I can quite explain," he said. "It's a feeling inside myself. It's something I can always turn to. It shows in my music. It's kind of a sacred feeling. Once you get it, it's hard to ever change it. I wouldn't change it for the world. The thing I remember best about church was the music and the overall picture of the message that they taught in church, which was, love your neighbor, love yourself. I thought that the best way to show that I do love my neighbor was to play my music. I think that without religion these people around this town here, especially my mother and father, I don't know what they would have done without the comforts of church. It gave them a reason to live and also a reason to die. That's sort of their whole life."

Then Tozer, Adams, and a cameraman took Roy, alone, to the house in the field outside town, on the Forsblad Ranch—or what was left of it. After Minnie and Bill Buchanan had retired and moved to town for more decent digs, the house where Roy grew up had languished. It had been painted white but that was long ago. Stripped of its windows and doors and more or less abandoned, it seemed to serve as a palpable image of the guitarist's childhood. It conjured the hold the place had on him. So did the tall, broad cottonwood that rose over it, giving protection and shade. At first Roy was uncomfortable before the camera, but with a little time he achieved a halting eloquence in explaining the place's influence on his life.

"This place here is the place where I probably spent most my life," he said, hesitantly. "We moved here when I was about five years old. We lived quite a normal life. We picked a little cotton, baled a little hay. It was a happy time in a sad sort of way. You know? The reason I left this place was, eh . . . "—and here he takes a long pause—"even when you love something you wonder what else you can do with what you learned. I loved this place, it's beautiful. You can have your solitude. It's also lonesome. I guess I left this place because I had something to do, something to prove, to myself. This place . . . [is where] . . . I learned the other side of life. But I had to get away. There wasn't much opportunity in Pixley for a guitar player, for one thing. I couldn't learn the different types of music that I wanted to know, unless I did travel. That was really one of the main reasons I did leave. So I could learn different styles.

"I haven't been home in about, I guess it's been 12 years. I was real nervous about the whole thing. Cuz I really didn't think I'd ever get to go home again. People told me, 'Things change.' But things hadn't changed one bit. I was kinda happy over the whole thing. Like I say, I was, I was scared. I don't know exactly what I was afraid of. I thought maybe I'd changed. But I don't think anything had changed, including me."

Asked about his long hard road, about how he had managed in the face of obscurity, Roy came as close as he ever did to explaining himself and his feelings about his life's work. "You set your own goals for success, and when you succeed it don't necessarily mean that you will be a big star, make a lot of money, or anything. You'll feel it in your heart, whether you've succeeded." This seemingly noble approach to anonymity also masked the profound disappointment he must have experienced throughout the 1960s, when anonymity wasn't a choice, but something that swallowed him in its maw. He addressed that, too, revealing cynicism. "I think probably the reason I never made it big is because I never cared whether I made it big. I didn't really give a damn. All I wanted to do was learn to play the guitar for myself. I didn't care about anybody else."

"I've had dreams in this place, not dreams that most people would understand," Roy said, picking at a blade of grass between his feet and gazing out over the fields beyond Pixley. "Dreams to do something I wanted to do. And I did what I wanted to do. I played like what I felt this place was. It became me. There was a closeness. Used to be so quiet, you could almost find God within your own self. You can get some real strange feelings out here. You can learn yourself."

"I wrote a song. It'll be included on my album. I had this place in mind. It's called 'The Messiah Will Come Again.' But instead of using this place, I generalized the whole world. Because the whole world is kinda like this place, to me. I think when you hear the song then you'll know why I think the way I do about this place, about every place, about everybody. To come home again is like steppin' out of a dream, steppin' into reality, or steppin' out of reality and stepping back into a dream, you're not quite sure. It's like a big dream. It's unbelievable. It's real. It's really great to come back here after I saw what I wanted to see. I don't believe this place will ever change. It wasn't meant to change. I don't think this place will change until I do. It's gonna be a long time."

"We were amazed," Adams said, many years later. "He'd be so quiet, then when the cameras rolled, he became so articulate." The documentary called for Roy to manifest his musical heritage in a series of gigs with players who'd influenced him. The producer managed to line up opportunities for Roy to sit in with Merle Haggard and his Strangers—including the venerable Roy Nichols—at Pat & Charlie's in Ridgecrest in the desert east of Bakersfield, with Mundell Lowe and his band at Donte's in West Hollywood, and with Johnny Otis in a club on Los Angeles' Santa Monica Boulevard. Tozer would also interview the guitarist in various settings, and tape it. Ultimately, the footage would be run with a live performance on a New York soundstage, which for a relatively cheap cost would make up half the TV special.

The crew first headed northeast to Pat & Charlie's, a country hall in Ridgecrest, deep in the desert. John Adams and Roy drove together ("I've never been someplace so hot," Adams, the New Yorker, recalled.) Offstage but on-camera, Adams asked Roy to explain his interest in this particular country music outfit. "I was always influenced by Roy Nichols," the guitarist said. "As a matter of fact I used to watch him and I'd get the chords and the basic things I needed. I also liked his lead playing, so I learned quite a bit off him."

Onstage at Pat & Charlie's Haggard introduced his special guest and let everyone know that the film crew would clear out in time to get the joint jumpin' with his regular show. "A portion of Roy Buchanan's early life was spent in Pixley, California, where he admired Roy Nichols' playing, which was part of the reason he became the guitar player he is," Merle intoned. "In spite of all that," Nichols chimed in, "he still made it!" The band launched into some good-natured country blues, which produced dexterous duets between Roy and Nichols. Roy showed he had mastered the chicken pickin' Nichols had pioneered, as well most of the blues bends and steel-guitar licks to which every country guitarist aspired. The band, including Nichols himself, and Norm Hamlett, Haggard's steel player, got a kick when, on "Travelin' Blues," Roy kicked into overdrive, throwing out squealing harmonics, which Nichols answered with his fanciest picking. Later Nichols would demand to know, "Where'd you get them bird sounds, Roy?" "I Love You a Thousand Ways" gave both guitarists a chance to strut their steel-guitar licks on their Teles. The most difficult part for Roy came when the moment demanded a few words. "This is one of the biggest thrills of my life, performin' with Mr. Merle Haggard and Mr. Roy Nichols and the whole group and I want to thank them very much for the honor of sitting in. I don't know what to say, just thank you very much." Roy hung around for the Strangers' set and tossed down a few beers while the crew loaded its gear for the haul back to the city.

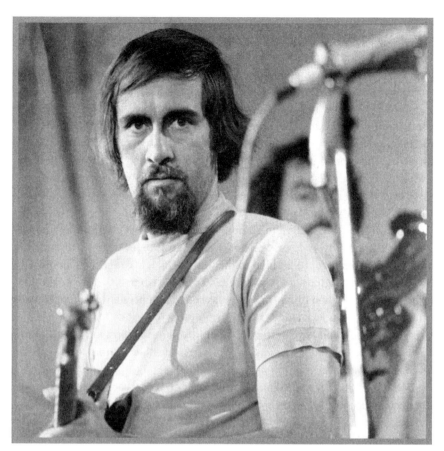

A WNET publicity photo, possibly taken in summer 1971, used to promote the Nov. 8, 1971, broadcast of the public television station's documentary on Roy's life.

Later, Adams and Roy drove back to their motel to get some sleep, but sleep wasn't in the cards for either. "This is when I first got frightened of Roy," Adams recalled, still puzzled—or disturbed. "Roy came over in the middle of the night and pounded on my door. Roy was pretty good at the Haggard session, except he drank a lot. When we got back, Roy's strangeness got to me. He came to my room. He's tore up and not making any sense. I said, 'Roy, go to bed.' He wanted to talk. I couldn't get rid of him. He seemed almost overbearing, physically. I was a little scared. I didn't know this guy at the time. He was acting odd. He told me later it was some stuff one of the musicians gave him."

The scene at Donte's was pretty loose and the group played around with a few uptempo numbers to which Roy added energetic jazz riffs that sufficed, but did not ignite. Then Lowe suggested a ballad, perhaps Roy knew one he liked? "Misty," came the response. What followed was an achingly tender rendition that captured both Roy's astonishing technical prowess in a genre he did not frequent, as well as the heartbreaking feeling he could impart to his playing. During that piece, Lowe put down his guitar and sat close, talking to Roy and encouraging him to really *play*. Later, after the program had aired—"Misty" had made the cut—Erroll Garner, author of "Misty," had told a friend at his home in Pittsburgh that Roy's version was the best he'd ever heard, besides himself. The documentary crew moved on to Santa Monica Boulevard, where the guitarist finally got to play with Johnny Otis, the man he'd seen with his Heartbeat buddies 15 years earlier. Johnny obliged, delivering the exhorting vocals and boogie piano that gave R&B its relentless and reassuring feeling. Otis lent the spotlight to Roy, and the band did rollicking versions of "Sweet Home Chicago," "Bye Bye Baby, Until We Meet Again," and "Ain't Gonna Worry My Life Anymore." Offstage, Roy recalled the days when the teenaged Heartbeats managed to glimpse the great Johnny Otis inside a Los Angeles club. Johnny, Roy said, was "one of the first great blues singers that really set me back on my ears . . . . I listened to him quite a bit. He could bend a note with his voice. Even though he didn't play guitar, I could listen to his voice and get ideas from it." The band then turned to a showcase blues number for singer and guitarist called "Goin' Down Real Slow," a nitty gritty piece ignited by Margie Evans' gut-wrenching vocals and Roy's searing fills, solos, and call-and-response with Evans, when he echoed her cries with his own. It is a classic blues performance captured on tape, and never released.

With the film they needed in the can, Tozer's crew flew back to New York while the Buchanans returned to their cramped apartment in Lanham, outside DC. Not long afterward Roy left Danny Denver's employ and began to headline the Crossroads with his own band. "Uncle George" Saslaw had seen Roy's drawing power and gave the guitarist weeknights at the club. For Danny Denver, the moment must have been bittersweet, to say the least. After all those years of giving Roy a job—the two had first played together in 1964—the gig was over and the guitarist got a big chunk of the week's business. Freed from Denver's strictly commercial country music, Roy gravitated naturally to a mixed bag of rock 'n' roll and roadhouse blues, with nods to country and jazz. He maintained a healthy mix of covers like his old favorite, "Johnny B. Goode," and Neil Young's recent "Down by the River," plus a few country standards, including "I Am a Lonesome Fugitive" and "Sweet Dreams." He also had, by this time, a handful of original compositions like the simple, autobiographical "Roy's Bluz," "The Messiah Will Come Again," and a haunting lament, "Since You've Been Gone."

TO PULL TOGETHER a band to help him fill the weeknight slot at the Crossroads Roy did not cast a wide net. He called on a few friends and their acquaintances. By this time he knew Danny Gatton well, and Danny's talented keyboard player, Dick Heintze, and the two joined in on bass and Hammond B-3 organ, respectively. Gatton recruited Mike "Pokey" Walls on drums. Chuck Tilley, who'd drifted in and out of the scene the past few years, got the rhythm guitar spot and—because no one on this roster could sing worth a damn—he would serve as lead vocalist. Crucial to this arrangement was Heintze's ability, and willingness, to take on the chores the ostensible bandleader—Roy Buchanan—would not. Heintze amiably put together arrangements for the band. The guitarist might express a preference for certain songs, but he was open to any his band members suggested. He might have a key or tempo in mind, but he was easy if the boys in the band wanted to try something different. He let Heintze work out the details, just as he allowed a local construction worker, Hal Davis, to make, or take, phone calls on his behalf. Suddenly he had a "manager" as well.

Pokey had respect and affection for Heintze, as did all who knew him. At that time he had a solo gig as "Dick Heintze at the Hammond Organ" at Tom Soros' New Orleans House. "He was a lounge lizard," Pokey recalled with a laugh. A talented lizard, too. "We'd be driving to a gig and I'd hear a song on the radio. I'd say, 'You know that one?' He'd say, 'Wait a minute.' He'd listen to it and say, 'Okay, we can do it.' I'd say, 'Should we do it in the same key as the record,' he'd say, 'Nah. B flat.' He was like a data recorder on an airplane." One explanation for his magical powers: Heintze, like Roy, had perfect pitch. It is said that when the speedometer on his vehicle gave out, Heintze kept the windows down to better hear the engine. By assessing its pitch, he could judge his speed.

The band didn't last, but during its brief incarnation there were some good times. By then Gatton had become a second lead guitarist, while local Don Monahan took over on bass. Pokey recalled one evening when the extroverted Cajun fiddler, Doug Kershaw, turned up at the Crossroads. "That was the best we ever sounded," Pokey said. "Kershaw has stage presence. He came in after his gig dressed in an Edwardian velour jacket with a blue candy flake fiddle. We're all wearing crummy clothes. He stood out onstage like a diamond on a goat's ass. That night Gatton is playing slide. The way Doug Kershaw is, he wants everybody to be happy. Roy? He just stands there and grits his teeth. Well, the band got to smokin', Danny's just rippin' ass on the slide on a dobro. It was just kickin' *ass!* Roy is just standing there. And Doug Kershaw goes over and puts his face right in Roy's face. He's got his fiddle up. Dee dee-dee-dee-dee, dee dee-dee-dee-dee. Kershaw's just smilin' right in Roy's face and Roy's face got beet red. But he started cuttin' loose—the most animated I'd ever seen him. I mean, Doug Kershaw's mood is infectious and everyone got crackin' up lookin' at Roy! I wished I had a recording of that."

Apparently Kershaw's desire to jam and, perhaps more importantly, his willingness to simply drop in made for a wonderful evening of music. Not everyone got the same cordial treatment. One night Leon Russell called down to the Crossroads to say he was in DC on a gig and asked if he might stop by to jam. By 1971, Leon—a keyboard wizard and songwriter from Tulsa—had led Joe Cocker's band on national tours. He'd settled on Muscle Shoals Studios in Sheffield, AL, as his artistic home, where he recorded the bulk of his debut solo album, released that May, titled, "Leon Russell and the Shelter People." In industry terms, he was hot. "He wanted to bring his entourage over to the Crossroads after their show at the Capitol Center," Pokey said. "Roy wouldn't come to the phone. He said, 'Pokey, you go talk to 'em.' Leon says, 'I want to talk to Roy, man.' I said, 'Roy, he wants to talk to you.' Roy said, 'I don't want to talk to 'em.' I said, 'Why not?' 'They just want to come over and steal my licks.' I said, 'Let 'em! You gotta be *you* to sound like you do. This guy's big in the recording industry. Maybe he'll like us and record us.' 'Nah, they just want to steal my licks.' I got back on the phone and said, 'He's kinda tied up.' Leon said, 'Who the hell *is* this guy? Fuck *him!*' And he hung up. That was the end of that."

Roy's nonchalance extended to his musical presentation. None of them had given any thought to a name for the band. "People'd say, 'What's the name of your group?'" Pokey recalled. "'Roy Buchanan.' 'And the *what?!*' So we came out one break, Chuck was talkin' about how he had this one dream. He hated spiders. We come out after that particular break and we were Roy Buchanan and the Spider Haters. That same night Chuck told us he had a dream that he'd been hired as a snake stretcher. My first remark, of course, was, 'Yeah, I've done that too, but I don't tell people about it!'—stretchin' your snake, ya know? We got a big laugh out of that. So we came out that break and this time it was, 'You've been listenin' to Roy Buchanan and the Snakestretchers.' That was just kind of a joke, but it stuck."

Meanwhile, that fall, Eliot Tozer had finalized the focus of his documentary: the canned film from Roy's California homecoming would be wrapped around and interspersed with a live-in-the-studio performance by the Snakestretchers. The WNET telecast would feature a special guest of Roy's choosing, and would be MC'd by the prominent rock impresario Bill Graham. It seemed somehow apropos of Roy's ambivalence to fame that on a television program to celebrate his own skills he would feature a special guest on *guitar*, but such was his generosity and genuine disinterest in the spotlight. At first many believed that that guest would be Danny Gatton, but Roy—either genuinely paranoid or advised to be realistic—seemed to have been leery that Gatton might upstage him, and settled on his young DC acolyte, Nils Lofgren.

The final Snakestretchers lineup had not come without some pain. Gatton's departure was inevitable. He had achieved a degree of technical mastery, applicable to virtually any form of music, and he had dreams of commercial success. His friendship with Roy had developed into a rivalry. According to Pokey, "Danny was a technical wizard. But Roy's guitar sang. He had soul. Danny was more of a trampoline act—he was a chicken picker, and frightening on slide. Danny was so jealous of Roy his teeth were falling out, especially because people would come to Roy and offer him opportunities." Though Gatton departed, his friend Dick Heintze remained. So far, Roy's weeknight gig at the Crossroads paid better than anything Gatton could offer, but Heintze's decision rankled Gatton, though the guitarist seemed more irritated with Roy than Dick.

Bassist Don Monahan also left at this time. There was no shortage of willing local players, and Pete Van Allen made his entrance, nearly completing the lineup that would appear in New York in early November. Van Allen, all of 22 years old, had been listening to R&B and gigging in various local bands for years. He'd even done a stint with the venerable Joe Stanley and his immortal Saxtons. ("Playing for Joe was like going to college and having the best professor you could have," he later said.) Van Allen had been to the Crossroads in the Danny Denver era. "I remember Danny Denver laying on his back on the floor, drunk as a skunk, singing 'High on a Mountain of Love' with hillbillies and women with beehive hairdos dancing around him. Roy is rolling his eyes, and playing guitar lines that sounded like they were coming from heaven. It was surreal!"

THAT NILS LOFGREN got the call to join Roy on his TV special is not surprising, given the younger player's reverence for Roy. "I got to know Roy [in 1971] and quickly fell in love with his playing," Lofgren recalled. "I thought he was the greatest guitar player I'd ever heard. It was the first time I'd heard harmonics sound like bells. He was a master who recognized an appreciative student with a thirst for his style of playing, and he treated me accordingly."

Lofgren led an ensemble composed of Bob Berberich, George Daly, and Paul Dowell, and they recruited Roy to do some rehearsing with them that summer at their friend Bob Dawson's mother's house on Spring Street in Silver Spring, MD. Dawson, a budding recording engineer, captured two demo tracks. The group taped an instrumental version of Don Gibson's country hit, "Sweet Dreams"—covered successfully by Faron Young in 1956, by Gibson himself in 1961, and by Patsy Cline in 1963—and a long spirited jam off the theme to Bobby Gentry's 1968 hit, "Ode to Billy Joe." On the first track Roy played in a sweet country-soul style that spoke eloquently of bittersweet love, while the second track evolved into a laid-back mood piece that gave Roy an opportunity for some of the psychedelic ramblings then in style. Outside in the blazing sun, a pregnant Judy sat in a lawn chair, waiting. She refused to enter the house, adamant that Roy finish whatever he was doing and come along. "We'd play for several hours," Berberich recalled, "Then she'd knock on the door and say, 'Enough!'" The tape got the band an audition in New York with famed producer Phil Ramone, who owned A&R Studios. Ramone said there would be no record deal without that virtuoso guitarist, and Roy had already moved on.

Roy still harbored a dangerous fondness for amphetamines, which in that place and time often came in the form of black capsules dubbed, variously, "black beauties" and, in the vernacular of both races, "nigger babies." These players all recall seeing the guitarist take "handfuls," washed down with Carling's Black Label malt liquor, yet remain seemingly unfazed. Berberich, however, did notice inconsistencies. "There were many different sides to his personality. When he showed up you never quite knew which persona he was going to be in. He could range from hyper-agitated to almost confrontational to being a sweet guy."

Unpredictable behavior and, say, gigs, did not mix well. As Grin, the band had been getting local gigs and Roy rehearsed with them for an upcoming engagement. The band would open for Small Faces, featuring future Rolling Stone Ronnie Wood, set for a roller rink at McGonigle's Seaside Park on the Virginia shore. Show time rolled around, but Roy failed to appear. "After our gig we were watching the Faces and I looked down [into the audience] and there was a very drunk Roy Buchanan in the audience," George Daly said. "I went over and said to him, 'Roy, where *were* you?' He says to me, 'I'm not Roy. I don't know what you're talking about.' Days later he came over to where we were rehearsing at Bob Dawson's on Spring Street. I said, 'Roy, what happened?' He looks at me and says, with that baleful sincerity that only a great artist on the downward slide can exhibit—he tells the truth, but it's so sad—he says, 'If I told you it wasn't me, it wasn't me.'" Afterward, the band scrawled the quote on the wall of Tom Guernsey's hippy pad, a basement apartment in Tacoma Park. "His art was a great gift and a burden to him," Daly said. "He brought me to tears once, playing all alone without an amp, just his Tele. We were playing a Byrds album, the first or second one. He said, 'I love this guitar [part].' And he started playing. He brought tears to my eyes. I remember at the time, when I was 20, saying to myself, 'I'll never forget this music I'm hearing.' The guitar was his voice. His guitar playing had some anger in it, but it also had great pathos, a solitary determination. He played like he *had* to play."

ONE NIGHT AT THE CROSSROADS the Snakestretchers were joined on the bill by another group, and percussionist Marc Fisher caught Roy's attention by adding flair to the Snakestretchers' rendition of Traffic's "Feelin' Alright." Fisher jumped groups and the Snakestretchers were complete. That fall the band gigged at the Crossroads six nights a week, five sets per night, 40 minutes on, 20 minutes off—not much different from the regimen that, over past years, had driven Roy to distraction. But being the headliner meant a degree of recognition that cheered Roy's somber soul, and the fact that he led his own band and could choose his own sets brought a certain relief. In fact, his comfort level even fanned the smoldering embers of his ambition. By October he'd decided—or agreed with someone else's suggestion—that the Snakestretchers ought to tape a few of its sets in an effort to capture Roy's way with a Telecaster. Someone rigged up a portable, monaural, reel-to-reel machine and crudely captured a few sets one week in October. "He was in good spirits over there at the Crossroads," Fisher recalled. "Things were starting to happen. And he was happy the way the tapes came out." The tapes made good listening, perhaps, but in no way were they of high enough fidelity to suit a legitimate record company. It's not clear whether the tapes were actually offered to Polydor, to which Roy still had a contractual obligation to produce a record, but in the end the guitarist blithely decided to go it alone. He picked a half-dozen songs, about 35 minutes' worth, and proceeded to have a local record pressing plant cook up a few thousand copies. That he may have first approached Polydor—and been disappointed by their lack of enthusiasm—may be reflected in his choice of a name for the record's label —B.I.O.Y.A., which stood for Blow It Out Your Ass. By January, when the band got a better offer to be the house band at My Mother's Place in Georgetown, the records were placed inside burlap bags garnered from a jeans promotion, stenciled "Roy Buchanan: Buch and the Snakestretchers," and sold for a few bucks apiece. From Roy's perspective, the record represented an effort to record exactly what he wanted, where and how he wanted it. He liked the comfort of the Crossroads and the way his guitar sounded there, and he didn't care for the antiseptic atmosphere of the studio. *Buch and the Snakestretchers* represented an artist's genuine, if somewhat naive desire for control, and an attendant abhorrence of interference by pesky producers, A&R men, and PR flacks—it was a true homegrown effort. From a music industry standpoint, however, the effort was not only a quaint gesture, but akin to a drink dashed in Polydor's face, and it prepared to sue Roy for breach of contract. *Buch and the Snakestretchers* had zero marketing and distribution power. Nonetheless, after the WNET program aired, the record achieved a buzz that reached outside of the DC area and served notice that Roy's obscurity had ended.

JUST PRIOR TO HEADING to New York for the WNET soundstage performance, however, the Snakestretchers were happily ensconced at the Crossroads, doing their low-key sets and enjoying a few beers and the occasional amphetamine. For the most part, Roy's vices were relatively in check, which was as good as it got. But Roy's shtick, delivered in interviews, that he had quit drugs altogether didn't go over all that well at home. Though he gave Judy the bulk of his earnings for rent and food for six children, there still wasn't enough to cover the basics for such a large family. Circumstances had improved and success seemed close, yet Roy had only the tattered remnants of ambition. Judy, on the other hand, saw it was time to push and push hard. While he worked at the Crossroads that fall, she drove him to work in the family station wagon and, often, picked him up again at 2 in the morning. When she appeared at 2 a.m. to find that her husband had already left and no one seemed to know quite where to, there was hell to pay. Using her best husband-hunting sense, she might look for him and find him, perhaps getting high at a nearby friend's house. Just as often she would return home in a huff. Roy could find his own damn way home.

The soundstage performance that would cap the WNET documentary took place on November 8. In the first week of November Roy and his family and the band all drove to New York City. A WNET press release stated, "This program will demonstrate that great, unknown talent exists, and it will be the showcase that some, unfortunately, never find." The program was actually titled, *Introducing Roy Buchanan*, but it acquired a misnomer, "Introducing the World's Greatest Unknown Guitarist"—which fried Roy. *Unknown?!* Damn, he'd been creating a name for himself for nearly 15 years! Still, the TV station's point established that, outside of certain rarefied circles, Roy's name was indeed unknown. A few choice accolades might

Roy smiling nervously as the WNET soundstage performance gets under way.

fix that. When, finally, the broadcast began, accolades tumbled in interspersed with a bit of testimony from Roy himself.

"He's probably just the most original country-style rock 'n' roll guitar player," testified the Grateful Dead's Jerry Garcia. "He has the nicest tone, the most amazing chops, technically. Super fast. And much neglected." Merle Haggard weighed in: "Yeah, I think he's got a lot of heart. And that's somethin' you can't fake. You know? If you have it, you've got it. If you don't you can't make it look like you do."

"He's been called 'great,' 'the greatest,' by those few who have been fortunate enough to see him," Bill Graham announced from the soundstage. "Apart from some bootleg albums he hasn't put out any of his own. He's played obscure clubs all around the country up until this time. So this is an evening of discovery for most of us, an evening of celebration for all of us. I'm privileged to bring on an artist who should be known by everybody: Roy Buchanan."

Roy had been outfitted with a blazer for the occasion, but his longish hair and Jack Daniels–style beard were well-matched with his battered '53 Telecaster. He and the band launched into a version of "After Hours," and though in retrospect he must have been mightily nervous—the music is tight, self-conscious—the essentials of his remarkable tone and feeling and technique still come through. When Bill Graham suggested applause for Roy's band, Roy led it. Then Graham intro-

From left, Chuck Tilley, Nils Lofgren, and Roy, conjuring up Junior Walker's "Shotgun,"
on the WNET soundstage during the live portion of the documentary.

duced Roy's guest guitarist, Nils Lofgren, who dedicated his first album to Roy, and the band launched into Junior Walker's classic '60s jam vehicle, "Shotgun." The band obligingly leapt into a suitably frenzied version, with Lofgren grabbing the lead . . . and keeping it . . . until it became apparent that he either wasn't able or willing to trade off with his host. Many years later Lofgren ruefully acknowledged that he'd gotten a little excited. Lofgren, who went on to a long and productive solo career, as well as fruitful associations with Bruce Springsteen and Ringo Starr, can laugh today. "That was a real big deal for me to go up to New York City," he said. "I was nervous and excited. I remember playing as fast as I could. I was into it, but I was a very immature player at that time and at some point, I was so excited that I was unaware that I got going and wouldn't stop. At some point Roy just had this *grin*. He could tell that I was too young to have an interactive dialogue with another guitarist. I was in my own world, frantically playing my Stratocaster and at some point it was obvious I wasn't going to have the good taste to trade-off licks, shut up, or whatever. But Roy realized it wasn't me trying to be rude. I was just an overly excited kid. Roy just started hitting a string and de-tuning it, kind of like, 'Well, there's no room here to play any music, why don't I just try some sound effects.' " Roy's technique sounded like a jet plane taking off and, under the circumstances, it actually added tension and texture to the frenetic jam. But great music this was not.

STILL, WITH THE BAND'S performance of the heartfelt "The Messiah Will Come Again," and long film segments of Roy's insights into his Pixley heritage, the presentation effectively delivereded an enigmatic figure. Roy's early professional days were left somewhat murky, though it was clear somehow that he'd paid—perhaps even overpaid—his dues as a journeyman. Between his gigs with Mundell Lowe, Merle Haggard, and Johnny Otis, and the soundstage performance, it was abundantly clear that this artist was cut from a different cloth. He was no rock star, just a soft-spoken, humble country boy with something to say and, once he strapped on a Telecaster, a way of saying it that seduced the spirit and boggled the mind.

As the show came to a close, the producers had to fade out on the band performing "The Messiah," which led to a deluge of phone calls. The program became one of the most requested in PBS' history, according to Adams. Back in Roy's hometown, the *Pixley Enterprise* alerted its readers to a rerun of the program just days later. The article featured a photograph of the old Buchanan homestead on the Forsblad Ranch, with the cottonwood tree Roy and Linda Joan had nurtured towering over it. "The owner of the property had made plans to chop the tree down," the *Pixley Enterprise* reported, "but evidently has decided otherwise. He heard of Roy's feelings in the subject . . . and said he would leave it standing. Roy loved his home in the country east of Pixley near Road 128 and he said that if they cut the tree down it would die as he did when he moved from there."

In the wake of the successful airing of the WNET special, Polydor offered to put its lawsuit aside and get Roy into a studio. My Mother's Place promised to boost his pay and provide a more congenial atmosphere for the audiences most likely to see Roy perform. Apart from these tangible offers, however, life remained pretty much the same as it had for most of the past year. But now Roy could no longer ignore the open door before him. Stepping through the door involved higher stakes, bigger dreams, and a commensurately greater danger of bitter disappointment. While he weighed his aversion to fame and the possibility that it all could turn into his worst let-down yet, Roy headed down to My Mother's Place to play five sets a night, six nights a week. He had hungry mouths to feed.

STEPPING INTO
THE LIGHT

J anuary in Washington, DC, could be bleak, but good fortune was coming Roy's way. The phone began to ring. Offers tumbled in to play concerts outside the DC area. These were not club dates, but actual concerts, with several thousand people in the audience, and fees in the thousands of dollars—more than he'd ever made in a single night in his life. Roy, often loath to assert himself, had to make decisions. He lacked professional management and, if he didn't do something about it quickly, the train would leave the station without him. Hal Davis still yearned to handle the guitarist's affairs, but Davis simply lacked the know-how and his jealous, parochial attitude threatened to choke off opportunity at the precise moment the world had arrived at Roy's doorstep.

Years earlier a Georgetown student in a music appreciation class named Jay Reich, Jr. had asked master jazz guitarist Charlie Byrd to name the best rock guitarist alive. Byrd directed Reich to the Crossroads. "For years there had been rumors about this guy," Reich recalled. "We'd heard that Clapton had gone to see him and ran out of the room screaming." Reich visited the Crossroads and heard what he needed to hear. Though he went to work for his father at an advertising agency in Pittsburgh, PA, after graduation in June 1971, Reich regularly made the three-hour drive to DC to see Roy play. "My heart was set on working with Roy, somehow," he would recall. Reich managed to get Roy's signature on a contract to play Pittsburgh's Syria Mosque in April 1972 and the show sold out. Pittsburghers embraced Roy and his gritty blues and roadhouse rock. Suddenly, Reich had more than Pittsburgh on his mind.

By that time Roy and the Snakestretchers had ventured forth, headlining at the Rhode Island School of Design in Providence, Philadelphia's Tower Theater, and a spring festival in Shady Grove, MD, with Delaney & Bonnie and Billy Preston. Reich brought Roy back to Pittsburgh in May for something dubbed the One World Festival at the University of Pittsburgh stadium, a disastrous date that impressed upon Reich the perishable nature of Roy's music. The roadhouse blues had to be delivered in an appropriate showcase, on a human scale. Roy could take a club by storm, even rivet an audience in a modestly sized concert hall, but his sound could not be projected across a football field, where the music's essence vanished in the wind. Reich now understood that to re-ignite Roy's career he would have to put together club and concert hall dates. To break Roy into the business as a solo artist, Reich needed to present his client in a prominent showcase and generate media response, as well as word-of-mouth buzz.

He set his sights on Carnegie Hall in New York. He gambled the $1,200 it took in those days to book the prestigious hall, and set a date for the evening of June 21. By early June Reich had the jitters. A modestly sized advertisement in *The Village Voice* touting "possibly the world's finest guitarist," a bit of hype courtesy of *Rolling Stone* magazine, had run twice, to little effect. "Stuart Werksman, Carnegie Hall's manager, told me, 'You're out of your *mind!* This guy doesn't even have a record out,'" Reich recalled. "He thought I was going down the drain with this plan." New York was known in the business as a "late town"—that is, because of the profusion of diversions, tickets often didn't sell until right up until show time. Desperate to make the event a success, Reich implored John Adams to have WNET rerun the documentary on Roy on the Saturday evening preceding the Carnegie engagement. The rerun played at 11:30 p.m. on June 17 and apparently a lot of New Yorkers were up at that hour. Ticket sales jumped. On the 21st night of June, a warm summer evening, every one of the 2,850 seats in Carnegie Hall was filled. Record company executives, music critics, pop music cognoscenti, family, friends, and the merely curious assembled, creating an air of expectancy that often filled the hall before a performance. His financial tightrope walk completed, Reich stepped to the microphone, a little nervous but greatly relieved. He said simply, "Here's Harold Lowder."

Harold was Roy's brother-in-law, the husband of Judy's older sister, Doris. At Roy's request, and in keeping with the down-home feel of the evening, Harold had agreed to provide an introduction. A stout man of medium height with thinning red hair, he'd donned a suit for the occasion. As he ambled to the microphone, he suddenly was conscious of the sophisticated audience focused on him. He cleared his throat, and explained his presence. "Ah, hello," he said, tentatively. "I'm here first to give mah blessing to mah favorite rock guitarist." A smattering of applause interrupted him. "I'm here to go through the necessary formality of introducing a group, and a man. I could at this point go into some, ah, comments about technical excellence, about craftsmanship, but I'd rather just tell you about a musical man who has something to say—a certain something to say, and a way of saying it with his music. I'd like to bring to you the heart and the hands and the rock guitar of Roy Buchanan and the Snakestretchers."

The audience responded warmly as five casually dressed young men with longish hair emerged from backstage and took their places. The leader, with his long brown hair, goatee, and dark brown eyes, stepped to the microphone. "First of all,

I'd like to thank everybody for comin' by," Roy said in his mild Southern drawl, as if it was just another weeknight at a bar in suburbia. "I really appreciate it. I really do. I always heard of Carnegie Hall, but I never really believed there was such a place." He paused at his own wonder. "I'd like to start off too with introducing the guys in the band, because we may not get any more applause after you hear our first number. I'd like to get it now. On organ we have Dick Heintze. On bass we have Pete Allen. On drums we have Ned Davis." Audience applause, nervous laughter from the young men onstage. "And we have my voice right here, Mr. Chuck Tilley." Roy stepped away from the microphone, but a second later he returned. In his nervousness he has missed something. "As usual, I forgot to turn my amplifier on," he announced. "But just hang on for a second and it might catch up with us."

Someone said, "You're on," and the band pounded out Dale Hawkins' 1957 hit "Susie Q." The earthy bottom end of Louisiana rock filled the concert hall, the backbeat considerably stronger than patrons of the venerable hall were accustomed to hearing. The band's Fender amplifiers were well-suited to the room's warm acoustics. At that point rock 'n' roll at Carnegie Hall was a bit of a novelty, even though an electric Bob Dylan, backed by the Band—featuring Roy's long-ago student, Robbie Robertson—had played the venue four years earlier. When it came time to solo, Roy gestured good-naturedly toward heaven before plunging in. He was tentative, out of his element. Just days before, he and the Snakestretchers had been holding down their five-nights-per-week gig at My Mother's Place in Georgetown. Before that, it was house band duty at the rough-and-ready Crossroads. Suddenly Roy was on the comparatively antiseptic stage of Carnegie Hall with spotlights banishing the shadows he preferred. The comforting clink of beer bottles was absent, as were the clubs' typically disinterested patrons. But beginning with "Susie Q," Roy methodically worked his battered Telecaster, giving his listeners a taste of where he'd been. He opened his next song, a country ballad titled "Together Again," with a series of steel guitar–like licks, evoking Pixley days, and the influence Jerry Byrd, Buck Owens, and Roy Nichols had on him. To fill out the portrait of his early career and warm up the rather staid crowd, Roy led the band in a fun version of Smiley Lewis' 1955 rhythm and blues hit, "I Hear You Knockin'."

Rock 'n' roll derives from the blues, so the portrait Roy painted of his musical heritage would be incomplete without a little dissertation on the latter subject. Roy knows blues. His native melancholia, seasoned by disappointment, has made him suspicious of good fortune. He had heard of Carnegie Hall, dreamed of playing there, yet until now "never really believed there was such a place." So when he and his band turned to a blues number that balmy summer night, he had a few things to say. Those watching closely saw Roy hook his right pinky around the Telecaster's volume knob and his ring finger around the tone control as he struck a note, bent it, and made it swell into a soft, mournful wail in A minor. A mood captured the concert hall as Roy's descending spiral of sinuous notes drifted out of his amplifier and made their way into his audience's psyches. The melody line to this composi-

Close-up of Roy at work on the '53 Telecaster at Carnegie Hall.

tion, "Since You've Been Gone," has a life-goes-swirling-down-the-drain quality that evokes the heartache and misery of lost love.

Heintze played variations to the haunting melody on his organ, creating a mesmerizing mood piece. Roy, protected for a moment from the glare of the spotlight, coaxed his Telecaster into an echo of Tilley's anguished voice. The guitarist dashed off a series of aggressive staccato runs followed by plaintive cries, reflecting both the anger and the need for love embodied in the singer's supplication. For a moment the performers and audience slipped the ordinary bonds of the well-lit concert hall and found confluence on an emotional level. Roy's seductive guitar work tugged at willing sensibilities. His detached expression could only hint at the source of these blues.

THE BAND LIGHTENED UP with Bill Haley's 1955 rocker, "Rock Around the Clock," another '50s rocker, "Linda Lu," and Chuck Berry's anthem, "Johnny B. Goode," accentuated by Roy's lashing Telecaster work. At first blush, the set might have seemed somehow inappropriate for the circumstances, but it represented a rock 'n' roll résumé. Few could claim, as Roy could, that he'd learned these songs when they originally hit the charts two decades earlier. These were his roots. But this concert was also to be a personal statement. Heintze struck a series of hushed chords on his Hammond B-3 organ. Roy set an introspective mood with a soft, fluid preamble on his guitar, quieting the crowd. He stepped to the microphone and, in his sometimes maddeningly soft drawl, recited the lyrics to his signature song:

> Just a smile, just a glance
> The Prince of Darkness
> He just walked past
>
> There's been a lot of people
> And they've had a lot to say
> But this time, I'm goin' tell it my way
>
> There was a town
> A strange little town they called the world
> It was a lonely, lonely little town
>
> 'Til one day a stranger appeared
> And their hearts rejoiced
> And the sad little town was happy again
>
> But there were some that doubted
> They disbelieved, so they mocked him
> And that stranger, he went away
> Now that sad little town that was sad yesterday
> It's a lot sadder today
>
> I've walked in a lot of places
> I never should have been
> But I do know that the Messiah
> He will come again

Roy shuffled a half-step back from the microphone and unleashed a series of dramatic, stately notes of bell-like clarity that rang out across the hall. His guitar cried out for redemption, raising goose bumps out in the audience. There were soaring questions, statements of devotion, furious arpeggios. The song ended on a series of soft wails that seemed to echo throughout the hall. "Thank you," Roy said. "I thank you very much." As if the crowd might disperse to pursue more pressing business, he added, "I hope you'll stick around." There'd be another set, and this was the standard prayer of a club's house band. Roy walked to the lip of the stage to talk with a handful of young fans. Backstage, later, well-wishers surrounded him. Atlantic

Roy working it out on his Tele at Carnegie Hall.

Records founder Ahmet Ertegun pressed his business card into Roy's hand and murmured promises of fame and fortune. A road stretched out ahead, almost exactly as long as the difficult, winding road that had brought Roy Buchanan to Carnegie Hall. Now he had to step into the light, for he could not return to the shadows.

HAVING SAID HIS PIECE, Roy decided to loosen up for the second set and have more fun. He talked to the crowd as if it were request night at the Crossroads. "You want somethin' fast or slow?" he asked. So it went. His eclecticism might have daunted a few. "Haunted House," an uptempo country favorite popularized by Gene Simmons in 1964, featured some vintage chicken-pickin', and was followed by "Hey Joe," a tribute to the late Jimi Hendrix, whose slow, soulful version of the song had scaled the British charts in 1966. Roy's version was even slower, somehow more menacing. Later, Roy himself would sing this selection—lending a sinister edge with his bland tone (hearing him sing "Yeah, I shot her" in a conversational tone could be chilling)—but at Carnegie Hall Chuck Tilley handled vocals, leaving Roy to give a particularly sensitive reading of the song on his old Tele. He began with slow, sad chords, at a languid pace. Suddenly Roy exploded into a fury of screaming guitar that stunned the audience. Once again, the singer intoned the lyrics. Roy strummed, slowly, but with a whiff of danger. He had captured the audience's attention and served notice that he was indeed Hendrix's peer. Few others could dream of playing the guitar with such ferocity. The ice was broken, a few minds blown. The band opted for a selection titled "Bad Boy," off Eric Clapton's recent debut solo album. There followed a slow blues jam. The audience called for a vocal number, and Roy acquiesced. "Roy's Bluz," in E minor, borrowed heavily from the lyrics to Clay Hammond's 1963 song "Part Time Love," popularized by Little Johnny Taylor. Roy obviously found resonance in the dark lyrics, which might be construed as autobiographical—the flip side to the sentiments expressed in "the Messiah."

My soul went down last Friday
Yeah, but it rose again today

Yeah, my soul went down last Friday
Yeah, but it rose again today

The people in the cemetery
They're not alone like me
You know some turn to dust
Some turn to bone
But me, I'm left here all alone

I've dreamed of heaven
Yeah, I saw my baby there

I dreamed, I dreamed of heaven
And I saw my baby there

You know she had real pretty eyes
And she had long, black wavy hair

If I go to hell
I'm going to speak very highly of you

Yeah, if I go to hell
I'm going to speak very highly of you

Cuz you've done some things pretty momma
That I don't believe that the Devil woulda do

Roy followed the tortured lyrics with blues licks that assured his audience he knew whereof he spoke. "We'll do a fast one after this one," Roy assured the restless and the young in the crowd when "Roy's Bluz" was over. He decided instead to squeeze in an old showcase tune, "Malagueña." This had been one of Roy's crowd-pleasers for more than a decade, a change of pace packed with breath-taking dynamics and visual tricks, including his one-handed pull-offs and hammer-ons that today are standard for any flashy rock 'n' roller. The audience rose to its feet. The evening had been one of discovery for them, and a coming-out for Roy. The Snakestretchers tried to finish up by thrashing their way through a rocking, unpolished version of "Slippin' and Slidin'," Little Richard's hit from 1956, but the band stumbled to a halt. They couldn't end such a historic evening that way! So they turned to B.B King's hit, "The Thrill Is Gone." Even while paying tribute to one of his favorite guitarists—mimicking King's distinctive Gibson picking—Roy still managed to leave his own imprimatur on the song. "Thank you very much. I love you very much," Roy mumbled into the mike and then, deeply relieved, he sauntered off the stage, Tele in one hand, Schlitz in the other. The audience stood and clapped for five full minutes. But Roy couldn't stick around. He and the Snakestretchers had to return promptly to Georgetown to their gig as house band at My Mother's Place. Meanwhile, *Guitar Player* magazine's annual poll results were in: Eric Clapton had been voted the year's No. 1 guitarist, beating out George Harrison, Carlos Santana, Terry Kath, Jimmy Page, and Roy Buchanan. Rounding out the top ten were Jerry Garcia, Alvin Lee, Frank Zappa, and Pete Townshend. With nary a record in circulation, Roy also took the New Talent category by a landslide over 12-string maestro Leo Kottke, pop singer Don McLean, and teenage bluesman Shuggie Otis.

THE ASSIGNMENT to produce Roy's first LP for Polydor fell to Peter Kieve Siegel, who had bridged the gap between the record company and Roy. Siegel played guitar and banjo. He appreciated vernacular music, thus he recognized the authenticity in Roy's music. His own parents had been involved in the folk movement since the 1930s, hip to a scene embodied by Woody Guthrie and, eventually, Bob Dylan and Joan Baez. By 1963 he'd recorded an album with the Even Dozen Jug Band for producer Paul Rothschild on Elektra. The band included Stefan Grossman, David Grisman, John Sebastian, Maria D'Amato (later Muldaur), and Josh Rifkin, all of whom went on to fame in various endeavors. Siegel recorded obscure folk and bluegrass players for tiny labels like Folkways, County, and Silverbell. In his search for native music he helped launch the Nonesuch label's Explorer series, making his mark by taping 15 LPs of south Indian music, making the first-ever record of Japanese shakuhachi music, documenting Swedish fiddle music. "I loved folk music, the blues, old-time country music, bluegrass, and what is now called 'world music,'" Siegel said. "I loved music I would call 'authentic,' true to itself." His aspirations as an engineer and producer led to a chance to clean and align tape heads at Elektra's New York studios, "like you would wash pots in a kitchen," he recalled.

In 1971 Siegel joined Polydor as an A&R man. Artists and Repertoire people decided who would record for a label and what they would record. Siegel and his predilections for authentic music represented a departure from the usual power-hungry hit-seekers who typically sought A&R powers. "I had strong feelings about 'severe' music, authentic music," he recalled with a touch of self-deprecation. "I was dedicated to bringing out an artist's essence, rather than imposing ideas. I tried to produce records transparently, so you wouldn't know I was there."

As Polydor prepared to sue Roy—into the studio, if possible—Siegel entered the picture. He thought he saw another way. Siegel traveled to Washington to speak to Roy in person, only to be greeted by a pair of redneck, self-appointed managers and an attorney pliant to their wishes. The trio explained that it would be their way or the proverbial highway, so Siegel ventured out to Bladensburg to the Crossroads to find the artist himself. "After his set I went backstage. I got him to understand that I knew something about his music and cared about it. The prevailing stereotype in these situations is that 'people from the record company' are idiots and don't know anything about the music, and that was not the case. I made it clear to him that I was hearing his music and that I knew the people who had influenced him. But he was very passive and I don't think he was in a position to say anything about anything."

Siegel returned to New York, frustrated. Polydor's legal department issued a summons to Roy to appear in court for violating his contract. Suddenly the label had the guitarist's attention. Wouldn't it be simpler to just go to New York and record an album than to wrangle in court? Compromise: Roy would bring the Snakestretchers to New York for two consecutive nights of recording in July and record exactly what he wanted to. This time he *did* have something to say, and he didn't want the record company messing with his sound. Polydor agreed. Siegel booked the Record Plant, Jimi Hendrix's former haunt, with respected engineer Shelly Yakus at the "boards," the recording console that transformed a studio performance into saleable vinyl.

The approach was simple: the band would perform the songs it played at the Crossroads live in the studio. There'd be no overdubs, no tinkering with the music. The session took place in Studio B, not the preferred Studio C, where Roy would record his second album. "We got them in there, miked them as well as we could and tried to have a convivial atmosphere and keep it moving," Siegel recalled. "During the sessions people were coming into the studio and saying, 'What *is* that?' They'd heard his guitar through the walls of the studio and it was really speaking to them."

Dick Heintze arranged the music and led the band through its club set. As far as Siegel could see, the band had made no preparations for recording. Roy performed his year-old anthem, "The Messiah Will Come Again," which with the hush of Heintze's Hammond B-3 and Roy's quiet vocals made a particularly effective studio track. The band developed a couple of moody blues riffs into full-fledged pieces dubbed "John's Blues" and "Pete's Blue," respectively. Particularly on the latter, the band set up a somnolent context while Roy simply let fly with inventive riffs, bending into his notes, bending out of them, picking a quirky path up and down scales, effortlessly reeling off pinched harmonics and other crazy sounds, just at the right moment. Tradition had its place as well: "I'm a Lonesome Fugitive," a hit for Merle Haggard in 1967, Hank Williams' "Hey Good Lookin'," "Susie Q," "I Hear You Knockin'," "Can't Judge a Book by Its Cover," and a few others cropped up in the course of two nights. A lot of it was just barroom music, meant to please a Saturday night crowd, or blow off steam in the studio. This was not innovative rock from a recently unearthed virtuoso. Still, the music drew on American blues and country traditions and its sheer variety provided Siegel with something to choose from. Clearly, Roy Buchanan was not the next Jimi Hendrix. No, it was something weirder: Roy could simultaneously be ahead of his time, and a throwback. Therein lay his strength, as well as a source of trouble for those with pecuniary interests in his art.

The vibe felt good, but nobody knew if they really had an album. "I asked him if he could think of anything else," Siegel recalled. "He said, 'Well, I have this country thing.' It turned out to be 'Sweet Dreams,' which I'm really glad I got to record." "Sweet Dreams," written by Don Gibson in 1956, had been a hit for country singer Patsy Cline in 1963. Roy played it as an instrumental, his guitar line emulating the singer's voice in its plaintive cry for understanding. Late one night, with tape left on a reel, Siegel sat Roy down in a chair by himself, miked Roy's Vibrolux amp and turned out a few lights for atmosphere. He wanted Roy to reach deep down into his roots and give him something from the heart. What sort of thing was he looking for? Roy asked. In the control room, Siegel hit a switch so he could be heard in the studio. "Whatever you want," he said. "You got a half-hour of tape in front of you." Striking a low E that blends with the barely perceptible hum of the amplifier, Roy finger-picked his way through themes at times playful, in turn sublime. He circle picked with the nail of his index finger, lending a reverence to the music. Utterly free-form, he sculpted a moody, spunky thing of beauty composed of riffs and half-forgotten snatches of melody. He built a melody from a dead-thumb bass line, a rhythm element, and a lead picked, somehow, over the top. Then he reversed himself, keeping a steady lead going while he picked out a bass solo. Roy's free-form improvisation lasted more than 12 minutes. It was a thing of breathtaking beauty and, of course, totally unsuitable for release. At least in that day. Dubbed "Dual Soliloquy," the track would be issued nearly 20 years later on the label's posthumous collection, *Sweet Dreams: The Anthology*.

Anxious to capitalize on the buzz surrounding its new artist, Polydor rushed the LP into production and distribution. The eponymous *Roy Buchanan* hit the racks by the end of August, a mere six weeks after the Record Plant sessions. Reactions varied. A writer for one of the Chicago daily newspapers suggested that Roy was "the rare example of a talent that cannot be captured on record." Likewise, Roy's eclecticism, a strength in performance, becomes "jarring" on an LP, the Chicago reviewer wrote.

Rolling Stone reviewer Tony Glover also found the record a mixed bag. "Roy is one of the few guitarists to come along with his own *sound*," Glover wrote. Though "technique triumphed over content" on a track such as "Pete's Blue," Glover had nothing but praise for "The Messiah Will Come Again," a "stone-beautiful gospel-sounding melody" that delivered "pure soul." Glover also observed that although "Roy played Carnegie Hall recently [and] other concerts may be on tap, I sorta hope he keeps playing bars . . . Music like this . . . seems to fit bars better than Carnegie Hall somehow."

THE FIRST LP'S SALES were promising, if not stellar, Roy was in a cooperative mood, and Siegel was certain that with another visit to the studio they could improve on Roy's first effort. So arrangements were made to return to the Record Plant in November. Siegel felt that with a greater effort at developing repertoire and with crack session musicians in support a second effort would bear sweeter fruit. When Roy returned to New York with Heintze, Siegel had gathered a few musicians he'd worked with before: Teddy Irwin on rhythm guitar, Don Payne on bass, and Jerry Mercer on drums. Chuck Tilley would sing on one track, Roy sang another. The rest would be instrumentals, pure blues. Roy and Dick had worked out a handful of them on the train to New York. "[Dick] brought a pencil and paper and I explained to him what I wanted," Roy said later. "It was recorded all live . . . I had more to say on this album than on any of the rest of them. I put more heart into it. It was my thing. Actually, my and Heintze's thing."

Drummer Jerry Mercer took his cues from Heintze. "Dick would say, 'Okay, now we're going to do a blues. We'll go two times through the 12 bars, then Roy will go into his solo, there'll be a keyboard solo, then back to the head. And we'd just sort of talk it through like that, and then roll tape! Maybe we'd run through them once or twice to make sure we had the right feel together, have an idea of where the solos were going to be. It was really a semi-jam! And I had no problem with that [approach]. I liked that. If they wanted to fly by the seat of their pants, there's an element there that always did attract me."

As producer, Siegel envisioned more purpose to the madness. "I like to get it to the point, the day before, where it's not quite there, and then go in and nail it," he said. "Roy just played the blues, which I thought was great. We would sit in the studio and I'd say something like, 'You ever play like Elmo' James?' and he'd play 'Tribute to Elmore,'" which made the cut when the album was assembled. "'Filthy Teddy,' I think, was a riff Teddy Irwin started playing. We would just encourage Roy to play something in a particular groove and make a piece out of it." As for "Five String Blues," the name came easily. "Listen to that song," Jerry Mercer said. "There's a place where he's reaching for a high note and there's a slight hiccup. He broke his high E string. He just kept playing, bending his guitar into tune. We never knew that he broke a string until we were walking into the control room and the string was hanging off his guitar. We said, 'When did you break that?' He said,

'In the middle of the solo'—a 'gosh, darn' kind of thing. And if you listen to the solo, it was brilliant."

Apart from the blues pieces, there was an original Roy number with autobiographical lyrics, and a reverential tone.

Thank you Lord, saw your sun shine today,
Bless you Lord, got to see my children play,
May not be the right way to pray,
But I want to thank you anyway

Upwellings of notes, "rushes," filled the background. The song offered an intimate look at Roy's sanctified inner life. He'd had an inspiration about a year earlier. "I'd been up about three days and nights, workin' at the Crossroads," he would recall in an interview. "We lived in an apartment and I was sittin' out on the balcony and I had my guitar and I saw my kids out playin'. The sun was just comin' up. I didn't finish the song that day, but when I sang it to Pete Siegel he said, 'Why don't you sing what you've got and make the rest an instrumental?' So that's how that one came about." According to Siegel, Roy's inspiration was not all divine. "On 'Thank You Lord,' he at first sang, 'And when the night comes and the moon shines above, I want to thank you Lord...' So I stepped into the studio and said, 'Man, you're going to get us *sued* by whoever wrote 'A Good Woman's Love.' He said, '*Damn!* Hawkshaw Hawkins, 1945. How'd you *know* that! Okay, I'll take it out.' He thought he'd never get caught!"

After recording and mixing and editing, Siegel had eight songs suitable for release, four for each side of the LP. "Filthy Teddy," "After Hours," "Five String Blues," and "Thank You Lord" filled the first side. The rocking "Treat Her Right," by Roy Head, opened side two, followed by "I Won't Tell You No Lies," which, with its moody organ work, showcased Heintze's genius for the blues. "Tribute to Elmore" and its lashing guitar work came next. The country ballad, "She Once Lived Here," closed the side with a few choice pedal steel–like licks from Roy's Telecaster. Though these simple 12-bar blues and country ballads broke no new ground musically, each worked as a vehicle for Roy's expressiveness and craftsmanship. The music's simplicity and honesty contrasted markedly with a lot of technically complex studio records being produced then that, despite their sonic cleverness, had little to say. Roy's second album offered American roots music, aged in oak casks, steeped in tradition, yet brimming with something compelling, if not wholly new, to say.

Once again, Polydor sped the album to market, releasing it in February 1973, only a few months after the actual sessions. The record was uniformly well-received. The *New York Times* allowed writer John Rockwell five paragraphs to review Roy's first two Polydor records. "If you like outsider-eccentrics in your rock and roll, Roy Buchanan should be your man," Rockwell began. The first record was "a little odd," and the second "a bit strange," he wrote. "Roy plays an insinuating kind of country rock, so laid-back that it almost falls asleep. What he does is exploit some aspects of the peculiar potential of an electric guitar in a way that nobody else has equaled . . . Roy's solos are remarkable for the intuitively musical way in which he bends the notes of a phrase into shape, sliding up and down the scale, twisting ornaments lazily around a note. It is slow blues perfected to a rare polish. But Roy doesn't ever do much more than what he can do very well. His 'singing'—or, more accurately, his growled, mumbled talking—is eccentric in the extreme: intensely personal statements about God that have little artistic impact . . . If Roy had a musical adventuresomeness to match his innate sensitivity, he would really be something to hear."

Stereo Review's writer, Neal Coppage, responded to Roy's emotional craftsmanship. "Roy Buchanan's *Second Album* for Polydor brings the electric guitar up to date . . . Roy's work calls for its own definition of good taste . . . He has his own unique brand of soul . . . " *Stereo Review* named the album among the "Ten Best" in all music categories for 1973.

While it was gratifying to have one's art appreciated, reviews of the *Second Album* also underscored that Roy clearly was not destined for the mainstream market his sponsors at Polydor wished to tap. That sowed seeds of discontent in the record company's executive suites. The suits had gambled that the sales of Roy's records would reflect his sensational level of word-of-mouth praise as The Next Great Thing. The records sold respectably well, but there seemed to be a feeling at Polydor that given the hype surrounding Roy's emergence the albums were underperforming.

WITH JAY REICH booking him into clubs and concert halls up and down the East Coast, Roy could finally afford to lay down his house band duties at My Mother's Place. The Snakestretchers were gone, suffering the ignoble fate of so many sidemen, fairly or unfairly charged with holding back the star.

Meanwhile, word of Roy's prowess in performance had gotten around. One of the Snakestretchers' last gigs had been a series of nights at New York's Village Gate. Roy played wonderfully, as he did throughout this period. With an advance on record sales from Polydor and steady, lucrative gigs, a financial burden had been lifted from his shoulders. He loved to play for people who wanted to hear him and it showed in his playing. At one of the Village Gate shows in late October, Bob Dylan and John Lennon, both denizens of New York City, were said to have disguised themselves and taken in a set. According to Roy, Dylan later called him at home but he didn't return the call.

When he resumed touring a couple weeks later with a gig in New York his lineup consisted of Dick Heintze on keyboards and Jerry Mercer on drums, with Junior Gill filling in on bass. Mercer knew how to fly by the seat of his pants, but even for him Roy's approach to his upcoming tour proved a tad improvisational. "Roy shows up," Mercer recalled. "He puts his little Fender amp on the chair and

'Roy's in business,' right? Up comes a guy named 'Rodney.' Dick says, 'Roy, this is Rodney So-and-So, he'll be the singer on this tour. Rodney, this is Roy Buchanan.' We start to play a song and Roy looks over at Rodney after a solo and says, 'Sing.' That was Roy's idea of giving direction! It's incredible for a guy at that level, who's putting together a group that's going to tour America, then go to Europe . . . Most people spend months preparing. They want everything squeaky clean, polished. Here's Roy with a band of strangers, practically. All you did was play and listen to Roy. You didn't play as if you knew what was coming next. You played carefully and you listened. My ears were huge on that tour. I remember focusing like mad. I'm a hard player. I hit hard. I've been a rock and R-&-B drummer most of my life. But with Roy some nights the only sweat was the sweat of concentration—just waiting and listening for the dynamics. Is he starting to roll? Is he looking for sharp accents or does he want everything hush-hush, just a whisper behind him? You've got your ears on Roy, your eyes on Dick. Dick is focused on Roy like mad. If Roy felt like whispering for ten minutes, he'd whisper for ten minutes. The job of the band was to stay tuned. So the show evolved, though we never rehearsed one song. And every night he called something that he never called on any other night. I'd never worked this way before. With Roy we evolved the arrangements onstage, by listening very carefully, and the arrangements began to grow."

ROY'S PERFORMANCES in this period drew on more than a score of songs, a lot of them pretty funky, from Little Richard's "Lucille" to Ray Charles' "What'd I Say," from Smiley Lewis' "I Hear You Knockin'" to Buck Owens' country heartbreaker, "Together Again," a hit for Ray Charles during his country phase in 1966. With "The Messiah," "Hey Joe," and "Roy's Bluz," the band had a powerful arsenal. Two performances that December at Pittsburgh's Heinz Hall revealed Roy in an explosive mood, coming out "with his pants on fire" as one reviewer later put it, delving into each number with an endlessly inventive flow of musical ideas and guitar techniques, toying with melodies in flights of unrestricted fancy.

THE SPRING OF 1973 brought an invitation to play the Montreaux (Switzerland) Jazz Festival where Roy was warmly received. The band moved on to Germany, then to London for a three-week stay and a series of performances in nearby towns. Near the end of the run Polydor planned to tape a performance at London's Marquee Club for a possible live LP. Londoners might have gotten a glimpse of the ordinary life behind the Roy mystique if they read a *Melody Maker* article on May 5, just days before the Marquee Club gig. Michael Watts had penned the music paper's "New York Report," and in an article titled "The New Guitar Man" he described a Roy encounter a couple weeks earlier at New York's Academy of Music. Backstage after the show a long-haired young man buttonholed the guitarist to talk technique. The guitarist is stoic. He's been there before. Then a young woman, one of those backstage specters who seem to have a lot to say about nothing in particular, suddenly required Roy's attention. For some reason, she pressed him: communication is *so* important. "I mean, especially in this city, where everything is so phony. Don't you [think so]?" she pleaded. Buchanan glanced at the Budweisers on ice just beyond his reach. "It's good if an audience feels it too," he offered, distractedly. "No! No!" the woman insisted, to Judy Buchanan's amusement. "I mean with boyfriends. You know what boyfriends are like. You have to keep him jealous to keep him, but that's not what I want to be into." She smiled. Roy glanced at the Budweisers. Finally, the woman left. "I always mess it up and say the wrong thing," Roy said. As the group left the dressing room for the ride to Roy's hotel, the guitarist donned a pair of rimless glasses, which lent him the appearance, Watts wrote, of a "Bavarian astronomy professor." When they reached the hotel, Judy declared, " 'Roy, I want you to come up to the room. I want to talk to you.' Roy vaguely nodded his head and wandered into the hotel bar, where he ordered a large Bloody Mary." Roy recounted his early days to a writer. Judy reappeared. "Roy, will you *please* come upstairs? I have something to say to you." Judy disappeared. When Roy finally sauntered up the stairs, he had one writer, three band members, and a cardboard box full of beer. Upstairs, somehow, another interviewer is waiting. When Watts caught Judy's eye, she smiled wanly. "Don't worry. I'm used to it by now."

Roy had achieved a degree of popularity in the UK with his first album. In fact, "Sweet Dreams" had risen to Number 50 on the British charts in early April. The same week, the teen heartthrob Donny Osmond's latest record had reached No. 1. Once ensconced in London, two Daimler limousines ferried the band to gigs in Manchester, Leeds, then to an overnight in Great Yarmouth, on the English coast. Eric Clapton's praise had preceded them, so turnout was "thick and ready" in Mercer's words. Still, somehow, the band fractured as the tour progressed. In an honest, professional effort to hone its performances, the band pressed for rehearsals. Roy promised to show, but didn't. "That really let the air out of the band," Mercer said. "The will to excel really died. When you're trying to build something around an individual like Roy you need to have Roy there!" But Roy preferred to avoid rehearsals. He believed they tended to over-prepare him for a performance and take the edge off spontaneity—a valid objection, and possibly a rationalization by someone too lazy to rehearse.

In the end, the Marquee Club performance was anticlimactic. The new singer, Rodney Juster, simply didn't fit. For the most part the band sounded disjointed and the tapes were deemed unworthy of release. (Nearly 20 years later, the track "C.C. Ryder," the lone gem from this concert, was released on *Sweet Dreams: The Anthology*.) Nonetheless, the Brits took a shine to Roy. In a review by David Lewis of a performance at London's Imperial College, published in *Melody Maker* a few days later, Lewis wrote: "At London's Imperial College on Saturday night he left a jam-packed audience gaping with astonishment as he casually produced the kind of guitar playing you can normally only dream about. Standing motionless and blandly staring down at his boots he did things with his beat up old Telecaster that you would not have thought possible. The guitar not only talked to the crowd, it sang, screamed and whispered as he twiddled the control knobs and slapped his fingers across the strings, flamenco style."

It was on this London sojourn that, according to Roy, he received an invitation from Paul McCartney to jam. Roy said that he told McCartney he couldn't make it. The guitarist had promised to take his daughter to the zoo that day. Seymour Duncan, who'd caught up with Roy at an American College gig prior to the Marquee Club date, had met Neil Young and members of Wings backstage, so the McCartney story was not implausible, though the plot seemed familiar. Roy had blown off the Stones, and others. Why not one of the Beatles? Enough preposterous stories about Roy had proved to be true, yet one could never be quite sure when he was bullshitting. Between his dead-pan Southern manner when he mentioned something astonishing and his astounding abilities on the guitar, one really couldn't be too sure. That's how Roy liked it.

WITH POLYDOR'S ADVANCE and Roy's tour proceeds, Roy and Judy moved from the cramped Lanham apartment to a multi-bedroom house in the country, outside Lovettsville, VA, 40 miles northwest of DC. For Roy and his clan, after years in excruciatingly tight quarters, the Lovettsville house was a dream come true. Finally they had a decent home of their own, with elbowroom, in the country. Roy acquired two mastiffs, which he loved to walk along the country lanes, though the dogs could intimidate strangers. As always, the dream came with a price. The Lovettsville house could only be sustained if Roy periodically left home for weeks at a time to tour the country. That meant he wasn't home to help parent the couple's six children, several of them entering their teens, and the kids missed their father. For Judy, it meant also that Roy and his band, who were, after all, rock 'n' rollers, would be debauching for weeks at a time—never a pleasant thought for spouses. Roy tried to limit the duration of his tours, but business was business. And that meant he had it pretty good. When Roy got tired of home, he could go on the road. When he tired of the road he could go home. Judy had no such choices. At the same time, material success didn't mean that Roy suddenly was happy. With the money came pressure to write and record and tour. Though tours could be fun, an escape from mundane days at home, traveling also inevitably meant mundane days on the road and the starkness of the Gypsy lifestyle, racing from town to town to entertain others. Sometimes the prospect of recording or touring put him into a real funk. "When we moved to Loudon County he'd get blue because he didn't want to record or go on the road or he didn't want to do something," Judy told author Mark Opsasnick. "So we'd take a little drive. I'd drive him out to Prince George County. He used to like the Italian Inn, over on Route 450. We used to go there for pizza and lasagna. In fact, Roy used to drive me crazy about pizza. He had to have a pizza practically every day of his life. I remember when we didn't have a pot to piss in we would gather our pennies and off we would go to get a pizza. Anyway, we'd reminisce at some of the old places where we'd lived. I'd say, 'Do you want to go back to living like that?' It would give him the incentive to go on."

DESPITE THE OCCASIONAL BLUE DAY, life was good and Roy finally had the attention he deserved, even if he wasn't entirely comfortable with it. "I'm not a star," he told *Down Beat's* Mike Kalina that spring. "I never could be . . . I never will be. I'm just a guitar player. This star business . . . scares the hell out of me." As for the financial rewards that came with his new recording contract and his tours, Roy said he was grateful for it, but "I'm not out there driving a pink Cadillac." In fact, he said, "I'm not really interested in the money a label can give me. I'm more interested in the sound I can get with the record company." Roy readily admitted to Kalin that he didn't practice. "The only time I play is when I get up on stage. My music's more spontaneous that way, and I play the way I feel. If I practiced day after day, I feel my music would get stale." His recent successes had him nostalgic for the Cross-roads, or so he said. "It's a nice, small place . . . It has a great atmosphere and is tremendous acoustically. And you can relate to the crowd because the place is real small. I miss the place . . . You miss something in the big concert halls. It's hard to feel the vibrations from the crowd. Don't get me wrong. I'm pleased to have the opportunity to play concerts because I can reach a hell of lot of people . . . And that gives me great satisfaction because more than anything I want people to not only hear my music but also like my music."

To get people to hear his music, of course, Roy needed a band; his latest had imploded on the spring tour of Europe. Dick Heintze remained available, and drum-mer Robbie Magruder, who had briefly filled in earlier that year on drums, also was ready. Magruder had grown up in the DC area playing in local bands, including the Misfits, who'd had their brush with fame in 1963. He'd known of Roy as a local leg-end since the late 1960s. When early in 1973 he first got a call to join Roy for a brief tour of the Midwest, he realized that the Roy gig was not for the faint of heart. Dick Heintze sent him a tape of *Second Album* to prepare him. Then Magruder flew to Cincinnati and climbed onstage in front of 2,500 people, having never even met Roy, let alone rehearsed any music. "I just showed up, terrified!" he said later, still amazed. That night, however, he realized he was working with someone who, despite his nonchalance, could really work a crowd. "It was magic what he could do with a single note," Magruder said. So, despite Roy's kamikaze approach to tour-ing, when the call came in at the end of summer, the drummer signed on.

Roy also needed a bass player, so Reich recruited John Harrison, a Pittsburgh native whose first love had been folk music before he got seduced by rhythm and blues. His father played piano and sax; classical music often filled the Harrisons' home. While his brother explored the drums, Harrison found an affinity for the bass guitar. When he reached Pennsylvania State University he formed a band called Homebrew and gigged at nearby clubs. He met Bill Pollack, an accomplished singer who took the stage name Billy Price and ran a smoking R&B band. Homebrew had opened for a number of Roy's Pittsburgh-area shows in the early 1970s. As Reich put together a summer 1973 tour he stopped by Harrison's apartment and told him he had the gig. Harrison had to be in New York in a week. "I said, 'Fine. When do rehearsals start?'" Harrison recalled. "Jay says, 'You don't get any rehearsals.' This is Roy's M.O. This is a source of amusement and, to be quite honest, a real source of frustration over the four years I stayed with him. Jay says, 'Talk to Heintze. He's the bandleader. He'll talk you through it.' Dick said, 'Look. Just get the records.' Basically, I locked myself in a room for a week and wood-shedded on those tunes. I also asked Jay: 'By the way, who's singing?' He said, '*You're* the singer!'"

On August 13 Harrison flew to Long Island and met up with the other members of the band for the first time at their gig at My Father's Place in Roslyn, a venue whose patrons would inspire Roy to peak performances over the years. "I asked Roy, 'Is there anything you want me to know?' He said, 'No, we'll be fine.' I'm shitting in my pants!" Roy's set of straight rock 'n' roll had the audience in a frenzy, and as Harrison belted out "Johnny B. Goode" he realized that the wacko he'd signed on with was winging it and getting away with it. "People went *apeshit*," Harrison said with evident satisfaction. The new foursome melded, he said, like "a real team. The best gigs we did were when we'd been out two or three weeks in a row and, just by playing all the time, you'd develop musical communication. Even without practice we'd invent all kinds of stuff and got really tight so it wasn't by the numbers. The band gelled. There were some unbelievably great concerts." Reich agreed: "The chemistry was good. We had a good time wherever we went. Roy was happy. I was happy. We made money."

After a brief tour of the East Coast and Midwest, it was time to head into the studio to fulfill Roy's obligation to Polydor for a third LP. But things had changed since the previous fall when Pete Siegel managed to generate just the right atmosphere for Roy's sessions. Decisions had been made, and business ruled. "Jerry Schoenbaum called me into his office and told me that he felt that Roy's *Second Album* hadn't lived up to its potential sales," Siegel recalled. "He saw Roy more as an Eric Clapton or Jimi Hendrix, with rock songs and singing, and he didn't think I was the producer for him." Siegel was out, but no alternative presented itself. Without a seasoned producer on hand, Jay Reich suggested that the road band hole up at Roy's Lovettsville house and find out if anyone had any songs. As usual, Roy had a few riffs. A couple ideas. No lyrics. Jay suggested that the band include blue-eyed soul singer Billy Price, from Pittsburgh, and so Price joined the sessions.

Price had grown up on James Brown and Otis Redding and, after the usual apprenticeship in teenage bands, he'd organized a hard-driving R&B band he dubbed the Rhythm Kings. Pittsburghers embraced them. Price first met Roy on a TV program out of New York called *Don Kirchner's Rock Concert* in the summer of 1973, where the singer had a classic Roy Buchanan experience. "The first time I ever performed with Roy was in a dressing room to do that show," Price recalled. "No rehearsal. They said they needed a singer for this thing. 'Will you do this?'

'Johnny B. Goode,' 'I Hear You Knockin',' and a couple of other things. That was my baptism."

When the invitation came to join the sessions for the third album, he accepted. He rationalized his participation as a career move. Making a studio recording with Roy Buchanan might garner national exposure for his Rhythm Kings. Where was the downside? Price soon found out. "The third album was thrown together in a kind of half-assed way," he said. "Roy didn't ever tell you what he wanted. He was anything but a leader. Writing songs for that album wasn't really 'writing songs.' Roy would play a riff and wait for me to sing something. That's the way we did lyrics. It was not the way we did things with my band. This was more intuitive. We didn't play the fuck out of the song first, before recording it, as we did for the Rhythm Kings."

Together, the band fleshed out six new songs to augment a few from their live set. A majority of the new creations were rhythm and blues or blue-eyed soul ballads with Telecaster work at times eloquent, often blistering, on the whole well-executed if somewhat melodramatic. With material in hand Reich convinced Polydor executives to hand him the producer's reins and the band headed to Shelly Yakus' Record Plant. Reich was consciously looking to cut tracks that would garner airplay; he was looking for a hit. The first track on the record, "My Baby Says She's Gonna Leave Me," revealed a glimpse of Roy's songwriting process: It was based on a riff he'd been toying with for years. Staples from the band's club set included "Hey Joe" and "Roy's Bluz." The latter, particularly, though a simple 12-bar blues, provided a vehicle for Roy's stunning blues chops.

Yeah, my soul went down last Friday
Yeah, but it rose again today
Yeah, I think I like life better
Oh, I might even decide to stay

Another significant piece on the album turned out to be a lilting country blues titled "Nephesh," the Hebrew word for soul. The song is simple enough, but in Roy's hands the guitar beseeches the listener, grabbing attention with its trebly piercing Telecaster siren call, searching for solace, speaking of devotion. It is naked, sub-verbal expression.

Unfortunately, the mix of songs was too eclectic to gel for an overall effect. One song that should have been a standout, Roy's version of "Hey Joe," suffered, as did other tracks, from too much flash. The recorded version was unbearably slow, and soft-spoken, with stabbing lightning bolts of guitar to add tension. But it ended in a blitzkrieg of high-speed guitar riffs that smacked of overkill. Jay thought pyrotechnics would sell records. Many years later, he acknowledged that *That's What I'm Here For* was "a blatant attempt to sell singles." Price was appalled. "The direction was ridiculous. Roy would play a very tasteful solo in the studio and then come into the control room. Jay would say, 'Roy, you've got to throw that fast stuff in there for the kids.'" Reich remains proud of certain tracks on the album and, indeed, "Roy's Bluz" is a raw tale of personal pain, as "Nephesh" is a remarkable piece of country soul. "It could have been a lot better, if we had taken more time," Reich said. "I was twenty-three years old and running the show. I'd never been in the studio before. [Polydor] expected so much from Roy and thought I could get it. As I look back at that record, from the cover to about 60 percent of the material, it was blatantly commercial for the sake of being commercial. We missed the mark."

At the Record Plant the band passed a diminutive figure in the hallway. It turned out to be John Lennon, there to mix his *Rock 'n' Roll* album. The former Beatle knew Roy's work, and not only did he offer to play on Roy's album, he invited Roy to play guitar on his current effort. As Robbie Magruder remembered, Lennon was mixing a record in Studio B when he found out Roy was recording next door and popped in for a visit. "He said he wanted to play. Roy says, 'Sure man, let me finish this track and then you can come on over.'" We do this track countless times, Roy hems and haws. Lennon comes back in, sits down in the control room. He just wanted to play rhythm guitar on anything on Roy's record. I remember this very vividly. Lennon had on this black satin jacket with huge, block, white letters on the back that said, 'FUCK OFF.' But he was a very pleasant, very cordial guy. Dick whispered to me to get his autograph. I said, '*You* ask him, man.' Dick hissed, 'I *can't. You* do it!' So I got Lennon's autograph for Dick's daughter. Well, once again, Roy played, drank a lot of beer. Lennon comes in, says he's tired, and he's going home. But when you're ready for me, call me and I'll grab a cab and come right down here. Roy is like, 'Fine.' Lennon split. Shortly thereafter Roy went back to his hotel. The next morning, 10 a.m., we show up to start recording again. Apparently Lennon was going to come and play. He definitely expressed his interest in playing on the record. But Jay had gotten a call at 8 a.m. that Roy had flown home. He didn't feel like playing that day. You have to wonder," Magruder added. For his part, Jay Reich insisted that Roy didn't blow off Lennon. "It just never came off. When he was ready, John wasn't. And when John wanted to do it, Roy was working on something else."

That's What I'm Here For was released in February 1974. Bill Holland, then writing for an alternative Washington, DC, weekly, *Unicorn Times,* reacted positively. He suggested that the new material sounded closer to the hard-edged sound of the raucous J. Geils Band or the finesse of Eric Clapton's 1970 venture, *Derek and the Dominos.* He liked the original songs—"on an artistic level they're strictly lightweight, but fun"—and called the band "a working unit." Holland had been a critic of Roy's early, weak bands, and now, he acknowledged: "For the first time on record there's a glimmer of a kick-ass band . . . The rumors should be dispelled—Roy *can* put together a good band, he *can* allow other musicians to come forward, and he *can* play damned fine modern rock and roll. This album should attract listeners who found his previous albums, and perhaps his general approach, too introspective for their 'get it on' tastes."

As larger publications held forth, however, the reviews were shorter and less admiring. *Stereo Review* had picked *Second Album* as one of the ten best records of 1973. But where Noel Coppage had lauded *Second Album*, he discerned a change in approach that marred the third effort. "It's awfully hard to say where the line is," he wrote, "but I think Roy Buchanan crosses it here, and demonstrates flash for flash's sake. His understanding of the electric guitar is broad and deep, and his ability to completely dominate the instrument is probably unique, but the main idea still should be to interpret the song. The band's new vocalist, Billy Price, helps that in a raw but competent way, and Dick Heintze's keyboard work continues to be exemplary, but I think Roy overplays."

Rolling Stone's influential and widely read review was published May 9, 1974, while the band toured the country at the peak of its performing powers. Reviewer Jim Miller said what he had to say in two paragraphs. "Roy Buchanan has problems," Miller began. "Playing from a broader stylistic base than most other rock lead guitarists, he has chosen to work with a narrow band just this side of hack barroom competence. Roy realized early that he couldn't sing; but his replacement, an inept fellow named Billy Price, has compounded rather than alleviated the problem. Price mauls every song he touches, which unfortunately includes most on this album. Roy's ringing tone still sticks out amid the vocal butchery. One of Roy's tunes, an instrumental called 'Nephesh,' closes the album on a hovering note of grace. But *That's What I'm Here For* generally sticks to a gloomy fare of gruesome singing and hackneyed 'original' compositions. Roy's mostly instrumental *Second Album* fared better." The band was devastated, particularly Billy Price. Blue-eyed soul obviously didn't pique the taste buds at *Rolling Stone*. Miller clearly understood Roy's "broad stylistic base"; he simply didn't like the material.

Rolling Stone's status and pervasive distribution amplified its impact. It mattered little to the band when, the following month, *Guitar Player* declared that "this record . . . gives testimony that Roy is definitely one of the greatest rock guitarists ever. The way he coaxes harmonics out of that old, beat-up '53 Telecaster, and bends, slurs, and shakes those strings make up a technique that is unbelievable. His imaginative approach to tone distortion (and he doesn't even use any modification devices) is at once humbling and illuminating in this day that finds a foot switch for practically anything. And Roy's riffs weave over and through each other with breathtaking subtlety. Every single cut on this album is worth hearing . . . ."

A certain amount of damage had been done. Jay Reich's faith in himself as a record producer was badly shaken, as was Billy Price's devotion to his genre and craft and he flirted with quitting the music business. And Roy? Too reserved to say. It was just a record, anyway. Performing live was the thing. He knew that records traditionally helped fuel demand for tours and served to keep one's name before the public, but that maxim had never seemed to work for him anyway. The audiences on tour pretty much showed up on the strength of word-of-mouth of the guitarist's incendiary performances, and their roars, in turn, told him all he needed to know. Besides, under his Polydor contract, he had two more albums to deliver. They'd surely hit it next time around.

EARLY 1974 TOOK THE BAND to through the Northeast, the Midwest, the West Coast, and back through the South, including Texas, always one of the band's favorite stops. The band's infectious rock 'n' roll energy, and its barroom set list, captured audiences everywhere it went. A typical set might open with Booker T's "Green Onions" (a showcase workout for Dick Heintze on the Hammond B3), proceed with Bobby "Blue" Bland's "Further On Up the Road," move on to Ma Rainey's "C.C. Ryder"—a nice serving of American roots music—before turning to a couple original compositions. "That's What I'm Here For" and "Please Don't Turn Me Away" gave Price a chance to strut his stuff. Roy would return to his favorites, including Smiley Lewis'"I Hear You Knockin'," Jerry Lee Lewis'"Whole Lotta Shakin' Goin' On," even Sly Stone's "Don't Call Me Nigger, Whitey," just to rile the crowd. Roy virtually always included "The Messiah," "Hey Joe," "Roy's Bluz," and "Tribute to Elmore" to please his hard-core blues fans. In an intimate setting, his soft-spoken introduction to "The Messiah" would be barely audible, but effective. In a larger hall, it would be all but lost and Roy was not inclined to enunciate or project his voice, leading an occasional, raucous concertgoer to shout "Speak up, boy!" Up front, where Roy stood in a spotlight, these rude intrusions only added to the moment's edge. But he never skipped a beat, never seemed flustered. From his pulpit on stage, hecklers seemed inconsequential. He'd learned that over the course of 18 years on the road. Besides, it was just a gig.

In March the band booked into Carnegie Hall for the second time. "We were in Columbus, OH, playing a college," Robbie Magruder recalled. "Judy didn't want to fly the band to New York and Jay is saying, 'This is *Carnegie Hall*. This is an important gig. You can't expect these guys to drive 24 hours and show up and play!' So Jay bought us all plane tickets out of his pocket to get us there." Roy's penchant for head games had not waned since the early days. "I was terrified to fly," Robbie added. "Roy turns to me and says, 'This plane is going to crash. We're going to be famous! Bigger than Hendrix! Can't you see it?' "

Each of Roy's Carnegie Hall gigs—there would be four, between 1972 and 1985—garnered legions of new fans. In spring 1974 that included this author. The New York area, as in other parts of the country, produced knots of devoted Buchanan fans. One such group, led by Peter Alpert of South Orange, NJ, included this author, Andy Stein, David Weisman, Charlie Cohen, and Marc Lester—all denizens of Maplewood. Having been raised on everything from Motown to the Beatles, Ray Charles to the Rolling Stones, with a particular focus of late on Jimi Hendrix, Cream, the Band, the Allman Brothers Band, and the Grateful Dead, we instantly knew we'd struck a mother lode. The pure electrifying excitement of Roy's piercing, soulful exclamations channeled through his Telecaster claimed first our attention, then earned our devotion. Throughout the spring the band played again and again throughout the New York area and, as fervent disciples, the Maplewood Mafia managed to attend.

At a time when rock 'n' roll had graduated to giant sports arenas, and chain link fences often separated audiences from artists, Roy's decision to play clubs and small theaters was wholly refreshing. Instead of a wall of industrial-strength amplifiers, here was the warm hum of a Telecaster plugged into a modest Vibrolux amp. Here was the funkiest, most creative electric guitarist on the scene and you could approach the stage and banter with him between numbers, if you were so inclined. Roy's authenticity and availability in comfortable settings set a powerful example, and it had a lot of impact on audiences. Roy clearly loved playing to an appreciative room and his fans returned the affection.

John Harrison has good memories of this period. "It was a wild time," he said. "A fun time to be around, because everyone was getting hip to Roy. We were treated great." Good vibes were not enough for Billy Price, who lamented the lack of preparation for performances and saw the cultish fascination with Roy in particular as detrimental to the band as a whole. "I grew up admiring guys like Otis Redding, James Brown, and Jackie Wilson," he said. "I always thought of myself as a vocalist *and* a performer. I did some of that with Roy but it wasn't accepted because people were there to hear him play the guitar. The more I stood out the more I felt I detracted from what people expected him to do. In that respect we got jaded very quickly." Dick Heintze sometimes chafed at the audience's reception as well, for he too lived in Roy's shadow. Following a well-received solo by Roy, Heintze might work over the keyboards with dexterity and nuance and feeling—all to dead silence, as the audience waited for Roy to resume blazing. Sometimes Roy himself generously led the applause for his organist, who scowled behind his beard but said nothing.

Despite the attention, Roy maintained his seeming indifference to the spotlight and new opportunities, which baffled Robbie Magruder. "Jay was Mr. Gung-ho, constantly pleading with Roy to do this or that. I remember sitting in a Toronto hotel room and Jay came in and blurted out that one of the Rolling Stones [Bill Wyman] had just called to ask Roy to play on his album [*Monkey Grip*]. Roy looked like someone had just said, "The hamburgers are here."

When June rolled around, Roy announced he was heading to the Record Plant West in Sausalito, CA, to record the fourth of five albums he owed Polydor. That would be the fourth record in two years, or one every six months—prolific by any standard, let alone for a guitar stylist without a penchant for penning his own material. The road band would take a house in Sausalito for a month, courtesy of Polydor, and gig up and down the coast, but they would not participate in the studio sessions. After the third album debacle, Polydor was making sure it got the most out of its much-touted guitar star. Ed Freeman had produced Greg Allman's first solo record and he got the assignment to get the best of Roy down on tape. He chose to record at the Record Plant West.

Freeman selected material ranging from funky R&B to electrified country blues, produced and packaged for the perennial possibility of radio airplay. The album's first side featured "Rescue Me," a 1966 hit for singer Fontella Bass, "I'm a Ram," a brassy number written by Mabon Hodges and Al Green, "In the Beginning," a reverential Roy original instrumental, and Ma Rainey's "C.C. Ryder." The flip side opened with "Country Preacher," by keyboardist Joe Zawinul of Cannonball Adderley and Weather Report fame. Then Roy rocked on Mike Bloomfield and Nick Gravenites' "You're Killing My Love." A down-and-dirty blues followed—"She Can't Say No"—co-written by Bill Sheffield and Roy, based on a riff Roy for years had been teasing out in performance. The closing track, "Wayfaring Pilgrim," took a wistful Roy riff and fleshed it out a la Freeman, with piano accents and synthesized strings.

Freeman chose a core of competent Los Angeles studio musicians to support Roy, including Bill Sheffield on vocals, Neil Larsen on keyboards, Kenny Tibbets on bass guitar, and Bill Stewart on drums. Famed percussionist Armando Peraza played congas on a couple tracks. The emphasis was on craft and taste, in contrast to the ostentatious overplaying on the previous effort. In that respect the album succeeded, with Roy providing well-crafted fills and solos and the song itself remaining the focus of attention. Still, it had been all Freeman could do to squeeze eight tracks—31 minutes of music—out of Roy.

The latest road band inevitably blew apart. Billy Price returned to the Rhythm Kings. Judy fired Magruder for fooling around on his wife. Dick Heintze got pissed when Roy announced he was going to record without his road band. That was the last straw for Heintze. "Dick didn't feel Roy was working enough," Reich recalled. "Dick had a family. He wanted to do something closer to home. So when he was home he was working with Danny Gatton. That's like working for Macy's and Gimbel's at the same time. That stuck in Roy's craw that this guy would work with Danny, because he thought Danny was taking a lot of his ideas. And I'm sure he was." So Heintze was out. Harrison understood Roy's position and, though the studio situation irked him as well, he hung in. "We ran into this all the time," Harrison said. "It was part of the frustration that kept growing. People would come in and say, 'I'd love to work with Roy, but I don't want his band on the album.' That really pissed us off."

When Roy hired Malcolm Lukens, a Heintze protégé from DC, to play keyboards, and Ron "Byrd" Foster, another Pittsburgher, to drum and sing, he had a band. With Lukens and Foster onboard a unit formed that would endure for three solid years—an eternity in the lives of club musicians. Lukens, eight years Roy's junior, had grown up in the DC area listening to classical music and boogie-woogie on his parents' radio, before turning to rock 'n' roll. He happened to be playing in Denver at a striptease club in August 1974 when Heintze called to tell him Roy had an open spot on keyboards. There was an upcoming gig at the Schaefer Music Festival in Central Park in New York, set for August 26. Both Malcolm Lukens and Ron Foster would meet Roy and the rest of the band for the first time at the Schaefer Festival gig. Ten years younger than Roy, Ron had grown up in the Pittsburgh area playing in blue-eyed soul bands: one was known as the Igniters, another the Marshmallow Steamshovel. By 1972 he recorded an album with Sweet Lightning for RCA. He too underwent the typical Roy initiation. "I'm at a fast food restaurant in Pittsburgh and Jay Reich comes in," Foster recalled. "Could I play with Roy that weekend in Central Park? I said, 'Let me think about it a second—*yeah!*' I'm sittin' backstage and Roy comes runnin' in. Jay said, 'Ron, this is Roy Buchanan.' I said, 'Mr. Buchanan, it's a privilege to work with you . . . .' And he says, 'Uh, let's go.' And we walked out on stage."

WITH RECORD SALES never more than modest, even leveling off since *Second Album*, Polydor experienced an inevitable letdown. Though Roy himself often said at that time that "Polydor couldn't sell a Beatles reunion," the label would have sold a hell of a lot more records if Roy had been smart enough to have John Lennon play on *That's What I'm Here For.* In any case, mutual disillusionment had driven a wedge between artist and label. "At that time I was looking into recording at Atlantic with Ahmet Ertegun, who was responsible for Otis Redding's career, and Eric Clapton's success," Reich said. "He was a legendary guy. He wanted to sign Roy. And I wanted to get out of the contract with Polydor. So I approached Polydor and I said, 'Listen, we're not getting anywhere on this label. Atlantic wants us, why don't you let us go?' He said, 'Well, you've got one more album on the contract.' Ed Freeman's album cost $75,000, which was a lot of dough at the time. They said, 'Why don't we do a live album on the cheap?'" Reich arranged for the band to play two shows at New York's acoustically friendly Town Hall on Nov. 29, 1974. Roy would share the bill with Larry Coryell and the Eleventh House. Arrangements were made with the Record Plant to have its mobile recording truck at the hall, with Shelly Yakus at the boards.

By this time the band had crisscrossed the country for three months, playing clubs and small auditoriums, and it had gelled and expanded its repertoire. All four players were steeped in blues, rhythm and blues, and roadhouse rock, so the sensibilities and songbooks each brought to the party overlapped nicely. The overall effect was barroom music played at a world-class level. The band's standard operating procedure would be to play whatever Roy felt like playing, including suggestions made for the first time right there on the bandstand. Unlike other bands Roy had suffered along with, this band had dynamics and a robust sound that fit with Roy's guitar work.

The evening did not begin auspiciously. "We had gone to the gig in one of those horse-drawn carriages," Byrd Foster said. "John and me and Roy and Jay and Malcolm. Malcolm at that time had a problem and he had that glazed look, and was kinda noddin'. Roy started gettin' nervous. He did not have a happy look. Didn't say anything. Jay says, 'Malcolm, are you all right?' 'Yeah, just tired.' Well, he went out there and played great."

After Coryell played a well-received set, Roy and his band took the crowded stage. Roy sported a white turtleneck and a blazer with broad lapels. Even Billy Price, who'd been called in to sing on the gig, got pressured into wearing a sport coat. These were men who worked in after-hours clubs their whole lives. Roy hadn't even tucked in his shirt for Carnegie Hall. The band began tentatively, warming up on an uptempo rocker by Roy's own hand, "Done Daddy Dirty." They turned in a perfect, if somewhat restrained performance of Roy Milton's "Reelin' and Rockin'," with Roy demonstrating the tasty rhythm guitar work behind Price's singing that he rarely got credited for. Next they turned to Junior Walkers' cha-cha dubbed "Hot Cha." "Some of the things Roy pulled off for that gig I'd never heard before that night," Lukens recalled, many years later. "Like that instrumental by Junior Walker and the All-Stars, 'Hot Cha.' He would yell to me, 'This is a fat-back in B flat' and off we'd go. I played rhythm on that one, the part a horn section would have played."

Though veteran Roy watchers, including this author, were struck by the restraint Roy showed at Town Hall, he was carefully delivering well-articulated takes for the live LP. Billy Price had suggested the obscure "Can I Change My Mind?" and the band now gave it a try, cold, and almost nailed it. Roy lit up the crowd with his new anthem, "Hey Joe," with a few bars of "Foxy Lady" thrown in to incite Hendrix fans. The rhythm and blues standard, "Too Many Drivers at Your Wheel," followed, as much to blow off steam as to please the crowd with something hard driving. The testosterone-loaded "I'm a Ram" followed, and it was tight. The band turned next to Bobby "Blue" Bland's "Further On Up the Road," with both Price and Roy delivering gritty, convincing performances. The set ended with a deft and heartfelt medley of "In the Beginning" from the Freeman sessions, and Charles Brown's "Driftin' Blues." They were relaxing now and playing music, finding the groove, less concerned with the tape rolling than with feeling the music.

During the break the Maplewood Mafia joined the band in the small dressing room upstairs. Charlie Cohen took photographs while another miscreant fired up a joint and passed it around. Even Roy, concerned about the recordings, relaxed and had a few tokes. When it came time to return to the stage, the band was in a new state of mind—feeling good, loose, in the groove. Before heading out the door, Roy signed an autograph for fan Bob Hayden. "Live happy, Roy," it read. As the fans trooped out front to take their customary positions directly in front of Roy's microphone stand, Marc Lester hung back. He could see his friends taking up their perch at the lip of the stage. As Billy Price passed him, the singer remarked: "Oh yeah, those are 'Roy's Rabbits.' They're always poppin' up."

n the second set the band knocked out a warm-up rocker, took another stab

Roy's fingers blur as he feels the music at Town Hall, New York, on Nov. 29, 1974.

at "Done Daddy Dirty," and delivered a stunning version of "Roy's Bluz," in which Roy had added new lyrics.

> *The train is always gone*
> *Always leaves at three o' nine*
> *The train is always gone*
> *Always leaves at three o' nine*
> *Well, I'm gonna tell a whole lotta people*
> *It's always left Buchanan behind . . .*

Roy delivered a stunning run of fierce blues licks, essentially telling the same story—being left at the station all alone—without words. With a few twists of the volume and tone knobs, his Telecaster sent up a mournful cry. With a few angry harmonics—how *could* she?!—he picked out an accelerating riff that raised a few goose bumps out in the audience. What followed approached the incendiary, mind-shredding blues guitar work for which Roy was becoming famous. A majestic and soulful rendition of "Down by the River" came next. (This track would be released on Polydor's 1992 *Sweet Dreams* box set.) The band tried "Further On Up the Road" again, but this time the fire was missing. Once again the band ran through "Hey

Joe/Foxy Lady," "Can I Change My Mind?" and "In the Beginning/Driftin' Blues." This time, "Change My Mind" had all the emotional impact it deserved, and the final medley packed a convincing wistfulness.

"THERE WAS A SENSE, listening back to the tapes, that Roy had held back," Byrd Foster remembered. "We were on our best behavior," John Harrison agreed. "The fire was still there. It was just a little more controlled." Jay Reich thought so too, though he suggested, "We didn't think the sets were as good as others he was doing on the road." Today a band might tape a dozen or so shows to get an album's worth of peak performances, but Roy delivered six sparkling tracks, about 30 minutes' worth, in one evening at Town Hall. Later, after taping an Evanston, IL, performance at the Amazing Grace Club in December, Reich added an explosive version of "I'm Evil" from that set to round out the live record. It somehow seems apropos of Roy's career that this throw-away, finish-off-a-damned-contract project arguably turned out to be his best album. *Live Stock* captured the magic of his live performances, while demonstrating his ability to deliver the goods on demand. The eclectic selections, ranging from soul to cha-cha to tortured blues to hard-driving rock, spoke to Roy's wide-ranging sensibilities. Everything seemed to fall into place on this one. Even the cover. Reich had a funky photograph on his desk from an Australian fan, featuring a well-worn brick butcher shop, with a marquee that read: "Roy Buchanan. LIVESTOCK." The tumblers fell into place in Reich's head. He had a cover and a title. For the back cover he opted for a shot of Roy and the band on stage at Town Hall taken from the balcony. Along the lip of the stage, the Maplewood Mafia stood out in silhouette. During the mixing process for *Live Stock* at the Record Plant, Jay Reich ran into Eric Clapton at the hotel where they both were staying. Clapton was in New York to mix "I Shot the Sheriff" and other tracks from his *461 Ocean Boulevard* album. "I ran into him in the hotel lobby, told him I was a big fan, grew up listening to him, and that I'd like to play him some of Roy's stuff that I was working on," Reich recalled. "He said, 'I'm awfully busy, but if you leave something in my mailbox at the hotel, I'll be sure I listen to it.' So I did that. One of the songs on the tape was 'Further On Up the Road.' The next thing I knew, Clapton was touring. I caught him in Pittsburgh and he played that song with the same arrangement as on Roy's album. I knew he'd gotten that from Roy, from that tape, because he left out the same verses of that song that Billy Price left out when he recorded it live. It wasn't Roy's song. It wasn't the most obscure song in the world. But a real gentleman would have called Roy up and said, 'I'm going to do it, too.' Or thank him or somehow acknowledge him. Or help Roy's career in some way." Perhaps Reich didn't realize that Roy himself had grabbed "Further On Up the Road" from the Hawk in 1961, and that the Hawk had gotten it from Bobby "Blue" Bland, who'd first belted out the Don Robey–Joe Veasey composition in 1957. Or that Roy had played Clapton's "Bad Boy" at his first Carnegie Hall show just two years earlier. Among truly great musicians, "stealing" was all a game.

With the Polydor obligation behind them, Reich and Roy were looking forward to a six-figure advance from Atlantic, engineered by Ahmet Ertegun. Reich also was pushing for Tom Dowd to produce Roy's debut for the new label. Dowd had recorded two of what many regarded as the finest rock 'n' roll albums of all time: 1970's *Layla and Other Assorted Love Songs* by Derek & the Dominos (Derek was Eric Clapton, joined by Duane Allman and friends) and the following year's *The Allman Brothers Band at Fillmore East*. With a new label dishing up more money than they knew what to do with, Tom Dowd on tap, and concert bookings throughout 1975, things looked rosy indeed.

A STREET CALLED
STRAIGHT

9

With Town Hall only a memory, the band continued its streak of live performances. Through the winter of 1974–75 Roy and his band careened from town to town, coast to coast, a raging rock 'n' roll machine that took corners on two wheels. The band's repertoire expanded, its textures deepened, and with a relentless schedule it grew squeaky tight—or, if the mood required, exquisitely loose. The band rocked with passion and precision. John Harrison's driving bass locked in with Byrd Foster's deft, rock-solid drumming. Malcolm Lukens' magic keyboards provided the perfect counterpoint to Roy's guitar work. When called on, Lukens could dance in the spotlight, or Foster could belt out gritty vocals. Roy's intuition gave him a feel for his audience, for the right song at the right time. Even the notes he played were just the right notes at just the right time.

Foster remembered this period fondly. "Guitar players are known to have egos," he said. "But I tell the guys I play with these days, 'I played with one of the greatest guitar players in the world, and when I sang, he shut up.' Roy would do nothing but just back you up. He would listen to you. I learned dynamics from that man. We would go from a whisper to a scream five times in a song. And he would direct it. After a while we all knew the cues. It was psychic."

When he first joined the band, the picture was slightly less rosy for Malcolm Lukens. For an extra $100 each week, he had to schlep the equipment from gig to gig in his van. He soon rebelled. Hauling amps and driving was an insult to Lukens' talent. Yet somebody had to do it, and Roy's dedication to playing clubs didn't generate the sort of box office receipts that justified even one roadie. At first, the schlepping didn't amount to much. The band traveled light, taking only Roy's Telecaster and amplifier, John Harrison's bass guitar, and Byrd's drum sticks and snare. The band's need for keyboards, drums, amplifiers, and a PA system was met at each stop with rental equipment. In the later '70s, when relative prosperity justified it, the band brought along bass amplifiers and speaker cabinets, a full drum set, and keyboards.

After repeated protestations from Lukens, and in recognition of the band's success, Reich recruited Pittsburghers Harry Homa and Jim Potts to serve as roadies. The duo became known as Harry the Foot and Humbug. Together they were willing and able to drive from city to city, state to state, hauling equipment and anything else the gig required. Foot and Bug served as all-purpose rock 'n' roll fixers: they'd transfer amplifiers and drums from town to town, rent instruments and PAs at each stop, obtain multiple cases of beer and whatever else was required, get the boys to the show on time, and do what they could to keep everyone out of jail.

For Homa, life on the road with the Roy Buchanan Band presented a mix of the mundane and the absurd. While Foot and Bug hustled the equipment into the van and took off for the next gig, often several states away, Roy and the other band members boarded a plane and flew. Roy insisted that in addition to his own plane ticket he had a ticket for his '53 Tele as well. It had its own seat, right next to him. "One time the flight was full and we had to check the guitar," Harry recalled. "Roy almost lost his shit because we had to check the '53. I opened the case and loosened the strings so the neck wouldn't bend. Roy was freakin'." Even with minimal equipment, Homa had his hands full just setting up each night. "Roy'd play through that Vibrolux amp which, with Telecaster pickups, can pick up someone fartin' three counties away. I had a lot of feedback problems and Roy wasn't makin' it any easier on me. He'd go up to the Vibrolux, plug in, and run his fingers across the knobs, turning everything up to 10. Finally, behind his back, I fixed the knobs so that when he turned it up to 10, it was actually on 8. At first we'd set the Vibrolux on a chair and turn it backwards. That softened his sound. Later, I unplugged the speakers from the Vibrolux, ran it through a Music Man cabinet with four 12-inch speakers and faced *that* backwards and miked it from the back to cut down on feedback. That finally worked, because Roy would just *wail*. Also, Roy couldn't stand red lights. He'd tell me, 'I can't see my frets.' I *never* saw him look at his frets."

To Homa, the spontaneity of each set—with Roy calling out whatever tune he felt like playing throughout the night—added to the band's dynamics. The roadie finally prevailed on the guitarist to begin sets predictably with "Green Onions" so he could set the PA levels. After the show was over, there were other concerns. "My first job was to get the '53 Tele out of his hands, because he'd be shaking hands with all these people who would just be grabbin' at the guitar," Harry said. Roy's sheer friendliness could be troublesome, too. "We'd be on tour and Roy would go out drinkin' and meet some busboy who wanted to be a musician," Homa recalled ruefully. "So Roy would tell him he could play with us that night—and then we'd have to get rid of him. It was like a kid finding a puppy!" But for all the hassles, Roy often paid back his crew the hard way. Homa recalled one occasion in Erie, PA, when the band had collected at a Holiday Inn bar after the gig. A couple rednecks were giving the musicians a hard time when Homa finally told them where to stick it. "I had to jump in and start punchin' the guy," Homa recalled. "Well, Roy jumped in too and backed me up. He wound up poppin' this one guy good! We thought he'd broken his hand, which scared the shit out of us. He was a real laid-back, intelligent, intense man. But if he believed in something, he'd do it. He didn't have to jump in like that."

Then there was the business end of things. Homa collected the gig money, took care of immediate expenses, and at the end of a week or two's run, stuffed the rest into Roy's guitar case, and sent it home with him for Judy to count. "I loved Roy, but she was impossible," Homa said, trailing off into unrepeatable comments on working for a man whose wife kept the books, and trusted no one. Not that Judy didn't have to get her back up, with her husband loose in every roadhouse across America, with a group of guys who all had the same things in mind.

Homa understood the delicate situation. "Another part of my job was to keep Roy from getting laid," Harry said simply. "I mean, Roy was so #@&$! honest he'd get laid, go home, tell Judy about it and, the next thing you knew, she'd be on tour with us for like two #@&$! weeks!" According to Lukens, the relationship embittered Roy at times. "Frequently after the show there'd be an interview with a local newspaper. Roy could bend four-note chords and put separate vibrato on each of the strings, or he could bend one note completely off the neck. So reporters would ask him, 'How did you get that kind of strength?' Roy would say, 'I just pretend that's my wife's neck.'"

"Places were sold-out everywhere," Harry added. "It was nuts. We were workin' a lot. Texas was always really good. The whole South. New York was good. Pittsburgh, of course. San Francisco was cool, too."

By all accounts, the band's visit to San Francisco in December 1974 began a tradition of fruitful visits, both personally and professionally. There were down-home friendships: the attorney Alan Scheflin now lived there and frequently hosted the band at his home. And a new acquaintance, Joey Covington, drummer for the Jefferson Starship, took the boys to shows or introduced them to his hipster cronies. There might be magical discoveries. It was on a trip to San Francisco that Roy stumbled across the work of the street poet Charles Bukowski. While not an avid reader, Roy went out and purchased one of Bukowski's collections of gritty prose. Enamored of the poet's style, Roy impressed his band mates with his latest discovery. "Roy was so proud of the fact that he turned us on to Charles Bukowski, one of my favorite writers," Lukens said. "Bukowski at that time would open for rock 'n' roll bands. He'd wheel a little refrigerator out on stage, open it and start knockin' back a few brews before he'd even say anything to the audience. This is the literary equivalent of Roy Buchanan. You can see how Roy saw himself in this guy. Bukowski was just as happy if the audience hated him. Roy was so proud that he'd discovered this great literary guy. There's humor and pathos at the same time in both men's work."

People discovered Roy. Bobby Flurie, an up-and-coming DC guitarist, had been playing with a local band named Cherry Smash in 1969 when he first sought out Roy. "He told me, 'It's nice to see so much talent in a young body'—I was pretty young at the time—and that befriended me to him," Flurie remembered. "He took me under his wing and showed me things. The one lick that really blew me away was the way he made his guitar say, 'I want my mama, I want my mama.' He knew there was no way in hell I'd be able to do those licks the same way he did. He taught me how to use the volume control. I was playing a Gibson and the volume knob was not within reach, so that made my technique different than his. He used the tone control at the same time as the volume control, which gave it that wah-wah effect. He had his pinky and ring finger on both tone and volume controls—there's *still* nobody who does that. But I learned that from him: to this day I use no pedals, no effects. It's purer. Any kind of effect I might plug in only diminishes the signal the guitar sends to the amp."

Flurie doesn't mind telling a few Buchanan stories on himself. In those early days in DC, Roy would make the young acolyte wash his hands—*twice*—before picking up the '53 Telecaster. That's okay with Flurie. "Roy was always very protective of his knowledge," Flurie said. "He never wanted to share his knowledge, because he was afraid someone would use that knowledge—certain guitar techniques—to their benefit, against him. That was the only knowledge he possessed, so there were very few people he would actually show what he did. But even if he did show you, you couldn't in a million years do it the way he did it. That's the difference between the brush stroke of one artist and the brush stroke of another artist. To me you just play what you play. And the people who can learn by observing it deserve to have it. It's not stealing. It's like being able to comprehend and grasp a certain knowledge. But there *are* people who will take your techniques and parade them around."

By 1974 Flurie was based in San Francisco, playing lead guitar for the Quicksilver Messenger Service. When Roy and the boys showed up, Bobby grabbed the opportunity to put in some hang time with them. One evening Flurie and Roy had hit a couple bars and retired to Roy's hotel room to talk guitar. "Roy says, 'Let me show you this guitar technique that's brand new. Somebody could really make a style out of it. I'm too much of an old dog, set in my ways. But I'd like to pass it on to somebody who can do something with it.' He then proceeded to nod out." Flurie sat bolt upright. "I said, 'Roy! *Wake up!*' He starts snoring. Then he wakes up long enough to say, 'See you later, man.' Next time I saw him it was a year later. I said, 'Roy, do you remember what you were going to show me? That new style?' He said, 'I can't remember for the life of me.' But that's when Eddie Van Halen came out with all his overstrikes. [Fretting the strings on the neck by tapping with the fingers of the right hand.] That's what Roy had been trying to tell me a year earlier."

While the band was in San Francisco in December 1974 Flurie took the boys places and introduced them to people, including an enigmatic character at the fringes of the rock 'n' roll world. "When I first hit San Francisco I went through various cultures, Haight-Ashbury and all that stuff," Flurie recalled. "I ran into Billy Roberts, who supposedly wrote 'Hey Joe.' When I went over to Billy Roberts' apartment he had walls and walls of tapes of takes of 'Hey Joe.' Hundreds of tapes, by everybody who'd ever done it. He lived on Fillmore Street. It's funny, Billy Roberts used to play it fast, not slow, like Roy. He did a fast version of it. I said, 'You know, Roy Buchanan is doing 'Hey Joe' now. He's a friend of mine, I could introduce you to him when he comes to town. Billy said, 'I'd like that.' So I brought Billy to the American Music Hall. Those guys hit it off really well. They started talkin' and I was gone."

That week Roy and his band played four nights running at San Francisco's Boarding House, a classic rock 'n' roll palace described by one writer as "the Dodge City Opera House married to a 1927 Berlin *nachtlokal*, where the cigarette grit of the ages blows through its rafters." At Reich's urging, Roy and John Harrison visited the offices of *Rolling Stone* to see if someone would cover the show and perhaps dispel the curse cast by the magazine's scathing review of Roy's third LP. The magazine responded, writer Jim Kunstler drew the assignment, and he attended one evening's performance. His review ran a month later in the magazine. He wrote, in part: "If Roy Buchanan has found his voice, he found it residing on the dark side of his heart. Standing stock still, or drifting stage right to his monitor, liquid danger and sadness squeezed out of his Telecaster. Amens and catcalls of gospel adulation echoed back to him out of the darkness. Buchanan's tale is the tale of the journeyman genius."

Writer John Wasserman also attended one of these shows on behalf of the *San Francisco Chronicle*. "Whatever demons stir inside the mind of Roy Buchanan are exorcised nightly when he walks on stage and pours out a hurricane of raw emotion the likes of which have been approximated in this music only by the late Jimi Hendrix," Wasserman wrote. "Sometimes soft and lilting, languid, the tone almost harp-like; sometimes tight, angry, piercing; sometimes fat and rounded cries of soulfulness; sometimes anarchical spasms of cacophony, notes indistinguishable from each other, great flaring bursts of intensity comparable to the music of no other, produced with a technique and arsenal that is, for practical purposes, unlimited. As Aretha sings, so does Roy Buchanan play. It is music and a dimension beyond." With this lavish praise, Wasserman ended his review on a sober note: "Roy has yet to find a record company or a record producer competent to handle his unique but often wasted talents. He is a great guitar player, the most viscerally exciting alive. He is not yet a great artist."

During one night's set, Roy brought his new friend, Billy Roberts, out on stage for an introduction. Later, Roy invited Roberts to "write me a song, too," and Roberts took to the studio to record a handful of demos for his new guitar hero. He hadn't exactly written "Hey Joe" for Jimi Hendrix, but this time he would write a song intended for Roy Buchanan to perform, one that somehow fit the Arkansas hillbilly in Roy. "Next thing I know," Bobby Flurie recalled later. "Billy said to me, 'Hey, Roy's going to do another one of my songs.'" This would be "Good God Have Mercy," which appeared on Roy's next album.

Scheflin recalled the period with a knowing chuckle. "Roy called me up and told me to meet him at the Boarding House, so I went down. When I got there, I looked around for him and there he was, sitting at a table in the middle of a large contingent of Hell's Angels. The Hell's Angels were country boys, too, so they dug Roy." Did Scheflin feel nervous? "Hell yeah! But when I realized what was going on, I thought it was pretty cool."

It was pretty cool, too, when the band encountered Little Richard in Memphis. "We had just done our gig and we went back to our hotel, which caters to musicians," Byrd Foster said. "Me and John Harrison are walking down the hallway and we pass a room. The door opens. I turn around, and there's *Little Richard* pokin' his head out the door. I screamed! I said, 'Hey John, there's *Little Richard!*' He says, 'Say *what?!*' So we're like 'Little Richard, you're the greatest! We love you! Yada yada yada.' Little Richard says: '*Hey!* How *you* doin'?! Come on *in*. Who you workin' for?' 'Roy Buchanan.' 'Oh *yeah!* I know him. He's great!' So there's Little Richard, his enormous bodyguard, a guy and his wife—she's a knock-down gorgeous woman, basically there as entertainment—and a baseball-size lump of cocaine on the coffee table. This is rock 'n' roll heaven, man! Little Richard says, 'I don't touch it no mo'. Hep yo selves!'

"Well, I hear Roy and Jay comin' down the hall and I stick my head out. 'Roy! See who we've met!' Roy greets Little Richard and they hug, they're smilin' and they just hit it off. Seems like they might have met before, in the old days. Well, they just start talkin' about how the Earth was made, biblical stuff. The babe starts getting it on with one of the band members, who takes her down the hall to the sauna with Little Richard's bodyguard in tow. We've been there a couple hours now. Little Richard and Roy are talkin' scripture and we're across the room, whiffing coke." Apparently the sauna-goers were having too much fun and Little Richard's bodyguard suffered a heart attack. The paramedics came, took him out on a stretcher. Very hush-hush. "We kept partying," one band member said nonchalantly.

Perhaps on that particular night, for Roy, talking scripture with Little Richard won out over other temptations. Over the course of a two- or three-week tour, however, he had ample opportunity to enjoy excess. Thus the transition from touring to returning home could be jarring indeed. When Reich, Harrison, Foster, Homa, and Potts flew home to Pittsburgh, Malcolm Lukens and Roy flew home together to DC. "We talked very little on the plane," Lukens said. "Sometimes it felt awkward. We were both sober, nobody was high or partying." Roy had reason to be pensive. Judy would have questions. He would not have a lot of good answers.

When a tour was over, weeks on end of reckless living came to a crashing halt. What passed for life on the road with the boys in the band did not even clear the threshold at home. Judy made damn sure of that and one can hardly blame her. Roy's travels meant he was working, bringing home the bacon—at least that which had not been consumed on the road. But it also meant he would be hanging out in a rock 'n' roll band, racing from town to town, drinking, getting high, and possibly committing adultery. As for the Buchanan's six children, they understandably came to resent their father's long and frequent absences from home. Roy was kind and warm and loving and thoughtful when he was present, but that just couldn't make up for all that time away.

As much as Roy enjoyed the thrills of the road, bandmates and friends say he truly loved being home, relaxing, doing ordinary things with his wife and children. He liked walking the two mastiffs he'd acquired as pets, big hunting dogs that spooked the local garage owner when he came out to Roy's place to jump-start the family station wagon. He finally had earned enough money to protect himself and his family from the world. Isolated from the tumult of the city, insulated from the old days of hand-to-mouth, the Buchanan clan thrived. When Roy and Judy were at peace with one another, life was pretty damn good.

BY THE MID-'70S, Roy's admirers included the biggest names in the business: Eric Clapton, Keith Richards, Ron Wood, John Lennon, Bob Dylan, Jerry Garcia, Kim Simmonds, Ritchie Blackmore, and a host of others. One of the others was Jeff Beck, who in a post-Hendrix, post-Beatles, post-Clapton era—Hendrix was dead, the Beatles had split, and Clapton had burned out on heroin—had gained an aura for being one of the hottest guitar slingers on the international scene. In fact, Beck was one of the few guitarists with the humility to recognize his debt to Roy's technique.

Beck was born in war-torn England in 1944, and picked up a guitar early on. By the late 1950s he was cutting his teenage teeth on American pop music, strongly influenced by guitarists such as Scotty Moore, James Burton, and Cliff Gallup. Beck may have heard Roy Buchanan on Dale Hawkins' "My Babe," perhaps even on a Temps' record. In 1965 he joined the Yardbirds, a group that epitomized British rockers' enthusiasm for the blues. The slot turned out to be his entrée into rock stardom, but when Eric Clapton left John Mayall's Bluesbreakers, Beck declined an invitation to replace him. He said his abilities weren't up to snuff. He formed his own group, with Rod Stewart as lead singer, and recorded a number of powerful, well-received solo albums in the late 1960s that featured his straight-ahead blues-rock axe work. He made his talents available to musicians as diverse as Donovan and Stevie Wonder, the GTOs and the Rolling Stones, Eddie Harris and Stanley Clarke. A short-lived but powerful trio, Beck, Bogert, and Appice—with Tim Bogert and Carmine Appice, the former rhythm section for Vanilla Fudge—brought him to a reassessment of his heavy-and-getting-heavier music.

By 1974, when he entered the studio to record *Blow by Blow*, Beck had made a journey from blues-rock to fusion and funk. He also had come to terms with his chosen role of lead guitarist while keeping at arm's length the Guitar Hero label and all the crap that went with it. As a musician aware of his musical roots and interested in exploring them, and as a devotee of the Telecaster, he had already discovered Roy Buchanan. This hillbilly with a Vandyke beard had a gutsy style and laid-back demeanor that made a lot of sense to the Brit. Beck told an interviewer, many years later, that he'd caught the WNET documentary on television in November

1971, while on tour in Boston with Rod Stewart. "We just sat there aghast for about an hour. It was some of the best playing I've ever heard. I just said, 'Who *is* this man?' The next time I saw Bill Graham I said, 'Tell me about Roy Buchanan.'"

What Bill Graham couldn't tell him Beck gleaned from Roy's albums, especially *Second Album* and *Live Stock*. On Beck's next album, *Blow by Blow*, he dedicated Stevie Wonder's "Cause We've Ended as Lovers" to Roy. Many observers believed that the track represented the spiritual and musical highlight of *Blow by Blow*. Released in March 1975, the LP skyrocketed up the charts, eventually selling more than two million copies. One reviewer noted the "Lover" track's "dreamy," "moody" feeling that nonetheless was "strangely moving," a la Roy's style. "I played that song with the same sort of vibe he had," Beck explained later. "I just took a page out of Roy's book for that and thought, 'Why not just play all the way through this thing?' Without hiding, you know? Like *he* did a lot of the time. He defied all the laws of verse-chorus-verse and just blazed." A few years later, in an interview with *Down Beat*, Beck said that in an earlier period he'd listened closely to Roy, Les Paul, and John McLaughlin. The thing that turned him on about Roy's low-key approach was that "Roy Buchanan has a real positive attitude in his music, and a nice, raunchy sound. When I saw him on television . . . we were in the middle of an onslaught and barrage of horrible teeny-bopper guitarists, [so] it was amazing to me that here was this unknown guy playing some of the best blues guitar that had been played for a long time. It just seems that all the wrong people get the big slices of the cake."

Though in subsequent performances with a Telecaster Beck clearly made use of Roy's trademark effects that utilized the guitar's tone and volume knobs, the Brit emphasized later that Roy's effect on him was less technical than it was inspirational. He'd found a new freedom after hearing Roy's approach. "I had that style already, pretty much in my head," Beck suggested. "That sort of stroking strings and making arpeggiated sorts of chords and bending notes at the end. But he actually made it more comfortable for me to play that style. That's really what I learned from him. You know, when you're a little nervous about putting a new thing out, you're not quite sure of yourself. So when you see someone like that, you think, 'Well, what was *I* worried about? I *can* do all that.' It sort of brought it out." Within the year the Rolling Stones would invite Jeff Beck to replace Mick Taylor, who'd replaced the late Brian Jones back in '69. Beck liked the band and he considered each member a mate. Yet he felt uncomfortable with the role and its possible toll. He declined.

When Roy entered the studio again in the spring of 1975 it was for Atlantic Records, the first of three albums in his new contract. Atlantic reportedly had paid in the low six figures for the privilege. The album would be recorded at four different studios, including two of Hendrix's old haunts—Electric Lady and the Record Plant, both in New York. Sessions began in the spring of 1975 and, after the band spent the summer touring, resumed in November. The transition to Atlantic had not gone according to plan. "When we signed to Atlantic we were promised Tom Dowd," Jay Reich stated flatly. Dowd had captured the best of Eric Clapton and Duane Allman's work on record and, Reich believed, had just the sensibility for recording his artist. Instead, Ahmet Ertegun assigned the production of Roy's first Atlantic LP to Arif Mardin, who had a fabulous track record of hits, having produced popular artists such as Aretha Franklin, the Bee Gees, and the Average White Band. "We couldn't tell Ahmet Ertegun 'No,'" Reich said. "Being such a smooth guy, he told me Tom 'wasn't available.' He said Arif would be better. He got me to believe it. That Ahmet himself signed Roy had created a good deal of buzz within the company. It was Ahmet's pet project. And I sold the idea to Roy. I promised Roy the world. I said, 'Roy, *this* is really going to make it for us.'"

With the label's founder and substantial resources invested in the project, Arif Mardin set out to create a hit for Atlantic. Rather than attempt to capture Roy Buchanan's road-hardened, vernacular music on record, Mardin sought to create a studio construction complete with contemporary disco rhythms. This was the mid-1970s, after all, and the backing tracks were filled with horns and a synthesizer that mimicked strings. In contrast to past outings, nine of 11 songs were penned by, or co-credited to, Buchanan. For the band, the good news was that they would play on the album, along with a bevy of studio players. Mardin liked Malcolm Lukens' playing in particular, which thrilled Lukens. Still, on half the songs studio aces Andy Newmark played drums and Will Lee played bass. Billy Cobham contributed percussion, as did Rubens Bassini, while the Brecker brothers, Randy and Michael, played horns. Five backup singers were recruited as well.

The results were uneven. The album opened with a driving rocker called "Running Out," co-written by Roy and bassist John Harrison, which often opened the band's live sets. The road band played together on this one and Roy clearly is comfortable with the driving beat—he delivered vintage Tele squeals, wails, cries, and stabbing fills to impart feeling to the music. With the second track—"Keep What You Got"—performed by studio players, the mood hits a wall. The song is pure disco and, while given a funky edge by Newmark and Lee and black female backing vocals, it is utterly foreign to Roy Buchanan and his music. It is pure, 100 percent, Grade A, Studio 54, glitter ball, *Saturday Night Fever* horse crap. The guitar break sounds like Roy, but the music conjures the image of a fat woman crammed into a pair of gold lame pants gyrating on the dance floor. The repetitive track did nothing more than signal anyone who cared for Roy's music that something was terribly wrong. But every Roy studio album, no matter how ill-conceived or antiseptically executed, contains a handful of gems. The next track, "Good God Have Mercy," sparkled. Written specifically for Roy by Billy Roberts, the author of "Hey Joe," its music and lyrics captured perfectly the guitarist's down-home idiosyncrasies. Roberts had sent Roy a demo tape of ten songs, of which Roy had checked off two to try. He settled on "Good God," which loosely fit him in a mythical, autobiographical way.

Down in South Carolina
In the piney woods
Where they make sweet turpentine,

There I first saw the light of day
Landin' on mah mind,

Runnin' in the sunshine laughin'
Rollin' in the red dirt cryin'
Said, mmm, mmm,
Good God have mercy

The song was propelled by a finger-picked acoustic guitar, a tremulous bass line, and mournful lead guitar fills that sounded like a train disappearing down the tracks. "They were both strange guys," Reich recalled of Roy and William M. "Billy" Roberts. "Billy came around a lot and he always said he wrote 'Hey Joe.' We were always kind of skeptical that he wrote it. Roy and me, we just looked at each other. But Roy came to believe that he did write it, because he sure loved that song, 'Good God Have Mercy.'"

One has to wonder what Roy's recording career might have been like had his producers pushed and pushed until every song on the album rose to this level of personal expression. He needed an advocate for his music, as Pete Siegel had been. Mardin did not push for Roy's essence, though when the guitarist appeared with his usual handful of riffs and snatches of lyrics, the producer gave his artist all the help he could. According to Billy Price, Arif Mardin later told Reich that Roy was the most difficult artist he'd ever recorded. "Arif said Roy would come in with just the barest shreds of songs. He said he had to put together everything for him."

The final track on side one, "Caruso," if not a gem on par with "Good God," at least had the feel of a Roy composition and it reeked of Roy's autobiographical mojo. "You just name it, and I done it." Roy intoned.

In retrospect, the first side of Roy's first album on Atlantic set a pattern for what was to follow: It was a hodge-podge composed of Roy's half-finished songs, a couple gems worthy of a gifted but quirky artist, and lots of material imposed or clumsily suggested by a producer insensitive to Roy's strengths, and hell bent—given the label's financial risk—on commercial success. Side Two followed the pattern. It opened strongly with "My Friend Jeff," Roy's tribute to his new, prominent admirer, an instrumental track that neatly captured the direction Beck had taken towards fusion, with a funky beat, duets between horns and guitar, and a somewhat contrived refrain that smacked of early 1970s power rock. ("That was really neat," Beck later said of Roy's gesture. "We hadn't spoken two words to each other.") With a few harmonics, an uptempo bridge, and some tasty organ work by Lukens, the track really began to cook and the band let loose for a good time. A funky groove continued with "If Six Was Nine," Roy's interpretation of the defiant '60s anthem by

Jim Hendrix. The almost reggae beat, wah wah bass-synthesizer, and quirky organ riffs made a hypnotic base from which Roy departed on a number of stylistic excursions. "Guitar Cadenza," an effects-laden solo, came next. The nearly note-for-note remake of "The Messiah" that followed was puzzling, as synthesizers and echo on the vocals only detracted from the bare bones original. Yet the side closed with a country boy's acoustic love song that provided Roy with a vehicle well-matched to his typically tentative vocals. "I Still Think About Ida Mae" had many textures, created in part by the deft, low-key organ and background chorus that snaked in and out of the music. The song, unburdened of any heavy guitar work, transformed itself into something approaching great music, an ethereal wisp of a tune that would have made a great ending to an album twice as strong as this one.

In the end, Arif Mardin had managed to get half a great album. Unlike Roy's earlier albums, the Atlantic material for the most part wasn't replicable on stage, nor did it belong in Roy's sets, since many of the tunes lacked a strong groove. It was telling of the difference, to Roy, between music made in the recording studio and music worth performing live, that Roy added only "Running Out" and "Good God Have Mercy" (and the latter only rarely) to his live sets in this period. "My Friend Jeff" and "If Six Was Nine" would have made excellent additions to the live set, but for some reason Roy chose not to perform them. Those songs, as well as "I Still Think About Ida Mae" and "Good God Have Mercy," also showed, finally, what Roy ultimately could do in a studio. But Mardin had his hit-making agenda and he worked with an artist notorious for not preparing for recording sessions—and that meant a scattershot album, a mélange of tracks that carried the hope that something might click with the record-buying public.

That was the career-oriented aspect of the record. Personally, Roy had reached a crossroads of sorts with himself. As he'd hinted at in "Caruso": *Made up my mind I's goin' get myself together, I was gonna straighten up . . .* he felt he'd turned a corner. He dubbed his album *A Street Called Straight.* "Roy came up with that," Byrd Foster recalled. "He was wrestling with sobriety at that point. He'd go on these stretches— 'I'm not drinkin' this week.' And he'd do fine. Maybe just to prove it to himself. I never saw him overboard on anything. He always took care of business. He wanted to take care of his family."

Unfortunately, as musicologist Colin Escott once wrote, Roy's street called straight "never ran for more than a few blocks." Therein lay deep frustration perhaps for the guitarist and definitely for those around him. With effort, he could lay off his favorite poisons for weeks on end. Eventually, in a haunting pattern, he'd fall off the wagon. That may have hurt inside. On the one hand, Roy was always glad to head out on tour with the boys and have a good-old time, fueled mostly by alcohol but with pot ever-present and cocaine increasingly making its appearance. But on those sober plane rides home to DC, Roy had to wonder what made him live like that, and why he couldn't be content with a "normal" life at home. In fairness, this affliction troubled many rock 'n' rollers and other Gypsies—why the fascination with and the need for the thrills of life on the road, and why the haunting dissatisfaction with life in a secure, comfortable home? Roy loved the road life, but recognized it could not be sustained, and he loved his home life, while realizing it would never be enough. To listen to his music, one imagines that at times these contradictions gnawed at his soul.

WHILE AT WORK ON *A Street Called Straight* at Atlantic Studios in New York, Roy was invited to stay late one night to observe a mixing session for the Rolling Stones. Gene Paul, son of Les Paul, had engineered Roy's sessions, then stayed to meet with the Stones. According to Reich, however, Roy had knocked back a few beers and in a good-natured way proceeded to make a few suggestions. Apparently that seemed a bit high-handed to the session's participants, which included Keith Richards, Ron Wood, and Eric Clapton. "By the time the Stones got there Roy was, uh, slightly intoxicated," Reich said. "He wasn't obnoxious, he was playful. He was a pretty difficult guy to dislike. But Roy had nothing to say to a guy like Ron Wood. Roy was only close to the people he knew and trusted. He wasn't one for small talk. And besides, he didn't really trust those guys. Roy felt he was in possession of all these musical ideas that he didn't want to expose to anybody who could exploit them before he did."

"I do know there was not a lot of warm feeling that evening between Roy and those guys. Remember, it was right after Roy felt that Eric Clapton had pinched 'Farther On Up the Road.' There's a paranoia that's understandable between these guys. Knowing how Roy felt about that 'Farther On Up the Road' thing . . . He didn't have the warmest feeling for Clapton anyway. It was almost as if we were impinging upon their turf. Which, in fact, we were."

NEARLY A YEAR PASSED before Roy ventured back into the studio. In the meantime he toured the country, ranging from California, Texas, and Colorado to Ohio, Tennessee, North Carolina, Georgia, Florida, and back again. His itinerary included some of America's funkiest clubs, those with a devoted local following that sustained the precarious business of hiring people like Roy Buchanan to rock all night: the Agora in Cleveland, Armadillo World Headquarters in Austin, My Father's Place in Roslyn, NY, Tobacco Road in Rhonda, NC, the Horseshoe Tavern in Toronto, Alex Cooly's Electric Ballroom in Atlanta, the Jai Alai Club in Orlando, the Electric Ballroom in Dallas . . . the list was long. Today that list is exceedingly short: many clubs from that era are long gone. "My Father's Place was a roadhouse, essentially a dump bar," John Harrison recalled. "You went upstairs to a dressing room behind the stage. Dressing room is not the right word. They were just dark, smoky rooms with threadbare furniture. Occasionally they would have some food for us, but not usually. They'd bring you something to drink. You'd come down the stairs to a small stage, high above the audience. The room was long, so with the stage lights on, you couldn't see very far into the audience, but you could hear them. The audience was

Roy had pockets of avid fans all across America. Bostonians loved Roy, performing here at Symphony Hall in January 1976.

there to have a good time, get high, and let it loose. Which is, of course, exactly what you want." Eventually, however, there came a price for rocking out every night. "After a while," Harrison said, "a lot of the places started to blend in with each other, in the haze of the light and the smoke and the beer and the energy of playing. The details of each place did not make much of an impression." That was life on the roadhouse circuit: Report for work in the evening, say, 9 p.m., when everyone else is done for the day. Hang out in a dark, smoky room with threadbare furniture, knocking back a few beers, perhaps scoring dope of one kind or another, either entertaining fans and groupies, or fending them off, while a crowd gathers in the venue, getting louder and louder as they get liquored and loose. Then, show time! Deliver a couple sets of rock and blues played so loud that the music seemed at times to rearrange one's internal organs, as the crowd goes berserk. By 1:30 in the morning the show is over, the club soon is closed, and the musicians move on to hotel rooms, private parties, another bar. Sometimes the sun rose before the night's festivities were through. Sleep all day and rock all night.

"Roy came out of that roadhouse environment," Harrison said. "The best shows we ever played were in those small clubs—the Agora in Cleveland, My Father's Place on Long Island—where the crowd was close enough that they became part of the show. When we did arena shows, it was tank city. You *had* to have audience contact. We were not showmen. Back in those days there was a lot of glam rock going on, and all we ever did was stand there and play." To the band's credit, that would be enough.

AFTER ROY AND THE BOYS had rocked the Agora, writer Joe Kullman noted: "In jeans and straw hat, shirt hanging out, [Roy] was so calm on stage he could have been playing alone out behind the barn after a long day plowing the north forty. But the flow of energy rippling from hand and guitar made up for his virtual non-movement on stage. He weaned sounds from his 1953 Telecaster that other guitarists wouldn't attempt without a wah-wah or echo chamber . . . ." At one point, as Roy intoned the words to "Hey Joe"—"goin' down to kill my old lady . . . "—some members of the audience shouted back, *"Kill her, kill her, kill her, Roy!"*

After the show, Kullman interviewed the guitarist. "As long as I can play where I want, make a living and support my family, I'm satisfied," Roy declared. Asked about his long road to recognition, he said, "I played as well in the '50s as I do in the '70s, maybe even better. Being a star is just a matter of the right time and right place." Who did Roy listen to among guitarists? "All of them," he said. "I think Jeff Beck is great, but he's the last of a dying breed. I mean Beck and Hendrix, the Cream and [Duane] Allman, they were the originals who started this thing in the '60s with the Marshall amps and all. I could have gone to the wah-wah and the Echoplex, but it wasn't my sound. I hook up to a small amp and make my own sounds. Besides, I had already done that stuff in the '50s." Of his own interests, Roy commented: "I'm a blues player, but I love rock 'n' roll, I like jazz, I like country. I'm not sure what category I fit in. Just say I like music . . . It's been music through all my life, that's my real addiction, one habit I never did break. But I never did want to."

Accounts from around the country in this period testify to Roy's ability to capture his audience's loyalty. Months later, in Austin, Tony Reay reported on a show at Armadillo World Headquarters for *Performance: The International Talent Weekly*. More than a thousand fans were turned away at the door at the 1,700-seat theater at one of two sold-out performances. After a local band warmed up the house, Roy and his band took the stage at midnight, and held the audience in thrall for two full hours. The band "literally riveted the audience to their seats . . . Now Roy Buchanan knows that he has a very special place in the hearts of the Texas people," Reay wrote. "As the crowd filed out, I asked one young lady if she had enjoyed the show and whether she would return to see him. 'Are you kidding?' she said. 'I'd give up front row center seats to the Stones anytime to see Roy Buchanan. And I *love* the Stones.'"

ROY GENERALLY got a lot of good press in the mid-'70s. In interviews he was open, honest, and articulate. In its June 14, 1976, issue, even *Time* weighed in on Roy with

*Roy's longtime bass player, John Harrison, belts out a rocker
at Lowell, MA, in June 1976.*

a brief piece. The magazine merely recounted the fiction Roy had told Tom Zito of the *Washington Post* five years earlier (echoed in *Rolling Stone*) that his daddy was a preacher man. *Time* naively suggested that *A Street Called Straight* "has generally been hailed as the first album that captures the excitement Roy can generate in public performances." (If anything, the album failed to do so.) Referring to a May 30 show at the San Jose Center for the Performing Arts, however, the *Time* writer aptly described the denouement to the show, a trademark of Roy's performances in those days. "At the end, having promised that the Messiah would come again, Roy moved slowly toward the back of the stage and, like a sort of rock Messiah, slipped off into the darkness." Notes from heaven hung in the air, but the stage was deserted.

GUITAR PLAYER FEATURED ROY on its October 1976 cover. Inside appeared a forthcoming article by Roy, as told to Lowell Cauffiel, that went a long way in describing the guitarist's craft. Sure, he repeated some of his favorite legends about himself, including how his father had been a fiddle-playing preacher, but he articulated as never before his techniques and the emotions behind them. Gone was the paranoia about people "stealing" his licks. He was giving them away.

"The churches really influenced me in a couple of ways," Roy told Cauffiel. "Gospel music and blues are closely related, really. The church was the first time I ever heard blues. Blues sort of started in the black churches, and what I ended up doing was mixing the white man's church music with the black man's blues to get that sweet feeling in my playing. Another thing was the preaching. At a revival, a good preacher would really get the people going with his sermon. Work the crowd. He would start out slow and quiet, and as he went along, he'd build his volume and speed and bring everybody to an emotional climax. It was fiery. I think music works the same way, bringing audiences to high points with your guitar playing, and the preaching probably had an influence on me in that way."

Of his chosen instrument, Roy said, "The Telecaster sounded a lot like a steel, and I liked that tone. If it didn't have the sound it does—if it sounded like a Gibson or a Gretsch—I'd never play a Telecaster. Because the others are easier to play than a Tele, but don't have the sound." Life on the road had been good for his music, he suggested. "I just liked to play with different guys, different fields of music. It helped me, because every band I played with was another challenge. I used to play with a lot of horn groups, and there wouldn't be any other chord man but me. I really learned rhythm guitar. I don't think you should sell anything short, even with records. Listen to it all. I was never any knock-out jazz player, for example, but what I did learn about jazz really helped me."

"There's a lot of great guitar players out there pumping gas," Roy told Cauffiel. "Once I was playing a carnival in Oklahoma City, and this real country-lookin' guy came up to me and said, 'I like the way you play. You feel like jamming a bit?' I don't remember who he was, but he also played piano with Hank Thompson. Well, that son of a gun came in with the oldest damn Gibson I'd ever seen, no cutaway or nothing. I couldn't even play rhythm for him. He was just all over the thing, and he was one of the greatest jazz players I'd ever heard."

Roy dubbed his own approach "unorthodox." "Basically, I learned through dividing the neck into positions, where the chords are in their various forms. It's a good way to practice. Take E, for example, and find the chord in each of its forms all the way up the neck. Then learn the scale in each position to go with it. I see everything in visual patterns in my mind. But it was always the chord that came first. For example, when I practice I'll play major, minor, diminished, and augmented scales. I really don't know the technical names for them, and I don't know what half the chords I use are. But I know for every chord there has to be a scale that fits it. And I find those notes on every position on the neck. You do this enough, you'll get the whole neck programmed into your mind. Playing by ear really is a feeling. But it only comes with knowledge of the neck. It has to be ingrained in your mind ahead of time. Rhythm also taught me a lot about playing leads. I always felt I was a better rhythm player than lead player, but was always called upon to play lead . . . I think there's more to music than just speedy leads, one straight drone. You have to know rhythm to be able to put together interesting solos."

Acknowledging that one of his specialties was making the Telecaster sound like a pedal steel, he spilled some more beans. "To get that steel sound, you don't use a lot of right hand, hard picking, but instead an easy touch real close to the bridge and the volume way up. And you get a little vibrato going. A lot of it, too, has to do with the tone of the Telecaster."

He credited Speedy West with pioneering the use of the volume control to make the guitar cry. "He and Jimmy Bryant, who was a real good guitar player, used to play together," Roy recalled. "West wasn't great technically, but Bryant was one hell of a player. So when it was Speedy's turn to play, he had to really do something impressive to keep the momentum going. So he would use the volume controls . . . ."

Though he didn't confide the makeup of his country mojo in the *Guitar Player* piece, Roy came one step closer to the connection between techniques and the emotional impact of one's playing. "The whole thing comes down to creating tension in your playing," he told Cauffiel. "Using different volumes, working a scale from top to bottom, bottom to top, and planning ahead. I set the listeners up with something simple to get their attention, then proceed to develop it. I have to beat the licks I've done before to reach a musical climax . . . You're setting people up, is what you're doing. You work them to that point—and yourself too. They know it's coming, and you can see it in their faces. Sometimes it boils down to just one note. One note can be as effective as dozens. Somehow—and this may sound farfetched—I have a feeling that all notes are contained in one. And if it's played with feeling, the reason it has such an effect on everybody is because it does have the other notes somewhere in it. It's the old 'bring-the-house-down-with-one-note' thing."

Roy made one more point to aspiring guitar players. "Homer [Haynes] of Homer and Jethro told me something one time. We were doing a show in Las Vegas. I said, 'I don't feel like I can learn anymore. I'm just not capable. I'm as good as I'll ever be.' Then Homer said, 'You remember one thing. The way you feel now means you're going to really *start* to learn.' I've never forgotten that. When you feel like you're slipping or can't do anymore, that's the knowledge that it's time to move on, keep learning."

IN MID-OCTOBER, after a short break from the road, Roy headed to New York City and Electric Lady Studios to work on his second Atlantic album. The first had garnered generally positive reviews and briefly attained the charts before slipping into obscurity. For the second Atlantic effort Tom Dowd was still "busy" and Atlantic had other ideas. Ahmet Ertegun summoned Reich to his New York office. "At the time I was 23 years old," Reich said. "When this guy said, 'Come to New York,' I went. I listened. I met with Ahmet Ertegun and Ramon Silva. Ahmet said, 'We've got a guy named Stanley Clarke who'd like to produce.' Well, Stanley Clarke had been with Return to Forever and the Mahavishnu Orchestra. We'd done some shows with them. I couldn't see it. I didn't like that kind of music. I still don't. I couldn't see it with Roy. But Ahmet and Ramon—I mean, they were from *New York*—and I thought they were on to something. Their taste seemed to be impeccable. Who was I to say that it wasn't going to work? They said, 'This is going to put Roy over the top.' I said, 'I'd really like Tom Dowd to come in and do some tracks for us.' They said, 'Stanley Clarke is dying to do the project.' So we did stuff with Stanley in Miami, in L.A., New York. The album must have cost a fortune. Ramon was there every step of the way. Roy's road band, which was on part of the first Atlantic album, got completely ignored. We had these session guys, some really good ones like Jan Hammer, Will Lee, who was a helluva nice guy *and* a good player. The Brecker Brothers . . . But for me, I couldn't sink my teeth into this music. Roy was trying like hell. He knew Stanley Clarke's reputation. To make a long story short, that record didn't work either."

The opening track on *Loading Zone*," The Heat of Battle," spoke to producer Stanley Clarke's goals for the album. Being a fusion bassist, Clarke had decided to thrust Roy, a soulful roots musician, into the musical maelstrom created by seasoned fusion players. Essentially, push the artist out of his genre and see if he rises to the occasion. Roy actually played the role well, exploding with mind-boggling runs up and down the neck, the notes nearly a blur. It turned out he could play jazz-rock fusion as well as anyone—but to what end? On the aptly named "The Heat of Battle," Roy is thrust into the role of, say, John McLaughlin, Lee Ritenour, Jeff Beck . . . but not himself. The flawless execution by his backup band of studio veterans—Jan Hammer on keyboards, Raymond Gomez on rhythm guitar, David Garibaldi on drums, and, alternately, Donald "Duck" Dunn, Dennis Parker, and Will Lee on bass—rather than improving the record actually contributed to its emotionally antiseptic feel. This time, with the exception of Malcolm Lukens, Roy's road band had virtually no role on the album. That riled bassist John Harrison and drummer Byrd Foster, who co-wrote one song for the album yet served only as a backup singer on it. This merely reflected the tight hold Atlantic kept over the recording process. The company had paid Roy a fat advance and it wanted a hit—the one it didn't get the first time. It installed a producer who "knew what to do with Roy" and equipped him with veteran session players to obtain the desired result. The label looked upon Roy's road band as if they were so many feral cats—a charge that, if partially true, didn't disqualify them from studio work. So this was "success": lots of cash for Roy, a slap at the band, and a very long way from the intuitive producing of Pete Siegel, who'd so effectively documented Roy's musical essence for Polydor.

"The Heat of Battle" made for a dramatic opening track, but the tension and excitement dissipated immediately with a couple of New Age–inspired tracks credited to Roy's pen that lacked both groove and guts. The side was saved by a quirky duet between Roy and Stanley. The producer, in the control booth, heard the guitarist fooling around with an infectious country ditty, and donned his bass and joined Roy in the studio. Dubbed "Adventures of Brer Rabbit and Tar Baby" by Clarke, who is black, the track exuded spunk and a sly humor that provided a rare moment of accessibility on the record. The side closed with "Ramon's Blues," a 12-bar excursion that featured Roy and Steve Cropper, a charter member of Booker T. & the MG's and Roy's contemporary and musical peer. While the dexterous soloing between the two veteran guitar-slingers pleased guitar devotees, the track's monotonous tempo limited its appeal. It was the sort of blues that, delivered in the after hours for an audience that had knocked back a few drinks, could ignite a room. Tightly crafting the same song in the studio rendered it harmless.

The record's second side opened with Booker T. & the MGs' 1962 instrumental hit, "Green Onions." After Lukens laid down a soulful organ introduction in deference to the original, Roy and Cropper methodically traded solos—Roy courteously let Steve take the first one—creating a fruitful conversation between instrumentalists. They conversed for eight minutes, until their ideas were spent. After the original studio session, Roy enthusiastically played a rough mix of the track for his friend, attorney Alan Scheflin in San Francisco. "Roy called me to come over to his hotel room. He's sitting on his bed in his coat, a big cigar sticking out of his face, and the broadest grin I'd ever seen. I said, 'What're you so happy about?' He said, 'Listen to this.' He and Steve Cropper had just jammed on a couple of songs, one of them 'Green Onions.' They were so proud of the mix they'd done. It was a beautiful tape. When it came out on record, I was appalled. Stanley Clarke had remixed it and speeded it up into a contest. All of that sultry, after hours, smoky feel of two players who were in no hurry to go anywhere was gone."

Perhaps the album's most successful track artistically was an instrumental dubbed "Judy" that came next. Composed by drummer Narada Michael Walden, the gorgeous melody gave Roy a chance to put some feeling into his playing and he gave it a heartfelt reading. Apropos of the album's patchwork quality, the next track was a rocking number, "Done Your Daddy Dirty," that the band used effectively as a set opener on the road. Laying it down in the studio was irrelevant. The album closed with a gutless New Age outing dubbed "Your Love."

Like the first Atlantic record, *Loading Zone* exhibited a hodgepodge of styles and moods, almost too disparate and, for many, too antiseptic to do Roy's music justice. Coming on the heels of *A Street Called Straight*—an album that alluded to a newfound dedication to the straight and narrow—*Loading Zone* seemed to send a different message. The cover photograph showed Roy with a world-weary look and his '53 Tele at a table in a bar, smoking a cigarette, beer close at hand. It seems the shtick about a "street called straight" had run its course. Perhaps the guitarist had gotten over a need to posture. He knew that we knew that he knew he had a problem. He liked to drink and get high. Everyone could just get over it. That was easy to say, but there were bad omens. Like in May 1977 when the great white blues man from Chicago, Paul Butterfield, perished from a life of drink. The time no longer was propitious for blues-based musicians and their craft, either. The mechanical oblivion of disco music was getting shoved aside by the angry cacophony of punk rock, which at least exhibited raw emotion, though it disdained melodic roots music with the same sneer it gave disco.

Though die-hard fans were disappointed with the sound and material on the Atlantic albums, the critical reception included enthusiasm for Roy's new sound.

In a *Rolling Stone* review in June 1977, Jean-Charles Costa assessed new records by Roy, Al Di Meola, Lee Ritenour, and Janne Schaffer. Costa panned all of them except Roy's. Costa wrote that Stanley Clarke "has had a positive, prodding effect on Roy's playing." Though Roy was known for his Telecaster squeal, "on some of these tracks his frenzied excursions into overtones, harmonics, and tight clusters of notes played largely in the upper register of the instrument move beyond traditional lead-gui-tar histrionics. One gets an acute physical sense of Buchanan literally shredding his way through the blues-rock clichés to get to a higher, abstract plane. He is trying to take lead guitar into another dimension and his sparkling work . . . augurs well for his continuing development." This constituted a rave review, for Costa questioned whether Di Meola's "obsessive zeal has produced great guitar music or aimless tech-nical perfection." As for Ritenour, Costa remarked, "[His] faultless renditions of unremarkable syntho-funk tunes don't inspire much of a passionate response."

John Adams at WNET expressed his thoughts on Roy's latest album in an April letter to the guitarist. "The album . . . shows a lot of work. It shows a desire to improve and clarify your music. Your curiosity and imagination combine to drive you to see what you can really do. You want to see what more can be done with the instrument and the music. Most players go so far, then run out of things to say. (Hendrix should hear you now.) I tingle at the prospect of new chapters from Roy Buchanan! They will come even though you are a lazy sonofabitch like the rest of us—though I suspect you aren't as lazy as you'd like people to believe . . . ." Adams suggested that "Judy" was the most successful track on the album and congratu-lated Roy on the "blinding, awesome, and frightening" leads on "Green Onions."

John Harrison, for one, was disappointed. "Everybody wanted to make some-thing of Roy," he said many years later. "They wanted to turn him into something. The Atlantic albums, if you listen to them, are really sterile. They all wanted to pop-ularize him. To me that was the wrong way to go. The excitement of Roy Buchanan's band always came in a live situation. You can't capture that roadhouse music on record. The musicians take as much out of the audience as they give. Roy was a quintessentially 'audience' musician. When the audience was on, and they dug it, he soared. He took all of their energy and put it through that guitar. That's why *Live Stock* is one of his best albums. The album transmits what really went on in that hall. It was a great show. When you listen to that album you get some of the energy that was in that room."

THROUGHOUT THE SPRING OF 1977 Roy and his band turned in a string of dynamic performances, many of them extending nearly two hours each. The band had added a few songs to its repertoire, including the recent "Good God Have Mercy" and Cream's "Sunshine of Your Love." The latter featured an uptempo segue that gave Roy, like Jimi Hendrix before him, a chance to show what *he* could do with Clap-ton's one-time showcase—he turned it into a shuffle all his own. They included Booker T. & the MGs' beautiful instrumental, "Soul Dressing," "Slow Down," the

Lawrence Williams song made popular by the Beatles, and they added a few bars of "Foxy Lady" to the end of "Hey Joe." Not exactly a spectacular development for a band that had been together four years. But this was not some progressive rock band whose music evolved rapidly, the sort of band for whom weighty, socially relevant lyrics and cutting-edge music were of supreme importance. No. The players in the Roy Buchanan Band were bad-ass barroom brawlers who knew how to rock a joint to its core. The lyrics to the songs they typically performed were frequently misogynistic. There was "Hey Joe": *"I had to kill my old lady, you know I caught her messin' round with another man."* There was Neil Young's "Down by the River": *"I shot my baby."* There was the blues that borrowed a lyrical format from *Second Album's* "Five String Blues." But what had once been: "Oh Jesus, this is my final plea" (presumably for salvation) had become: *"Oh baby, this is my final word. If you bring me down one more time, you'll hear the loudest sound you've ever heard."* Roy's melancholy guitar work left no doubt that the narrator hated to do it, but the message lingered: *Sometimes these things just got to be done.* These were men singing about women, without the thin veneer of political correctness. Women could sing their own songs.

LIKE YOUNG CANADIANS, Brits, and Europeans, Japan's youth couldn't get enough of that gritty American rock 'n' roll. It had been that way since Roy had first visited with Bob Luman in 1959. Jay Reich arranged a 14-day tour of a half-dozen Japanese cities for June. The boys were all warned about Japan's strict policy regarding drugs. In 1980 Paul McCartney—long-revered by Japanese audiences—had his bags searched upon arrival at Tokyo's airport for a tour and a half-pound of marijuana turned up. He spent a week in jail until he was allowed to leave the country. He had gambled that as an international celebrity his bags would not be searched. So no one entering Japan was immune to scrutiny. In fact, the Roy Buchanan Band's contract was written so that if any member got arrested for possessing or using any illicit drugs, all fees from the entire tour could be withheld. Once they arrived safely, however, someone discovered that Malcolm Lukens had brought methadone over in a shampoo bottle.

THE BAND PLAYED three or four gigs in Tokyo, then moved on to Sapporo, Nagoya, Niigata, and Osaka. Polygram International taped most of the tour, resulting in a solid record of the Roy Buchanan Band at its peak. The shows were set for 6:30 p.m., a nearly incomprehensible time for rock 'n' roll vampires. "We were all just waking up," Harrison recalled. "We hadn't even copped a buzz yet. And the crowds were, of course, very sober. Japanese audiences would make polite applause at the end of every song. We thought, 'We're bombing big time!' Then at the end of every show they would go berserk, rush the stage, throw gifts at us. Very strange cultural thing, but wonderful." As Byrd Foster noted, "It was like being Elvis when we got there. You still had to walk down the steps from the airplane to the runway. There was a banner that read: 'Welcome Roy Buchanan Band.' All these geisha girls came running out and gave us flowers." Before each gig the promoter gave each member of the band an envelope with 100 Yen in it. The message? "Give 100 percent." "We had such good camaraderie," Byrd said. "And it seemed Roy respected us. It seemed like he really enjoyed working with us. I like to think we made him comfortable. We had a lot of laughs."

Tapes from these Japanese performances reveal Roy at the apex of his powers. The band's camaraderie translated to musical conversation. The interplay between guitar and organ, the deft handoffs between soloists, the lock between bass and drums, the rollicking, steamrolling momentum the band generated made it the equal of any group in rock 'n' roll. Malcolm Lukens proved to be a fountain of musical ideas and his background work and fills were as imaginative as his solos. John Harrison's bass playing supplied a good deal of the swagger and menace that lay at the heart of good, pounding rock 'n' roll, while Byrd Foster's drumming could range from a tasteful accompaniment to quiet blues to the sharp accents needed to punctuate dramatic passages in dynamic numbers such as "Hey Joe." Byrd's vocals fit the music perfectly.

The sets in Japan included the usual standbys, such as "Sweet Dreams," "The Messiah," "Hey Joe," "I Hear You Knockin'," "Farther On Up the Road," "My Babe Sez She's Gonna Leave Me," the magnificent "Soul Dressing," lots of down-and-dirty 12-bar blues, "Green Onions," "I'm Evil," "Change My Mind," "Since You've Been Gone," "Down by the River," even "Susie Q" and "Johnny B. Goode." At one show in Osaka, the band ran through every song it could conjure in the course of a performance that lasted more than two hours.

Throughout his solo career, Roy never moved swiftly to add material or evolve his sets. Yet, over time, plenty of new music got woven in. In the months preceding the Japanese tour, he added a couple favorites loved by the entire band. There was the 1950s hit by New Orleans' Earl King, "Lonely Nights," where Roy could lay back and, with a few simple countrified notes in the lower registers, give the song a whole new feel. He worked in a precise, sensitive instrumental reading of B.B. King's "The Thrill Is Gone." And there was an Elmore James–like R&B romp with improvised lyrics dubbed "My Sweet Honey Dew."

Polygram edited the tapes down to a 45-minute LP. *Live in Japan*, however, would appear only in Japan. It has never been released in the United States. The LP opened with "Soul Dressing," an enchanting melody in an entrancing tempo that showed just how tight and cerebral the band could be. Rollicking "Sweet Honey Dew" came next, followed by "Hey Joe/Foxy Lady"—which featured an unexpected and moving nod to "Shenandoah"—and the thunderous "Slow Down." Side two opened with "Lonely Nights," "Since You've Been Gone"—an old Snakestretchers' number re-dubbed "Blues Otani"—"My Baby Says She's Gonna Leave Me," and, as an encore, a wonderfully heartfelt reading of Roy's melancholy instrumental version of Don Gibson's "Sweet Dreams." Each track offered a window onto Roy Buchanan's soulful talent, and reflected how the band had gelled.

After *Live in Japan*'s release overseas, Roy told American interviewers the record represented his best work. Of course, he knew that no one in the States had heard the record. His perspective seemed to be: the best stuff I've ever played, you'll never hear.

In FACT, the difficulties in getting a hot-selling Roy Buchanan record out of the Atlantic sessions had come home to roost. Fingers were pointed. Roy and Judy laid responsibility at Reich's feet. Perhaps the reasoning was: "How could you *let* me make that lousy record?" Reich had not yet turned 30. "There was a disappointment between Roy and Judy, perhaps with me, because with *Loading Zone* we didn't make the right record," Reich said. "Roy called me up—it was a difficult thing for Roy to do—and he said, 'Listen, I think you should find something else to do.' We parted company. I was devastated. Working with Roy was by far the best thing that had ever happened to me. I liked the lifestyle. I liked being associated with him and everything that entailed. I thought, 'Well, maybe my presence is inhibiting him. Maybe he'll go on to do great things and make zillions of bucks.'"

At virtually the same time, John Harrison saw the graffiti on the bathroom wall. "I'd been with him for four years, we'd made a bunch of records, traveled all over the place, and I really felt that we had gone as far as we could. Having done it for four years, it was time for me to move on. I was close to 30 at the time. I wanted to exploit my filmmaking career. So I signed off."

Roy fired Malcolm Lukens for the third time. The keyboardist's erratic behavior became too vexing to tolerate, even for Roy. There must have been some fear on Roy's part that his own tendency towards addiction might draw him into the same potentially deadly circle Lukens then occupied. Roy had problems of his own. He didn't need Malcolm's as well.

The Buchanans decided that someone with more experience than Reich should handle Roy's management. They discovered the hard way there were no immediate takers. The two recent albums had disappointed the hit-makers and the accountants at Atlantic and, though he didn't know it, Roy's stock had begun to tumble.

LOST IN
THE WILDERNESS

10

*I*n reaching for more, Roy wound up with less. Having fired his manager, he found no one willing to step into the void. Those who once had intimated they might be interested suddenly were busy. After dismissing his keyboard player for the third and last time and losing his bassist to ambition, his entourage consisted of precisely one drummer/vocalist—the faithful and talented Byrd Foster—and one road manager, Harry Homa. In the fall of 1977, upon his return from Japan, Roy's situation abruptly changed from leading one of the hottest working bands in the country to having a whole lotta nothing. He called Foster and asked if the drummer could rustle up a band. Byrd said he knew players in, of all places, Pittsburgh. Foster's pal Fred DeLu agreed to contribute his talents on the Hammond B-3. Al Britton McClain signed on to play bass. *Presto!* A new band.

As for a manager, Roy and Judy decided they would save money if they kept that salary in-house. Judy would manage Roy's career for him. Problem solved. Steve Simenowitz, a fledgling attorney in New York, had befriended Roy back in the early 1970s, and he thought perhaps the problem had *not* been solved. "Judy had business cards printed up," Simenowitz would recall. "The cards said, 'Roy Buchanan, legendary guitarist.' Under that they said, 'Management: Judy Buchanan.' I said to her, 'Legendary' is the kind of thing other people say about you. You don't say that about yourself!' That was emblematic of their mom-and-pop approach to a need for major-league management."

Roy needed not only professional management, but a degree of supervision. When not under his wife's watchful eye his predilection for excess now went unchecked. His habit of pounding down the better part of a six-pack of beer before sauntering on stage was well-known. Now cocaine appeared on the scene with increasing frequency and in disheartening quantities. "Blow" had been part of the jazz scene since the 1930s, in an era when cocaine was routinely used for medicinal purposes. In that day the coca plant provided the coca in Coca-Cola. As for the rock 'n' roll scene, cocaine in powdered form had really begun to circulate as an illicit narcotic since the late 1960s. By the late 1970s it seemed to be everywhere, particularly at the clubs and roadhouses where Roy performed.

Cocaine provided users with a seemingly benign rush of pleasure. Used carefully, it could be invigorating, even enhance performance. Naturally, as with all things, these gifts came with a price. Taking a little led to taking more. And a lot of cocaine eventually warped a user's judgment, twisted his thinking, and numbed emotions. Priorities inevitably got reordered, with cocaine at the top of the list. The sudden abundance of cocaine on America's black market kept its cost relatively low—if not really affordable, then at least obtainable. Roy's notoriety attracted the sort of folks likely to carry ample supplies. The backstage scene, long an attractive den of iniquity for musicians, sank further. Few could resist the temptations of the rock 'n' roll dressing room, where sex and drugs were the coin of the realm. Roy Buchanan did not, or could not, resist.

Roy's new group hit the road in spring 1978. DeLu and McClain's love for soul, R&B, and rock 'n' roll made them kinsmen of Roy's from the start. If the band initially lacked the deep groove the previous ensemble had honed over four years' time, it found its own way soon enough. DeLu and McClain's first gig with Roy took place at the Ivanhoe Theatre in Chicago. They soon learned Roy's standard operating procedure—there would be no rehearsals. "Byrd gave me some tapes of Roy's music a week or two before the first gig," DeLu recalled. "And that night Roy made a list of the songs he would play. He didn't play *one thing* off that damn list."

The band's travels took them once again to the familiar stops Roy had been making regularly since his re-emergence in 1972. This time, however, the touring might have felt more like work, less like fun. Same old places, same old routine. Things *had* changed. Roy was pushing forty. But there was no sense worrying about it, the rock 'n' roll life still beat cutting hair. Through the Northeast, the far West, the South, the band rattled from town to town, having a good time, never asking where it all might lead. That was another crucial element of the rock 'n' roll lifestyle: one lived for the pleasures or perils of the moment, without looking ahead, or behind.

Texas always treated the band right. One night in January 1978 Roy booked into Panther Hall in Fort Worth on a double bill with Dallas-area guitarist Bugs Henderson. During the first show Roy managed to set the audience and promoter on edge by playing three songs, then casually disappearing to his dressing room for a half-hour interlude. As nearly everyone in the house reached the limits of their patience, Roy sauntered back onstage and finished his set in jaw-dropping style.

Henderson taped the second set of the evening, which opened with "Stormy Monday." By this time every member of the band was in a howling state. As Al Britton McClain recited the lyrics with a soulful gusto, he skirted close to the edge of raucousness—the band was not far behind their leader in backstage dabbling—as Roy worked up stunning, jazzy fills behind him. The music was soulful but charged.

Roy played a few leads so tip-toe soft one can hear his pick on the Telecaster's strings. For ten minutes he fluidly explored variations on the melody, mixing leads, rhythms, even percussive effects on his Telecaster. DeLu added a dash of gentle jazz piano and the band sounded ready to cook. Suddenly, however, Roy somehow broke his guitar strap, which gave him an excuse to disappear backstage yet again as his band mates provided a five-minute interlude of laid-back jazz. When Roy regained the stage, "Stormy Monday" still in progress, he stepped to the microphone and blurted: "Think future! Think future! It's important!" And: "Uh, people, I guess the preacher thing is kinda in me, ya know? There's two rules you gotta live by. There's only one god and one Lone Star beer. So love yourself like your neighbor. And you got it comin'. And the second [rule] is"—and here Roy hesitated for a moment, as any good storyteller would, however high they might be, before bestowing a revelation—"God is not logical. But listen: logic is something God gave Man to understand his own problems with." Stunning blues licks exploded from Roy's guitar. McClain picked up the song without batting an eye, though his guitarist had just been trying to explain the mysteries of the universe. But as McClain attempted to finish singing the lyrics, Roy suddenly drowned him out with wild banshee blues licks that grabbed the spotlight. McClain bravely carried on, though at one point he declared, "I can't sing!" as Roy's guitar screamed again, out of turn. Nearly 20 minutes later, the first song of the set was over. "Oh *yeah*," Roy called out. "I love ya so much! I'll bet ya we love you more than you love us."

Roy began the next song, "Honky Tonk," with some super-heated guitar work, the volume turned up to ear-splitting levels. "*Yeah!*" he shouted. "*All night!*" Then, as was sometimes his wont, he improvised lyrics. "Oh baby, you don't have to go, but you can pack your rags if you don't love me no mo'. . . " When it came time for Roy to solo there lurked an air of danger—*will he make it?!*—but he peeled off the melody and a few quirky permutations with verve. As he reeled off his dexterous lines, however, there was an almost imperceptible glitch in his run of notes. They were not perfect.

Suddenly Roy interjected the knife-edge rhythms of "Green Onions," and he was off on the kind of slashing, stabbing leads that would make Hubert Sumlin himself sit up and take notice. Bugs Henderson came out onstage to jam and plugged in his Gibson. Roy startled him by grabbing the Gibson and handing off his Tele. Roy proceeded to burn it up on the Gibson while Bugs gave the Tele a run for its money. The two guitarists traded solos for a few minutes, before Roy stepped back into the spotlight. The guitar switch baffled Bugs. "We played really different guitars," he would recall. "At that time I played with pretty big strings. And Roy used his Tele with real tiny strings on it, which for his style of playing is necessary. The swap was bizarre." But the soloing that followed established that Roy could play most anything on an unfamiliar instrument that he could do with his '53 Telecaster. After the mind-riveting explosions of "Green Onions," Roy turned to his old standard, the lullaby-like country melody "Sweet Dreams." He hypnotized the audience with the sweetness and simplicity of his reading, making his Tele cry as never before, soothing nerves jangled by the evening's fierce soloing. With a set of sixteenth notes, he segued into "The Messiah." Though he slurred the words, there was a poignancy to the moment. The crowd called out encouragement, giving up atavistic cries of *"R-o-o-o-y!"* After riveting cries for redemption, Roy quieted his guitar. "Bye-bye baby . . . bye-bye baby . . . even though I love you . . . " he sang, cryptically. An hour-long tightrope walk was over.

"I remember that night in particular because my wife was pregnant with my son, Buddy, who's my drummer now," Bugs said. "Roy came over to rub her stomach and he told us, 'It's going to be a boy.' Later that night she went into premature labor. We left the gig and went to the hospital. That turned out not to be the night, but I always remembered that. Roy was a real strange guy. He was always regaling me with stories, but I never knew if they were true." But there was no disputing the veracity of Roy's guitar playing. "You couldn't nail him down and say, 'Roy plays blues guitar,' or 'Roy plays rock guitar.' He was just a great guitar player," Henderson said. "He grew up in a different time, when they just played good songs on the radio. He loved all kinds of music and you could hear it in his playing."

THE BAND TOURED THE COUNTRY that spring and summer, gradually feeling more at ease with each other personally and gelling musically. One taped performance from the Agora in Cleveland on May 15 reveals a band that had achieved that runaway freight train quality that only desperately talented electric musicians can conjure. They added to their repertoire a pounding "Love Me Two Times," "Walkin' Talkin'," "1841 Shuffle," even Jimmy Reed's funky "Big Boss Man." For a precious moment, this band sounded as good as any Roy ever had.

Touring, despite its temptations, remained the bright spot in Roy's career. The situation with Atlantic had soured. The final disappointment had been his third and, as it turned out, final LP for the label. *You're Not Alone*, produced by Raymond "Ramon" Silva, had been released in April 1978. Critically, it did not hit many nerves. This time the album was recorded, mixed, and mastered in one studio— Atlantic Studios in New York City—perhaps to save money, given the high cost of the first two records. One ensemble of studio players recorded the entire album: Ray Gomez played acoustic and rhythm guitar, studio veteran Willie Weeks played bass, and Andy Newmark did the drumming. Veteran producer Jimmy Douglass assisted Silva with capturing Roy's power and volume. Keyboardist and Cat Stevens collaborator Jean Roussel helped the guitarist flesh out a few of the riffs Roy brought to the session, teasing out a few songs. Side one featured four instrumentals. It opened with a forgettable excursion into studio spaciness, then launched out of the solar system with Roy's potent reading of Joe Walsh's power-guitar anthem, "Turn to Stone." This was a convincing excursion into vintage '70s fusion-rock that stacked up nicely to anything Jeff Beck had done on *Blow by Blow*. It was also one of the rare tracks that made it from an Atlantic record to Roy's performance repertoire, becoming a crowd favorite. The next track, "Fly . . . Night Bird," is a quiet, contemplative piece that features Roy's soulful yet bittersweet touch, and is perhaps the strongest track on the album. Both tracks conveyed a new facet of Roy's talent but, unfortunately, they were the album's sole highlights. The last track on side one, "1841 Shuffle," was simply an uptempo guitar workout that had migrated from stage to studio, suffering in the process. The same could be said for "Down by the River," the opening track on side two. The next piece, "Supernova," was an uptempo guitar scorcher that, though primitive, marked the only time on the album Roy and the band really cut loose.

By this time Roy had become thoroughly disenchanted with Atlantic. He'd had three producers in as many records, while the label cast about in vain for a winning formula. Each producer had tried for a different sound, even different genres, without creating a coherent product with broad appeal. Roy's cachet in the recording industry crested. Three less-than-stellar records in a row dissipated the aura of mystery and fascination the industry had bestowed on Roy since his deliverance from anonymity in 1971.

There was plenty of blame to go around. Arif Mardin, Stanley Clarke, and Ramon Silva, Roy's respective producers, must have reluctantly reported to Ahmet Ertegun that despite Roy's earnest cooperation, the guitarist did not bring sufficient material to the sessions. It was a struggle to get something definite out of the man. It had been maddening, in some cases, to work with someone of such eclectic tastes and talents, trying to record something coherent that would sell in the commercial record market of the mid-1970s.

The process and the result disheartened the guitarist. "Roy told me at the time he disliked having record companies telling him how he had to play, or what he had to play," Seymour Duncan said. "They were trying to make him into a guitar hero. It was like trying to turn Roy, a Cadillac, into a Porsche—trying to slick him up. He went along with it as much as he could. But deep inside he resented it, or felt flustered by it. Listen to the first four albums he made with his Telecaster, the emotion he put into it. Later on he was just recording to record. It's a shame that when you have a family, house payments, you have to get kids' clothes for school, sometimes you do things you don't really want to do. I felt bad because he lost that sparkle that he had."

Later, three albums too late, it dawned on Roy that he had to *want* to record. He had to enter the studio with a strong sense of precisely what he wished to accomplish if he expected more from the medium. At this stage, however, all he could muster were complaints about the way he was being handled by the label—appropriate criticisms, to a degree, though Roy's view omitted a necessary measure of personal responsibility.

In San Francisco in August for an appearance, Roy spoke to Sheila Rene, a DJ for KSJO's *Live Wire* program. Roy seemed to open up more with female interviewers, and the Rene interview is one of his most articulate and candid exchanges on record. His responses to her questions are at once sly and earnest and they present a snapshot of his outlook at this juncture. Rene must have touched a nerve when she enquired about Roy's songwriting endeavors, for his answer quickly turned to comments on his Atlantic albums. "Well, I actually have hundreds of songs that I've worked up," Roy offered. (This would be news to anyone who'd worked with him in the studio!) "To get a record company to buy the idea of lettin' you do it is another problem. Once in a while I can get some of my things on, sometimes I can't. [Often] the material is already picked for me. I don't have much choice. But things will change. Especially on the next album, one way or another. 'Cause I intend to do my own thing and ain't nobody goin' to stop it . . . I've had these ideas I've been workin' on all my life, really, but especially hard in the last six, seven years. I've reached the point now where I'm just going to do it. I gotta do it. Even if I have to do everything myself . . . It's going to be done."

Sheila Rene asked him why he didn't tour more often, given the demand for his music. "I've always had this theory that I learned to play music because I loved to play," Roy responded. "And I've always been lazy and not liked to work. So if I play too often, it turns out to be work. I can't see any point in making it [into] work. The way I go out now, I go out to have a good time." As for his audience, the guitarist confessed, "I walk out there strictly to entertain them . . . I watch their faces and try to please them. That's my goal when I'm out on stage."

As Rene pressed on, Roy revealed more. Asked about his original influences, Roy cast his mind back to his Pixley days. "I'll tell you the truth, okay?" Roy promised, before weaving fact and fiction. "There was a church about a block away [from our home], it was a holy-roller church, where they play the guitar wide open and they scream and shout and roll on the floor. And I heard that music at night and I didn't know what it was. But I liked it. I used to go around back and collect the guitar strings that got thrown out the back. My dad saw me doing it and he said, 'You like guitars, huh?' I said, 'Yeah.' So he bought me one. I was about five at the time." Are sons of preachers as wild as rumored? Rene asked. (By this time, Minnie Reed Buchanan had been ordained as a lay minister in the Assembly of God church in Pixley, so Roy could answer truthfully.) "They're the most rebellious, stubbornest, hard-headed, spoiled brats. I was spoiled to death as a child."

Is it harder for a guitarist to make it, as opposed to a vocalist with a band? she asked. "Yeah, [vocalists] can talk with their mouth and say things where regular people can understand it," Roy said. "It doesn't take much feeling. But if you've got something to say from the heart, and you've got nothin' but wood and steel to say it with, that makes it a little harder." You want to do it the hard way? Rene suggested. Roy laughed. "It chose me. I didn't choose it, to be honest with you. I just wanted to play, that's all. I'm really thankful that people like my playin'. I've really been fortunate . . . [and] I just stuck to my own little thing." How'd that "thing" come about? Roy reckoned he'd listened to the firmament of guitarists. "I try to find a route right through the middle of all of them." He and his '53 Tele seemed inseparable. Did he have a pet name for it, like B.B. King and his guitar, "Lucille"? "I never went in for that namin' stuff," Roy chuckled. "It's just a piece of wood with steel in it. And you hit it with a piece of plastic and it vibrates in a certain direction to make tones, and it comes out a certain way. So, it'll wear out someday."

Roy knew he had to pursue another deal with another record label. A deal meant cash advances, and a record that would help keep him touring. He did what he could and called the handful of recording industry figures he'd met over the past decade. No one offered anything tangible. For one thing, his track record on Atlantic sent a discouraging message about his commercial potential. His lack of professional representation could not have helped. Roy even tracked down Pete Siegel and questioned him. Could he get Roy a record contract, and produce another album for him? "He was looking for a deal and I had nothing to offer him at that time," Siegel would recall. "There weren't a lot of little labels doing interesting stuff." Siegel expressed the frustration that many had experienced, particularly the guitarist's record producers: "Roy always complained about being overproduced. Later, he admitted it was his own fault. He let them do it. He didn't have to do that. In 1975 [prior to the Atlantic contract] he was the hottest thing. He could have done anything he wanted. He was really frustrating in that way because he wouldn't come out and say, 'This is me.'"

Performing would be Roy's bread and butter, as always. He had little choice but to press on with his occasional one- or two-week long forays across the country, responding to a steady though precarious demand for his services, and living the only life he knew. That meant a road regimen of one-night stands at clubs in towns where he'd built a reputation. The clubs were glad to have him. Despite his much-vaunted status as something of a cult guitar figure, his fans would pack virtually any club, damn near anywhere in America. His itinerary no longer included the halls and theaters that might have made the economics of such a life more rewarding, but that was okay with Roy. He'd been playing for his supper for more than 20 years. He could handle it. Still, racing from town to town had lost a bit of its luster. Even a "lifer" like Roy occasionally flinched. Things just weren't the same. Foster could never be sure *what* Roy was thinking when his guitarist was in a pensive mood. But when Roy felt like talking, he sometimes surprised Foster. "One night he come up to me and said, 'Did you ever think of killing yourself?' It startled me. Where did *that* come from? I mean, we've all had times when we say, 'I wish I was fucking dead!' But I never had the urge to carry it out. So I said, 'How about you?' He took a deep breath, 'Naw, man, that's the coward's way out.'"

It seems Roy longed for the band of friends who had once coalesced around him and made the last five years the best of his life. He phoned John Harrison in Hollywood and tried to lure back his favorite bass player. "It broke my heart," Harrison said later. "I really agonized over it. I told him, 'You know what, Roy? I wish you hadn't called. I don't want to go through this.' My partners and I had just committed to making a feature film. In the end I couldn't do it to them. But it was a real temptation." The other calls went the same way. People had moved on. And Roy still had a gig to play. For the time being he had the faithful Byrd Foster, and Fred DeLu and Al Britton McClain were hanging in there, though Roy's call to John Harrison indicates *he* wasn't completely satisfied.

With no record deal, but a smoking touring band, the obvious became apparent: Recording live had worked so well with *Live Stock* and *Live in Japan* that taping a couple of the band's sets on the road might be the ticket to his next album. Though it would be expensive to have an eight-track recording made of a couple gigs on the road, the alternative—no record deal and the fading cachet of personal appearances—spelled doom. Perhaps with tapes in hand Roy could strike a deal. Somehow—the financing remains unclear—arrangements were made with the local firm of Onion Audio in Austin to tape a couple of shows in September at one of Roy's favorite haunts, the Armadillo World Headquarters. Before reaching Austin, the band toured the West Coast where, apparently, Roy in his unassuming way was pushing the lifestyle a bit too hard. Over the first two nights of September 1978 Roy, Byrd, Al, and Fred rocked the 'Dillo to its foundations on another double bill with Bugs Henderson. It was the late 1970s, and Roy was making an attempt to overcome the blue-jeans-and-flannel-shirt look of earlier days, so for the 'Dillo engagements he dressed in a driving cap, wide-lapelled polyester shirt, and dress jacket. The new duds did not seem to impede his talents. Roy led the band through super-heated versions of his standard set from the last two years. He threw in an edgy, uptempo version of Jimmy Reed's "Big Boss Man," invoking a John Lee Hooker–style shuffle before turning this easy blues groove into a killing floor of leads. While his rhythm section held the bottom, Roy stepped forward and picked ferociously, hypnotically, giving an astonishing performance. "Yeah, baby," Roy drawled. "Looks like it's closin' time agin . . . ." His guitar screamed this time, where once it had simply cried out. The boys had been dabbling backstage again. Suddenly tired of playing, he started rapping: "Rain. Snow. Minnows. Triangles. Circles. Pyramids. Algebra. Math. Apologetics. Philosophy. Einstein. Curved. Austin. City Limits. Tell it to 'em one more time, guitar . . . " Now Roy's Tele laughed and cried, soared and wailed. The music had a supercharged quality. And so it went that night. After the show, Roy and his party sauntered over to Antone's, another Austin fixture, where the great electric bluesman Albert King was holding forth. King invited Roy up onto the bandstand, but Roy refused. "A white man can't sing the blues," he is said to have told the crowd. "You have Albert King to listen to. He's the real thing."

ROY BROUGHT THE ARMADILLO TAPES to New York and, with assistance from the perpetually helpful John Adams from WNET, the two men hunkered down at National Sound studios to mix an hour's worth of music from several hours of tape. Unfortunately, upon playback, it became apparent that the performances were hyper, ragged, and raucous. The backstage scene in Austin had hit fever pitch and poisoned the flavor of the shows. Roy's guitar work screamed and shouted when it should have whispered and wailed. The performances, though often explosive, somehow lack the easy groove, the cohesiveness, that marked his earlier live recordings. On one level, that was okay. The band had simply delivered its raw club set, jamming on each song, cranking up the audience. On another level, however, this free-wheeling approach—it's clear the players are jacked up on *something*—did not produce music suitable for commercial release by a major label.

The Armadillo taping debacle spoke to larger issues. *Live Stock* and *Live in Japan* had succeeded because the band was tight and Roy more or less sober. Now, the relative innocence of 1974—a concept possible only in contrast to 1978—was long gone. Roy had picked Austin to record in because Austin was a good time and the band always enjoyed playing there. Yet the town also provided the temptations that could interfere with a successful recording. Though the artist and his band mates had all kinds of fun, an expensive attempt to capture an album's worth of stellar live performances went for naught.

In the wake of the Austin gigs, the local *River City Sun*, an alternative weekly, ran a story extolling the virtues of the music that had been captured at the 'Dillo. The writer, E.O. Wilson, mentioned that when Jerry Garcia had played the Armadillo several years earlier the leader of the Grateful Dead stated flatly that "Roy wrote the book" on electric guitar. In appreciation for the 'Dillo audience's support, Roy said, through Wilson, "I want to thank you from the bottom of my heart. It's good when a tree falls and someone's there to hear it."

The good news was there were plenty of people out there to hear Roy's tree when it fell. The sobering news was that people also were there when Roy stumbled, as he did now with increasing frequency. For one thing, Roy indulged his old habit of abruptly firing his whole band. Suddenly, Fred DeLu and Al Britton McClain were gone. Roy called Byrd Foster to let him know that *he* hadn't been let go. "We'd have a few beers," Foster said, "and everytime he'd fire me, he'd give me a raise!" Good times aside, Roy was on a streak to nowhere. Gone was the one crucial standard that had always sustained him: Don't get too fucked up to play. At the Park West club in Chicago on Feb. 1, 1979, Roy clearly had a debilitating head start on his favorite poisons by the time he hit the stage. He came out blasting on a new song, "Doctor of Rock 'n' Roll"—another mythically autobiographical piece—then suddenly digressed into a series of near-incoherent blues raps. The band turned out a sloppy version of Sam and Dave's "Hold On," then a feeble "Green Onions." "Goodnggght!" Roy slurred into the microphone before shuffling off the stage. "*Bullshit!*" screamed a fan. "*You suck!*" Another fan: "*A half a fucking hour? Booo!*" Though Roy returned to perform "Whole Lotta Shakin' Goin' On" and "I'm Evil," a spell had been broken. A month later he played Creations in Orange, NJ. When his guitar—an unidentified model, but no longer his trademark '53 Tele—kept buzzing disconcertingly, he got shit-faced, stopped playing, and began to taunt the audience. In a sorrowful display, Roy removed his shirt to make muscles for the crowd, handing off his guitar to someone in the audience. "I was there," John Adams said with asperity. "I was pissed at him and embarrassed for him because he had a piece of shit guitar that wouldn't play and he got pissed. And he got drunk, took off his shirt. He was acting like a punk rocker. And you know something? The audience was loving it. And the more the audience loved it, the more ridiculous he got. I told him later, 'Roy, I'm never mad at you. Just disappointed.'" At the Pinecrest in Shelton, CT, later that month, Roy played two smoking sets, but there was anger in his tone. The second set opened with an incendiary blues. "Yeah, the next time I try suicide baby," Roy roared over a fiery riff, "I'm goin' take you with me . . . ." No, things were not as they used to be.

Not even Roy's trademark guitar made it through this tumultuous time. He permanently retired his '53 Telecaster and took up playing its cousin, the Fender Stratocaster. To devotees of electric guitar, such a shift is akin to a seismic event. The two instruments' sounds are quite different and Roy's musical identity was bound up in the Telecaster's cutting yet sweet tone. The Strat delivered a wonderful sound all its own—a little rounder, a little fuller, perhaps, than the Tele—and it inspired its own devotees, including Jimi Hendrix, Eric Clapton, and Buddy Guy. In fact, the Stratocaster became many rock 'n' rollers' guitar of choice. But the difference between the two was unquestionably one of sound. The Telecaster cut, the Stratocaster seduced. Why would a guitarist whose signature sound was inextricably bound to one model switch to the other?

There are various stories regarding Roy's reasons for leaving his vintage Tele at home. Roy himself said: "The reason I quit even taking my guitar on the road is that I was robbed three times. It was just a streak of [bad] luck . . . ." One night during recording sessions in New York around this time Roy walked alone back to his hotel carrying his '53 Tele under his arm. Someone jumped him and tried to wrest away the instrument. Roy responded in true Tele-owner fashion: He axed the would-be thief. "I've always known the guitar can be used as a weapon," Roy told the New York newspapers. "When that guy found out I wasn't afraid to use it as one, he split pretty fast. That old wood is pretty hard."

Another account had Roy merely making the best of a bad situation. He purportedly handed over his beloved Tele to his friend Danny Gatton, whose guitar tech ruined the instrument by tinkering with the pickups. "I could see a change in him," Seymour Duncan said later, believing the latter to be the truer account. "I don't know what happened to him. Part of it is that when your 'race horse' dies— you know it and it knows you—there's some loss of inspiration. Roy's race horse was the Tele." Still, that wouldn't explain the switch to the Stratocaster. There were plenty of vintage Telecasters around for purchase. This was a conscious decision to explore new territory, branch out a little. Perhaps this guitar stylist was entitled to a midlife crisis, and to cast about for a new sound, with nothing deeper at work.

Roy told writer John Swenson for *The Complete Music Magazine* that his newfound affection for the Stratocaster was a qualified love. He spoke of the Strat in terms of its poor contrast with his vintage Tele—which he spoke of in the past tense, perhaps lending credence to the story of the damaged pickup. "The treble pickup in the Telecaster was cleaner and it had a lot more slicing or cutting power than the Strat, especially with the type amp I use," Roy said. "The Telecaster I had has a larger neck than the Stratocaster. I have to do things now with this new guitar to get the sounds that I got with the Telecaster, such as playing a little bit louder and using a dash of fuzz here and there, and the wah-wah." In other words, he had to work harder to get his sound with a wholly different model, but he'd get it just the same. That reflected the force of his style: A casual listener would have never known he'd switched guitars, as he bent the Strat to his will.

IN EARLY 1979 Roy somehow managed to return to Electric Lady studios to work with Raymond "Ramon" Silva on some studio material, a little of Roy's, a bit of Ramon's. Though the sessions produced several finished tracks, the result was akin to some of the amorphous New Age sounds developed on the Atlantic sessions. Roy shopped the tracks around, in vain.

At this juncture he had no record deal, no experienced management, not even a band—just his drummer and singer, Byrd Foster, still hanging on. Once again, he turned to John Adams at WNET and got help putting together auditions. He soon rounded up a band led by New Yorker Paul Jacobs. Jacobs was a keyboard player, guitarist, and singer who'd attended the Juilliard School of Music and made his mark with Meatloaf and Edgar Winter, both singers steeped in the art of funk and jive. Jacobs had grown up in Queens listening to rock 'n' roll and studying classical music, and he had been involved in music theater. Roy also hired bass guitarist Gordon Johnson, a Minneapolis, MN, native who'd played with, among others, Dizzy Gillespie and Maynard Ferguson. Once again, Byrd Foster delivered the goods on drums and traded vocals with Jacobs and Roy.

Despite a few missed opportunities, Roy still delivered the goods most nights. He instantly developed a close musical rapport with his new ensemble. The band went out on two-week jaunts to different regions of the country, first to the Northeast, then the Midwest. Roy returned to the Park West in Chicago and turned in a searing performance to make up for his earlier misstep. The new unit could rock or play blues well enough, but between Gordon Johnson and Paul Jacobs the band also developed a jazz sensibility that Roy really enjoyed exploring. There was plenty of clever interplay between guitar and keyboards, and Gordon Johnson's funky bass work brought spunk to the party. Ironically, this new unit was even less cohesive personally than past ensembles, yet it provided Roy a chance to investigate new sounds.

In November 1979 Bill Adler, *The Boston Herald American*'s pop music critic, wrote a perceptive piece about a Buchanan performance a few days earlier. Adler's insights into the music and Roy's performance gave no hint that something might be amiss. "The world's greatest guitar player? Debates used to rage pretty furiously in the late '60s and early '70s when there were a lot of guitarists around and room for them to strut their stuff. Jim Hendrix, Eric Clapton, Jeff Beck, Jimmy Page, Michael Bloomfield; every red-blooded rocker had his favorite. Well, times and styles change, and most folks today don't put much of a premium on the powerfully and elaborately strung-out guitar solo. But those who continue to care showed up in force at Jonathan Swift's Monday night to investigate for themselves the legend that is Roy Buchanan. He isn't, to begin with, much to look at. Most of the night Buchanan stood way over on the right side of the stage, a rather pudgy, impassive figure in blues jeans, shirt and hunting vest, sporting sideburns and a fastidiously trimmed, brown-and-gray Vandyke beard, and wearing a snap-brim cloth cap. He wasn't given to behind-the-neck guitar stranglings and appeared loathe to play on bended knee. No, Buchanan is your basic no-brag-just-fact monster, and it was his playing, after all, not his onstage histrionics, that earned him tributes from the Becks and Claptons and Pages before most of us knew of him."

"Beginning with a long, speedy, convoluted cadenza, Buchanan drew up suddenly and kicked the band into a blues so slow you could run circles around it between beats," Adler wrote. "A master of dynamics who gets a terribly affecting vocal quality out of his Telecaster guitar, Buchanan started out very soft and low, as if the bad news had hit him like a punch in the gut and it was all he could do to eke out, 'oh, oh, oh.' Catching his breath, Buchanan began to get louder and faster, angry now as he ripped off stinging riffs, majestic and elegant as he finger-picked a cascade of notes that slide into a long, greasy scream that peaked way up upon the bridge before easing gingerly into something exhausting but triumphant. Still, for all the feeling that informs Buchanan's virtuosity, there was something narcissistic about his flying fingers and the ecstatic response their every lick wrought. The young college crowd came to be dazzled by flash, and encouraged the legend's emptiest noodling with hoarse shouts of approval. Unimpressed, Buchanan took it all in with a mild Mona-Lisa smile and kept on playing."

By mid-December 1979, Roy's band members went their separate ways for the holidays, Paul Jacobs home to New York, Gordon Johnson to Minneapolis, Byrd Foster and Harry Homa to Pittsburgh. Roy returned, once again, to the house out in Lovettsville, VA. Over New Year's, he had occasion to leave the house and head out for a little drinking at a few of his favorite bars in Leesburg, ten miles from home. This time Roy wound up in police custody, badly injured. Greg Stocks, the Loudoun County police spokesman, told reporters in 1988 that Roy had been arrested on Jan. 1, 1980, for public intoxication and placed in the Loudoun County Jail. Judy told author Bill Milkowski in 1989 that she talked to Roy over the phone when the guitarist made the customary single call from the jailhouse. "He was having a time with somebody," she said. "I asked him, 'What's wrong? Calm down! I'll be there in a half hour." By the time she arrived, Roy was unconscious and had to be taken to the hospital. According to the police, he had attempted to hang himself in his cell with a sleeveless undershirt. Later, he was examined by a psychiatrist.

"He had bruises on him," Judy recalled. "It was obvious that he was beat up. He was aching in his back and sides from where they had kicked him." Billy Price ran into Roy in Richmond, VA, one night when both were playing in town early in January. Roy looked beat-up, all right, Price said many years later. Roy told him he'd "run into trouble with the cops."

John Adams felt he was closer to the situation. "I was like family. I never heard from them unless something awful happened. Both of them. I used to yell at them. 'How come I only hear from you when something horrible has happened?' Over New Year's I got this screaming call from Judy in the middle of the night. I was the first person. Of course, Roy and Judy both said later it was police brutality. But her statement to me at first, over the phone, at 2 o' clock in the morning, was 'Roy's hung himself.' *He* always told me that the cops beat him up." Adams paused. "He wanted out."

At the Rainbow Music Hall in Denver in mid-February, Roy showed no outward signs that something had been terribly amiss just a month earlier. Yet his blues were as bitter as ever:

Yeah the light used to shine bright,
Yeah, well, now the light is gone,
Yeah the light used to shine bright,
Yeah, well, now the light is gone,
Guess I'll just play my guitar,
And play some old lonesome song

Later in the show he played another blues.

Felt so bad last night
I had to get on my knees and pray
Felt so bad last night
I had to get on my knees to pray
'Cuz you was on my mind,
I don't think I'll ever get away
Yeah, the next time I try suicide,
Yeah, I'm gonna do it right this time,
I'd rather be deaf, dumb, and blind,
Yeah anything to get you off my mind.

Roy continued to pay dues on the road, from California to Connecticut in March and April. In April, at Toad's Place in New Haven, CT, Roy turned in a great performance that was broadcast over the local FM station. After a couple tunes, however, it was clear Roy was getting loaded. "All right, we're startin' to get a lil' bit bett-terr," he slurred. "Hope you didn't mind us practicin' tonight." In the middle of "Hey Joe" Roy recited a few bars to the Beatles' "Eleanor Rigby," then, during a loose blues rap he got into his patented stream-of-consciousness mode. "Beer!" he yelled into the microphone. "I want a beer. I feel like the blues, too. Blues ain't nothin but the reds turned inside out . . . .Have you ever watched the walls throb, and the ceiling looks like it's going to melt, and the dog is talkin', the one you used to own, before he got killed? Then you're startin' to get a little taste of the blues . . . .It doesn't take much to get the blues, all you got to do is think about, like, messin' around—15 minutes' worth ain't worth it—except sometimes on a cloudy day you watch the storm comin', you like to hear the rain on the tin roof, and you think about nothing else but everything else, and if you did think of everything else what would you be thinking of, it's like looking through a powerful telescope, you see the back of your head shinin' baby"—wild riffs explode from his guitar—"I felt a kind of freaky thing one time, I fell in love with a ghost, and nobody made love like she did, everything that you thought of and could put in one brain, she had, and you knew it was something real because she wasn't, except in the spiritual state which, like, really grooved . . . .You should go to New Orleans, like, I went there in '55, or was it '56?, in Shreveport, right across the river, however, tell you what I'm going to do for ya, I'm not going to tell you exactly what it's going to be, because, like, I'm going to take my time at it, you know, we did it several times before we were born, I'm one of those little amoebas that believes in reincarnation, I remember you, so I'm going to play it for you the way we used to"—his guitar shrieks again—"imagine I'm thinkin' about you all this time"—guitar scream—"I'd like to do a song I wrote for Janis Joplin. I never got to meet her. It's just that I really liked her a lot . . . ." With that, finally, Roy burst into a guitar solo that segued into an instrumental version of "The Messiah." The road, more than 20 years long, had Roy in its maw.

In early 1980, with the cooperation of owner Shelly Yakus, Roy managed to secure recording time at the Record Plant in New York City for a self-produced album—finally, a twist of fate in his favor. With a few tracks in the can, Roy contacted Gary Marx at a small local label in Minneapolis known as Waterhouse Records. After flying to Virginia to hear the tapes, Marx agreed to press it and market it. The plan was to record the rest of the album, then hit the road. One twist: The Silencers, from Pittsburgh, had recruited Byrd Foster in the pursuit of greatness. "We were like secret agents," Foster said, laughing. "We had shark-skin suits, thin ties, sunglasses. We had a chance to record for CBS. I told Roy I had a shot at something and he said 'Go for it.'" Richard Crooks, a studio musician from New York, and Dan Brubeck, son of the famed jazz pianist, helped fill in.

Roy made his typical preparations for the sessions: he simply assembled his new band at the Record Plant. As Jacobs recalled: "Roy said to me, 'Oh, by the way Paul, I want you to sing. Byrd is leaving the group. He literally handed me the lyrics to 'My Babe' and said, 'Okay, the tape is running. Let's do it!' I thought it was a little strange to find myself singing the title track to a record I had never heard in my life. Roy was not very well organized going into the studio. He didn't have any material ready. He said, 'Hey, do *you* have any material?' I started playing this song on the piano—'It Should Have Been Me'—that I'd played with another artist and Roy said, 'That sounds like a cool song.' Next thing you know, we were recording it. It was very bare bones, live-in-the-studio. Spontaneous. We did the whole record in two days." The self-produced album of material Roy had been working on "all his life" amounted to just a couple of worthwhile tracks: a remake of "My Babe," the Dale Hawkins' hit from 1958, a Doris Day number, "Secret Love," nearly 30 years old (on which Roy used a wah wah pedal for the first time in a studio), and a Carlos Santana–esque flamenco-like instrumental. The rest was rock 'n' roll that Jacobs and the rhythm section conjured on the spot.

After the sessions for *My Babe*, Foster departed for good. Gordy Johnson said he knew a drummer in his hometown of Minneapolis, and Gordy Knutsen came aboard. That gave Roy a band of musicians he hadn't known for more than a few months. Musicians often find an instant kinship, but Foster had been with Roy for six years, minding the beat and belting out vocals. Whether or not Roy realized it right away, Foster's departure created a void in the music and represented a loss of friendship as well. The next and last of the old crew to leave was Harry Homa. He'd had one too many hassles with Roy's manager, Judy. "I loved Roy, but she made it impossible." Homa recalled. "Later, I was tending bar in Pittsburgh and Roy came in to see me and he asked me to come back, but I told him I couldn't deal."

To promote the *My Babe* album Waterhouse taped an interview with Roy that gave the guitarist a license to spin his favorite yarns, and, uncharacteristically, to brag. He claimed to have left home in 1955 at age fifteen, when actually he had been 16 or 17 and the year was 1956. Roy went on to say that *he* formed the Heartbeats and even worked the Johnny Otis show. He'd recorded blues records in the 1950s that were released only in Europe. Really? his interviewer asked, innocently. "Okay, I can't remember the names of some of the labels," Roy responded, relying on pure mojo to deflect further questions. "A lot of the blues things, I can't remember what half of 'em's called."

As for the focus of the new album, Roy harked back to his roots. "I knew [the public] would like ["My Babe"] if they got a chance to hear it. I enjoy the song . . . . So that's the first thing we recorded when we went into the studio." The point of the exercise was control over the recording and producing process. "I've always wanted to produce my own album, but they said, 'What does Roy know about producing? All he knows is how to play the guitar.' We did it at the Record Plant in New York [because] I had recorded there before and I knew that they knew the sound I wanted."

Roy also spoke to his fans. "I would like to tell people that I appreciate 'em stickin' by me all these years, because without nobody to listen to the music, there is no music."

When lobbed the pitch he should have hit out of the park, however, Roy may have surprised his Waterhouse Records host. Would *My Babe* lead to commercial success? "Commercial success doesn't really mean a lot to me," Roy said. "For a lot of reasons. I'll give you one example. I see musicians come and go. And I mean big ones, like Peter Frampton. There was a time when Peter Frampton used to open for me. Then he got so big that he wanted me to open for him. I wouldn't do it, but he wanted me to. Just a few months ago, he wanted to open for me again. My leverage has always been the same. People, they like a religious experience. I don't really care about being a Top Forty thing. If it happened I wouldn't bitch about it; it'd be great. I really just want to make good rock 'n' roll music. I'll be playin' rock 'n' roll when they put me away."

Waterhouse released *My Babe* in November. Roy may have been onto something: either people *were* ready again for "My Babe," he was having a comeback after a recording absence, or some combination of effects was in play. The record garnered lots of attention from reviewers all over the country. Perhaps they wouldn't need to put him away anytime soon after all. Near the end of November, *Billboard* reported that the top requests to DJs across the country that week had included Bruce Springsteen, the Police, Rod Stewart, and Pat Benatar. The "breakouts"—the most surprisingly popular albums played on album-oriented stations—were topped by Roy Buchanan's *My Babe*. The record did particularly well in the Northeast and Southwest. In Philadelphia Roy ran third to albums by the Alvin Lee Band and REO Speedwagon, but bested Creedence Clearwater Revival, Blondie, Bruce Springsteen, the Police, Pat Benatar, and the Eagles. In the Tucson, AZ, market "My Babe" was the third most-requested song after Jimmie Mack and the Jumpers and Blondie, but ahead of Jon Anderson, Loverboy, Bruce Springsteen, Steely Dan, the Police, and Dire Straits. Not bad for a balding, middle-aged guitar wizard whose record was the result of hacking around in the studio for two days with a new band.

The press seemed predisposed to kind words, though there were reality checks as well. *Creem* captured Roy's situation well: "Buchanan's career ain't exactly been booming lately, he's no longer on a major label and he's not recording with big-name session men, either. All he's done here is to put together a fine, funky band that excels at the barroom blues 'n rock that is his specialty and lay down one of his best albums ever." One Toronto paper thought it caught the spirit that infused *My Babe*. "This is party music, not meant to be analyzed. [It's] meant to be drunk by and danced to. If you like guitar played with real balls . . . get this record."

In the Long Island, NY, entertainment weekly *Good Times*, Bill Milkowski weighed in with a thoughtful assessment of where Roy had been during his Atlantic years and what he'd done with *My Babe*: "Buchanan has come up with what might be his most commercially viable product ever. *My Babe* rocks hard, sounds punchy and clean, and features something that Buchanan had never given much credence to in past LPs—hooks . . . Rather than dominating the scene throughout the album with his awesome riffs, Buchanan lays in wait until finally jumping in with virtuoso technique. It's a nice balance, giving this album a sense of being recorded by a band rather than by a soloist plus an anonymous group of studio musicians."

Other reviewers were skeptical. There were those who could not help but analyze the record in light of Buchanan's origins and promise and track record. These reviewers did not intend to get drunk or dance to the album. In New York's *Trouser Press* magazine, Jerry Milbauer spelled it out. "Roy Buchanan is one hell of a guitar player. He can take an old chestnut like 'Secret Love' and float delicate notes, bend them around the block, sustain them forever, and then strum staccato like a mandolin player in a gondola, all the while improvising a heartbreakingly beautiful new melody. Unfortunately, when it comes to making albums, Buchanan is hampered by a serious lapse in taste in material, arrangements, and sidemen. The biggest mistake here is vocalist Paul Jacobs, who scatters his plastic grunts through plodding, soulless and totally unswinging [tracks]. Buchanan's guitar work, perhaps negatively inspired by his surroundings, consists of recycled rock clichés delivered, seemingly, by rote . . . .One wonders if being a sideman for somebody like the Stones isn't really the proper place for Buchanan after all."

Back on the road, Roy's club performances continued to earn awed endorsements from the most demanding quarters. Stuart Goldman wrote in the *Los Angeles Times* of a mid-December 1980 date at the Roxy: "During the course of one solo, Roy executed Flamenco-like arpeggios, stinging harmonics and Wes Montgomery–like octaves, then bent the strings to intervals normally reserved for pedal steel. Then he turned around and played a verse in an open-stringed classical mode, throwing in a bit of Merle Travis finger-picking just for good measure. His real appeal, however, is simple: Roy plays from the heart."

Roy flew from Los Angeles to Pittsburgh before returning West to Phoenix— a not uncommon pattern in those years. "Judy had us playing the South in the summer and Canada in the winter," one band member recalled with a laugh. In Pittsburgh Rex Rutkoski of the *Valley News Dispatch* caught Roy on the phone, and the guitarist responded with a surprisingly candid interview. Could Roy describe the difference in his approach to the studio, versus performing, Rutkoski wondered? "If you've had a hit record," Roy told the writer, "that doesn't mean that you're going to be up there forever. It just means that you've had a hit record and you've got some people who act like they love you for a while." In contrast, Roy said he was happiest "anytime that I'm onstage and seeing people happy, seeing them enjoy the music. That's one of the joys of being able to play music, getting out in front of people and seeing their happy faces. As I have said many times, I wouldn't trade one of my 'cult' following for a million of someone else's pop following. All 'cult' means, anyway, is a very loyal following. I feel the same way about them. I'm very dedicated to them. I try to play what pleases them. Sometimes," he added, "I feel like I am speaking for the audience when I play. I understand what they feel . . . I don't think that anybody has captured that feeling and sound on record. I want to accomplish that feeling and get it down on record. This album [*My Babe*] is a start toward that. I think it's a definite start in the right direction."

Roy allowed that being a musician and filling the role of family man was "terribly hard." "You have to love your family and make the best out of it that you can," he said. "I couldn't leave my family, but I couldn't let my music go either. It worked out pretty good for me, fortunately."

Before hanging up the phone, the guitarist defined his own terms for success. "It's being able to do something that you get paid for that you would do for nothing. Like me, playing the guitar. I would go insane without it. That's my life. I was born to play."

That may have been so, but Roy's somnambulant stage manner continued to mystify observers. In Phoenix, he spooked Andrew Means of the *Arizona Republic*. Though the guitarist seemed affable backstage, "Onstage he retreated into a private world, wearing his guitar like a mask. While the crowd went wild at his blistering guitar work on 'Hey Joe'... his singing was almost expressionless, as if he were under self-hypnosis."

ROY HAD FAITHFUL AUDIENCES across the US, and by this time he had developed a critical mass of fans in Europe, Japan, and Australia as well. The Aussies in particular loved Roy and his raucous roadhouse blues. In early 1981 Australian Concert Entertainment invited the guitarist for a brief tour in late June and early July. The trip took the band to seven cities in 12 days—from the Sydney Capitol Theater to the Gold Coast Playroom in Perth, to Thompson's Hotel in Mooloobaba, to Her Majesty's Theater in Brisbane and a few stops in between. ACE advertised Roy as "the Supreme Exponent of Rock Guitar." "The houses were wonderful," Paul Jacobs would recall. "As a blues guitarist, I never heard anyone play better than Roy, and I've seen Hendrix play. He obviously had a very special, emotional connection to what he played."

Unfortunately, the band was beginning to unravel. After the group returned to the US it booked into the Keystone in Berkeley, CA, in November 1981. From the very start, though he played well, as always, Roy clearly had had a snootful of something, and he salted the set with stream-of-consciousness raps. Opening with "Susie Q," Roy interjected before his solo, "This is the way Howlin' Wolf did it"—an allusion to his long-held belief that Dale Hawkins and James Burton had copped a lick off Howlin' Wolf to create "Susie Q." Before his second solo, he told his audience, "This is the way the Hawaiians did it"—an allusion to his own lap steel approach to the Telecaster. Who in the audience, though, could have known what he was talking about? Before the song ended Roy did more verbal riffing, this time alluding to Jimi Hendrix: "I love the Voodoo Child, he's really wild, got lots of style, my voodoo child . . . Susie Q, Red House baby you know I love you too . . . Oh Susie Q . . . ." When he played "Good God Have Mercy" Roy introduced the song by telling the audience he'd met Billy Roberts and convinced him to write him a song. Just talkin' to his audience. Later, during his usual rendition of "Hey Joe/Foxy Lady" he recited the lyrics to Hendrix's "Red House." At the end of the show, after tearing the house apart, Roy gave the crowd what they'd come for: the dynamic confessional, "Roy's Bluz." The striptease, in Bobby Flurie's words, was over. The G-string was coming off. Roy squeezed his usual hair-raising licks from the Tele, then he paused, stepped to the mike and, in a gap in the music big enough to drive a truck through, asked whether the audience preferred a classical ending, a jazz ending, or a blues ending? Before anyone in the crowd could respond Roy delivered the song's final, anguished screams. Roy had walked the tightrope walk one more time and made it to the other side.

THE SUMMER OF 1982 marked a new phase in this journeyman's career: Have guitar, will travel. Having dismissed his band, Roy would fly to random, one-night stands, or strings of them, that his wife cobbled together. At each stop he'd play with a local pickup band provided by the promoter. The bands had to know Roy's songbook—his original compositions and a deep list of the rock 'n' roll classics—and possess a certain degree of proficiency in the ability-to-rock department. Roy would fly in and proceed to take the stage with three or four strangers. Mission: Rock the joint. Typically he'd play two sets. He could expect to personally net considerably less than a thousand dollars each night, after expenses.

In the early 1980s, with 30 years of road work and ten solo albums behind him, going it alone across the country meant slippage. Roy had no band, no professional management, and no record deal. He was just another working stiff—almost. Fortunately, he spoke the universal language of rock 'n' roll, and, with little assistance, could ignite a club. That was a skill with market value. He even toyed with electronic effects, and the audience. In May 1982 in San Diego he tried out an effect pedal and the audience yelled back, "*Turn off the echo!*" Roy replied, "No no no no no . . . " Things might be a little slim, but he hadn't lost his sense of humor. Times were changing. The club business began to falter—the economy stalled, strict drunk-driving laws were in vogue, competing entertainments arose, and America became a little more insular. Journeymen were on the run.

ROY HAD LONG SINCE shed his paranoia about people "stealing his licks." When *Guitar World* approached him for a feature on the "noble monster," the Telecaster, he assented. In the magazine's November 1982 issue he explained precisely how he used the volume and tone controls to achieve his patented cries. He knew that others could make the sounds he produced. But they could never know how and when to use them in the startlingly original style that was his alone. Roy now understood that, and he was secure in his genius. In the interview, he praised the earliest American electric guitars. "The main thing I like about these guitars is their simplicity," Roy told Noë Goldwasser. "The most sought-after guitars nowadays [are] the old Les Pauls and Strats and Telecasters—just guitars with pickups." To get his patented cry, "you pick the string hard and bring the volume up or down at the same time. You can bend into it and you can bend out of it. You can bend up to a note and you can also bring it down. You can add a little vibrato by grabbing the guitar like you were a country boy and shaking it real hard after you've plucked that note. The idea is to not hear the pick. You actually hear the effect of what the pick has done." Things were far different from a decade earlier when Roy adamantly refused to face his audience for fear—the shaman's fear—of having his magic understood, and, therefore, made ordinary. Nowadays he had nothing to hide.

ROY'S NEED FOR A BAND reached the attention of Michael Flanagan at the Harvard Square Talent Agency in Cambridge. Flanagan made some calls. One reached Scott "The Cat" Anderson, a 28-year-old Boston rockabilly singer and Telecaster player. Scott had once dubbed himself "Scott Elvis," but finally settled on "The Cat"— meaning the Man, the coolest dude in town. He'd grown up on a diet of Elvis Presley and Roy Buchanan and he'd been catching the guitarist's local appearances since the early '70s. By the time Flanagan called him, Anderson had been opening for classic rock acts such as the Ventures, Ricky Nelson, Frankie Valli, and Sha Na Na. "Michael asked me if I'd ever heard of Roy Buchanan and would I be interested in fronting a band for him," The Cat recalled. "I leapt out of my sneakers! I told him I'd *loved* Roy since the first time I'd heard him. I told him it would be the greatest thrill that ever happened to me."

The Cat, who served the new ensemble on vocals and guitar, brought along some well-worn cohorts. Henceforth, when Roy toured the East Coast, Andy Paley from Boston played drums, Russell Keyes played bass, and Russell's brother, Bobby, played rhythm guitar.

THE GUITARIST FLEW into Pittsburgh for the band's first gig at Mancini's. Roy met The Cat for the first time there and, together, they worked out a set list. The Cat then brought in the band and hashed out chords and keys. The process took about 15 minutes, according to The Cat. Before Roy disappeared he asked the band, "Do you boys like to drink?" The Cat smiled. "Yes, we *sure* do," he assured his new employer. Thus began a year of mutually assured destruction. These boys were out to rage and they did so with a savage glee. Roy felt right at home.

Paley saw another side to Roy, offstage. "You know, he was known for that high screamin' Telecaster sound, but after hours he'd just sit around and play beautiful, laid-back, mellow jazz chords." Another band member said Roy wasn't always mellow. "Roy was one of those guys who could push people's buttons. If he saw somebody in uniform? He loved to get fights going. He would never get his ass kicked— but somebody *else* would!" Everyone in the band was single but for Roy. The guitarist's status as a long-term married man showed, according to The Cat. "Judy took care of absolutely everything. To be fair, Roy needed someone to take charge of his life. I think of her as Vince Lombardi and him as the football team." Judy had learned from years of experience how to keep tabs on the money. For his part, Roy had learned how to siphon off enough to sustain a black budget—a fat wad of $50 and $20 bills—for occasions when he might need a little cash. "We probably did about 160 shows together," The Cat recalled. "If we didn't do massive amounts of cocaine at about 150 of 'em, I'd be surprised. We did it every single night. There'd always be someone around who sold the crap. Unfortunately. There was no way around it. And we were really into it."

The ensuing year passed in a blur. Despite the band's dangerous lifestyle, the music blossomed. Roy had never played better. The Cat and Roy, nearly a generation apart, nonetheless drew on the same deep rock 'n' roll songbook and they both loved to rock the house. Sets included "Green Onions," the Ventures' "Walk Don't Run," Larry Williams' "Dizzy Miss Lizzy," "Rock Around the Clock," the Drifters' "Money Honey," Jerry Lee Lewis' "Whole Lotta Shakin' Goin' On," "Secret Agent Man," even the theme to "Rawhide." It was bar band material played at a world-class level, guaranteed to entertain. Roy naturally brought his own wonderfully dated repertoire, from "After Hours" to "Sweet Dreams," from "Hey Joe" to "1841 Shuffle." Talking to The Cat one night in Toronto, Roy revealed that he had several Telecaster Custom guitars. Which one did The Cat want for himself? Anderson picked one out and, in response to Roy's generosity, managed to secure two boxes of Cuban cigars. "That was his big thing," Anderson recalled. "The trip to the cigar store." Roy loved his stogies.

Despite the band's extracurricular activities it gelled with thumping accuracy. Night after night the boys tore up clubs on the East Coast circuit, from DC to Hamilton, Ontario, stopping off in Baltimore, Philadelphia, New York, Boston, and a couple dozen hamlets between. With a tight rhythm section and The Cat adding another talented Telecaster to the mix, the sets were robust, sweaty. You had to have a taste for rockabilly singing, or The Cat could drive you mad. He was intent on stirring things up. The new quartet, with two guitarists, had its own hard-edged sound. Roy had played with a keyboard player for the past dozen years, so this represented a new sound. Because The Cat and his cohorts had been a working band before they hired on with Roy, the downside—at least for some fans—was that Roy played the sideman as often as he took the lead. For Roy, that was the *upside*. Playing the sideman suited him after years out front. Taking the front, obliged to sing "Hey Joe" at the demand of some ninny in the front row, could be a *huge* drag. He loved nothing more than to back up a good singer and just be part of the band—and still get the front man's pay. With The Cat out front singing in the spotlight, Roy could relax and concentrate on his craft. He still sang his handful of songs, some of them his personal favorites, some of them crowd-pleasers. Ablaze in every way, the band raced up and down the East Coast. Roy must have enjoyed himself, after all, making a living doing what he loved—something, in truth, he'd do for nothing—and that counted for a lot. Certainly his sense of humor was intact. At the Stanley Theater in Pittsburgh in late December 1982, there were loud but conflicting calls for various Buchanan classics. "Hold it, hold it," Roy said. "Hands, please." Then he picked his way into a blazing shuffle.

As thrilling as performing with Roy Buchanan was for Scott Anderson, however, it was the after-hours hang time that lingers in memory. "Roy and me used to talk about Telecasters and old records 24 hours a day," he recalled. "One time he asked me, 'You have any Jimmy Bryant records?' I said, 'Yeah.' I'd found a couple in mint condition at an antique store. So he traded me his two James Burton solo albums for two Jimmy Bryant records. He was so happy!"

"Roy always took the time to help me, to teach me," The Cat added. "He showed me his secret techniques. He never did that with anyone. We'd stay up all night and he'd play my Martin D-35. The best playing he did was not on stage. I might say, 'Roy, play me the beginning of 'Cry Me a River' by Julie London. It'd be three o'clock in the morning. He'd play all these things note-for-note. He'd do the same thing during sound checks, stuff we'd never done before. He'd do Chet Atkins' 'Chinatown, My Chinatown.' He could play it all note-for-note. Roy said he'd been doing those songs since he was twelve years old."

Life on the road with Roy Buchanan proved to be a bit of an adventure, even for a durable lad like The Cat. One night after a gig at the Cambridge, MA, club Jonathan Swift's in spring 1983 the band dispersed and Roy headed up the street, cigar in one hand, Tele in the other, to a club where Carl Perkins was performing. Carl Perkins had been at the Creation, recording "Blue Suede Shoes" in 1956 for Sun Records. He and rock 'n' roll were synonymous. There might have been an acquaintanceship between the two from the early days, but in any case Perkins certainly knew who Roy Buchanan was. From the stage he beckoned to Roy, and Roy obliged, to the delight of the crowd. After the show Roy stayed on as the backstage scene developed. He had a noon gig the next day on the same bill as soul-belter Lou Rawls at the University of Massachusetts, up the road in Amherst. By noon the next day, however, The Cat had to have assistance breaking down Roy's motel room door to rouse him and get him to the gig on time. "Roy was not in a good frame of mind," Anderson said, still wincing after all those years.

On another excursion the band flew into Houston for a gig at Rockefellers, an old movie-theater-turned-rock-palace. After levying a heavy tax on the in-flight beverage cart, the musicians reached their hotel, knocked back a few more rounds, then checked into their rooms. The Cat and his band mates soon emerged, as planned, to seek dinner. Roy didn't show. "I didn't think anything of it," The Cat recalled, "because Roy enjoyed his own space. So we went out for dinner and returned to the hotel. Roy wasn't there. We checked out the venue for the next night. Still no Roy. We checked out a few bars. Now it's midnight. I'm eating the worm out of a bottle of tequila. Roy is nowhere to be found. Now we're getting scared. We called the police. They couldn't look for him until a certain amount of time had passed, when they could declare him 'missing.' We called the morgues. Houston has about 20 of 'em. God only knows what might have happened. Finally, we spoke to Harvard Square Talent and it turned out Roy had called Judy, who called Harvard Square. Roy had gone out, didn't know where he was, and just checked himself into another hotel for the night. To be fair, that's something that anyone who toured a lot could have done. Still, Roy had a knack for that sort of thing. That's one of the things I loved about him so much." One night on the road the two were yukking it up in The Cat's motel room, in his words, "doing dirty deeds." "He was sitting on my bed, not realizing it. Finally he took off his shoes, took off his shirt, and got under the covers. He said, 'Aren't you *ever* going to your room?' I said, 'Roy, this *is* my room.'"

What sorts of things kept life on the road interesting? The Cat hesitated. Well, there'd been that time at the Stanley Theater in Pittsburgh the night before New Year's Eve 1982. "Someone in the audience threw a World War II–type smoke bomb onstage. We're up there playing 'Blue Christmas' of all things, because I liked to do a lot of '50s stuff, rockabilly, and Roy would play whatever I wanted. All of a sudden the smoke started coming close. Roy and I were laughing. It got closer. We're really starting to laugh. You couldn't see one inch in front of you. People are climbing onto the stage because the exits were behind us. Suddenly, a bunch of firemen surround us on the stage—they have their special coats and hats on—and they have their axes in hand." The Cat emitted a wry chuckle. "The marshal comes over and says, '*YOU STOP PLAYING RIGHT NOW!*' And we don't stop. So they grab our road manager and raise his hands so we could see they were about to clamp the cuffs on. All you can see are these hands coming out of the smoke, with a set of handcuffs dangling over them. So just before they cuff him, we stop. We ended up in the alley with the crowd, passing around a joint. But the show was over."

And there'd been that time when, backstage, The Cat stumbled upon Roy and a "300-pound biker chick" in the bathroom of the Old Waldorf in San Francisco. The woman was offering the guitarist something that, ironically, even these boys considered evil—heroin. The Cat grasped the stakes and cold-cocked her. "Down she went," he said with evident satisfaction. He was too late. Though at first Roy appeared to be fine, he soon keeled over onstage. The band scooped him up and carried him, with his guitar still strapped to his body, into the dressing room. Roy did not return to the stage. Out in the audience, Alan Scheflin was concerned, and chagrined. He'd brought family and friends to see the guitarist he'd been raving about for years. Instead they saw the soles of Roy's shoes as he was carried out.

THAT FALL THE BAND turned in a string of sizzling performances in the Northeast, including a couple of stellar sets at New York's Lone Star Cafe on October 3. Despite the wear and tear, this band was squeaky tight. Among the rock 'n' roll, raucous blues, and cha-chas, Roy even worked in a reverent version of "Amazing Grace," stilling the restless crowd with his quiet touch.

The following week, at Jonathan Swift's in Cambridge, Bill Lawrence—the German jazz guitarist who'd repatriated to America in the '60s—showed up with a new Telecaster adorned with Bill Lawrence brand pickups for his friend. Lawrence, whose reputation for greatness was known to few outside jazz circles, climbed onstage for a few numbers. Typically, Roy would take a solo and then bow to his second guitarist, whether that be The Cat or Bobby Keyes. There'd be give-and-take. Paley recalled only one exception. "Bill Lawrence came to our gig and sat in. Here's this old German guy playing some classic swing blues and Roy is working with him. That's when Roy motioned to Bobby to stop playing. And Bobby is an amazing guitar player."

Bill Lawrence could see "the lifestyle" consuming his fellow artist and he appealed to Roy's common sense. Later, Roy recalled that "Bill spoke to me like a brother. He said drugs were hurting my talent." Roy often liked to tell this story to interviewers—as long as it suited him—to illustrate that he'd changed his ways.

The band evolved as the rhythm section came and went, or The Cat and Roy would "parachute" into a gig using a local backup band. For a time the two hooked up with Tommy Hambridge on drums and Dave Broderick on bass. On one of the band's stop-overs at the Bayou Club in Washington, DC, local guitarist Tom Principato—then an aspirant, today a master—opened the show. He had a chance, finally, to see Roy at work close-up, and he was both awed and perturbed. "He was as radical as Hendrix, for his era," Principato said, harking back to Roy's roots. "There was nothing remotely like Roy Buchanan. I just call it the 'Tele from Mars.' He obviously was coming from those great, traditional, reserved players. He was like the same thing, only with a bottle of Jack Daniels. Whereas Hendrix had the advantage of the guitars and fuzz boxes of his day, here was Roy with an old Telecaster and a little Fender amp. Definitely the barroom thing. Nobody ever controlled harmonics like he did. Nobody ever made them zing out so strongly and clearly, and he was the first. His best stuff was just pure inspiration. It just poured out of him." Nevertheless, Principato couldn't believe his eyes when Roy showed up at the Bayou with a Tele under his arm. No case. No spare guitar. No nothin'. "Here Roy was, an established guitar legend," Principato sputtered. "He broke a string in the middle of the show and he just motioned for the band to keep playing. He didn't unplug and go backstage. He had no guitar tech. He just reached into the pocket of his jacket and pulled out a handful of string envelopes, knelt down, fanned them out on the stage floor, and picked out the one he wanted. The band is playing, the place is packed. And you are privy to Roy Buchanan changing a string. Right there! It surprised the hell out of me. For a performer of his status, he should have had someone to help him."

ON THE WEST COAST, for tours in 1982 and 1983, The Cat and Roy joined up with drummer Jaco Marcellino, lately of Sha Na Na, and Michael Dehoney, who'd drummed for blue-eyed soul singer Delbert McClinton. Bass guitarist Freebo, a widely respected player who'd spent years with Bonnie Raitt's band, signed on for these West Coast tours. Years later, Freebo retained vivid impressions of Roy.

"I'd been hearing about Roy for quite a number of years as a legendary, killer bar musician who played a Telecaster and could've done anything he wanted to, but just seemed to prefer to play the blues in bars. Having met him and played with him and gotten to know him and gotten some insight into his psyche, to me he fits into a category—people who are incredibly talented but have either a fear of success or a fear of failure. Whatever it is, it's fear. We all have it. That's no judgment. But there's a question of overcoming it. In Roy's case he just couldn't accept the responsibility of going out there and being in the spotlight. He could deal with a small spotlight, but when it came to the big things he didn't know how to respond. His destructive nature just wouldn't allow him to go to the next level. Whenever Roy got into a situation that could have become a really good situation, one that would have gotten him to a place where 'now's the time to shine,' he would sabotage himself, and blow it."

Freebo thought there were big themes at play in Roy's predicament. "To me he is a classic example of an American tragedy. He was really good at what he did and he loved what he did. The world comes along and says, 'Man, you're really good. You should be more than this.' He says, 'Well, I'm not sure I want to be more than this.' Kind of like he was a small-town guy and he wanted to stay a small-town guy. The first time I played with him, the rehearsal, he said he'd had a problem with drinking and that he wasn't drinking. He was the nicest, sweetest guy, humble, played his ass off, real easy to deal with, quiet but right there with you . . . We did the gig and then an old buddy of his came backstage and said, 'Hey man, let's smoke this joint.' Everybody kind of looked at each other, like, 'Is he going to do it?' Nobody's going to say, 'Hey Roy, *don't do it!*' It was up to him. And I watched the downward spiral. It started with a joint and went on from there. He got through the joint, started drinking and, by the end of that evening, he was a completely different person. All this anger started coming out, anger that you just never detected in his usual demeanor. The rest of the tour was kind of tricky. There were two characters in there and they were fighting each other. I found that tragic, because he really was a genius. He didn't know where to go with it. Part of him wanted to be out there big time and part of him really didn't want to be out there big time. He was caught in a no-man's land. He had his little demons and I don't think he ever figured out how to work on them. I'm not sure he realized he could stop drinking. Sometimes a fork in the road can make all the difference."

When in San Francisco Roy could always count on seeing his friend and fan Alan Scheflin. And he always made sure to visit his eldest son, known as Roy Junior, or Little Roy, who'd pursued an alternative lifestyle in the Bay area. The best he could do to help his struggling son was to give him his love, his time, and a little cash. When in Los Angeles, he often saw Alan Clemmons, son of Phil Clemmons, his former brother-in-law. He told the younger Clemmons he had a recurring dream: He'd find himself high on a mountaintop playing guitar, but there was no one there to listen. "That was a fear of his," Alan recalled. "Almost a phobia."

A fork in the road did arrive, this time for The Cat. Earlier, Roy had asked Jay Reich to return to booking shows for him, and in early 1984 Jay managed to do so. He was dismayed to find Roy "pretty far gone." Reich nudged out The Cat by cutting back his pay until the singer/guitarist was forced to look elsewhere for work. Today, three decades later, The Cat still ekes out his living cadging time in the studio and gigging for his supper in the Boston area. From his perspective, Jay figured he had saved Roy's bacon. But what he didn't see and perhaps didn't want to know was that Roy had been not only a willing participant, but a leader in the madness of the past year.

Getting kooky on the road was all well and good until it involved large amounts of cash. According to Roy's old friend, attorney Steve Simenowitz, the guitarist possessed the endearing, though vexing qualities of the absent-minded professor. "He was a nightmare to work with, professionally," Simenowitz said, bluntly. "Roy did a concert in New Haven, Connecticut. The Agora Ballroom. I drive up there, pick him up. He's going to stay at my house that night, then I'd take him to the airport. He had to go to DC on the shuttle the next morning. We get to my house in East Meadow [Long Island], and he says, 'Oh shit! I forgot the money from the tour. It's at the Holiday Inn in New Haven.' I say, 'You're *kidding* me. How much money?' He says, '$18,000 and some change.' He left it under the mattress. He says, 'Let's call the hotel. Judy will kill me.' He started flippin'. I said, 'Let's absolutely not call the hotel.' I get on the phone to the New Haven police department. I identified myself and said, 'We've got a little situation here.' I wasn't an attorney yet, but I said, 'I have a client here who inadvertently left a large amount of money under the mattress at the Holiday Inn.' They said, 'We'll check it out.' I said, 'I'm not kidding. Look in the newspaper. We were there.' So I get a call 40 minutes later. It's Lieutenant so-and-so. 'How much did you say was there?' I said, '$18,423.' He says, 'Yes. It's here.' We had to drive back up there to get it. Later, we got him to the airport. He hopped the wrong shuttle, ended up in Boston. He was having a bad-hair day."

CATCHING
AN ALLIGATOR

Roy happened to be blowing the roof off Albert's Hall in Toronto in early 1984 when the force of his guitar created a break in the clouds. Bruce Iglauer, founder of Alligator Records, the Chicago blues label, happened to be visiting with Derrick Andrews, who managed the hall. Having just completed a distribution deal with Warner Music Canada, Iglauer had been celebrating with friends at a nearby restaurant. So when he stopped by Albert's Hall to say hello to Andrews, he was feeling no pain. He proceeded to take a nap on Andrews' office sofa. Outrageous sounds—loud, wild ones—from the club below pierced his sleep and he ventured downstairs to have a look. "I was smashed," Iglauer said. "Roy at that point was going through a period of being totally sober. So the first time I met him I had to lean against a wall to remain standing, and he was cold sober—the opposite of our relationship later on. Roy talked about how he really perceived himself as a blues player. We kind of agreed that we ought to get to know each other better."

By this time Roy had largely given up looking for a record deal. Suddenly, Bruce Iglauer appeared from nowhere and left his business card. Having spent nearly 30 years as a professional musician—the equivalent of a Ph.D. in cynicism—and being thrice-burned by his last major label, Roy was in no particular hurry to get in touch with anyone. Sometime later that year, however, his curiosity, the embers of ambition and, perhaps, a sober assessment of his finances made him pick up the phone and call Iglauer. "I explained to him that I couldn't really get my sound in the studio," Roy later told journalist Dan Keplazo. "I told him I didn't like overdubs. I just like to play live. That's when it happens for me. He said, 'That's the way we like to do it, too. Why don't you just record like you're playing live and leave the rest to us? When you say it's right, we'll go with it. I think we'll get your sound.' I said, 'Okay.'"

In March 1985 Roy booked into the Aragon Ballroom in Chicago to open for Johnny Winter, then touring in support of his first album for Alligator Records.

Iglauer was on the guest list and he intended to speak again with Roy about recording for Alligator. At the hall, which held several thousand, Roy took the stage before Johnny Winter. Iglauer sat in the balcony with his friend and co-producer at Alligator, Dick Shurman. "In the middle of a drum solo Roy's amp went out," Iglauer recalled. "He was strumming rhythm and no sound was coming out. He looked back at the amp, but no one realized what was going on. I left the balcony, cut through the service kitchen to the backstage area, pulled the fuse, got another from Johnny Winter's man, shoved it into the amp and turned it on. The light went on and it was making noise again. I was a genius! Roy looked at me appreciatively. Nobody had done anything and he was a guy who needed things done. There I was, putting my energy where my mouth was. That was a bond-sealer for us."

Having his friend Dick Shurman along helped. "When Bruce and I ran into each other at the Aragon, he latched onto me," Shurman said. "He told me, 'Roy will be reassured that someone will be working on this project who knows his history and understands who he is.' After the set we went backstage and talked to him and hit it off real well." Though Alligator so far had been all about traditional Chicago blues, the label had been branching out to include roadhouse blues men such as Lonnie Mack and Johnny Winter. Roy Buchanan fit into the pattern. "Those guys were taking Bruce to a place he'd never been, commercially," Shurman said. "They had a blues itch to scratch and we helped them scratch it." In subsequent discussions, Roy agreed to a three-record deal. Alligator appeared to be an appropriate home for his music.

Bruce Iglauer had founded Alligator in 1971 to record Hound Dog Taylor & the House Rockers, and over a decade and a half he'd contributed mightily to the health of the Chicago blues scene, resuscitating the careers of myriad local players. Iglauer, a native of Cincinnati, had discovered the blues in 1966 at age eighteen when he saw Mississippi Fred McDowell perform. Now, through personal relationships with the artists, he attracted a diverse roster of singers and players to his growing label and earned widespread plaudits for the records he made. Grammy nominations began to roll in.

Dick Shurman first ran into Iglauer in Chicago in the summer of 1970. "I was riding around with two buddies, Louis Myers and Billy Boy Arnold, and we were talking about whether Junior Wells had played harmonica on a certain Muddy Waters 78. So when we got to Pepper's Lounge on the South Side, the first thing we did was march up and ask Junior. He was sitting there with this young, earnest-looking guy. This was Bruce." In 1968 Shurman had struck up a friendship with guitarist Otis Rush. "He used to pick up me and my tape recorder every Friday and take me out to the West Side and I would tape him all night long. Blues people aren't like rock people. They don't have that *attitude*. They don't separate themselves from the audience." By the late 1970s Shurman had produced records by Otis Rush, Eddie C. Campbell, and Louis Myers. He'd brought the Texas Telecaster player, Albert

Collins, to Alligator. By the time Iglauer and Shurman met with Roy at the Aragon, they had worked together on four Albert Collins LPs and Johnny Winter's first Alligator album.

Six weeks after the Aragon Ballroom encounter Roy returned to Chicago with a guitar, a handful of cigars, and a few cassettes. He had ideas for songs. He also brought a clear head. He'd decided that Bill Lawrence was right. He resolved, once again, to make the most of the opportunity before him. He set his heart on staying straight throughout the entire process. And he did.

Iglauer and Shurman wanted to ensure that Roy had a satisfying recording experience. He had told them of his frustrations with the Atlantic sessions. "We'd say, 'Why did you go along with that?'" Shurman recalled. "And he said, 'Hey, they gave me all that money, I figured I'd do whatever they wanted.' Roy was very much into going along with the program. The hardest time Bruce and I had with him was to get him to tell us what he really wanted. He was so eager to go along with us. I was used to Johnny Winter and Albert Collins and they'd get their backs up. We'd say, 'Please Roy. Tell us what you want.' He came to realize that we really meant it." As Iglauer recalled, "He told us he wanted to make a blues record."

The three men began by gathering one weekend in the living room of Shurman's home outside Chicago to select material for the sessions. First they listened to the cassettes Roy brought along, which contained melodies or snatches of song, perhaps a hook or two, all of them instrumentals. "He told us he had garbage bags full of these cassettes in his basement," Iglauer said. "He would sit and play and when he came up with a good idea he would throw it on cassette. When he was ready to record he'd grab a few cassettes, kind of like a random thing. So Roy played these for us and we would say, '*That* sounds like one we can work up into something,' or 'Nah, that sounds too conventional or like something you've already done.'" In an environment conducive to exploring his ideas, the guitarist really turned a corner. "With Roy there was never a shortage of song ideas," Shurman said. To augment Roy's material and provide diversity Shurman delved into his vast collection of blues recordings to find suitable songs for Roy to cover, keeping in mind the guitarist's limited vocal range.

"When I think of working with Roy I think of two things," Shurman said. "The smell of cigar smoke and Lemon Pledge. Roy loved to smoke his cigars and Bruce, who is now an inveterate cigar smoker, he'd be firing up cigars Roy brought him. My wife would just cringe when we'd have our pre-production weekends here because of the smoke. Roy used Lemon Pledge on the neck and strings of his guitar for lubrication. So I always knew it was a Roy project if the air was full of cigar smoke and Lemon Pledge."

For Iglauer these pre-production sessions opened his eyes to the world of fine cigars. "I always tended to smoke cheap shit," he confessed. "I didn't know what the possibilities were. Roy got me interested in better cigars. I'm sure he's cost me thousands of dollars as a result!" Iglauer would scribble down the names of cigar brands Roy recommended in the margins of his personal phone book, where they remained for another decade.

In the end the two producers and Roy came up with five original compositions, all instrumentals, and four covers, two of which would be sung by guest vocalists. Roy at that time had been gigging regularly with two superb New York City union musicians: Jeff Ganz on eight-string bass and Ray Marchica on drums. Nonetheless, Shurman and Iglauer picked a handful of Chicago studio professionals to make the record. They selected a young Criss Johnson to play rhythm guitar, and Chess Records veteran Morris Jennings on drums. For bass they picked Alligator veteran Larry Exum, who had a gospel background. Bill Heid got the job on keyboards. Known mostly for his jazz work, Heid also earned a spot in the Guinness Book of World Records as "World Champion Hitch-hiker." From 1964 to 1986 he obtained 1,083 rides covering 324,280 miles. (Heid didn't "thumb" rides, but simply approached cars at stoplights.) Appropriately, he hitched his way into Chicago from Ann Arbor for the Buchanan session. For vocalists, Iglauer brought in Gloria Hardiman, a veteran of local gospel and blues scenes, and he promised Roy he'd round up the great R&B crooner Otis Clay for a guest appearance.

A brief rehearsal session at Dress Rehearsals in the city on April 18 gave the ensemble a chance to explore the songs on the list, and a few more. The goal was to be familiar with the material going into the studio, then try to catch the song on tape as it gelled. First the players developed a lovely, shimmering melody in C that Roy had created. They tried out a thunder-footed theme in F sharp that came to be titled, "Sneakin' Godzilla Through the Alley," a tongue-in-cheek, Iglauer-inspired play off Allen Toussaint's "Sneakin' Sally Through the Alley." Roy used his nylon pick to scrape up and down the lower, wound strings, to create visual imagery with a demented riff. "When a Guitar Plays the Blues," a Roy Lee Johnson number, got a workout. Gloria Hardiman sang "Why Don't You Want Me?" a torch song that Denise Osso wrote specifically for the project. "One of the main things Bruce and I wanted to do was to get top-quality vocalists for Roy, because that was one area in which his records had been inconsistent," Shurman said. The band tried out an infectious, funky boogie in E as well, another one of Roy's ideas. It would be dubbed "Chicago Smokeshop" in honor of one of Roy's favorite destinations. Some of the material was considerably more complicated than typical 12-bar blues. "Roy had a wider definition of blues than most of the people we worked with, which was fine," Shurman pointed out. "But consequently a lot of his tunes were more adventurous and varied structurally than most blues projects." That proved instructive to the younger players.

Two days later the gang reassembled at downtown Chicago's Streeterville Studios to lay down tracks. "When we brought Roy into the studio for the first time he said, 'What kind of tone do you want?'" Iglauer recalled. "We said, 'Yours!' And he said, 'You mean you just want me to set it the way I like it?' We said, 'Yes! Of course! If we wanted you to sound like another guitar player, we'd hire another guitar player!' He was taken aback that we really wanted him to be himself. Of course there were lots of different 'himselves.' He could be comfortable playing a zillion notes per second, or playing very few notes. He was comfortable being melodic and comfortable being almost anti-melodic. It was clear to me the longer I knew him that the more rocked-out stuff was what he thought the people wanted, more than what *he* wanted. Wanting to please is certainly a big part of the Roy story."

To enable Roy to get his patented performance effects in the studio his amplifier was placed in a vocal booth and turned to maximum volume. "Apart from setting his amp and using a delay pedal, he did it all with his hands," Shurman said. "All he used was a newer Tele with the Bill Lawrence pickups," Iglauer added. "Bill and Roy were very close at that time. Bill was sort of Roy's stay-sober sponsor."

Once the musicians were seated and ready, Roy came into his own. "Roy ran the show," Shurman noted. "Not in a heavy-handed way. But he was the guy explaining the concepts and doing most of the organization of the songs. I'd be out on the floor with the band, while Bruce would be in the control room. I like to give the artist a chance to pull stuff together and not impose stuff on them. It has to start with the musicians. We'd start with the artist's concept of the song and just tighten it up." Engineer Justin Niebank proved to be a long-time Buchanan fan and he told the two producers Roy had to be the best guitarist they'd ever worked with—or at least his favorite. Niebank would have a strong hand in the album's eventual mix.

The band got right to work on Pee Wee Crayton's "Country Boy," a track Dick Shurman had picked for Roy that, in the guitarist's hands, sounded considerably more sinister than Crayton's 1954 original, titled "Runnin' Wild." "I dug that one out and Roy took right to it," Shurman said. With its faintly autobiographical story line, Roy delivered a controlled, articulate, and imaginative take—the only one necessary, it turned out, after a playback confirmed the magic everyone had heard.

I'm a little country boy,
I'm runnin' wild in this big old town,
When I make love with my baby
I don't want a soul around,

They call me country
I'm from a country town
Girls are crazy 'bout me,
They love what I'm puttin' down

I woke up this morning
Ew, my head was bad
I just can't tell you 'bout the good time that I had

I'm a little country boy,
I'm runnin' wild in this big old town

As the evening wore on, Otis Clay arrived to perform the soulful ballad "Nickel and a Nail," by his friend O.V. Wright. After Clay recited the emotional lyrics with his gritty, beseeching R&B voice, Roy stepped in and created a solo that echoed all the singer's emotive power. The performance, everyone agreed, was a highlight of the sessions. When Clay sang the song pain was writ large across his face, but Roy, as usual, appeared nonchalant. Later, one of the band members was overheard to ask Roy how he could remain so calm when his guitar belched fire. "I'm screamin' inside," Roy responded.

THE NEXT DAY the band reconvened, this time with veteran tenor sax man Sonny Seals on hand. After running through the old rocker "Big Boy Pete" (Roy had been playing it since 1962) they turned to a rocker in G that nearly blew the roof off Streeterville. Roy and Sonny traded off solos until there were smiles all around. It would appear on the album as "Short Fuse." Among other songs worked out that afternoon was a lilting blues in C that drew on classical and country influences. Shurman had asked Roy for "something pretty with a lap steel feel to it." Roy's effort began with a hypnotic message of lazy contentment, then rose to an attention-demanding eloquence. Roy dedicated the song to his first and only teacher, Mrs. Presher. He may not have known how to spell his childhood teacher's name, or he may have attempted to get some mythical mileage when he suggested the spelling "Mrs. Pressure." As the session wound down, Iglauer and Shurman knew they needed a track to cap off everything. They had in mind the Roy Lee Johnson song, another autobiographical number for Roy, "When a Guitar Plays the Blues." "I had the Roy Lee single of that song, which is pretty well known to rhythm and blues collectors," Shurman recalled. "I originally brought it to Bruce for Albert Collins, who recorded it on his *Don't Lose Your Cool* album. So Bruce liked the song enough that when the Roy project came along I think he had the idea to give Roy a shot at it. Bruce had certain songs that he was determined that somebody was going to do a great version for him. I don't think he was crushed by Albert's version and I think he thought Roy might have a different take on it, which he did. That intro Roy played wasn't anything Albert would've played." "That intro" was a magnificent, haunting demonstration of Roy's prowess as a Telecaster player. He coaxed a series of ethereal scales from his instrument, using the volume and tone knobs to create an entrancing, cello-like effect, which gives way to a heavy descent into screaming electric blues, a bit more aggressive than Johnson's laid-back, swinging original.

Before packing up, Roy decided to have a little fun with his own rollicking take on Elmore James' "Hawaiian Boogie" by laying his Telecaster in his lap, affixing a nut extender under the strings, and using a bar to play lap steel. Two minutes of the exuberant jam would close the LP, which would be aptly titled, *When a Guitar Plays the Blues*.

Apart from a few distractions, the sessions had run smoothly. When edited down they yielded a compact, kick-ass 40 minutes of music—a pretty close call, as very little material had been dropped. "On this first album Roy stayed around for the start of the mixing," Shurman recalled. "We wanted him to have a hand in everything. But by the end of the first day his comment was, 'My god this is boring. How do you guys stand it? I trust you. You guys take it from here.' A common reaction from a musician." Still, the artist and his producers managed to enjoy some hang time. "We'd get together, go out to dinner," Shurman said. "We had some very nice times. One of the things about Roy that was not true of Johnny Winter, in particular, was that Roy was so ordinary-looking. People probably thought he was my uncle, the professor. He'd have his corduroy jacket, the beret. He was very nondescript and as a result we could go anywhere. If you tried going somewhere with Johnny Winter, everybody wanted to fuck him, fight him, get him high, give him a tape, or something. With Roy you could go anywhere. One night we went to the Cubby Bear across the street from Wrigley Field to hear Paul Butterfield to see if we should bring him in for a project. Nobody came up and said, 'Oh wow, you're Roy Buchanan!'"

FROM ITS RELEASE IN SUMMER 1985, *When a Guitar Plays the Blues* looked likely to garner the sort of attention and praise Roy had long deserved. The album entered *Billboard's* pop charts with a bullet signifying fast sales growth, and though it never climbed high it remained on the charts 13 weeks. It would eventually sell more than 100,000 units worldwide, highly respectable sales for a modestly sized blues label and a relatively obscure artist.

"It's the sound . . . I've been looking for, for years," the guitarist told Joe Carey for *Down Beat*. "It's something I'm really proud of. I've hit this creative thing. For the past year I've enjoyed music more than at any time of my life." He added, with a touch of mischief, "I hope it's a comeback. All of a sudden, it's fun to play again."

The *San Francisco Bay Guardian* called the album "refreshingly sharp and consistent." "Buchanan uncoils line after gleaming line of biting and intensely squealing notes, building his solos into dense, dizzying squalls propelled by a tight Chicago blues rhythm section. His more reflective pieces reveal a lyrical melodic sense honed by inventive guitar dynamics. Buchanan's mastery may have finally caught up with itself, and this is the album where you can hear it best."

An anonymous critic for the *San Diego Reader* suggested that an entire generation of rock guitarists was about to get its comeuppance. "To this day Buchanan hasn't gotten near the recognition he deserves. That may be about to change. On his latest album . . . Buchanan forever lays to rest any questions about his rightful place in the guitar-players' pantheon . . . Unlike some blues masters who build slowly to an emotional climax, [on this record] Buchanan comes out with his pants on fire and never lets up . . . Buchanan pushes past the hordes of journeymen guitarists like a man trying to catch a train. [He] serves notice . . . that he is the architect of many of the styles associated with the likes of Beck, Clapton, Mike Bloomfield, and the rest . . . .After thirty years in the business, Buchanan is poised to elbow his way to the front of the long line of guitarists whose playing bears his signature."

Roy's simple honesty made him eminently quotable. "I think there's been a resurgence in the popularity of the blues lately," he told Mike Joyce of the *Washington Post*, citing the success of blues-based popular performers such as George Thorogood and Stevie Ray Vaughan. "They sure help old codgers like me." Roy was then 46. "When the kids start listening to them they also start looking into the music to see who else was around." *Guitar Player*'s August issue featured an interview with Roy and offered readers its bonus Soundpage—a floppy square of vinyl with a single track etched into it—containing "Blues for Jimmy Nolen," a rollicking roadhouse shuffle, Roy's tribute to an acknowledged influence. "I owe Jimmy a lot," Roy reaffirmed. "He was my first real influence in the blues."

In the *Guitar Player* piece, Ashley Kahn observed: "Roy Buchanan remains one of American's most technically awesome and explosively soulful guitarists. He continues to command an undying loyalty among fans and fellow guitarists alike . . . With *When a Guitar Plays the Blues*, Roy creates a blues potpourri that reaches beyond the standard 12-bar, three-chord limits to cover a variety of uptown and down-home grooves. His bristling, trademark tone and emotion-charged solos are up-front throughout. Two tracks [even] capture the most personal, emotive vocal style Roy has ever recorded." What was different between the new album and past efforts? Kahn asked the guitarist. "On this one," Roy said, "we wanted to sound like we do live . . . [and] the engineer made my guitar sound like it does onstage—real loud, but clean . . . .Man," he bragged, "I haven't scratched the surface of my material yet."

Asked about composing, Roy shed light on his creative processes. "I usually do it without an instrument. I can picture the fret board in my mind. I'll hear these melodies, and I know what they're going to sound like on guitar. I won't pick up the guitar and say, 'Today I'm going to think up a lick.' It's sort of the opposite of that. There's a story about Thelonious Monk. The guy would be walking in the park and suddenly would have to find a piano. He would go into a place, say, 'I just thought of something,' write it down, and be gone two minutes later. That's what I do. Think up a lick first, then pick up the guitar."

That guitar was different these days, Kahn pointed out. "I know," Roy laughed, "everybody thought I was born with that old one . . . .In the past five or six years, Fender has put out new Teles that are better than the old ones. Now they've got the big frets that everybody wants. In the old days, all they had were maple necks; you can get the new units with rosewood fingerboards. All you have to do to make them sound as good is to get a good set of pickups—as simple as that." What kind of pickups? "Bill Lawrence pickups, definitely," Roy said. "By the way, two years ago Bill took me aside and talked to me like a brother. He told me that drugs and drinkin' were hurtin' my talents. That changed my life. Nobody had ever talked to me like that before. Now I'm playing better than ever, I feel better, and I'm learning more, thanks to Bill." Roy also let it drop that he was taking lessons from a young hotshot in Buffalo, NY, named Dave Whitehill. *Lessons?* Kahn asked incredulously. "He's in his early thirties, and he can play anything," Roy testified. "He showed me how to get a lot of different sounds." Roy also had some advice for budding guitarists. "Don't do drug things or alcohol. I don't want to come off as a goody-goody, but I did this whole album straight, and that's the reason I'm so proud of it. It was me, and not some drunken slob playing guitar. You can only hurt your own talent. The other advice is try to listen to all the different styles of music you can—don't limit yourself to one. Just listen to it all, and eventually you'll incorporate it into your own style. It'll just come automatically."

The buzz over *When a Guitar Plays the Blues* peaked when the recording industry nominated the album for a Grammy award as 1985 Blues Album of the Year. As a nominee Roy joined other distinguished blues artists, many of whom he'd long admired, including B.B. King, Bobby "Blue" Bland, Big Joe Turner, and fellow Alligator artists Koko Taylor and Johnny Winter. Nobody could argue with the winner: B.B. King's *My Guitar Sings the Blues*. But the nomination alone legitimized Roy's maiden effort on the label and, however briefly, kept the record on the charts.

After signing with Alligator Roy bought a Cadillac and in his spare time he would drive north over the nearby state line to Frederick, MD, which had a vibrant nightlife with music, friendly people, and cozy bars. In Frederick Roy ran into his old keyboardist Malcolm Lukens, who'd made his home there and did some bartending when he wasn't gigging. As Lukens recalled, "He'd bought his Cadillac, finally. He told me, 'You know, I've always been a hillbilly at heart. I had to get a big old black Cadillac.'"

BY THIS TIME ROY had spent six months playing with his power trio composed of bassist Jeff Ganz and drummer Ray Marchica. Ganz and Marchica were two New York pros Roy had hired in December 1984 after asking his old friend John Adams for help in putting together a top-notch band. Ganz had grown up on a diet of rock, jazz, blues, and Broadway show music. In time he would play for a diverse number of artists including the Village People, Johnny Winter, mambo king Tito Puente, jazz saxophonist Gerry Mulligan, and Bo Diddley. Ganz observed later that his eight-string bass worked well in the trio format. "The eight-string bass is the bass cousin to the 12-string guitar," he pointed out. "The strings are in pairs, tuned in octaves, and each string has a partner tuned an octave higher. So you play two notes at the same time. You could play in a guitar trio and not hear big holes. The higher octaves hinted that there was more going on than what was actually going on.

"I was not a huge fan of Roy's, to be honest," Ganz continued. "I didn't love those early recordings. It all seemed very clean and tame to me. I thought, 'Okay, this will be pleasant.' Then we got into the RCA recording studios where we rehearsed and the place just exploded when Roy started to play." As for playing with a "legend," Ganz added: "Roy was very quiet, self-effacing. Being my age, when your heroes become your peers, it's not an easy transition to make. When you're 14 and going to Johnny Winter shows, then, next thing, you're playing with

Johnny Winter . . . You're not quite sure whether to shower endless praise on the guy or be one of the guys. It's hard to know exactly how to act. With Roy that disappeared faster than with a lot of other people I've played with. Because he really didn't have any airs. He loved to hang."

Ganz and Marchica, like many before them, experienced the "Buchanan procedure" for new bandmates. On Dec. 7, 1984, the three gathered at RCA Studios in New York City for a rare rehearsal, where they toyed with various mainstays of the Buchanan songbook. The following evening the band played its first gig, at the Capitol Theater in Passaic, NJ. Within a week the band played Tramps in New York City, and a tape of the performance reveals that the trio already had hit its groove. In a rocking set they delivered a blazing shuffle, a menacing "Green Onions," a rocking "Done Daddy Dirty," "Hot Cha," a slow reading of Henry Mancini's "Peter Gunn." Ganz even sang Bobby Darin's "Dream Lover," a throwback to Roy's early days.

Despite the occasional pop tune, the music had made a 180-degree turn from the easy-going rockabilly sound Roy had explored with Scott "The Cat" Anderson. Now the band's sound had a harder edge, a jazzier, funkier sound. Ganz's Hondo eight-string bass added fuzz and crunch. Marchica's penchant for electronically generated tom-toms with echo added a modern element as well, though that element irritated not a few longtime fans. Roy himself began to utilize effects on stage for the first time in his life. He typically traveled with the Telecaster Custom that Bill Lawrence had given him and played it through a Boss delay pedal, which Roy believed would help attract a new generation of fans.

The approach seemed to be working, if reviews were any reflection. After a performance at the Bottom Line in Greenwich Village, *Variety* described the dynamics of the new unit. "At a time in which many record companies are getting mileage out of marketing artists as unsung American legends, blues/rock virtuoso Roy Buchanan has a legitimate claim to being the real thing. This quiet, reserved, 45-year-old musician, who never looked the part of a rock star even in his younger years, was as wild and untamed as ever once he picked up his Fender Telecaster for the SRO one-nighter. In Roy's hands the instrument takes on an extraordinary range of expression, wailing, weeping, sobbing or howling at a touch . . . .Typical of the evening was Booker T. Jones' 'Green Onions,' which Buchanan quickly brought to a violent boil, raking his fingers across the fret board in an explosive display of sonic fireworks . . . ."

THE BAND HIT all the usual haunts and a few new stops on a streak that lasted from December 1984 to July 1985. Roy seemed energized by the power and enthusiasm of his younger band mates and felt again the thrill of dazzling a crowded club with virtuosity and gut-wrenching blues. In this new context, with new material and a new sound, he continued to advance his guitar playing and explore new places. At Cabaret Metro in Chicago in late July, Roy discovered completely new terrain late in a blues in E. Though he began by gracefully swinging on a country-style blues, he

Roy demonstrates his ability to bend strings until they shrieked, at Carnegie Hall, in December 1985.

gradually put an edge on it. On the break he delivered an ample sample of his trademark chicken-pickin' and harmonics before pushing the band into a rollicking double time. Then he changed tempo and direction and feel again, turning to whimsical, sweet country picking before kicking off a funky interlude in which he alternately dueted with Ganz or danced above the rhythm, creating music that had never before issued from his guitar. This kind of turn-on-a-dime playing, the toying with rhythm and feel, hadn't been possible with some of his earlier bands. His new trio's prowess allowed him to evolve. Where his sound in the 1970s fell solidly within the parameters of roots music's simplicity and sincerity, the new band had all the bristling edginess of a wildcat on acid. Nowhere was that more apparent than in its fierce rendition of Henry Mancini's private eye TV show theme, "Peter Gunn," which began with a menacing rumble from Ganz, only to be hijacked by Roy's riveting, whiplash leads. The piece gave him plenty of room to explore sounds for their own sake at the highest volumes, shredding not a few minds en route. With his new band Roy toured the country's clubs as a legendary American axe, intent on cementing his reputation and raising a little hair. Audiences ate it up. "The people who came to see Roy were not, let's say, also going to the opera," Ganz laughed.

In time, however, the bassist learned there was more to Roy Buchanan—a lot more—than the nightly mind-blow suggested. "One night we were in Milwaukee during Summerfest and after our performance we all went over to a club and ended up playing the jazz standard 'Autumn Leaves'—not the stuff that he was known to do. But this guy could do anything. He had the most amazing ears I've ever seen."

Fortunately for Roy, the era of mom-and-pop management had passed. Bruce Iglauer had steered him to Teddy Slatus, who then was managing Johnny Winter's affairs. The arrangement made sense on a practical level, if not a musical one. Slatus, out of New York City, excelled at helping musicians with mundane details, though he had little grasp of Roy's craft. No matter. Slatus brought professionalism to booking tours and took care of the logistics that musicians typically were incapable of dealing with. Though the Buchanans and Slatus rarely saw eye-to-eye, the new manager rescued Roy from the wilderness and put him back on a solid business footing.

This new level of professionalism, however, applied strictly to Roy's business affairs. In practical terms, he still had a club-circuit trio without the economies of scale that provided for help on the road. Where Ganz's effervescent personality earned him the role of onstage emcee, he also got stuck with handling "arrangements" for the band. "In 1985 I was the 'road manager,'" Ganz recalled. "That was hell. I was checking people into hotels and all that. It sucked. We had no tech people with us and we were using rental gear the whole time." Ganz didn't have to schlep the gear, or drive, but that was small comfort. "The actual 'road manager' was too young to rent a car," the bassist laughed. "He was a 'party animal.' Sweet guy, but a real ingestion machine. I did a lot of the driving. When he drove I was scared shitless." As for the star of the show, all was not as advertised. "We were told, when we first got into the band, that Roy had recently become sober," Ganz observed. "There was no playing the guitar with the beer bottle, or drinking a pitcher of beer while playing 'Peter Gunn.' But there wasn't any sobriety that I was aware of, either."

In fact, demons *were* reappearing, re-emerging from the recesses where they lurked. Dark and shadowy, they remained elusive to their host, and inexplicable to those around him. The mystery to observers was that things were going so well for Roy. Why go back to drinking and drugging to excess? Perhaps the chains of habits too light to be felt in the Dale Hawkins days had, three decades later, gotten too heavy to break. Perhaps the guitarist fell into the familiar trap of believing that as long as his playing flowed and the gigs went well he was free to indulge himself to his heart's content. The lifestyle informed the playing, debauchery fueled the blues, and backstage lunacy inspired new guitar licks. It was all of a piece.

Roy could get into trouble as innocently as grabbing a cold beer before the show. But one cold beer always led to another, then a few more, then perhaps a joint and a snort of coke. The demons called. Too often, Roy responded, leading to an all-night wrestling match that always left him high and dry at some disturbingly familiar crossroads a long way from home. Over time that made for a pretty rugged existence. *I woke up this morning, Ew, my head was bad, I just can't tell you 'bout the good time that I had . . . .*

Still, Roy was a survivor. The occasional hair-raising night of partying did not diminish the genuine pleasure he took in having a new record deal, a new band, and a real manager who could put things together for him. Roy loved his work and warmed again to the stage. It was 1985 and the year had begun well with a quick tour of Europe. Pickup bands awaited them at the Paradiso Club in Amsterdam, the Rockpalast in Hamburg, the New Morning Club in Paris, the Tavastia in Helsinki ("*the* place to play in Helsinki," one local attested), and the Dominion Theater in London, where locals Martin and the Dainties backed Roy. Greeted at the Dominion by thunderous applause, Roy shot back: "Don't encourage me, I might stay here all night." (Later, his American friends asked him about the quality of rock 'n' roll bands in Europe. "They're *horrible!*" Roy replied with a smile.) Back in the States, he toured the country with Ganz and Marchica until October, then the band did a short stint in Australia in early November. Tony Convey, writing in *Muse* magazine on Roy's visit to the Canberra Workers' Club, called Roy "one of the great masters of the electric guitar." The song "Mrs. Pressure," Convey added, was the evening's highlight. "This exquisitely wrought melody, with its gleaming bell-like tone and sighing liquid harmonies, is a masterpiece in the timeless tradition of Django Reinhardt's 'Nuages' and Jimi Hendrix's 'Little Wing.'" Convey also noted a contrast that over the years had puzzled so many. "Talking to Roy afterwards it was hard to reconcile this humble, middle-aged man with the wrenching, highly charged music that had just flowed from his fingers."

THE LAST THING on the year's schedule was a December 6 date at Carnegie Hall with Lonnie Mack and Albert Collins. The show, dubbed American Guitar Heroes, was the apex of a short tour of the East Coast. Before the show the producers got the three "heroes" to sit down together and tell stories. Albert Collins' and Lonnie Mack's stories paralleled, even intersected, Roy Buchanan's story.

Albert Collins, born in Leona, TX, in 1932, was the elder statesman. He'd begun his professional career in 1952. He had put in 16 years on the road, always at the periphery of fame when, in 1968, he was playing the Ponderosa Club in Houston. Members of the blues-rock band Canned Heat found him there and spirited him to San Francisco to open for them at the Fillmore West. With a new, wider fan base Collins' career got a transfusion.

Lonnie Mack, born in 1941 in Harrison, IN, was at 44 the junior "hero" on the bill. In 1963 his instrumental remake of Chuck Berry's "Memphis" climbed the charts and he spun across the country in his Cadillac with his 1958 Gibson Flying V, milking his fame. He had more hits, including "Wham!," and five years of one-night stands. An article in *Rolling Stone* in 1968 re-ignited interest in his talents and he signed with Elektra, eventually doing A&R work for the label. He dropped out, only to reappear in a Pennsylvania-based band with Buffalo native and former Hawk Stan Szelest. Mack had plans to record an upcoming Texas talent named Stevie Ray Vaughan, who instead got snapped up by Epic. He'd "retired" to the Cincinnati clubs by the early 1980s, when he too got a boost from signing with Alligator Records.

Mack, for one, had had an epiphany after playing the Fillmore in 1969, opening for Crosby, Stills & Nash. The rock 'n' roll scene, to an extent, would be a hell of a lot easier to cut than the old roadhouse circuit. "We just played long songs and screamed and hollered a lot and jammed a bunch," he recalled with a wry smile. "Basically, this music is simplicity. If you have to think about it, you're doin' it wrong." As to the current gig at Carnegie Hall, Mack remarked laconically, "Things have changed a bit, but the roots of it still seem to hold." It was his first meeting with Roy Buchanan, but he spoke for all three men when he described the vagaries of the business. "You got to stay out there forever. You got to love what you're doin'. Cuz if you don't, it'll kill you . . . .Like I always say, 'I'm a lifer,' and I know both these guys are too. We've all been playin' forever. It's like all you do. I tried doin' some straight jobs for a while and it bored me to death. So I get to the point where I ain't happy at home, but then I get out on the road and stay too long and I ain't happy out there and want to go home. That's it. You just got to keep doin' it."

Later that evening, a packed house greeted a humble Albert Collins. "This is the highlight of my life, ladies and gentlemen," he announced from the well-lit concert hall stage, the antithesis of the smoky clubs to which he was accustomed. "Thank you so much." With songs like "If Trouble Was Money (I'd Be a Million-aire)," Collins filled the hall with down-and-gritty blues. And he pierced the staid atmosphere by stepping off the stage and walking among the audience, wailing on his Telecaster, a long cord trailing behind him. Lonnie Mack, the best singer of the three, came out next and with songs like "Stop (Hurtin' Me)/I'm Just Your Fool" told haunting stories of the impermanence of love.

Roy came out last, in respectable dress shirt and trousers, a black vest, and, because he had begun losing his hair, a black fedora. He cradled a brand-new Tele-caster. It had been more than a dozen years since he'd taken the stage at Carnegie Hall. For some reason—Ganz suggested that, by this time, his New York union pay rates might have undercut his usefulness to Roy—Ganz and Marchica were not asked to play this particular gig, and Roy had instead brought in Cary Ziegler on bass—an acquaintance from Maryland who'd toured with his own band, Crack the Sky, and played with Edgar Winter—and Paul Wilson on drums, a denizen of the music scene in Frederick, MD. Both men had grown up on the era's rock and the

Roy's return to Carnegie Hall in December 1985 on a "Guitar Heroes" bill with Lonnie Mack and Albert Collins got mixed reviews when he diluted his set of roots music with Led Zeppelin's hard rock.

DC region's soul music and had played a handful of dates with Roy that fall. For the Carnegie engagement, Wilson got a bird's eye view of Roy's approach to big moments. "We couldn't get him to rehearse. I mean, here we are, playing Carnegie Hall. It's being videotaped. And I haven't a clue what's going on!"

Roy opened his set with "Green Onions" and gave the audience a taste of his patented harmonics, machine gun–like staccato runs, and a few mournful cries. "Short Fuse" off the first Alligator album came next, another showcase for the guitarist's sometimes mind-numbing runs up and down the neck. He conjured the cello-like volume swells that introduced the incendiary "When a Guitar Plays the Blues." A dozen years earlier he had sent sinuous notes snaking through the recesses of the hall; tonight he made his Tele scream in anguish. Having created some tension and momentum to his set, though, he turned things over to his bass player, who belted out Led Zeppelin's "Whole Lotta Love." No doubt Roy and Ziegler thought they'd pierce the hall's stuffiness with a hard rock number, but the shift away from the evening's traditional music proved jarring to many in the crowd. Iglauer, for one, felt Roy showed a lack of appreciation for the evening's tone, and did not take full opportunity to showcase the roots music that had sustained the three performers. The producer earlier had told a film crew that the American public "still wants direct, emotional roots music," but here was Roy cavalierly tossing out a Led Zeppelin song. "Led Zeppelin to me is the cartoon version of the music I love," Iglauer said many years later. "The general sense of Roy's set was that it was a letdown. It wasn't the climax of the night. The audience was ready for wherever he would take them. I was disappointed he didn't make more of a personal statement, particularly on the heels of tight sets by Lonnie Mack and Albert Collins."

AFTER THE SHOW ALLIGATOR RECORDS hosted a party at S.I.R., Studio Instrument Rentals, a rehearsal room downtown. The caterer assured Iglauer and his crew that there were sufficient beverages for 200 people for two hours, but just as the party began to roll—"It was a *party!*" Iglauer said, still jazzed—the booze ran out. A handful of Alligator staffers grabbed handcarts and ran to the nearest after-hours delicatessens and carted back cases of beer. When they found the studio too crowded to re-enter, they simply passed the cases of beer into the crowd like a bucket brigade. "There's this huge jam session with Albert Collins and Roy got up to play," Paul Wilson recalled. "Some guy got up to play bass and he was absolutely god-awful, some kind of derelict. He was so bad he blew the whole jam. There are hundreds of people there. Anyway, I went back to my room early. Cary comes in that night and he says, 'Paul, you won't believe this!' I said, 'What?!' He says, 'Man, that bass player was *Jaco Pastorius!*' "

The party didn't break up until 5 a.m., and Iglauer ended the night by stuffing garbage bags into a dumpster outside S.I.R. Roy lurched off to find his hotel room. Jaco Pastorius—one of the great electric bass players of the age—continued his descent into madness.

BY THIS TIME ROY AND JUDY had moved from their Lovettsville digs in the northern Virginia countryside to a three-bedroom town home Judy picked out in Reston, VA, a leafy suburb ten miles west of the DC city limits. The couple's children had grown up and moved on and the Lovettsville house had become a financial burden. They'd bought the place in flush times with money from the Atlantic contract, but the deal with Alligator simply couldn't sustain their old lifestyle. The new place in Reston had two bedrooms upstairs, a split-level kitchen/living room area on the main floor, and a finished basement where the kids could stay and Roy could retreat to pick on one of his guitars and make practice tapes for the next Alligator session.

The new digs and their suburban surroundings would take some getting used to. Compared to the elbow room they'd enjoyed, the town house was a tad cramped. Roy would escape by walking through a copse of trees that separated the home at 2325 Harleyford Court from a local mall, which featured a restaurant called Fritzbee's and its quiet bar. Or he'd take the family station wagon to the nearby Fair Oaks Mall, where he could shop for cigars at John B. Hayes, Tobacconist, then retire to the Ruby Tuesday's upstairs for a few beers. Reston was leafy, but it was not the country. There'd be no more jaunts to Frederick for a good time.

Though he missed his excursions to Frederick, a walk through the woods to a nearby bar appealed to him. It didn't work as well for Judy, who had grown tired of, though resigned to, the ups and downs of life with a wayward musician. And it wasn't just Roy's drinking that bothered her deeply. "In the 1980s he got into coke, which concerned me more than any other drug he took," Judy told writer Bill Milkowski. "I saw a change in him. He got more of an 'I don't care' attitude. I'd always been able to reach him under any circumstances but when he took coke I could never reach him, and that scared me."

AT THE END OF FEBRUARY 1986 Roy gathered up another handful of cassettes and packed his bags for Chicago. It was time for Lemon Pledge and cigar-smoking with the boys from Alligator.

"On the second album we wanted to learn from what we had done before," Iglauer said. "We didn't have a lot of brilliant ideas but, to me, if you take a great musician and a batch of memorable songs he can work with, you're doing a good job. You don't have to have a theme for everything. The theme is good music."

Iglauer brought back the rhythm section from the first record, Morris Jennings on drums and Larry Exum on bass. For keyboards, Iglauer reached back to Roy's days with Ronnie Hawkins and the Hawks to pull in Stan Szelest. Hawkins had once dubbed Szelest, "Lon Chaney on helium," for his wild hunch over the keyboards. These days players nicknamed him "Mount Rushmore," for his road-weathered countenance. "Lonnie [Mack] had taken Stan to Texas to work on Alligator's *Strike Like Lightning* record," Iglauer recalled. "Lonnie hooked me up with Stan. I loved Stan's playing." Szelest and Roy went back more than 25 years, so that was good for chemistry. The delicate role of supporting guitarist went to Donald Kinsey, lead guitarist for one of Chicago's great bar bands, the Kinsey Report.

One choice remained: they would need a guest vocalist. Both producers recognized that with two vocalists on the first LP, the marketing possibilities had been limited. They needed one singer to provide vocals and a commercial identity for the record. "You need radio airplay to have a hit record," Iglauer said. "An independent record label, as Alligator was back then, doesn't get a lot of airplay. You also don't get national radio hits with 46-year-old bald guys who can't sing. Radio needs songs and for Roy it wasn't so much about songs, it was about guitar playing. We needed a singer." Dick Shurman thought that commercially, they'd have their best luck with a white singer, so he suggested Delbert McClinton, the Texas-based rhythm and blues belter. The preparations at Dick Shurman's house fleshed out a handful of Roy's instrumental ideas—mostly uptempo guitar workouts on some highly charged melodies—and they emerged with a repertoire for half an album. Shurman had some ideas for McClinton, who would arrive at the studio once the band found its groove. McClinton would not accept a flat rate for his services. The price for singing on four tracks, any of which might garner airplay and become a hit, would be a slice of the album's royalties. Iglauer agreed.

In late February the band put in a couple of evenings at Dress Rehearsals running through the instrumentals Roy had penned. Roy brought both his new Telecaster-style custom, actually made by Guild, and a gold-topped Les Paul, which he frequently used for rhythm. Among other things, the band ran through "Peter Gunn." Roy gave the Mancini theme a frightening serving of his whiplash-style leads, complete with overtones that seemed to exceed the boundaries of the human senses. A lot of guitar players had recorded wild versions of the "Peter Gunn" theme—including Duane Eddy, Jimi Hendrix, and Link Wray—but Roy *owned* it. "We talked about Link Wray," Dick Shurman recalled. "I sensed there was some kind of rivalry between the two. Roy claimed that Link got some of his ideas from him, but I never got the whole lowdown." On the first day of March, the players moved over to Streeterville studio to record. The first day the band ran through the instrumentals and all but one were master takes. At Alligator, instrumentals inspired a creative naming process. When Mindy Giles, Iglauer's assistant, said the first song—a funky "Huey Smith thing," in Dick Shurman's words—sounded like a cross between Eric Clapton in Cream and Steve Cropper in Booker T. & the MGs, they dubbed it "Cream of the Crop." An uptempo boogie driven by Roy's slide seemed to combine Roy's gentle touch with his razor edge and so was titled "Petal to the Metal." A playful romp with fun, even acrobatic leads did not survive its first name. "Dick and I both like plays on words," Iglauer said. "On 'Jungle Gym' there's a vocal scream near the end. I said, 'That sounds like a banshee scream.' The word 'banshee' seemed liked an exciting word to have in an instrumental title. And Roy quite calmly said, 'We had a banshee out on the farm in Virginia and it used to keep us awake nights, screaming. We had to move.' He said it like, 'We had gophers tearing up the lawn.' I thought he meant it, so I changed the title of that track to 'Jungle Gym.'"

While the band took a break, Roy sketched out a Bach-like theme that combined deft, somber rhythms with achingly beautiful leads. It seemed only an idea, but when Roy demonstrated he had complete, two-tracked guitar parts worked out in his head, they captured the piece's intricacies on tape. "Basically," Shurman said, "Roy was just having a duet with himself, a really pretty one, one of the prettiest songs I've ever worked on." Iglauer added: "The two guitar parts interlocked perfectly. I think 'Matthew' is a true mark of Roy's genius because the conception was so complete and he did it so quickly. The whole thing was a vision." Roy named the song for a grandchild, Matthew. He and Judy had legally adopted Matthew as their children left the nest.

It had been a productive day in the studio. Shurman had a strong feeling that these particular players made a truly great studio band. Still, the situation did not lack technical hurdles. "I remember Roy would lay down these rhythm parts for Donald, who is a top-notch guitar player, just off-hand, like, 'Here's what I want you to play,'" Shurman said. "Roy would knock off these patterns, and Donald would say, 'Whoa! Wait a minute!' They had to simplify fifty percent of it down. For his part, Stan was pretty quiet. As far as he was concerned he never played anything right, though we could never hear anything that needed to be repaired. You didn't have to say much to him. He knew what we were doing."

The following day they captured a fun, near-perfect rendition of "Beer Drinkin' Woman." Despite Roy's limited vocal range, he had to sing *something* on the record. So Shurman pulled out a Chuck Berry version of this old Memphis Slim song. To dress up this good-humored, well-grooved song, Roy opened it with a series of cascading open-string pull-offs, a technique he'd learned from the young and talented Dave Whitehill. Many years later, Whitehill recalled with a mischievous grin, "Sometimes Roy would play this or a similar one I taught him in a show, but I wouldn't know when he was going to do it. I knew he would throw that lick in to freak me out, but I never knew when, so it was like, 'Where's Waldo?'"

The recording process had gone well, but Iglauer felt something was missing. "We needed something slow and powerful for variety and, because, after all, this *is* a blues label," he said. "I thought of two on my way home one night and the next morning I threw them on tape and stopped at Roy's hotel on the way to the studio. Later, he came to the studio and said that Albert King's 'Drowning on Dry Land' just *hit* him. It was like the story of his life. It had been a big Stax Records hit for Albert on black radio. Donald Kinsey had an arrangement that he'd done with Albert. So he showed everyone his arrangement and we cut it really fast. Most of the vocal, if I recall, we cut live in the studio. Roy was playing his Les Paul." The track was a highlight for Shurman as well. "We got a really spirited, slow blues vocal out of Roy on that. Everyone laughed because he sat in a chair during the take, but while he soloed he had his feet lifted way up in the air, a sure sign he was feeling the music." After having fun with a boogie featuring Roy's fluid slide work, the band packed it in for the night.

The next day the players reassembled with Delbert McClinton. He'd arrived from Texas earlier in the day to meet Roy for the first time and talk over that evening's recording plans. "When I met Roy he was settin' down in a coffee shop in this hotel in Chicago," McClinton said in a 1988 radio interview. "And he had a big cee-gar stickin' out of his mouth. I think he had that cee-gar stickin' out of his mouth every minute that I knew him that he wasn't talkin'. When he'd be doin' the session? Big old cee-gar stickin' out of his mouth. He had a pocketful of 'em. When I meet somebody I don't know, and they impress me, somehow it means more than meetin' somebody already knowin' their image. I guess that's what made it so much more fun in the studio with Roy. The fact that we weren't that familiar with each other, but when we did the first lick in the studio, [we said], 'This is going to be fun. We're not going to have *any* trouble with this.'"

The evening's first tune would be Joe Simon's country soul tune, "Chokin' Kind," which Shurman felt would fit McClinton's vocal sensibilities. The lyrics told of the protagonist's fear of love that was the "chokin' kind." Next the crew dug into one McClinton suggested: Willie Dixon's "You Can't Judge a Book by Its Cover," a hit for Bo Diddley in 1962. Shurman encouraged the singer to stay in the studio, to feel at home with the band, and to engage with Roy by trading off vocal and guitar riffs. The song became the album's hit record, garnering the level of airplay that

Iglauer typically could only dream of. Unfortunately, Alligator's marketing and distribution channels just weren't adequate to meet the demands of the moment. "It showed everybody the limits of what Bruce could do," Shurman recalled. "His whole distribution and promotion setup wasn't geared toward really trying to have a pop hit. He had a certain level that was exemplary for a blues label, but he wasn't set up to crank out enough, and pay enough, and cover enough territory to really give it a shot in the pop market."

The next evening's sessions began with a take of "Baby, Baby, Baby," a song from Aretha Franklin's first Atlantic album in 1967 that Delbert had suggested when first approached about the project. Shurman remembered the singer nailing the song in one, possibly two takes. "He walked into the control room, having put the vocals straight down in the first take, and said, 'Let's see if that's worth shit.' We listened to the playback in the control room and it was brilliant. He just shook his head and said, 'I guess I just can't sing this song.' Bruce and I didn't know whether to laugh or cry."

"One of things that struck me during the sessions for the second Alligator album was how much Roy enjoyed being an accompanist," Iglauer said. "I think he enjoyed having a situation where, like a jazz player, he had a melody upon which to improvise. On a song like 'Baby Baby Baby,' for example, there was that specific vocal melody off which he could improvise. He liked that *a lot*." The evening ended with three great vocal tracks in the can. Another brief session two days later and the recording process was finished. "What stuck out to me in the mixing process, and I mentioned it to Bruce," Shurman said, "is that the unedited, 13 tunes we cut for the second album were shorter than the nine edited tunes we had for the first one. The tunes on the second one were a lot more tightly focused." In the midst of the sessions came horrible news: Richard Manuel, once the heart and blue-eyed soul of the Band—the former Hawks—had committed suicide in a Winter Park, FL, motel bathroom, after yet another gig on the road, this time at the Cheek-to-Cheek Lounge. By all accounts the group had played two great sets that night for an avid crowd of fans, which had gone wild for Manuel's reading of "Georgia on My Mind," the 1960 hit for Ray Charles. Manuel had battled melancholia and his own demons for years, making several attempts to break free of drink and cocaine. And, certainly, the Band was not what it once was. They had held the rock spotlight for nearly a decade when, in 1976, Robbie Robertson made his permanent departure after "The Last Waltz" concert at San Francisco's Winterland. Ten years later the remaining band members had to work considerably harder to generate the old magic. For his part, Robertson had desperately wanted to avoid just the situation Richard Manuel found himself in during the early hours of March 4. According to statements members of the Band made afterwards to the press, Manuel had appreciated the crowd that evening, even taken a little shit about his return to drinking from bassist Rick Danko. He told organist Garth Hudson how much he'd enjoyed working with him over the years, but Hudson missed any signs of trouble. He sat on the edge of Levon Helm's bed at 2 a.m. and talked about people, and songs. An hour later he tied his belt around his neck, fastened the buckle, then looped the other end around a shower rod and tucked the loose end under. Then he sat down, hard. His wife found him later that morning. Manuel's death came as a brutal reminder to anyone who cared to consider it that life on the road with a couple of bad habits could eat a man alive.

Roy knew that story too well. His dedication to remaining straight throughout the recording process had slipped. "The first album was a big deal to do sober because he felt so good about it," Iglauer observed. In contrast, Roy's behavior on the second album was "back-and-forth." When it came time to name his just finished album Roy suggested *Dancing on the Edge*. It seemed to fit.

THE MUSIC TRADE PAPER *Album Network* initiated industry buzz in a prerelease review in early May, saluting Roy as "one of rock's greatest players," and praising McClinton's "git-down-on-yer-knees-and-sing-from-the-gut vocal testimony." Upon the record's release in June, *Billboard* noted, "The premier roadhouse guitarist is slingin' enough fire to burn down the juke joint." *Guitar for the Practicing Musician* rated the album "storming" and lauded Roy's "blistering" guitar that sent "razor sharp, trebly tones slicing through the air. The entire album bristles with energy....Buchanan builds his whirlwind solos with an ease and sweaty grace that reinforces his standing as a master technician . . . ." *Guitar Player* liked the selection of material and the "clean and uncluttered" arrangements that gave Roy's trademark sound "plenty of room in the spotlight." More accolades: *College Media Journal* awarded the record honors for best blues album of 1986. (Among this award's nominees were Ry Cooder's soundtrack for *Crossroads*, John Lee Hooker's *Showless*, Albert Collins, Johnny Copeland, and Robert Cray's *Showdown*, and the Fabulous Thunderbirds' *Tough Enough*.) *Dancing on the Edge* also garnered a New Music Award. Roy attended the televised awards ceremony and was asked to say a few words. "I want to thank you all very much. I'm a blues player and I came to play, rather than talk. God bless you." Roy then took the stage and improvised several haunting melodies to thunderous applause.

Robert J. Hawkins, a writer for the *San Diego Tribune*, put things in context when he blurted in print: "It's just a damn good thing Alligator Records has developed a side interest in resurrecting great guitarists in their, uh, maturity. In the past year, the Chicago-based label has recorded Buchanan, roadhouse rocker Lonnie Mack and Texas blues-rocker Johnny Winter . . . .Last year Alligator issued Mack's *Strike Like Lightning*, produced by Stevie Ray Vaughan, and Buchanan's self-produced [sic] *When a Guitar Plays the Blues*. Both were fresh breezes cutting through the dead still air of rock 'n' roll. Roy has come back with *Dancing on the Edge*—a soulful shot of the blues."

This appreciation for the great roadhouse players of the day inspired the Great American Guitar Assault tour, which packaged a few roots players who individually couldn't sell the bigger halls. In making real music economically viable, the tour's promoters put together Roy, Lonnie Mack, and Dicky Betts, one of the founders of the Allman Brothers Band, for 14 dates in 27 days. The tour began in Chicago on May 29 and stopped off in Davenport, IA, Cincinnati, and Pittsburgh before proceeding to St. Louis, Phoenix, San Diego, Seattle, Portland, OR, Salt Lake City, and Denver. At Parker's in Seattle on June 18 Roy included "Roy's Bluz" in his set. The original lyrics intoned, *The train it leaves the station, always leaves at three-oh-nine, you can tell all the people, it's always left Roy behind.* This time Roy sang, *You can tell all the people, it ain't gonna leave Roy behind.* He wanted to codify his new outlook despite occasional tumbles from the wagon. And he undoubtedly meant what he said. But when it came to shedding bad habits, talking the talk was always easier for Roy than walking the walk.

AFTER A SMATTERING of outdoor summer concerts including the San Francisco Blues Festival at Fort Mason on September 19, Ganz, Marchica, and Roy jumped a plane for Japan. They played ten dates in 20 days, beginning as soon as they got off the plane, jetlagged, in Sapporo. They traveled south to Tokyo, Nagoya, Kyoto, and on to Osaka and Kobe on Osaka Bay. "My favorite Buchanan comment happened as we're walking through the airport at Tokyo International at Narita and there's nothing in English," Ganz said. "Roy looks around and he turns to me and he says, 'Now you know what it's like to be illiterate.'" Ganz, like John Harrison before him, was nonplussed by the Japanese audiences' reactions. "They were very sedate at first. Then, by the encore, they were *insane*. It was like throwing a light switch. There were," he mused, "cultural differences." Roy appreciated those differences. In an interview upon his return, he noted that he'd had a birthday in Japan in September 1959, and again, his 47th, just a month earlier. "They really like the blues a lot. They actually like it better than Americans. They just get engrossed when you get to playin'. And they don't come to get drunk or get high, because they don't allow that over there. They come strictly to listen and they're mesmerized by the blues. I always have a good time."

The shows began at an early hour and, therefore, as in 1977, they were not marred by the band's ability to absorb sake—or anything else. "We're gonna rock your brains out," Roy would announce to his Japanese audiences upon taking the stage. It was hard to believe that only three men created the music that followed: razor sharp, deeply rhythmic, it had momentum and texture. Ganz's eight-string bass lines muscled their way to the forefront, especially when he conjured the sounds of a Hammond B-3 organ. With Roy employing spectacular technique and a delay pedal, the band sounded like a handful of instruments, you just weren't sure which ones. Despite the heaviness and sharpness to the music, the volume was kept reasonable and the sound had a pleasant, good-time feeling to it. On "Country Boy," Roy sang playfully, "I'm a little country boy, runnin' wild in Tokyo."

BACK IN THE US, the band continued its tear, from DC to Vancouver, British Columbia, and from San Diego to New York City, stopping off at home only briefly as the tour stretched through October into early November.

The band disintegrated after a gig at New York's Bottom Line. There'd been too many hassles along the road. One night in Great Woods, MA, in October, the band waited backstage after the show for Roy to materialize after meeting and greeting fans. An hour passed. There'd be only one ride to the hotel that evening. "We're waiting. We're waiting," one person present recalled. "Finally, Roy comes in and announces, 'I just tried crack!'" The sidemen were losing patience. At the Bottom Line gig, "something didn't go down right," Jeff Ganz recalled. "But at that point I'd had enough."

Thinking back on his experience with the Master of the Telecaster, Ganz grew pensive. "I use my own set of standards to judge emotion. If it gets me, it gets me. I could tell when Roy was bullshitting. Then there were times when notes he would play would send shivers through me. Roy was like many guitarists of that vintage. They just want to stand there and play. They didn't want to pay attention to showmanship of any kind. Sometimes I got the vibe that it was, 'Stand up there and play,' and in parentheses, 'Collect the money and go home.' For me, at that young age, I was a lot more serious about trying to be a band. Roy was just happy to be playing the guitar. That's a double-entendre. He saw the writing on the wall. Roy was not a blatant, bitter guy. Resigned, to a point, perhaps. But I could give you five diametrically opposed observations about Roy and they would all be correct." No one could stay mad at Roy for long, including Ganz. Somewhere along the road, at an outdoor gig at the Equestrian Center in Prince George County, MD, Roy's old stomping grounds, the guitarist gave his bassist a book on the *Bowery Boys*. "Roy and I were both *Bowery Boys* freaks," Ganz laughed. "We had this thing in common and he bought it for me. I asked him to sign it, but he just wouldn't do it."

The year 1987 brought relentless tours. Roy first embarked with Dave Broderick on bass and Tommy Hambridge on drums, then segued to playing with Cary Ziegler and Vince Santoro. Demand for his services kept Roy on the road from January 1987 clear to May. Roy retained his sense of humor and often teased his audience. At Rockefellers in Houston, TX, on February 5, someone called out a request: *"Hey Joe"!* Seemingly astonished, Roy asked, "Is *Joe* here?" He introduced his favorite Neil Young song by calling it "Down by the Liver." And there were antics. "We went to Richmond, Virginia—very conservative surroundings," Santoro later recalled. "We were in the band room, waiting for the audience to get keyed up and we looked at each other. We all had that feeling we had to do something wacky. We found these tablecloths, green tablecloths, and we wrapped them around ourselves like tunics from the neck down. And we promised each other we'd wear them at least through the first couple of songs. Sure as shit, Roy put that thing on and went right out on stage!"

A window into the life of a traveling "legend" is contained in Teddy Slatus' contracts for the new year, 1987. If a club owner or promoter wished to secure the services of the Telecaster Master, the Doctor of Rock 'n' roll, Mr. Roy Buchanan, that could be done—for a fee. In addition to the fee, which was based on the venue's capacity and ticket prices, the interested party would have to provide a guitar amp (Roland JC 120, Marshall with reverb 100 watts, or Peavey Twin with reverb), two bass amps, and a set of Yamaha or Ludwig drums. In the dressing room, the host was required to provide two cases of beer (Heineken or Molson), two gallons of natural, non-sparkling spring water, assorted soft drinks, coffee, tea, sugar, lemon, honey, and fresh milk. There would also be a deli platter with bread ("*no* white bread"), and condiments. Don't forget the ice, cups, plates, napkins, forks, knives, and spoons. Add three towels. "It would be appreciated," the contract also stated, "if you would supply us with the following information: address and phone number of venue; times for sound check and shows; name of stage manager and phone number; closest hotel to the venue that you would recommend; and phone number." It was lonely out there on the road. Roy Buchanan, "the Artist" in the contract's parlance, could use a little information, a few beers, and an amp. For a fee, he'd fill your club with people who liked to drink and raise a holy ruckus.

At this point Roy was working almost exclusively with Cary Ziegler and Vince Santoro. They'd hit a groove musically and personally. Ziegler, a Baltimore-area native, had grown up on rock and soul and Roy's early records when the call came from Teddy Slatus. Ziegler's experience with Roy echoed that of so many others'. The leader needed a drummer, and quick, for an upcoming gig at DC's Warner Theater opening for the classic '70s band, Bachman-Turner Overdrive. "I kept waiting for someone to call about rehearsals," Ziegler said. "Finally, Roy calls and says, 'I'll see you at 5:30 at the Warner Theater.' That night! So here comes Roy. He's late. I'm sweatin' bullets. No sound check." Somehow, the band clicked. "I sang a bunch of songs. Roy was great that way. He let you do whatever you wanted. Being on stage was a treat. Every night he'd amaze me." Vinnie Santoro had been drumming for country pop-rock artists like Roseanne Cash and Rodney Crowell when he got the call. He'd grown up all over the country as an Army brat, but spent his formative years in Alexandria, VA outside DC, listening to the Beatles and Motown, the Four Tops, and Jimi Hendrix.

After the Warner Theater show the trio toured the West Coast, Texas, the South, and the Northeast with John Olds now running interference as road manager. They had *fun*. Even the long tedious drives to out-of-the-way gigs acquired the character of an addled family vacation. "We would be in the station wagon, driving down the road, with me and Cary in the back, Roy in the front and John driving," Santoro said. "Me and Cary would be just jukin' around, havin' fun, smacking each other. Roy would lean over to John and say, 'Pull the car over and split up those two.' We'd have to stop the car and Roy would get in the back seat with one of us, 'cause in the daytime he was just like your old man. He wanted everything calm and collected. He was very internal, he didn't want any part of horsing around. He'd often fall asleep on the drive with a cigar in his mouth. He was like a little old man in that respect. So I dug him. But then, at night, on stage, he just exploded. Those were the good extremes he went through."

En route to one of the many gigs the trio played in this period at the Lone Star Cafe in New York City, Barb Santoro, Vinnie's wife, saw more to the enigmatic guitarist than his wild-ass guitar playing. Barb herself worked as a singer in the torch ballad tradition, and she punched a tape into the van's cassette player of one of her favorite female singers from the 1950s. Roy lit up. "I could tell he had a sentimental feeling about that time and that music," Barb said. "I knew he liked those sexy, sultry, sensuous female singers. On 'Baby Baby Baby,' which Vince sang, Roy played these exquisite, heart-wrenching solos that pulled on me. He made me cry. That's when I realized that he had played with jazz singers before, because he really listened to the vocalist. He had a great sensitivity as an artist. Not like those guitar whizzes that are so anxious to get their chops in, and get the singer out of the way so they can do their thing. I got the sense he loved the finesse of the music. But for Roy, ultimately, that jazzy, quiet, muted sound was too confining. He had become a guitar shredder at that point. He would go out there and scream on the guitar. That's what people wanted him to do. The audience egged him on. He was a people pleaser, he wanted people to be happy. When he would do 'Baby Baby Baby,' people in the club would be talking so loud during the whole thing, because they couldn't care less about a beautiful ballad, they wanted to hear screaming, rockin' stuff." Backstage, the star had little chance to escape the trappings of a rocking bluesman. "There was a whole entourage of people who would show up," Barb recalled. "Roy was a funny combination of being 'Everyman,' a regular guy, and being from another planet. He loved these rednecks, men and women, who'd known him for years. They considered him 'theirs.' They popped up everywhere and they were 'friends of Roy's.'" The attraction was mutual, and the result was preordained, not to the benefit of either party. *Woke up this mornin', Ew! my head was bad, I just can't tell you 'bout the good times I had . . .*

THE TRIO TOOK ADVANTAGE of an offer to visit Europe, and they played ten dates in two weeks at the end of April with stops in the German cities Bonn, Bochum, Hamburg, Frankfurt, and Stuttgart; Zurich, Switzerland; Paris; and Amsterdam. Teddy Slatus arranged for a Volvo tour bus with bunks and a shower. "Very easy," Ziegler said. "Big bunks. Fluffy blankets. An English road manager and an English driver. We hit every 'serious' town in Germany, Switzerland, and France. Amsterdam—with its coffee, hash, and eight million bicycles—was my favorite." A little incident in Hamburg illuminated Roy's different take on life. "Here's a story that shouldn't get anyone in trouble," Santoro laughed. "In Hamburg, they have a district for prostitution, the 'Something-strasse.' It's an experience. One night both Cary and Roy decided, 'I've got to experience this.' They both met girls and went up to hotel rooms. First Cary came back to the tour bus, all pissed off. 'That bitch! I want my money back!' Turns out the women take you upstairs for 50 or 100 marks and they *talk* with you. 'For another 50 I'll do this.' So he was pissed. On the other hand, Roy came back, the same thing happened to him, and he was okay with it. He said, 'Didn't you ever just want to sit down and just talk to them?' He meant it. Roy loved to sit down with a stranger and just yak."

Roy didn't mind having some fun with his young band mates' heads, either. "Roy had stories about the Devil," Ziegler laughed. "Spooky ones! We were riding this tour bus through Germany and it looks like Transylvania. Eerie. The shadows were just right. And he looks up at this castle and says, 'Uh-oh.' Vinnie and I look at each other. '*What?!*' 'Oh man,' Roy says. '*This* is where it happened.' He talked about cats entering his room, surrounding him. It would get real spooky." "He met the Devil," Santoro agreed, matter-of-factly. "He mentioned this several times." Not certain what he had on his hands, Ziegler tried to tape Roy's spiel one night. "He caught me and took the tape," Ziegler laughed. "He didn't do anything, but he was on a roll."

Being on a roll with the guys in the band was one thing, but once they returned home, drinking and carousing had an impact. "He used to come home very drunk," Judy told Bill Milkowski. "He could be very violent. Especially with me. One particular night . . . when Matthew was probably two years old . . . Roy started in with me, then he went downstairs and got his gun, which scared me to death. That night I was afraid of him. I'd never had to call the police until that one time. And all they did was come and ask him to leave, but they said they couldn't make him leave. He said, 'Can you take me to a hotel?' So they supposedly took him to a hotel, but he was back in 20 minutes. And things were okay. But the thing of it is, when guns were involved, that scared me."

AT THE END OF MAY Roy reached into his green garbage bag, grabbed a handful of cassettes, packed his bags, and headed once more for Chicago. Roy insisted that he work again with the band that worked so well on *Dancing on the Edge*. As usual, a guest vocalist would be needed. Delbert McClinton was unavailable. Shurman suggested veteran soul singer Johnny Sayles, while Bruce Iglauer proffered local singer Kanika Kress, herself an aggressive guitarist. In the end, both would sing on the record.

When it came time to record, however, there was a bit of confusion over the artist's vision for the record. "We were getting conflicting signals from Roy on what direction he wanted to take," Shurman recalled. "As often happens, the joy of scratching an aesthetic itch like the blues began to fade as the financial limits became more apparent, especially to Judy, I think. Understandably, I think, she was a lot more interested in having Roy maximize his earnings than his creativity. No doubt Teddy Slatus shared some of those sentiments. In contrast, Roy was telling us that he really liked working with a black rhythm section. He had musical integrity about what he wanted to do. These were the conflicts." Roy had it his way: He and Stan Szelest were the only white boys on the record.

The band spent two days at Matt the Cat rehearsal hall to run over the songs Roy, Shurman, and Iglauer had picked out. They'd worked four of Roy's ideas into songs: two high-energy guitar-heavy outings, "High Wire," the aptly named "Flash Chordin'," one slow blues called "the Blues Lover," and a sparkling, pensive gem dubbed "Sunset over Broadway," which featured Roy's hypnotic, steel guitar–like licks and volume swells. They tried out Link Wray's "Jack the Ripper," Johnny Heartsman's frolicking "Goose Grease," and Peppermint Harris' equally good-humored version of Dr. Clayton's "Ain't No Business," the latter two featuring Roy on talking-style vocals.

As before, the band entered the studio to capture master takes just as it got a feel for the material—not a minute sooner, not a day later. They now added Bobby "Blue" Bland's "That Did It" in preparation for Johnny Sayles' appearance. With one night's exception, Roy played masterfully. On the night in question he explained again to his patient but irked producers why he played better half-drunk. Uncharacteristically, a little sloppiness showed. It didn't spoil the recording process and Roy was careful to indulge his taste for cocaine off the premises. Nonetheless, "I was pretty upset," Iglauer recalled. "He was very surreptitious about it. But there was beer in the studio." Only one song, "That Did It," required an overdub, how-ever, and that was because of a broken string during the solo. "During the record-ing for 'Ain't No Business,' I remarked that it had some nice Gatemouth Brown touches," Shurman recalled. "Roy was getting a little tipsy and he wanted to know if he should call Gatemouth and apologize to him for stealing his stuff!" Rough mixes in the ensuing days showed that they had ten tracks in the can and another session was set for August to get Johnny Sayles to perform with the band, in an effort to capture Bobby "Blue" Bland's "That Did It" and "25 Miles to Go," a hit for Edwin Starr in 1969. Kanika Kress performed only one number, Otis Redding's "These Arms of Mine," but it proved to be the album's shining moment. "Many gospel singers hit a note a little flat and bend up to the proper pitch to create ten-sion," Iglauer observed, "but Kanika would hit sharp and bend down, and it made for an unusual feel in her vocals." Roy listened, echoing her heartache with notes so tender they tugged on one's emotions. The guitarist's melodic eloquence flowered as never before and his comfort with the recording process showed. He hadn't played his feelings in the studio this well since *Second Album* a decade and a half earlier. Though some longtime fans lamented the uptown blues gloss on the Alligator ses-sions, desiring instead the Cajun picking and rawer sound of days gone by, the artist had moved on.

After a handful of outdoor summer dates, Roy and his trio took the rest of the summer off. In October they hit the road again, touring Texas and Florida, then, as winter set in, heading to Canada for Ontario and Toronto. In Toronto, Ronnie Hawkins and Robbie Robertson popped in on Roy backstage at the Horseshoe

Tavern. "After our show we walked back into the band room, a dark, dingy little room, and there was Ronnie Hawkins, Robbie Robertson and Nick Wexler, Robbie's manager at that time," Santoro said. "They were like kids, like high school buddies. Chattin', laughin', and back-slappin' and stuff. Roy was the quieter one, but the one who said the profound things. They were just tickled to see him. He would mutter things under his breath that drove them wild." Ziegler heard one story that spooked him. "They asked Roy, 'Remember the time you drove an ice pick through your left hand, on purpose, and it missed everything? Didn't fuck you up at all?'" Roy remembered. It had been pure luck he hadn't permanently injured his hand, but it was another incident that added fuel to the myths that still swirled about him. For Robbie Robertson the evening had been pure serendipity. "When I was in Toronto," Robertson later recalled, "Ronnie Hawkins said, 'Come with me, I want to take you somewhere.' He took me to this club and Roy Buchanan was playing there. This is the first time I'd seen him since [the early 1960s]. And he played just amazingly that night. It was wonderful to hear him and wonderful to see him again. It brought back to me all of the things that I realized that he did back then. Now, there are so many people to copy from, but at the time it was like taking it out of the air. [He got] a little influence here and a little influence there, but he took it 100 yards further."

SUNSET OVER BROADWAY

12

*I*n January 1988, seeking to make hay while the sun shined down with good fortune, Roy embarked on an ambitious series of tours. He wasn't getting any younger and his audiences, though loyal, weren't getting any larger. He had virtually nothing put away for retirement and, like every rock 'n' roll lifer, he had recurring thoughts of quitting the road. The guitarist began a busy year in New England. February sent him clear to Australia for a month. He returned and crisscrossed the United States and Canada. As spring, then summer rolled along, he flew from gig to gig, from Buffalo, NY, to Portland, OR; from Vancouver, BC, to Charlotte, NC; from New York City to Fort Lauderdale, FL. He worked 20 dates a month for six months in a row. He might not have been *the* hardest-working man in show business, but he was close.

Roy was booked solid from January into August when, after an outdoor festival in Guilford, CT, on August 7, there was a break for a couple weeks. According to the plan Teddy Slatus put together, Roy would resume touring in support of his *Hot Wires* album with a date with Johnny Winter at a Toronto blues festival in late August. He intended to renew his contract with Alligator and head back to Chicago that fall to work on his fourth album for the label. After that, who knew? It would be a full year indeed.

Throughout the spring and summer Roy was accompanied by Cary Ziegler on bass and vocals. Vinnie Santoro and Ray Marchica alternated on drums, as Santoro's Nashville duties with singer Rodney Crowell limited his availability. In January the band stopped at Hammerjacks in Baltimore, where a young music writer and fan, Ty Ford, caught up with Roy for an interview. There was the usual jive—"How does it feel to be a legend?"—but Roy answered Ford's questions simply and honestly. Had the audience for roots music faded during the past decade? "Yeah, well, I think

Roy considers his next move in a January 1988 appearance.

when rock 'n' roll gets exhausted, then the young people start looking for different things. In the '50s there was a blues resurgence, then [again] in the '70s, and it's happening again in the '80s. Kids are sort of restless. They're tired of drum machines, the synthesizers, and they've come across the blues. It's honest music, it's got a good beat. It always comes back around." He recalled his Pixley roots, named his influences—Mrs. Presher, Merle Travis, and Jimmy Nolen—and patiently described his style for what must have seemed like the umpteenth time. He remembered it all out loud for the tape recorder, courteously, unabashedly, more or less accurately. He did not need to mythologize this time. As for the band with Cary and Vince, Roy said, "These guys have me listening to *their* sound. I'm sort of fitting in with *their* feelings right now. We're not trying to set out to sound like anybody else. That's why I'm excited with these guys. I think we're finally getting it. I think if the music is good enough, and has the right feel you can be commercial and keep your dignity, too. We're sort of shooting for that."

What about "the all-time biggest Roy Buchanan story"—that he turned down the Stones? "That was a long time ago," Roy said. "For some people, that seems to be the big event of my life. That was almost 20 years ago. I'd hate to think that all I've ever accomplished is saying 'no' to the Rolling Stones."

How did the guitarist feel about his acceptance by black audiences? "That's a good question," Roy replied. "I *have* been played on the black stations. When I play, I don't try to copy any of the black guys. A lot of people say I'm not a 'purist.' Well, there's no such thing as a white purist. I'm playing white guys' blues, the way I feel it as a white person. I guess there's some black people who like it, and maybe some who don't."

BY THE TIME TY FORD'S interview appeared in print in *Maryland Musician* in February, Roy, Ziegler, and Santoro were en route to Australia for a month-long tour. The plan called for 19 dates in cities along Australia's eastern coast—Sydney, Melbourne, Queensland, Gold Coast, Brisbane—then a flight up north to Cairns, across the continent to Perth and Bunbury and Rockingham on the Indian Ocean side, then back east to Adelaide, and return engagements in Melbourne and Sydney. Then it was off to Christchurch, on New Zealand's South Island, for a pair of dates, and one in Auckland's Town Hall on the North Island. The promoter, Oz, acted as if the circus had come to town. "You Must Hear To Believe!" one advertisement roared. A small classified ad in one of Melbourne's dailies shouted: "THE MAN THAT TURNED DOWN THE ROLLING STONES!!!" The hype probably wasn't necessary. Australian fans already loved Roy and his rough-and-tumble roadhouse repertoire. And there was an extra, added attraction on this tour. Santoro had shaved his head smooth as a cue ball. "The day before we were leaving the country my wife and I said, 'Come on! Let's do it!'" the drummer recalled. Meticulously shorn, Santoro went to Dulles airport to meet Roy. "He looked right through me," Santoro recalled of his rendezvous with his boss. "He didn't even know it was me." When Roy and Santoro got to talking, the guitarist related the time back in Toronto in 1961 when he'd not only shaved off his hair, but his eyebrows as well. Santoro's smooth dome planted an idea in Roy's head.

Australia offered many delights and a few hazards. Geoff, the band's assigned driver, tried his best to work his way through a fifth of vodka each day while piloting, or attempting to pilot, the band's van. "That drove us over the edge," Santoro said. The Aussie audiences, however, made up for the terrifying rides. "If I had to leave this country," Ziegler vowed, "*that's* where I'd go." Even Ziegler, a rock 'n' roll veteran, was in awe of the zest for life displayed in the clubs down-under. "These people drink for a living," he exclaimed, still astonished more than ten years later. "When we walked into our first gig there was a pool of blood on the floor. The situation had the potential to blow up on you."

Hazards aside, there *were* delights along the road. At the start of the tour, on Feb. 14th, the band booked into the Corner Hotel in Melbourne to do a show. As it happened, veteran rock juggernaut Pink Floyd had played one of its elaborately staged performances in a huge stadium in town that evening. When Floyd guitarist David Gilmour caught word that Roy Buchanan himself was gigging at the Corner Hotel, he arranged for members of the band—masquerading as "the Fishermen"—to join Roy on stage after his set. They settled in for a couple of long blues jams before a crowd of perhaps 200 people. "It was a pretty wild night," Santoro recalled. "We'd done our gig and these guys walked in and said, 'Hey, we just want to jam.' It was the three of us and the three of them. We went through a couple of blues numbers and had a blast. Roy and David seemed cut from the same cloth. Gilmour had that same innate feeling for the music that Roy had. We closed up, the crowd went nuts, and then we filtered upstairs into one of the offices. That's when I found out these guys were absolute indulgers. We just hung out and did what musicians do after a show. It was good to see guys that age just rockin' like hell."

Australia may have been halfway across the globe, but the backstage temptations still found Roy; he didn't have to go looking. "He could get wacky," Santoro said. "He'd disappear into his room with someone and later he'd be walking around with no shirt on, sweatin' like a dog. We had a party once in his room where he was just lit up. I'm not going to say it was the norm, but it happened." On those occasions, Roy's generosity knew no bounds. "He'd gotten into this Australian didgeridoo music," Santoro said. "It's played on a big long tube, up to eight, ten feet long, that the aborigines blow into. It goes 'Owowowowowowow.' [Low, throbbing, strange sound.] He got hold of a tape of didgeridoo music that he was absolutely taken by. He put it in the cassette deck he carried with him, cranked it up, and all night long he'd walk up and down the halls of the hotel we were staying in. He'd put the speaker up to people's doors and turn it up and blow it into the rooms. I said, 'Why are you *doing* this?' His explanation was, 'I want to turn people on to this music.' It was like *four in the friggin' morning!* He was nuts about it. It was moving him. And he wanted it to move everyone else, too."

The Australian shows were well-received. After the Cairns Civic Centre show on February 21, reviewer Rick Rogers wrote in the local paper that the band's performance "left the sellout audience gasping . . . . Buchanan and his boys poured their hearts out in a performance that surely knocked a few bricks out of the theatre's walls." In an interview at the venue prior to the show Roy expressed a few thoughts about the future. After an upcoming US tour he intended to tour again in Europe and Japan. There was a possibility of playing in Moscow. Among current players he appreciated, he mentioned George Thorogood, Robert Cray, Stevie Ray Vaughan, Eddie Van Halen, and Joe Satriani. As for his own craft, he felt there was more yet to do. "I'm in the process of learning, trying to grow, trying to reach for something else," he said. "I see another step. Hopefully, I'll be able to get that together. 'Cuz I've started, like, hearing in my mind again. Something new. When I say different, I don't mean to change what I am. It means, be a little more versatile with the tone, don't just slap it back to the first pickup and say, 'That's it, I refuse to do anything else.' Express it in a few different ways."

As for drugs, he averred, "It was so stupid to ever do anything like that. It messed up my music. I won't hire people who get really screwed up. It's no good. I want my music to sound good. I care about my music."

"His explanations of things were pretty interesting," Santoro observed. As with Jeff Ganz before him, he heard Roy tout the benefits of sobriety without walking the walk. When it came to music Santoro could appreciate Roy's new direction. "It's true. You go through changes. That's a fact. That extended to his playing and his equipment. Roy started using a Roland JC 120 guitar amp when we worked together. He could turn it up and he was happy with the sound. Historically he had been a Fender guy. Musically, Roy grew tired of 'The Messiah,' 'Hey Joe,' and his other early stuff. He was chameleon-like in that sometimes he *did* want to do that stuff. He'd drop back and punt. He was such a crowd-pleaser that if he sensed people wanted to hear it, he'd play it. But he got a big charge out of doing stuff like 'Down by the River' and the Led Zeppelin stuff. We did that rock 'n' roll stuff because *he* liked to do it. Cary and I weren't going to influence what he wanted to play. We'd come up with ideas, and if he felt like playing it, we did it."

AFTER THE AUSTRALIAN TOUR Roy took the plunge and shaved his head like Santoro's. Roy was already badly balding and he'd been fashioning what was left into a face-saving comb-over for years. There might have been other factors in his decision to go with the smooth look. The opinions of those who claim to know are evenly divided: Some say it was simply a reaction to impending baldness, others insist it was part of a midlife crisis, or an effort to shame himself into staying straight. "There was some of [the latter] going on," Santoro said. "Maybe he needed a little impetus, and maybe this was it. When he finally did it, the band must have looked pretty interesting—two shaved guys, one unshaved guy."

In March John Adams had occasion to visit DC and he dropped in on Roy and Judy in Reston. The trio went out for dinner in the country. "While I was taken aback by the shaved head, I sensed something deeply wrong with Roy," Adams said. "Despite an attempt to be himself, he seemed distant, troubled. He had never been the same since his daughter's baby's death."

The previous November, Roy had accepted an invitation from Adams to play guitar on *Shake, Rattle, and Roll,* a television film tribute to old-time rockers such as Jerry Lee Lewis, Ben E. King, Chubby Checker, the Shirelles and, not incidentally, Roy Buchanan. Roy was happy to do anything to repay Adams for his many kindnesses. The producer brought Roy to Nashville's Opryland television studios for several days of filming. "The day before we taped *Shake, Rattle, and Roll,* I got a phone call from Roy. He was calm, but in the background Judy was screaming. Roy's youngest daughter's baby had died. Crib death. I had to take them to the airport. Roy said, 'I'll come back.' He did, the next day, and he was magnificent, very controlled. But I don't think he ever recovered from that. Somehow he blamed himself for the infant's death."

In spring Roy's trio opened for a new incarnation of the Band on a brief tour that took them all through New England and across Canada. The tour featured three of the five original Band members, Levon Helm, Rick Danko, and Garth Hudson. Richard Manuel was dead and Robbie Robertson had quit long ago. Guitarist Jim Weider, a native of Woodstock, NY, and student of the great American roots players like Roy, had recently joined the Band.

Roy, Ziegler, and Santoro—"two shaved guys, one unshaved guy"—delivered their high-energy set, with Roy weaving in his share of zingers and mind-boggling blues screams, making sure everyone knew that middle-aged fogeys could rock, too. The Band rocked for an hour, then invited Roy back onstage for a little good time boogie, a chance for everyone to strut their stuff. The Band's deep songbook provided plenty of fodder for a barn-burning. As the evening grew long the ensemble might close out with a raucous, rhythmic version of the vintage Johnny Otis hit, "Willie and the Hand Jive." It had been mother's milk to them all for 30 years and they gave it everything, with Rick Danko on his fretless bass beaming and bouncing, Levon Helm belting out the vocals from his position behind the drums, and the professor, Garth Hudson, towering over the Hammond B-3 at the back of the stage. Roy and Jim Weider traded Tele licks until the night grew old.

Playing the same bill was like old-home week for the older players. For Weider, it was a chance to hang out with someone who'd pioneered the Telecaster's role in rock 'n' roll. When he met up with Roy for the first time on that spring tour with the Band, Weider had questions. He asked Roy whether he had indeed taught Robbie Robertson how to play "pinch" harmonics. "I showed him the *wrong* way," Roy joked. Roy didn't mind telling a few stories from the old days, some of them even true. In the course of conversation, Roy expressed curiosity about Richard Manuel's death. "I told him Richard had been doing really great," Weider said. "He had been getting his solo trip together and had a record coming up. Roy was friends with the Band, with all of us, but especially the older guys, with Richard. So he was curious about Richard's death. 'Well, what did he do? How did he do it?'" Roy demanded details, and he got them.

THAT SPRING ROY was playing almost exclusively with a new Telecaster-style guitar custom made by the Fritz Brothers of Mobile, AL. Although he was known for the battered '53 Tele he no longer took on the road, Roy told one interviewer in May, "My goal is to show people they can make new ones better than the old ones."

Earlier that spring, Steve Bloom, a writer for *Guitar World* magazine, caught up with Roy at New York's Henry Hudson Hotel on 57th Street. Roy had just polished off a meatball sandwich and was getting ready to take his obligatory nap prior to his appearance that night at the Lone Star Cafe. In Bloom's article, published in June and titled, "A Guitar Hero Ain't Nothin' But a Sandwich," the guitarist talked about his enthusiasm for his new sound. "Some people say that Roy Buchanan doesn't sound like he did when he was playing the old Telecaster," he said. "They don't

Roy in Cincinnati in 1988.

stop to think that I'm not *trying* to sound like I did with my old Tele. I'm trying to sound new and refreshed. I used the old Tele for a long time and everyone sort of got to expect it. But I can get the old Tele sound out of the new one. It's just that I don't want that sound anymore. I think I've pretty much exhausted what I can get out of that old Tele sound."

"Right now I'm alternating between a new Telecaster, a Gibson Les Paul, and a custom-built [Fritz Brothers] guitar," he continued. "The custom has EMG pickups, the body's a copy of a Tele and so is the neck, except for the headstock . . . . You can take any of my new guitars and get sounds out of them that you can't start to get out of an old Tele. For instance, you have more of a selection of pickups as far as the toggle switches go, or you can use both pickups, and you can slam it forward from rhythm to lead without losing volume." "I like a variety of necks," he added. "On my Les Paul I have a real chunky neck. I have a couple of Teles with chunky necks and a couple with thin ones. On the last album [*Hot Wires*] I used the ones with the big necks, so I'm sort of used to it right now. Maybe three months from now I'll come back to liking a thin neck again. A lot of people just want to have one guitar. I think they're cheating themselves. Why not have the best of both worlds?"

Roy's enthusiasm for new guitars and new sounds seemed to reflect a generally positive outlook. Many years later, Santoro mused: "I wasn't so close to him that I knew his thoughts. But there was no difference to Roy between the beginning of my stint with him in February 1987 and the end of my stint with him in June 1988. He seemed to be enjoying doing what he was doing. I never saw a depressive state in the guy." When Alan Scheflin caught up with Roy in June in San Francisco, the attorney found the guitarist excited over some new material he'd written. He was eager to return to the studio, perhaps as early as September. "We had a good talk," Scheflin said later. "In general, his spirits were high." But, the attorney recalled, the death of Roy's granddaughter hurt him deeply. Sometime that spring Roy and his trio stopped in Chicago to play a gig and Dick Shurman caught up with them. "Roy talked to me a long time about music being a healing force and that that was what he wanted to do, use his music to 'heal the world.' He wanted his music to have that religious power."

ROY HAD IDEAS. He mentioned to numerous people that he wanted to record an all-instrumental album when he returned to Chicago that fall. He'd also remarked to Cary Ziegler that he might pursue recording a live album, perhaps another recorded in Japan. For Iglauer and Shurman at Alligator, nothing was settled except that they would be working together again soon. "We all had this thing about Roy and Jeff Beck," Shurman said later. The idea was inspired in part by the guest spot that the flamboyant guitar star, Stevie Ray Vaughan, had played on his mentor Lonnie Mack's 1985 Alligator album, *Strike Like Lightning*. "If they [Roy and Jeff Beck] were both in Chicago at the same time we wanted to record them, but it never happened.

After we did the third one, Roy called me and went into this real fervent thing about how he *really* wanted to record with Les Paul, which certainly would have been interesting. Who can say whether a fourth Alligator LP would have been an instrumental one or not?" Shurman added. "We also talked about bringing in some outside, name producer for a fresh approach." One issue was the gap between the sound and repertoire achieved on the Alligator recordings and Roy's road show. "There *was* a contrast between what he was recording and what he could, or would, play live," Shurman said. "We knew it would be better for his career to make him a record that he could replicate more easily on stage."

The producers had just gotten feedback on their last effort in the form of mixed reviews for *Hot Wires*. It wasn't easy to pigeonhole the Alligator albums. *Down Beat*, with its jazz and blues sensibilities, suggested that *Dancing on the Edge*, with Roy's guitar and Delbert McClinton's vocals, was "a hard act to follow. But *Hot Wires* manages to hold its own, and then some . . . .Buchanan's virtuoso licks are less overtly psychedelic than on *Dancing*, but they're still mind-boggling, making up in searing intensity and quirky invention what they lack in down-home feeling." *Guitar Player* offered a less confident endorsement. "Blues purists will likely be disconcerted with the spacey, flanged licks that pepper the opening, 'High Wire,' and with Roy's vocal style (about as bluesy as Lou Reed) on 'Goose Grease.' But, contrary to Alligator Records' packaging, Buchanan is not a blues guitarist—which is not to say he isn't bluesy and isn't a hell of a guitar stylist. When he plays it straight, Buchanan does a more than passable job, but he's at his best when he twists the form around his own eccentric personality, as on 'Country Boogie.' Soul covers such as Edwin Starr's '25 Miles' seem pointless; it would be nice to hear more of Buchanan's country/Cajun side next time."

In January and again in March Roy entered Streeterville's studios to record a number of tracks in support of a French film titled *Saxo*. The film traced the fictional story of a young, guitar-playing female singer, and in January Roy and Kanika Kress, his *Hot Wires* vocalist, got the call to record a half dozen songs for the soundtrack. Though Kress indeed sang and played guitar, her Saxo role was to stand in for blues legend Etta James. As for Roy, the project seemed to signify that he'd finally dropped his long-standing resistance to working on other people's projects, opening a world of possibilities. In late March, Roy joined his old Snakestretchers compadre, drummer Marc Fisher, at the Crossroads in Bladensburg, MD, to record a few easy-going instrumental tracks to promote his new Fritz Brothers Bluesmaster guitar.

Master guitar craftsman Roger Fritz planned to create models in a wide variety of categories: Roy Buchanan Acoustic-Electric, Roy Buchanan Lapmaster Lap Steel, Roy Buchanan Deluxe, Roy Buchanan Custom, and a Bluesmaster Model. The Bluesmaster, naturally, was Roy's chosen model. Roger Fritz immediately sent one of the first production Bluesmasters to former Beatle George Harrison, to see if he'd like it and, perhaps, say so. In fact, Harrison's actions spoke louder than words: In 1991 he took the guitar on a tour of Japan.

APRIL, MAY, JUNE, AND JULY were spent crisscrossing the continent, from Raoul's Roadside Attraction in Portland, ME, to the Commodore Ballroom in Vancouver, BC, from the Coach House in San Juan Capistrano, CA, to the Musician's Exchange in Fort Lauderdale, FL—with stops at the Merry Widow Cafe in Bridgeport, CT, the Little Bear in Evergreen, CO, the Stephen Talk House in Amagansett, NY, the Double Door Inn in Charlotte, NC, and Nightstages in Cambridge, MA. According to his standard contract, Roy required only a fee, a little information, a couple cases of beer, a deli platter, towels—his requests were simple and modest. In return he'd bring down the house and sell a *lot* of booze. Have guitar, will travel.

Marc Fisher caught up with Roy at the Tobacco Road club in Miami on July 21, and he was invited on stage to add maracas. Fisher made the gig at the Musician's Exchange in Fort Lauderdale the following night as well. That night Ziegler called attention to Roy's immaculately shaven head. "Roy looks good, doesn't he?" The crowd applauded, Roy grinned. As for Roy's skills, Fisher remarked, a decade later, "He was fabulous. A little worn from touring." As for Roy's occasionally erratic behavior on that stretch of the tour, Fisher had seen it all before. "Roy never got disappointed about falling off the wagon. It didn't bother him." Still, *something* bothered him. On July 13 he stopped at home to see Judy, and to see his psychiatrist, who prescribed 25 tablets of the antidepressant Elavil, in 50-milligram form. "Take as directed," the label intoned. "Do Not Drink Alcohol." Roy finished his July tour of the Northeast and then took a week off before his outdoor gig at the Guilford Fairgrounds in Connecticut. On August 3, Roy visited his psychiatrist again, who this time prescribed the anti-anxiety drug Inderal, in 20-milligram doses. Judy spoke with the psychiatrist, who said he thought Roy was "doing great." They postponed making another appointment, but agreed that Judy would nail one down for September, after Labor Day. The psychiatrist also suggested that Roy see his general practitioner for a complete physical.

THE GUILFORD SHOW would be staged in the leafy country ten miles east of New Haven. Sponsored by the Guilford Police Union, the program was advertised as "Guitar Wars." The bill offered the locally based funk- and soul-driven Shaboo All-Stars with Matt "Guitar" Murphy as featured guest. Kal David and his Gibson Firebird guitar would lead the Fabulous Rhinestones. The program was set to begin about 2 p.m. and, in the late afternoon, Roy would close the show.

Roy had become dissatisfied with a string of pickup drummers and he wanted a tight band for the outdoor show, so a few days prior to the gig he called his old friend and former drummer, Tommy Hambridge. Tommy and his band were in Bangor, ME, on a three-day run when the phone rang. Roy told Tommy he needed him for an upcoming show in Connecticut on Sunday. Tommy had a Thursday, Friday, and Saturday night engagement in Bangor. As Hambridge later recalled, "I said, 'It's impossible to do it.' He said, 'Whatever you have to do. Fly into Hartford and I'll pick you up.' I said, 'I'm not sure I can do this.' He said, 'Please? Just do this.' I said,

'All right. I'll work it out.' So I played that last night in Bangor, took my snare and drum stick bag to the Bangor airport and slept in the airport so I could catch the very first flight the next day at 6 a.m. I jumped a few planes, and ended up in Hartford. Roy showed up in a white stretch limousine, courtesy of the promoter, with Cary Ziegler and John Olds. We went to Guilford and checked into a hotel. I remember sitting on the bed in the hotel room. Roy's got his guitar out, goin' 'I can't wait to play.' I said, 'I can't wait either. What are we going to do?' He said, 'We'll do *this*. Do you want to do *that*?' I'm like, 'Great!' We were totally psyched. He was in a good frame of mind. The promoter had a huge spread of lobster, corn, and barbecue waiting for us at the show, under a tent. I was starvin'! So we went over and I was the second to last one out of the limo. Roy grabs me by the arm and says, 'Hey Tommy, let's go find ourselves a good cheese steak sandwich.' I said, 'Roy! I'm exhausted, I'm starvin'. Look at this feast they have for us! It's free! It's ours!' He said, 'Let's just go to McDonald's or something. We can hang out and talk.' I said, 'Roy, are you *crazy?!*' So I went in and hit the buffet and he stayed in the limo, which was air-conditioned. Later, I thought, 'Maybe he just wanted to talk. Maybe he had nobody to talk to. I mean, we were real good friends. We hadn't seen each other in a while. But off he went and came back with a meatball sub, or something. That was one of the great things about Roy. Promoters would take us to the swankiest restaurant in town and we'd order filet mignon and Roy would ask for a meatball sandwich. Anyway, we parked the limo next to the stage and stayed in it. It was cold! Matt 'Guitar' Murphy was on, playin' with the Shaboo All-Stars. People would come up to the passenger side window where Roy was and talk."

Before taking the stage, Kal David had a chance to pop into the air-conditioned luxury of the white limousine and talk to Roy, guitar player to guitar player. "We spoke about the fact that he had just come out with the 'Roy Buchanan Bluesmaster.' He had a couple of them sitting in the car there and we were checkin' 'em out," David said. "They were beautiful and he was really excited. He had just shaved his head, so obviously he was having some sort of identity crisis or something. I shared with him that I really enjoyed his work with Bobby Gregg, on a record called 'The Jam.' And that a lot of guys from my neck of the woods in Chicago—all the guitar players—picked up on 'The Jam.' We all played it at our gigs. You know the intro to that thing is pretty different and kind of hard to play until you master it. It's like a Chet Atkins thing. It was Roy's thing. I told him that I had appreciated his work over the years, and that I owned some of his records. He was very warm and friendly, just a sweetheart. He was so excited about these guitars that he couldn't wait for me to try one. He played great and I'm glad I had a chance to talk to him. He had a way to read a crowd, and he did it the way they wanted it."

David Foster, singer for the Shaboo All-Stars, had booked Roy many times into the Shaboo Inn in Mansfield, CT. He knew his friend Joe Lemieux would enjoy the show so he gave him a stage pass. That gave Lemieux a chance to take pictures from directly in front of the stage. "The people were there to see Roy," Lemieux said. "We were just in awe of his playing. He was definitely the highlight of the day. And he seemed pretty at ease."

Roy OPENED with his favorite warm-up, "Short Fuse." "It was reckless abandon," according to Hambridge. "He told the crowd, 'We're going to rock your brains out.' I lit up. I was thinking, '*This* is going to be *nuts!*' And it was incredible. The place was in a frenzy." Roy followed with the good-natured "Country Boy," then he lit into Link Wray's "Jack the Ripper," a tour-de-force of blazing guitar. "All right," Roy said, "Right now we're going to feature Cary on vocals on one called 'Susie Q.'" Cary Ziegler is no Dale Hawkins, but the spirit was alive and when it came time for the guitar break, Roy gave another trademark demonstration of controlled fury. Then he unleashed the sinister bass line and mind-twisting contrary bends that propelled "Peter Gunn," the private eye theme turned into science fiction. With the band amplified to intergalactic levels Roy mercilessly scraped his bass strings and sent the signal through a delay pedal, which pushed the edgy, uptempo song over the top. When everyone had recovered, Ziegler gave a slow, sensitive reading of Neil Young's "Down by the River." Roy always played this song simply and with feeling. It was just the sort of tragic ballad to draw out his most hypnotic playing, and that afternoon in Guilford was no exception. As the last notes faded, the crowd, mesmerized, was notably slow to respond. But this was a party, so Roy let fly with Dave Whitehill's patented cascade of pull-offs to introduce the rollicking good-time shuffle known as "Beer Drinkin' Woman."

The afternoon passed as in a dream. Roy conjured up the haunting, cello-like volume swells of "When a Guitar Plays the Blues," and his guitar's plaintive cries slipped across the park, rippling through the thousand or so people standing by the stage or laid out on blankets in the green grass. After lighting up the park with crazy licks at the highest volumes, Roy launched into an extended excursion into the realm of pure sound. To release the sonic tension he'd created, Roy segued into the easy groove of Bill Doggett's "Honky Tonk," then handed the vocals over to Hambridge, who launched into "Good Golly Miss Molly"—just good-time party music— until Roy grabbed back the lead with the menacing sounds of Booker T. & the MG's "Green Onions." A minute later, Roy signaled Hambridge to take a solo and the guitarist sauntered over to the edge of the stage to get a light for his cigarette. Walt Albert, who had gone to the show with David Foster and Joe Lemieux, was hanging out to one side of the makeshift stage. As Hambridge soloed, Roy stepped over. "He bummed a light off me," Albert recalled. "He was really cool. We were just rappin', shootin' the bull. He was real down to Earth." Lemieux, standing in front of the stage, snapped a picture of the two. Then Roy stepped back to center stage and brought Cary Ziegler's slap bass solo back into the song's driving melody. "Wonderful applause," Roy gushed, as the crowd leapt to its feet yet again. "We've had a request for some Jimi Hendrix," Roy acknowledged. With that he rocked into "Hey Joe" in a more impatient tempo than the days of old. As he rolled his strings and brought the song to a close he gently asked the crowd, "You want some more of that stuff?" "Yeah!" came the response. Suddenly, Roy roared disconcertingly into the microphone: "GIMME SOME MORE!! *I WANT SOME MORE!!*" With that, the band rocked into "Purple Haze." Ziegler intoned the lyrics—"Feelin' funny, but I don't know why"—and the audience yelled back without skipping a beat, "'Scuse me, while I kiss the sky!" The call-and-response on Hendrix's 1967 hit single was mother's milk to this crowd. Roy was feeling the music and he crafted leads, then feedback, harmonics, and a grand cacophony that pushed the song beyond recognition before bringing it to a close. "Thank you," Roy grinned. "Now we'd like to do one of our older ones." With that he hit the stately signature lines to "The Messiah" theme and gave a spine-tingling reading, with his new Telecaster emitting forlorn cries. As Roy delivered the soulful crescendo at song's end, the guitar let out another scream before ending on a poignant note. "God bless you. Goodnight. I love you." Roy moved away from the microphone and stepped off the back of the stage. Of course, this wasn't a nightclub, and everyone could see Roy chatting with fans behind the stage's three-foot risers. Roy took a minute to cool off in his air-conditioned limo, parked stage-side. Then he re-emerged to play an encore, a fierce rendition of "Sunshine of Your Love." "This one's for all you old hippies out there," he joked. When the thunderous riffs of "Sunshine" faded, Roy launched into a knock-down, drag-out blues, "Drownin' on Dry Land."

I'm goin' down
Yeah, my nose is in the sand
A dark cloud just came over me
And I feel like I'm drownin' on dry land

The Tele screamed an anguished scream while Ziegler and Hambridge held down a virile bottom end. "Good night. Take care of yourself. Love ya," Roy murmured. Then he was gone.

"WE ALL HAD TO GO BACK to Hartford to catch a flight, under a time crunch," Hambridge recalled. "We did the encore, got offstage, it was beautiful. We were on a high. The sun was blazing. We got in the limo. People were just swarmin' around. Cary, me, Roy, John Olds, and the driver. People were walking away from the site with their coolers. They're banging on the windows. 'Hey! It's Roy Buchanan! Come on, party with us!' Roy wanted a beer, and perhaps something else. The last time I saw Roy, he got out of the limo, and John got out with him. They were going to take another car, or something. Cary and I looked at each other. We were going to miss our flights. Cary says, 'We gotta go, man.' The last thing Roy said to me was, 'Can you do Poughkeepsie in a couple weekends? I got a show with Johnny Winter.' I said, 'Absolutely!' I gave Roy a hug as he got out. It was festive, and he was going to hang with the people. Roy was up, man, he was *up*. He wanted to stay and party. My vision is of him just disappearing into the crowd."

*By summer 1988 Roy sported the cue ball look. Here he works
his new Roy Buchanan Bluesmaster at the Guilford Fairgrounds
in Connecticut on Aug. 7, 1988.*

AFTER THE SPECTACULAR success at Guilford and the exchange of energy with the audience—and the opportunity to mingle with admiring fans—home life might have seemed a bit mundane. Strumming his guitar, smoking a stogie, and, to be honest, drinking were his favorite pastimes. On Sunday, August 14, Roy went to the grocery store, then he went to the basement to make demo tapes of his latest musical musings. That morning he wrote something with a classical theme and he made Judy come down and listen to it. Judy told him she was proud of him. About 12:30 p.m. he took the couple's car to the Fair Oaks Mall. He thought he'd select a few cigars, Judy wanted some hairspray, and he could have a few cold ones. Sometime that afternoon he arrived at Ruby Tuesday's restaurant and bar and proceeded to get a buzz on. As usual, one beer led to another.

About 9:20 p.m., Judy later recalled, Roy arrived back at 2325 Harleyford Court accompanied by a man she had never met before. Roy seemed to be in a good mood, if somewhat trashed. His companion, however, seemed more than drunk. Something about his intoxication—"on coke or something," she suggested—bothered her. The two men went downstairs to the room where Roy kept his guitars and his tapes.

In the old days it had not been unusual for Roy to bring home strangers. Since they'd moved from the country into the Reston town home, such behavior was rare—although Roy continued to give out his phone number to "friends he'd never met," according to Dave Whitehill. Judy simply changed it with some frequency. Judy eventually followed the celebrants downstairs and asked the stranger to leave. She felt that, in his noncommittal response, he refused her. "I thought, 'Well, maybe the police can make him leave.' So I called the police to see what could be done about getting him out. One thing led to another on the phone. The woman said, 'How did this stranger get in there?' And I said, 'My husband let him in.' And they said, 'Well, we can't make him leave. Have they been drinking?' One question after another. So then my littlest, [Matthew] who was three-years-old then, went down and told Roy I was on the phone to the police." Roy charged up to the kitchen on the main floor and grabbed the phone out of Judy's hand, pulling the cord out of the wall. The Fairfax County dispatcher had gotten the message, however, that all was not well at 2325 Harleyford Court. A potential domestic disturbance was under way, and at least two officers were sent to respond.

"Just about that time I realized that person was downstairs by himself," Judy told writer Bill Milkowski a year later. "I sort of got around Roy and went downstairs—he was always paranoid about people stealing tapes—but I couldn't find him." Judy ran back up the stairs and, sensing no one on the first floor, looked out the front door. The stranger was driving away slowly in a dark-colored car, with his lights off. Judy couldn't read the license plate. "Roy brushed by me and said he was going," she said. "He went up towards the road, the main road [Glade Drive]. I had the feeling he thought this guy was gonna wait for him or something. I guess that's where the police picked Roy up—down the street."

Roy had walked, or stumbled, a hundred feet to Charter House Circle and turned right. A minute later he reached the gently sinuous Glade Drive and, instinctively, he turned right and headed west along the sidewalk. Roy negotiated a path overhung by maples, oaks, and elms, barely rustling in the still night.

AT 2325 HARLEYFORD COURT, Judy thought it was probably about 9:45 p.m. when two Fairfax police officers arrived at her door. The official incident report states that the "call timing" actually was 10:40 p.m.—an hour later than Judy thought. Roy had been arrested near the home at about that time. Officers Charles Ponsart and Shawn Meban made contact with Judy. Officer Meban, a female, came inside and asked questions while Officer Ponsart stayed outside. "I figured he was looking for Roy," Judy recalled to Milkowski. Officer Ponsart soon re-entered the Roy town home and told Judy they'd found Roy. Officer Meban asked Judy if she wanted Roy home. "I said I was a little bit leery of him and that they could take him to one of our children's homes, or to a hotel, like the year before," she recalled. The officers got up to leave and Judy rushed after them. "I said, 'Lemme go out and talk to him before you leave.' They said, 'He's already in transit.' It took a minute for that to dawn on me, what that meant. 'In transit?' How can he be in transit? I thought he got in the car with you?' Officer Ponsart said, 'No. One of our backups picked him up.' That's when I told them, 'Well, be sure to radio them and tell them that he's Roy Buchanan and that I want him watched.' I told Officer Meban that he was famous, but she said she'd never heard of him. I also told her he was under a doctor's care. They assured me that he would be in a cell with 15 to 20 other people in front of a sergeant's desk. They assured me I didn't have to worry."

To this day the Fairfax County Sheriff's Department will not release the names of the two officers who served as backup to Ponsart and Meban that night. The two unidentified officers arrested Roy Buchanan for public drunkenness and headed for the Fairfax County Adult Detention Center, less than ten miles south. The peace officers might have headed west on Glade Drive to reach the well-lit and very public Reston Parkway, where they could turn left and head south. Along that stretch, Reston Parkway segues into Lawyers Road, then into West Ox Road. West Ox Road runs into Highway 50, the Lee-Jackson Memorial Highway, which cuts southeast to Chain Bridge Road, where a quick jag south gets one to the Fairfax County Adult Detention Center—the county jail. Alternatively, had the peace officers had any reason to take a back route, they could have left the Reston Parkway immediately and made a jog east to Fox Mill Road, a two-lane blacktop that winds through a well-wooded residential area where the houses are set back 50 yards and more from the road. Fox Mill Road winds and twists and the rolling terrain adds a bit of roller-coaster ride to the drive. The road snakes through Fox Mill District Park and the Little Difficult Run Stream Valley Park, then passes Scott Crossfield Elementary School and the Vale Valley Farms. A quick dogleg and the road becomes Waples Mill Road and then the Lee-Jackson Memorial Highway. The distance along this more secluded route is nine miles and the elapsed time, driving leisurely but steadily, is about 20 minutes at the outside—a bit longer than the well-lit, more direct route. Upon arrival at the Fairfax County Adult Detention Center, the police cruiser and its alleged miscreant eased down a recessed driveway that led to electronically controlled garage doors. The driver stated his or her business and the doors opened, allowing access to a secure, underground reception area. On the left, behind windows, sat three magistrates, who processed incoming arrestees. To the right, also behind glass, sat a deputy who controlled the garage doors and the cameras that swept the area. The peace officers had to disembark with their arrestee here, file past the magistrates, and enter the jail through a door made of vertical bars. Presumably, several magistrates and a deputy witnessed the officers arriving with Roy at—according to the police—10:45 p.m. Inside the barred door, deputies sat at desks on the right. Chief Deputy Carl Peed later told Roy's brother, J.D., that, according to witnesses, Roy was "talkative to the deputies and admitted having had too much too drink." Directly across from the deputies in charge of booking prisoners are two large holding cells where intoxicated arrestees are held until processed—the drunk tank that Officer Ponsart had suggested to Judy her husband would occupy. For some reason, Roy was escorted to the receiving cells. The cells are arranged on the inside and outside of a U-shaped floor plan. Cells alternate, so that a prisoner looking out through the vertical slit in the cell door, or the horizontal slot through which food is passed, would see only a blank wall. Each cell is ten feet by eight and a half feet. On one wall a concrete bunk covered by a mattress extends two feet off the ground. In a corner is a stainless steel toilet and sink. According to those who have seen the cells, they have no windows. The doors are solid steel but for an 18-inch-high vertical slit "window" at chest height to serve observers, and a horizontal slot covered by a one-inch mesh screen for passing meals and paperwork. The cells are well-lit by a bright, fluorescent bulb on a high ceiling, perhaps 16 feet up, covered by a wire security housing. The walls are smooth. The climate is controlled so that, despite the fetid August night outside, the cells in summer are not too warm.

After booking, Roy was taken to receiving cell R-45. The time, according to the police, was between 10:50 and 10:55 p.m. If police statements of time are accurate, no more than 20 minutes had passed after Roy's arrest on Glade Drive. If Judy's time frame is correct, Roy reached the receiving cell about an hour after his arrest.

A subsequent incident report stated that Roy had been observed in his cell at 10:53 p.m. A "floor check"—when deputies visually check on prisoners in the receiving cells—at 11:05 p.m. that night purportedly found that all was normal. But at 11:16, according to the police, Roy was found hanging by his T-shirt, which they said he had tied around his neck and then looped through the one-inch grate in the cell door's horizontal slot. Investigators subsequently suggested that Roy had dropped himself hard to the ground but been suspended by four to five inches, resulting in a severe ligature to his larynx, essentially crushing it, choking himself. The police managed to take a number of Polaroid photographs of Roy at the scene before he was taken to a nearby emergency medical facility. The police reported that deputies and medical personnel immediately started cardiopulmonary resuscitation. A rescue squad from the Fairfax Fire Department arrived at 11:23 p.m. and continued CPR while the medics transported Roy to an emergency room at Access of Fairfax, a facility three blocks away operated by the Fairfax hospital system. Roy, 48 years old, was pronounced dead on arrival at one minute before midnight.

You know the light used to shine bright,
Yeah, well, now the light is gone

When Officers Meban and Ponsart left the Buchanan residence it must have been nearly 11 p.m. Not long after, Judy was in the dining room when she was struck by fear. "It was as if somebody was watching me," she said later to Bill Milkowski. "I turned around, but I didn't see anybody. Something inside me said, 'It's Roy.' And all of a sudden I got really panicky, so I ran back upstairs and tried to call everybody, and I couldn't get anybody."

John Olds returned her call about 1 a.m. Judy explained that Roy had been taken to jail on a public intoxication charge. "John, they've arrested Roy and I don't wanna have to deal with him," John heard her say. "Can you pick him up?" John was used to the tone of the request. "I was the guy who came to their house and took her husband away for weeks on end," he later recalled. John dutifully called the Fairfax County Detention Center a little past 1 a.m. and was transferred several times until someone told him they'd have to call him back. Olds called again. "I said, 'Look, can I come by and pick up Roy Buchanan?' They put me through to the sergeant or captain or somebody in charge, and he said, 'Mr. Buchanan has expired in jail.'" John called Judy, who'd just had another visit from the police. This time the officers didn't have any questions. They sat Judy down and broke the news of Roy's death. Meanwhile the Buchanans' daughter, Jenny, who lived nearby, had come to the town home. Judy's sister, Doris, and her husband, the late Harold Lowder—the man who'd introduced Roy to the audience at Carnegie Hall 16 years earlier—traveled to Reston from nearby Silver Spring and stayed until morning. At daybreak they all drove to the morgue, where they were kept waiting. The doctors were performing an autopsy, they were told. That disturbed Judy, because she had not authorized one. Then they allowed her to view her husband's body from behind a glass window. "We couldn't see anything, just his face," she said later. "They had his head all wrapped up, his neck wrapped up. All you could see was his face. And I could see that his nose had been bleeding and I asked them about that and they said that was normal from a hanging." Asked later if she believed the police's version of events, she said, "Cover-up? I'm sure it is. For all I know he could've resisted arrest and they could've done a choke hold on him." Roy left behind Judy, seven children, and five grandchildren.

AN AUTOPSY—the examination of a body and analysis of its contents to establish the cause and circumstances of death—was established procedure for the death of a prisoner in police custody in Fairfax County. Two doctors conducted the exam beginning at 8:30 a.m., about the time Judy arrived to ascertain that her husband indeed was dead. The autopsy report indicated no sign of trauma to the heart, lungs, liver, spleen, gastrointestinal tract, pancreas, kidneys, skeletal system, scalp or skull. The report noted a "depressed skin furrow on anterior and left side of neck." The cause of death was listed as "HANGING." The two doctors did not sign and submit their report until August 29. A pharmacist performed toxicology work on Roy's body fluids. His blood alcohol level registered .20, a forensic confirmation that Roy had been legally drunk and probably, despite practice, quite intoxicated. The pharmacological report indicated the absence of morphine, cocaine, or other illegal drugs in his system.

JUDY STEADFASTLY rejected the official cause of Roy's death and she kept him in an above-ground vault while she explored legal and forensic avenues to justice. Should he be buried, the body would decay, forensic evidence would be lost, and the cost of exhumation would be prohibitive. Also, Roy had expressed to Judy a fear of being buried below ground and had asked to be placed in a mausoleum. Several days after his death, Judy had a burial service. The Money and King Funeral Home in nearby Vienna arranged for the ceremony. At the funeral at Columbia Gardens Cemetery in Arlington, VA, a knot of Roy's closest colleagues had assembled: Judy and the children, now all in their 20s, John Olds, Jeff Ganz, Cary Ziegler, Dave Whitehill, Elwood Brown, Teddy Slatus. Whitehill in particular had a hard time with the proceedings. Roy's former band mates carried the heavy coffin to the vault where the body would reside until decisions were made, or time ran out.

"It was a closed coffin," Cary Ziegler said later. "Judy opened it up for the band and all the close friends to see. It was obvious that he'd had his head bashed in. There were bruises on his head. I saw them. They were there. There's no question. Roy had always said, if he 'ever got caught again, he's fightin' his way out.' There's also no question he probably provoked it." Jeff Ganz also saw injuries. "I was one of Roy's pallbearers. He did have welts on his head." Dave Whitehill was repulsed by the entire proceeding. "The funeral was really suspicious. Roy had shaved his head a few months before that and you could see bruises on his head. It was obvious that he was mishandled by somebody."

A YEAR LATER, finances forced Judy to make a decision—mausoleums, especially for two, were beyond her means. Though she'd tried to find legal and financial help and moral support in her drive to answer unanswered questions, too little arrived to stem the tide of events. After a year of holding out, Judy had Roy's body moved from the vault to a grave on Azalea Avenue, Section C, in Columbia Gardens Cemetery in Arlington.

Meanwhile, the statute of limitations on wrongful death suits elapsed. Soon after Roy's death, Judy had hired an attorney to look into legal options. But the attorney backed away as it became clear the case had too many shaky elements, including Roy's history of excess and the incident in Loudoun County on New Year's Day, 1980, that police had alleged was a suicide attempt. A second attorney later reached the same conclusion. Judy also looked into obtaining the services of a forensic pathologist, but she could not pay the fee of many thousands of dollars.

The official story of Roy's death does have nagging discrepancies. Why the difference between Judy's sense of the hour on August 14—about 9:45 p.m.—and the police's, which was an hour later? Was that a mere mistake on Judy's part? Everyone who knew him predicted that Roy, drunk, would not be civil in dealing with law enforcement officers. Was he really jovial in the booking room, as the police spokesman reported? Or was he brought in already injured? The legacy of police misconduct in America's cities is shameful and pervasive, and in some places it has been found to be more the norm than the exception. Yet it is difficult to believe that two officers, several magistrates and deputies, and doctors performing an autopsy could witness foul play and remain silent for more than a decade. Conversely, fairness to Roy makes it perhaps equally difficult to believe that a man five feet, ten inches tall, weighing 220 pounds, could be sloppy drunk and jovial, then ten minutes later manage to tie a noose around his neck from his T-shirt, thread it through the grate on a chest-high window in his cell door, knot it, and drop himself to the ground, effectively crushing his windpipe. What about the bruises Roy's band mates observed on his head? "I've had my share of run-ins with the law," Whitehill said. "I've had the displeasure of being caught in a chokehold. And I've heard the inside deal on coverups: 'Accidental asphyxiation' from chokeholds becomes a 'hanging suicide.'"

THE STAKES IN Roy Buchanan's case remain high, all these years after his death. At the very least, the Fairfax County Sheriff's Office has not provided full information on the incident, including the names of the two officers who took Roy to jail, and the results of its own internal investigation into Roy's death. Without that full disclosure, doubts will always linger as to the truth of the incident that ended Roy Buchanan's life.

IN THE ABSENCE of convincing evidence for any one of several unsavory scenarios, the sentiments of Roy's family and friends and colleagues breaks evenly down the middle. Half are convinced he took his own life, and half are certain he could never have done it. The symmetry to these disparate views is disquieting.

"He was a sweet and wonderful guy and a brilliant guitarist," Billy Price recalled, "but also deeply troubled. I wasn't surprised when I heard about his death. Although it's true that his personal life seemed to be improving, he was always on a pendulum that swung in the other direction after each period of personal or professional success. I believe the story that I heard: that he fell off the wagon, ended up in a drunk tank in Fairfax, and hung himself because it seemed like a good idea at the time. The cops may well have roughed him up, but I doubt very much that they killed him."

Paul Jacobs, Roy's keyboard player in 1980–81, had a similar take. "My personal opinion is that nobody killed Roy. I had an understanding that Roy could potentially be dangerous to himself. I think Roy lost his life as a result of his own actions."

Many of Roy's closest friends cannot accept suicide as an explanation for his death. "They say he hung himself, but I don't believe that," Judy told Bill Milkowski in 1989. "I mean, there's no way that I think that Roy took his own life. I'll never believe that . . . .I'd like to clear his name. Even if he killed himself, it's still their fault."

Sonny Pekerol, Roy's band mate from 1966, also is adamant. "Roy loved his music. He loved his life, his wife, and his children too much to do that. He'd never do that."

Some have mixed emotions. "In all honesty," said Tommy Hambridge, "when this happened I said to myself, 'Roy did *not* do this.' Six months later I said to myself, 'Maybe he *did* do it.' But that's a cop-out. Maybe there was a struggle, he got beat up, and then he said, 'Fuck it.' Something had to trigger it. I mean, Roy's walking around drunk, and two cops pick him up—that's like throwin' gasoline on a fire. Yes, he could get crazy—sarcastic—when drunk. I can picture a trooper slapping him, 'I'm not getting your jokes.' And Roy not letting up."

Set aside the theories and what's left, Hambridge said, is the impact Roy had on those around him. "When he died, the world was, like, 'Here's this virtuoso who no one knew.' To me I lost this special guy, a friend. I've played with a lot of amazing guitar players—Danny Gatton, Ronnie Earl, Duke Robillard—and nobody played like Roy. *Nobody.* I was blessed to have played with him. But also blessed to be able to hang out with him, to have lunch with him, to talk to him. He would bring me cigars. 'Have you tried this one?' We used to smoke cigarettes—I don't anymore—and he'd call them 'fags.' He'd say, 'Do you know in England they call them "fags"?' He'd say that *every time I saw him.* I'd say, 'Roy, I *know* that. You already told me.' When he died, I thought about those times. It wasn't like onstage, playing 'The Messiah.' I thought about him sitting on my couch in my apartment, entertaining my friends with his stories. Talkin', playin' records. He was a gentle, unassuming guy. He liked cigars and guitars, that's what I tell people. He had magic and he could mesmerize an audience and all that shit. But he was also just this guy. Sometimes we'd be sitting up in a hotel room, late at night, and he'd be playing the guitar. He'd play the prettiest little melancholy stuff. I'd be thinking, 'Man, if we could just bottle this . . . .' It wasn't the screaming stuff. Like 'Amazing Grace'—it was just comin' out of his soul. And we'd fall silent. Then he'd say, 'You know, the action on this thing isn't what it should be . . . .' I'd say, '*What were you just playing?!*' He'd say, 'Oh, I don't know, I was just tryin' to feel the neck down here by the pegs . . . .' "

IN THE END, there's just music sweet music—the music Roy listened to, the music he made, and the music he inspired. The loss hit home for J.D. Buchanan. "I never saw Roy take a drink. I never saw Roy smoke. I never saw him going after a girl. He was a quiet kid. Whatever happened, it's a terrible waste." As Dave Whitehill lamented, "He was a real character, but he had a heart of gold."

"He could make the guitar cry like nobody in the world could," Robbie Robertson told National Public Radio after Roy's death. Harking back to the time the two first met, Robertson recalled, "He opened up my mind to styles. He had been places and heard people that I hadn't been exposed to. He opened up a whole new world for me. But he was also a very selfish guitar player. He didn't want to show you *nothing*. I'm saying this in the best sense of the word. [Roy probably said to himself] 'I crawled on my hands and knees to learn this. I'm not going to pass it on to you.' But I stole as much as I could!"

"He had the best chops of any guitarist I've ever seen and got more sounds out of a guitar," Dick Shurman said. "He also played the sweetest music I've ever produced, when he chose to do so."

"I remember the genuineness behind Roy's attitude," John Olds would recall. "He wasn't tryin' to be a star. He would never turn away from an autograph or a photo or a chance to talk to somebody. He stayed on that level with his friends and with the people he played to. He never separated himself from them. And I believe that's part of the reason that he became such a legend, without getting all the fame and the pop star image."

As Pete Siegel remembered, a half-dozen years after Roy's death: "He was a gentle, courteous man. He was one of the few musicians I've ever known in whose hands a guitar really seemed to come alive."

"Roy wanted to play guitar," Seymour Duncan said. "That's all he ever cared about. Roy never had someone who understood his music looking out for his business interests. People liked Roy's playing, but they never understood where that playing was coming from. It was *Roy*. Roy would play a note and bend it within a beat, not necessarily on the beat . . . It's like a wave in the ocean. When you feel the wave, you adjust yourself so that you're rockin' with it. It's almost instinct. A lot of younger guys have no patience. They want to get up and be a gunslinger and shoot all the targets down at one time. Roy would wait for the right time and when he does hit it, he *gets* you. You're unaware of what he's going to do, but he'd get you. He was so great at that. He'd hit one note, and I'd laugh, I'd say, 'I'll be damned! *Listen* to that!' Thank God people got recordings of him, so these young kids can see what guitar playing is all about. He was the best white blues player I've ever seen. Roy had a very instinctive imagination, a gift to translate what he heard in his head and bring it out in his guitar. That's a very hard thing to do. 'Nephesh' is someone talking. People don't get it. If it's 12-bar blues or a shuffle, it's what you say within it. The thing with Roy is, whatever he's playing, it could be white, black, blue or purple. He's a white man playing the blues. Roy understood something about it. He would know how to control a situation. People have to listen, really listen, to what he's saying with his guitar. He just had inside him what he believed in. Roy used and transformed his own melancholy, his depression, his loneliness, into art. How much of Van Gogh's depression inspired his paintings? There's a very fine line between being insane and being creative. Maybe in this period we're in, people aren't into the style of guitar playing that Roy did. But there'll be a time when things come around and people are going to want the real McCoy. Roy put down the definitive tone for what a guitar should sound like. When you've heard Roy Buchanan play, you never forget it. He creates a permanent place in your soul. He was saying something to you in a language we may never understand for another million years. But he was saying something with each note, which makes an impression. I think about Roy Buchanan every day. I think about the tone he had on his old Telecaster. Roy Buchanan is going to be a legacy like Charlie Christian, or Les Paul. Maybe he didn't sell records like Madonna. But if I had to go to my grave with one record, I'd take a Roy's *Second Album*."

THROUGH THE MEMORIES of those who experienced Roy Buchanan's musical gift, or simply his friendship, and through his recorded legacy, where his spirit leaps from musty tapes and grabs the listener somewhere it matters, the music lives. You can hear America—from the green hills of Ozark, AR, to the endless fields outside Pixley, CA, to any street corner in Los Angeles, Shreveport, LA, or Washington, DC—in every note he played. As the world gets smaller and narrower and colder, and a smothering sameness creeps into everyday life, Roy's guitar still speaks of a bigger, bolder time and a place that have all but vanished. In his brief life he had found a few things that mattered, and he told us about them with his guitar.

Thank you Lord
Saw the sun shine today
Bless you Lord
Got to see my children play
May not be the right way to pray
But I want to thank you anyway.

Acknowledgments

*I*n the spring of 1974 my friend Peter Alpert included me on a trip to Carnegie Hall to see Roy Buchanan perform. Since then I've been grateful for the camaraderie of characters like Peter, Andy Stein, Charlie Cohen, Mark Lester, Bob Hayden, Tommy Strauss, Jon Leiberman, and others in that early crew who made the effort to get to Roy's shows—and hear all the music we could—whatever that took and wherever that might lead us.

More than 20 years later, in the fall of 1995, Peter and I were together once again, driving north through California's San Joaquin Valley en route to a memorial for Jerry Garcia. We stopped off in Pixley to see Roy's sister, Betty. That visit sparked this project. Over the next five years I made numerous field trips across the country to Arkansas, California, Mississippi, Washington, DC, Maryland, Virginia, Pennsylvania, and New York to soak up American places and speak with as many of Roy's family, friends, and colleagues as I could find. In the process I drank up lots of country, met great people, and made a few friends.

I sincerely thank those who helped me tell Roy's story. So many people still hold Roy Buchanan and his work in such high regard that they trusted me implicitly to give an honest account. When I mentioned the guitarist's name, people welcomed me and told me what was on their mind.

A sense of place is important to this story, so some people must be acknowledged by where they live. In Ozark, AR, Roy's brother J.D. and his wife, Shirley Buchanan, were open to my visits, questions, and company. Roy's aunt, Willie Buchanan, and her son and cousin to Roy, Charles Buchanan, were down-home, as were Phillis Buchanan McCartney, Doodles Buchanan, Edna Patterson Gossage, Johnnie Pearl Buchanan Parker, and Austin Law, who told me about the old days. J.W. Gilbreth showed me branches on the family tree. Local historian Norman Powell explained the territory. The clerks at the county courthouse were helpful and, as always, interested that someone was interested in their records. Ozark librarians like Nancy Smith lent a hand.

In North Little Rock, AR, Dale Hawkins proved to be a righteous brother. In Heber Springs, AR, Rollo California and Norma Fantasia treated me like family. In Mississippi, genealogist Barb Cerveny, the local USGenWeb Project participant, advised me on locating the Buchanans' roots in Panola County, where the Delta air is thick and sweet.

In Pixley, CA, Betty Buchanan became a friend, showed me the old homestead and the picks Roy used for his lap steel lessons in the late 1940s. L.D. Cox and Freddie Ramirez remembered their boyhood pal, as did Bobby Jobe, whom I traced from Delano, CA, to Amarillo, TX. Mrs. Marge Karle, wife of Bill Buchanan's employer, recalled the Buchanan clan. Marvin and Paul Kirkland remembered their ace lap steel player. Albert Dung, Jr., at Pixley Union School, lent a hand, as did librarians in Pixley, Tulare, and Bakersfield. In Bakersfield, Bob Price of the *Bakersfield Californian* offered help. Norm Hamlett and Fuzzy Owen spoke to me of Bakersfield's early days. Linda Joan Buchanan, in Nevada, shared her time. In Hemet, CA, Phil and Alan Clemmons shared memories. Seymour Duncan in Santa Barbara, CA, fired me up. "I'm not Tom Wolfe," I told him. "Tom Wolfe isn't writing a book on Roy Buchanan," he responded. In San Francisco, Alan Scheflin provided camaraderie, shared the fruits of his labors and trusted; he compiled the book's discography; his wife, Jamie Caploe, and their daughter, Hallie, opened their home and the chocolate stash. From Northern California, Spencer Dryden had cool stories.

In Washington, DC, John Gossage shared tapes, photographs, insights, and the art of conversation. Mark Opsasnick personally introduced me to the area's club-based musical history, answered queries with his encyclopedic knowledge, and caught my mistakes. Tom Principato showed me hospitality and shared thoughts.

In Frederick, MD, Bobby Flurie and John Burdette shared their love of the music. Niagara Falls' humble Dave Whitehill offered an open hand and a generous heart, and his technical advice on Roy's music and techniques proved indispensable. In Pittsburgh, PA, Bill Pollack—aka Billy Price—was friendly, kind, and helpful. In Boulder, CO, Jeff Mason faithfully helped convert analog tapes to a digital format. In Denver, Rob Selleck kept stashing my computer diskettes in his cellar for safe keeping. Bob Davis in Massachusetts shared his remarkable tape collection. Librarians provided resources wherever I went, as they always do.

Others gave in ways too diverse to declare. I thank them no less: Scott "The Cat" Anderson, Bob Berman, Gary Bolin, James Burton, Jerry Byrd, Annette Carson, L.D. Cox, Charlie Daniels, Kal David, Stan "Dee" Doucette, Tom Drake, Bob Embrey, Tom Finnegan, Marc Fisher, Ron "Byrd" Foster, Jeff Ganz, Tom Guernsey, Tommy Hambridge, John Harrison, Jerry Hawkins, Ronnie Hawkins, Bugs Henderson, Bill Holland, Gary Hollowood, Bruce Iglauer, Paul Jacobs, Hal and Herb Kalin, Merle Kilgore, Kees de Lange, Bill Lawrence, Joe Lemieux, Nils Lofgren, Kevin Loftus, Harold Lowder, Malcolm Lukens, Robbie Magruder, Fred Mastroni, Marc and Dean Mathis, Bing McCoy, Jerry Mercer, Bill Millar, Billy Miller, Ed Montini, Butch Moore, Mr. Big, Bob Nirkind, Ari Niskanen, Joe Osborn, Troy Page, Andy Paley, Sonny Pekerol, Perry Petrone, Wallace Presher, Jim Pulsifer, Freddie Ramirez, Jim Reed, Jay Reich, Mark Renusch, Deano Reynolds, William M. "Billy" Roberts, Ebet Roberts, Robbie Robertson, Walter Salb, Vince and Barb Santoro, Dick Shurman, Pete Siegel, Steve

Simenowitz, Joe Stanley, Danny Studen, Christie Tarr, Pete Van Allen, Margaret Lewis and Alton Warwick, Jim Weider, Stan Weinberg, Bob Weisburgh, Charlie Whaland, Paul Wilson, Ernie Winfrey, Joe Zani, Cary Ziegler, Tom Zito. And, of course, everyone interviewed in this book.

Fellow writer Bill Milkowski generously shared his interviews with Judy Buchanan and his own investigative files, lent encouragement, and provided publishing contacts. Thanks to my kindly agent, Barb Moulton, to Jay Kahn, Dorothy Cox, Amanda Johnson, and the gang at Backbeat Books for their interest.

John Gossage, John Adams, Alan Scheflin, Dave Whitehill, and Seymour Duncan kindly consented to read this book in draft form, offer their insights, and keep me honest. No thanks would be complete without a nod to Dave-o, Mr. Fox, and the Dokdor of Rock 'n' Roll. They believed.

Once again, thank you Roy for music that mattered. Would that we could sit down now over a beer and have a long talk. I gave the book everything I had, and your music sustained me in my labors.

During the course of this project I found love and lost love, and life went on. Perhaps that's as much as you can ask for—*any* day can be a good day. Have mercy.

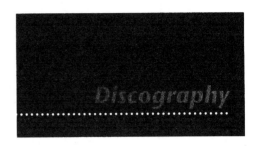
Discography

Compiled by Alan W. Scheflin

This discography is not comprehensive. Roy Buchanan played on innumerable sessions, many of them poorly documented or unreleased. Only records for which there is reliable information are listed. For the Dale Hawkins tracks, Scheflin relied on Ray Topping's discography. Discrepancies remain: For instance, Hawkins recalled to Phil Carson and Cub Coda that "My Babe" was recorded in Chicago, but Colin Escott says Hawkins told him the session took place in New York City.

Singles

1958, KWKH Radio, Shreveport,
Louisiana: Dale Hawkins
My Babe [Checker 906]
Take My Heart [Checker 913]
Someday, One Day [Checker 913]

1959, Philadelphia: Dale Hawkins
Our Turn [Checker 929]
Lifeguard [Checker 929]
Liza Jane [Checker 934]
Back to School Blues [Checker 934]
Don't Break Your Promise to Me
[Checker 940]
Hot Dog [Checker 940]

1960, location unknown: Dale Hawkins
Poor Little Rhode Island [Checker 944]
Every Little Girl [Checker 944]
Linda [Checker 962]
Who [Checker 962]

1961, New York: Dale Hawkins
Grandma's House [Checker 970]
I Want to Love You [Checker 970]

1958-1961, Shreveport, Louisiana:
The Brothers (Marc and Dean
Mathis).
Lazy Susan [Argo 5318]
Deep Sleep [Argo 5318]
Sioux City Sue [Argo 5329]
My True Love [Checker 995]
One Lonely Heart [Checker 995]

1958, Shreveport: Jerry Hawkins.
Swing Daddy Swing [Ebb 152]
I Got A Heart [Ebb 152]
Cha Cha Chu [Ebb 157]
Lucky Johnny [Ebb 157]

1959, Los Angeles: Bob Luman.
Class of '59 [Warner Bros 5081]

My Baby Walks All Over Me
  [Warner Bros 5081]
Buttercup [Warner Brothers 5105]
Dreamy Doll [Warner Brothers 5105]

1959, Shreveport, Louisiana: Al Jones.
Loretta [Imperial 5589]
I Was Too Late [Imperial 5589]

1960, Philadelphia: Roy Buchanan.
After Hours [Bomarc 315]
Whiskers [Bomarc 315]

1961, Philadelphia: Roy Buchanan.
Mule Train Stomp [Swan 4088]
Pretty Please [Swan 4088]

1961, Philadelphia: Cody Brennan &
  the Temptations.
Ruby Baby [Swan 4089]
Am I the One [Swan 4089]

1961, Philadelphia: Freddy Cannon.
Teen Queen of the Week [Swan 4096]
Wild Guy [Swan 4096]

1962, Philadelphia: Danny & the
  Juniors.
Medley: The Twist/Mother's Club Twist
  [Swan LP 506]
When the Saint's Go Twistin' In
  [Swan LP 506]
Tallahassee Lassie [Swan LP 506]

1962, Philadelphia: Bobby Gregg.
The Jam Pts. 1 & 2 [Cotton 1003]
Potato Peeler [Cotton 1006]

1962, location unknown: Paul Curry.
Route 66 [Cotton 1007]
Honeysuckle Rose [Cotton 1007]

1963, Philadelphia: Bob Moore
  & the Temps.
Mary Lou [ABC-Paramount 10428]
The Shuffle [ABC-Paramount 10428]
Braggin' [Daisy 502]
Trophy Run [Daisy 502]

1964, Washington, D.C.: The British
  Walkers.
Diddley Daddy [Try 502]
I Found You [Try 502]

1971, Washington: Danny Denver.
The Shoes That Jesus Wore/Spring Is A
  Woman [Wrayco Records 202]

1972, New York, Record Plant: Roy
  Buchanan.
Sweet Dreams [Polydor 14178]
Haunted House [Polydor 14149]

1973, New York, Record Plant: Roy
  Buchanan.
Rescue Me/I'm A Ram [Polydor 14265]

1976, New York, Electric Lady Studios:
  Roy Buchanan.
Keep What You Got/Caruso
  [Atlantic 3342]

1977, New York, Electric Lady Studios:
  Roy Buchanan.
The Circle [Atlantic 3433]

1977, Los Angeles, Clover Studios:
  Roy Buchanan.
Green Onions [Atlantic 3414]

1978, New York: Roy Buchanan.
Down by the River [Atlantic 3489]

1979, New York: Steve Simenowitz.
Hinei Yamim/Hinei Mah Tov
  [ECO Records MRS 101]

Albums

1970: *Danny Denver: Live on Stage at The Stardust Inn*
[Go-Go Records LP 101; CW 597]

1970: *The Best of Danny Denver*
[Wrayco Records WLPS 209]

1971: *The Joey Welz Rock 'n' Roll Revival: Revival Fires*
[Palmer Records PLP 13404]

1972: *Buch and the Snake Stretchers/One of Three* [Bioya Sound Records]

1972: *Esther Mae Scott:*
[Bomp One RI 3384]

1972: *Roy Buchanan*
[Polydor 831 413-2 CD]

1973: *Second Album*
[Polydor 831 412-2 CD]

1973: *That's What I Am Here For*
[Polydor 831 837-2 CD]

1974: *In the Beginning*
[Polydor 831 838-2 CD]

1975: *Live Stock*
[Polydor 831 414-2 CD]

1976: *A Street Called Straight*
[Atlantic SD 18170 0698]

1977: *Loading Zone*
[Atlantic SD 18219]

1977: *Live in Japan*
[Polydor MPF 1105 Japan]

1978: *You're Not Alone*
[Atlantic SD 19170]

1980: *Jewish Blues: Out of the Woods*
[Nova MRS 111]

1980: *My Babe* [Waterhouse 12],
[CD: ERA Records 5005-2]

1985: *When a Guitar Plays the Blues*
[Alligator 4741 CD]

1986: *Dancing on the Edge*
[Alligator 4747 CD]

1987: *Hot Wires*
[Alligator 4756 CD]

1989: *The Early Years*
[Krazy Kat KK CD 02]

1991: *Rockin' at Town Hall*
[Country Routes RFD CD 06]

1992: *Sweet Dreams: The Anthology*
[Polygram 314 517 086-2]

1993: *Guitar on Fire: The Atlantic Sessions* [Rhino R2 71235]

1995: *Oh! Susie Q—The Best of Dale Hawkins* [Chess/MCA CHD-9356]

1995: *Roy Buchanan "Live"*
[Charly CD CBL 758]

1996: *Malaguena: The Collector's Edition* [Annecillo Records 1113-2]

1997: *Bugs Henderson: Legendary Jams*
[Taxim Records TX 1035-2 TA]

1999: *Roy Buchanan: Before and After*
[Rollercoaster Records RCCD 3034]

2001: *Roy Buchanan: Deluxe Edition*
[Alligator ALCD 5608]

Bibliography

Taped Interviews with Roy Buchanan

Kahn, Ashley, WKCR, Cincinnati, Nov. 24, 1984

Keplazo, Dan, Buffalo State College, 1986

Red Rooster Lounge, KBCO, Boulder, CO, 1985

Silverstein, Mike, WJAS, Pittsburgh, 1972

Steele, Allison, WNEW, New York, Aug. 14, 1977

Unknown interviewer, Albert's Hall, Toronto, WDF, 1985

Unknown interviewer, Cairn Civic Center, Cairn, Australia, Feb. 22, 1988

Unknown interviewer, unknown location, Sept. 14, 1971

Unknown interviewer, Waterhouse Records, promotional interview for
    My Babe, 1980

Books

Bane, Michael. *White Boy Singin' the Blues: The Black Roots of White Rock* (New
    York: Da Capo, 1982; 1992)

Carson, Annette. *Jeff Beck, Crazy Fingers* (South Africa, self-published, 1998).

Cohodas, Nadine. *Spinning Blues into Gold: The Chess Brothers and the Legendary
    Chess Records* (New York: St. Martin's Press, 2000).

Dixon, Willie, with Don Snowden. *I Am the Blues: The Willie Dixon Story* (New
    York: Da Capo, 1989).

Gillett, Charlie. *The Sound of the City: The Rise of Rock and Roll.* (New York:
    Pantheon Books, 1970; reprinted 1983).

Guinness Book of World Records 1990. (New York: Sterling Publishing, 1990).

Guinness Encyclopedia of Popular Music, edited by Colin Lankin. (England,
    Guinness Publishing, 1992).

Hannusch, Jeff. *I Hear You Knockin': The Sound of New Orleans Rhythm and Blues*
    (Ville Plata, LA: Swallow Publications, 1985).

Hawkins, Ronnie; Goddard, Peter. *Ronnie Hawkins: Last of the Good Ol' Boys* (General Distribution Services, Inc., August 1990).

Helm, Levon with Davis, Stephen. *This Wheel's on Fire: Levon Helm and the Story of the Band* (New York: William Morrow, 1993).

Hoskyns, Barney. *Across the Great Divide: The Band in America* (New York: Hyperion, 1993).

Lomax, Alan. *The Land Where the Blues Began* (New York: Dell, 1994).

Malone, Bill C. *Country Music USA* (Austin: University of Texas Press, 1968; revised 1985).

Opsasnick, Mark. *Capitol Rock* (Mark Opsasnick, 1996).

Paris, Mike; Comber, Chris. *Jimmie the Kid: The Life of Jimmie Rodgers* (New York: Da Capo, 1977).

Stanley, Jerry. *Children of the Dust Bowl.* (New York: Crown, 1992).

Trynka, Paul. *The Electric Guitar: An Illustrated History* (San Francisco: Chronicle Books, 1995).

Valkoff, Ben, compiler, Phil Carson, editor. *Eyewitness: The Illustrated Jimi Hendrix Concerts, 1968.* (Nijmegen, Netherlands: Up from the Skies Unlimited, 2000).

Wallis, Ian. *The Hawk: The Story of Ronnie Hawkins and the Hawks* (Ontario: Quarry Press, 1992).

Wheeler, Tom. *American Guitars: An Illustrated History* (New York: Harper Collins, 1992).

Whitehill, Dave. *Roy Buchanan Collection* (Milwaukee: Hal Leonard Publishing, 1998).

Wyman, Bill, with Coleman, Ray. *Stone Alone: The Story of a Rock 'n' Roll Band* (New York, Viking, 1990).

Periodicals

Adler, Bill, "Buchanan, Guitar, Add Up to Greatness," *Boston Herald American* (Nov. 8, 1979).

Album Network, review of *Dancing on the Edge* (May 9, 1986).

Allen, Greg, "'My Babe Is Really Rocking and Rolling," *The Press* (Atlantic City: Nov. 21, 1980).

Allen, Henry, "Legend of Buchanan," *Los Angeles Times* (Nov. 9, 1971).

Anthony, Michael, "Lou Reed's Work Finally Collected . . . " (review of *My Babe*), *Minneapolis Tribune* (Jan. 2, 1981).

Baltimore Sun, obituary (Aug. 17, 1988).

Bass, Kelley, "Roy Buchanan Brings Out the Best in Fans," *Arkansas Gazette* (Feb. 22, 1987).

Berman, Robert, "Roy Buchanan," *Guitar Player* (March 1972).

Billboard, "Sweet Dreams" No. 50 on British charts (April 7, 1973).

Billboard, review of *Dancing on the Edge* (June 14, 1986).

Billboard, obituary (Aug. 27, 1988).

Bloom, Steve, "Roy Buchanan: A Guitar Hero Ain't Nothin' But a Sandwich," *Guitar World* (June 1988).

Boston Globe, review of Nightstages performance (Dec. 30, 1986).

Boston Herald, obituary (Aug. 16, 1988).

Bourke, Chris, "When a Guitar Plays the Blues," *Rip It Up* (Christchurch, New Zealand: 1987).

Bradshaw, Tom, "Jerry Byrd," *Guitar Player* (March 1972).

Bream, Jon, "Legend in Guitar: Public Catching Up with Buchanan Sound," *Minneapolis Star* (Jan. 9, 1981).

Buchanan, Roy, "A Long Lost Lesson," *Guitar Player* (July 1993).

_____, "Jimi Hendrix: A Tribute" [as told to Gene Santoro], *Guitar World* (Sept. 1985).

_____, "Roy Buchanan's Guitar Tips," *Guitar Player* (Oct. 1976).

Burleson, Robert, "Buchanan: Beyond Blues," *Guitar Player* (1988).

Carey, Joe, "Riffs," *Down Beat* (Nov. 1985).

Carson, Phil, "Hey Roy: Where Are You Going with That Guitar in Your Hands?" *Univibes* (Nov. 1995).

_____, "Jimi Plays the Hilton," *Univibes* (Aug. 1996).

_____, "American Axe: The Life and Times of Roy Buchanan," *Vintage Guitar* (Aug. 1999).

Cauffiel, Lowell, "Some Personal Playing Hints," *Guitar Player* (Oct. 1976).

Chipkin, Kenn, "Roy Buchanan: Relearning the Blues," *Guitar for the Practicing Musician* (Dec. 1985).

Considine, J.D., "Despite His Astounding Technique, Roy Buchanan Found Fame Elusive," *Baltimore Sun* (Aug. 17, 1988).

Convey, Tony, "Roy Buchanan, Canberra Workers' Club," *Muse* (Dec. 1985).

Coppage, Noel, "Way Out There with Roy Buchanan," *Stereo Review* (July 1973).

Costa, Jean-Charles, "Killer Guitars," *Rolling Stone* (June 30, 1977).

Crescenti, Peter, "The Jeff Beck Sheet," *Sounds* (Oct. 9, 1976).

D.F., "Roy Buchanan: Hot Wires," *Guitar Player* (Jan. 1988).

Davis, Patricia; Evans, Sandra. "Guitarist Found Hanged in Va. Jail: Artist Faced Alcohol Charge," *Washington Post* (Aug. 18, 1988).

DeCurtis, Anthony, "Richard Manuel: 1943–1986," *Rolling Stone* (April 24, 1986).

Deeb, Gary, "Ray [sic] Buchanan: Pickings Slim on Great Guitarist," *Buffalo Evening News* (Nov. 9, 1971).

DeWitt, Howard A., "Dale Hawkins: Oh Suzie Q and Beyond," *Blue Suede News* No. 40 (Fall 1997).

Dolan, Mike; Basham, Tom, "Grinding It Out Locally: The Washington Nightclub," *The Argus Dimension: Supplement to University of Maryland Diamondback* newspaper, Vol. VII, No. IV (Feb. 25, 1972).

Dougherty, Steve, "A Haunting Suicide Silences the Sweet, Soulful Voice of the Band's Richard Manuel," *People* (March 24 1986).

Down Beat, review, *Hot Wires* (July 1987).

Down Beat, obituary (November 1988).

Embrey, Bob, "The British Walkers," *D.C. Monuments* (1996) Issue 2.

Emerson, Dan, "Roy Buchanan Finds a Groove," *Sweet Potato* (Jan. 21–Feb. 4, 1981).

Evans, Tom; Evans, Mary Anne, "Guitars: Music, History, Construction and Players," *Facts on File* (New York: 1977).

Everett, Todd, "Roy Buchanan," *Record Review* (April 1981).

Flippo, Chet, "I Sing the Solid Body Electric: The Rolling Stone with Les Paul," *Rolling Stone* (Feb. 13, 1975).

Folsom, Harry, "Exclusive Interview with Roy Buchanan," *Harmonix* (Aug./Sept. 1982).

Ford, Ty, "An Intimate Interview with the Legendary Roy Buchanan," *Maryland Musician* (Feb. 1988).

Gavin Report, review of *Dancing on the Edge* (June 6, 1986).

Gladstone, Howard, "Robbie Robertson," *Rolling Stone* (Dec., 1969).

Glover, Tony, "Roy Buchanan," *Rolling Stone* (Sept. 28, 1972).

Goldman, Stuart, "Pop Beat," *Los Angeles Times* (Dec. 20, 1980).

Goldwasser, Noë, "Telly Talk," *Guitar World* (Nov. 1982).

Granit, Robbie, "'Blow by Blow': A Mature Jeff Beck Cleans Up His Act," *Circus* (June 1975).

Guitar for the Practicing Musician, review of *Dancing on the Edge* (Nov. 1986).

Guitar Player, review of *That's What I'm Here For* (June 1974).

Guitar Player, review of *Buch & The Snake Stretchers* (Aug. 1992).

Guitar Player, review of *Sweet Dreams* (Jan. 1993).

Guitar World, Jimi Hendrix: A Tribute, "Roy Buchanan: The Hillbilly Master Blaster" (Sept. 1985).

Guitar World, obituary (Nov. 1988).

Harrington, Richard, "Roy Buchanan, a Study in Blues: The Gifted Guitarist and His Road Less Traveled," *Washington Post* (Aug. 1988).

Hawkins, Robert J., "Buchanan Acclaim Long Due," *San Diego Tribune* (June 11, 1986).

Hildebrand, Lee; Kaiser, Henry, "Jimmy Nolen: A Rare Interview with James Brown's Longtime Sideman, the Father of Funk Guitar," *Guitar Player* (April 1984).

Hill, Jack W., "Buchanan Finally Sets 'Home' Date," *Arkansas Democrat* (Feb. 8, 1987).

Hinckley, David, "A Rock Dream Ends in a Nightmare," *Daily News* (New York: Aug. 17, 1988).

Hodenfield, Jan, "A Call for Buchanan," *New York Post* (July 9, 1974).

_____, "Love Story," *New York Post* (Jan. 22, 1975).

Holland, Bill, "Dick Heintze," *Unicorn Times* (Nov. 1974).

Holland, William (Bill), "Roy Buchanan," *Unicorn Times* (Feb. 1974).

_____, "Roy Buchanan Still Needs Arranging," *Washington Star-News* (Nov. 24, 1974).

_____, "So Who's Roy Buchanan?: A D.C. Guitarist on His Way," *The Washington Star* (Nov. 27, 1970).

Horning, Ron, "The Moving Shadow of Richard Manuel," *Village Voice Rock 'n' Roll Quarterly* (1986).

Joyce, Mike, "Buchanan, Playing It Straight," *Washington Post* (~1985; date unknown).

_____, "Roy Buchanan: Telecaster Master," *Washington Post* (March 19, 1985).

_____, "Roy Buchanan," *Unicorn Times* (Feb. 1981).

Kahn, Ashley, "In Session: Roy Buchanan Gets the Blues," *Guitar Player* (Aug. 1985).

Kalina, Mike, "Music . . . ," *Pittsburgh Post-Gazette* (~1975).

_____, "Two Guitarists Offer Mixed Bag at Mosque," *Pittsburgh Post-Gazette* (June 22, 1974).

_____, "Wanted: Roy Buchanan," *Down Beat* (June 1973).

Kanzler, George, "Guitar World Loses a Passionate Performer," *Newark Star-Ledger* (New Jersey: Aug. 28, 1988).

_____, "Four New Discs . . . " *Newark Star-Ledger* (Dec. 7, 1980).

_____, "Rock Guitarists Prove They Are Masters," *Newark Star-Ledger* (Dec. 10, 1984).

Kawashima, Dale, "Roy Buchanan: The Starwood, L.A.," *Cashbox* (July 6–7, 1979).

Kienzle, Rich, "The Electric Guitar in Country Music, Its Evolution and Development," *Guitar Player* (Nov. 1979).

_____, "Steel: How Hawaiian Hula Came Down Home and Gave Birth to the Nashville Sound," *Country Music* (Jan. 1976).

"Kirb.," *Variety*, review (Dec. 4, 1974).

Kullman, Joe, "Buchanan: A Calm Master," *NOW* (Sept. 19, 1975).

_____, "Buchanan's Addiction to Music," *NOW* (Sept. 26, 1975).

Kunstler, Jim, "Roy Buchanan Makes the Rafters Sweat," *Rolling Stone* (Jan. 16, 1975).

La Roche, Marianne, "Guitarist's Slow Blues Delights Rock Fans," *Washington Star* (Aug. 26, 1971).

Lawrence, David, "Fritz Bros. Roy Buchanan Bluesmaster," *Guitar World* (Dec. 1988).

Lemieux, Jon, "An Interview with Roy Buchanan," *Music Machine* (Jan. 22–Feb. 4, 1988).

Lewis, David, "Brilliant Buchanan," *Melody Maker* (May 12, 1973).

Los Angeles Reader, review of *When a Guitar Plays the Blues* (Jan. 31, 1986).

Los Angeles Times, obituary (August 1988).

Marshall, James, "Dale Hawkins: Human Tornado," *Hounds Eye View* (Oct. 1997).

Maryland Musician Magazine, obituary (Sept. 1988).

McClain, Buzz, "The Strange Death of a Local Guitar Legend," *The Journal* (Washington, DC: Aug. 9, 1991).

Means, Andrew, "Guitarist Plays with Professional Detachment," *Arizona Republic* (Dec. 17, 1980).

"Media Man," "All the Latest Poop," *Newsreal* (Jan. 1981).

Menege, Mike, "My Babe," *Sweet Potato* (Dec. 1980).

Milano, Brett, "Roy Buchanan: Passion and Modesty," *Boston Globe* (Aug. 17, 1988).

Milbauer, Jerry, "Roy Buchanan: My Babe," *Trouser Press* (April 1981).

Milkowski, Bill, "Danny Gatton: The World's Greatest Unknown Guitarist," *Guitar World* (Jan. 1989).

_____, "Johnny Winter/Roy Buchanan," *Down Beat* (August 1984).

_____, "The Lonesome Death of Roy Buchanan," *Guitar World* (Sept. 1990).

_____, "My Babe," *Good Times* (Dec. 16–25, 1980).

Millar, Bill, "An Oldie But Goodie," *Goldmine* (Feb. 15, 1985).

_____, review of *Roy Buchanan: The Early Years*, *Goldmine* (date unknown).

Miller, Jim, "That's What I'm Here For," *Rolling Stone* (May 9, 1974).

Mills, Donia, "In Search of Grin," *Woodwind* (April, May 1971).

Moore, Milton, "Roy Buchanan: Dumb as a Mud Oyster," *Boston After Dark* (Nov. 21, 1972).

Nashville Banner, review (Aug. 30, 1985).

New York Daily News, "Rock Dream Ends in Nightmare" (Aug. 17, 1988).

New York Times, review of Carnegie Hall (June 23, 1972).

New York Times, obituary (August 17, 1988).

Newsreal, review of *My Babe* (January 1981).

Obrecht, Jas, "*Buch and the Snake Stretchers*," *Guitar Player* (Aug. 1992).

_____, "Roy Buchanan: Sweet Dreams: The Anthology," *Guitar Player* (Jan. 1993).

O'Brien, Glenn, "The Search for the Golden Guitar" (publication date unknown).

Oppel, Pete, "Unlike a Rolling Stone," *Fort Worth Telegraph* (date unknown).

Palmer, Bob, "*Second Album,*" *Rolling Stone* (April 26, 1973).

_____, "Slim Pickings for the World's Greatest," *Rolling Stone* (July 18, 1974).

Paul, Les, "That's Our Man!" *Guitar Player* (Sept. 1975).

Pierce, Michael, "James Burton," *Guitar Player* (March 1972).

Pike, Jeffrey, "Roy Buchanan Talks About Practicing, Playing and the Public," *Guitar* (July 1973).

Pixley Enterprise, story on upcoming WNET special (Nov. 3, 1971).

Pixley Enterprise, story on WNET special rebroadcast (Nov. 13, 1971).

Prime, John Andrew, "Who's on Bass? Joe Osborn," *Shreveport Times* (Feb. 9, 1986).

Reay, Tony, "Buchanan Is Back," *International Talent Weekly* (Jan. 23, 1976).

Record World, story on Buchanan getting mugged for guitar (Nov. 15, 1980).

Record World, "Albums Picks": *My Babe* (Dec. 6, 1980).

Ressner, Jeffrey, "Roy Buchanan: 1939–1988," *Rolling Stone* (Sept. 22, 1988).

Richardson, Derk, "Microgrooves" review of *When a Guitar Plays the Blues,* *San Francisco Bay Guardian* (Oct. 9, 1985).

Rip It Up, review (Christchurch, New Zealand) (March 1988).

Rockwell, John, "Buchanan? Crazy," *New York Times* (late 72, early 73).

_____, "Buchanan's Talent as Guitarist Lifts 'Village' Rock Show," *New York Times* (Jan. 1, 1973).

_____, "'Guitar Explosion' Attracts the Young," *New York Times* (July 1, 1973).

_____, "Guitars, from Soft to Boisterous," *New York Times* (July 8, 1974).

_____, "How the Electric Guitar Became a Way of Music," *New York Times* (July 15, 1974).

Rohter, Larry, "Jeff Beck: The Progression of a True Progressive," *Down Beat* (June 16, 1977).

Rolling Stone, "Random Notes" (March 4, 1971).

Rolling Stone, review of Georgetown concert (May 13, 1971).

Rolling Stone, story on PBS special (Dec. 9, 1971).

Rolling Stone, stories on Carnegie Hall, Buchanan at No. 6 in guitar poll results (July 20, 1972).

Rolling Stone, obituary (Sept. 22, 1988).

Russell, Rusty, "Elvis and Scotty," "Elvis and Everything After," *Guitar Player* (July 1997).

Rutkoski, Rex, "Buchanan Maintains Low-Key Career," *Valley News Dispatch* (New Kensington, PA: date unknown).

San Diego Reader, "Readers Guide to Music Scene" review of *When a Guitar Plays the Blues* (Nov. 1985).

Santoro, Gene, "Roy Buchanan, the Hillbilly Master Blaster," *Guitar World* (Sept. 1985).

_____, "Roy Buchanan Lets You In on Some Trade Secrets," *Guitar World* (Jan. 1985).

Scaduto, Anthony, "Roy Buchanan, Legendary Blues and Rock Guitarist," *New York Newsday* (Aug. 17, 1988).

Scheflin, Alan, "Roy Buchanan," unpublished manuscript.

Scherman, Tony, "Youngblood: The Wild Youth of Robbie Robertson," *Musician* (Dec. 1991).

Sievert, Jon, "Questions," *Guitar Player* (Dec. 1988).

_____, "Roy Buchanan, Bluesman," *Guitar Player* (November 1988).

_____, "Roy Buchanan: Dancing on the Edge," *Guitar Player* (August 1986).

Singer, Karen, "Roy Buchanan's 6-String Prayerbook," *Bridgeport Post* (Connecticut: May 15, 1988).

Smith, Jim, "Buchanan's New Breakout," [Toronto] (April 1974).

Stereo Review, review of *Second Album* (~1973).

Stereo Review, review of *That's What I'm Here For* (~1974).

Swenson, John, "Back to the Blues," *Complete Music Magazine* (~1980).

Sylvester, Bruce, "Roy Buchanan: His New Style Fits Fine," *Boston Globe* (Nov. 2, 1972).

Taylor, J.R., "Flecks on a Future Wave," *Village Voice* (July 18, 1974).

Thompson, Lynne, "Ohio's Agora: 30 Years of Live Music Magic," *Goldmine* (March 15, 1996).

Time, "A Messiah on Guitar," (June 14, 1976).

Tozier, Rich, "Guitarists Try to Heighten Low Profiles," *Bangor Daily News* (Maine: Nov. 29, 1980).

Vandenberg, Paul, "Rock Musician's Contribution Remembered by Friends, Family," *Beacon Herald* (Stratford, Ontario: March 10, 1986).

Variety, review of Village East show (Jan. 10, 1973).

Variety, review of *Roy Buchanan* (Sept. 20, 1972).

Variety, review of Village Gate (New York) show (Oct. 25, 1972).

Variety, review of Academy of Music show (April 18, 1973).

Wald, Elijah, "Good Rock from a Benign Uncle," *Boston Globe* (Dec. 30, 1986).

Wale, Michael, "Roy Buchanan: Guitar Ace," *Zigzag* (~1972).

Washington Star, concert notice, with Grin (Aug. 25, 1971).

Wasserman, John, "Raw Emotion from a Superb Guitarist," *San Francisco Chronicle* (1975?).

Watts, Michael, "The New Guitar Man," *Melody Maker* (May 5, 1973).

Weitzman, Steve, "Beck is Back!!!" *Guitar World* (June 1989).

Whipping Post, review (March 1974).

Whitehill, Dave, "Riffin' with Roy Buchanan," *Guitar Player* (July 1993).

_____, "Roy Buchanan, 1939–1988," *Guitar World* (Nov. 1988).

Wilson, E.O., "Buchanan, Henderson Cut 'Dillo Albums," *River City Sun*, Austin, TX (Sept. 8, 1978).

Wilson, John S., "Roy Buchanan TV Rerun Warms Hall for Guitarist," *New York Times* (June 23, 1972).

Woodard, Josef, "Requiem for a Heavyweight," *Santa Barbara Independent* (California: Sept.1, 1988).

Woods, William C., "The Greatest Rock Guitarist in the World," *Washington Post* (April 27, 1971).

Woodwind, "Roy Buchanan: Magic in the Big Apple" (Washington, DC: July 12, 1972).

Wright, Michael, *Audio*, review of *Dancing on the Edge* (Oct. 1986).

Zimmerman, Kent, *Gavin Report* (May 12, 1986).

Zito, Tom, "Roy Buchanan: He May Be the Finest Rock Guitarist in the World," *Washington Post* (Dec. 9, 1970).

_____, "Roy Buchanan, Heavy Axe," *Rolling Stone* (Feb. 18, 1971).

Courtesy of Betty Buchanan: 7, 11, 18
Courtesy of J.D. Buchanan: 31, 36
Courtesy of the Shreveport Louisiana Hayride Company: 35
Courtesy of Billy Miller, Norton Records: 46, 49
Courtesy of Bo Berglind/American Music Magazine: 57
Courtesy of Scott Anderson: 70
Copyright *Washington Post*. Reprinted by permission of the D.C. Public Library: 82
Courtesy of Stan Doucette Estate: 90
Photograph by John Gossage: 93, 128, 129, 134, 136,
Photograph by Bob Berman: 113, 114
Courtesy of John Adams/WNET: 121
Photograph by Charles Cohen: 157
Photograph by Gary Bolin: 172
Photograph by Bob Davis: 174
Photograph by Ebet Roberts: 219, 223
Photograph courtesy of Ron Foster: 238
Photograph by Dean Reynolds: 243
Photograph by Joe Lemieux: 250

Index